# PEOPLE AND SOCIETY IN SCOTLAND

## I
## 1760–1830

*Edited by*
T.M. DEVINE
*and*
ROSALIND MITCHISON

A Social History of Modern Scotland
in Three Volumes

JOHN DONALD PUBLISHERS LTD
IN ASSOCIATION WITH
THE ECONOMIC AND SOCIAL HISTORY
SOCIETY OF SCOTLAND

ISBN 0 85976 210 6

*Also in this series:*

**People and Society in Scotland, II: 1830–1914**
edited by W. Hamish Fraser and R.J. Morris

**People and Society in Scotland, III: 1914 to the present**
edited by Tony Dickson and J.H. Treble

Reprinted 1991
Reprinted 1994

Printed and Bound in Great Britain
by J. W. Arrowsmith Ltd., Bristol

# General Introduction

Modern Scottish historical studies have experienced a vigorous phase of unprecedented growth over the last quarter of a century. Scholars are addressing a novel range of issues and themes, fresh perspectives on established topics are common and innovative methods are helping to transform the nature of research investigation. The subject has, in consequence, a new intellectual vitality. Of course, much remains to be done. Indeed, one of the fascinations for the professional historian is that so many key areas still remain unexplored. This contributes both to the challenge and the excitement of ongoing research in the archives and libraries. But substantial advances have already been made in the serious study of Scottish society since the eighteenth century and have produced results which warrant exposure to a wider audience than the readership of learned journals and scholarly monographs.

In 1985 the Economic and Social History Society of Scotland and John Donald Publishers agreed to publish a three-volume social history of Scotland from the middle decades of the eighteenth century to the present day. It is intended that the series should appear over a cycle of three years from 1988. Each volume has two editors and all contributors are recognised authorities in their respective fields. The project as a whole was supervised by an editorial committee appointed by the Society, consisting of T.M. Devine, Chairman (Strathclyde University), Anne Crowther (Glasgow University), T. Dickson (Glasgow College of Technology), W. Hamish Fraser (Strathclyde University), Rosalind Mitchison (Edinburgh University), R.J. Morris (Edinburgh University) and J.H. Treble (Strathclyde University).

The series is intended to appeal to undergraduate and postgraduate students, lecturers, teachers, archivists, museum staff, local historians and others with an interest in the social history of modern Scotland. Each author attempts to convey the results of recent published research while at the same time introducing insights, interpretations and evidence from their own personal investigations. None of the various themes are analysed in an exhaustive fashion but contributors provide in the notes at the end of each chapter references to the most important published work in the relevant field as a guide to further reading. Individual chapters convey something of the vitality of the subject at its present stage of development. Historical analysis inevitably produces variations in opinion, method and conclusion and these are honestly revealed in the different approaches adopted by different contributors. The editors made no attempt to iron out contrasting interpretations of key issues. The resulting volumes are therefore not so much bland textbooks as studies which reveal the 'state of the art' in modern Scottish history.

T.M. Devine
*Chairman*
*Editorial Advisory Committee*

# The Economic and Social History Society of Scotland

Over the last few years there has been a remarkable increase in both popular interest and serious research in Scottish historical studies. A series of major books have appeared; local history societies are flourishing: museums continue to improve in both quality and quantity; in television and press there is a new fascination with Scotland's history.

The subject is now taught in seven of the eight Scottish universities and curricular changes in school examinations ensure that more attention is devoted than ever before to the study of Scottish historical development. The Economic and Social History Society of Scotland was formed in 1983 to provide a national focus for much of the current research which is being undertaken in this expanding field. Its current membership of around 500 includes professional historians from universities and colleges, schoolteachers, undergraduate and postgraduate students, representatives from local history societies and museums, and members of the public with an interest in Scottish history. Most come from the United Kingdom but there are several also from Australasia, Canada, Europe, Ireland, Japan and the U.S.A. Members automatically receive a copy of the Society's journal, *Scottish Economic and Social History*. The first issue was published in 1981 and annual volumes of approximately 150 pages in length have appeared since then. The journal always includes the following items.

★ Three to four main articles. These are either based on original research or contain critical evaluations of recent work on major themes. In the last four years essays have been published on the Highland Clearances; the Union of 1707; Early Modern Towns; Urban Elites; the Clyde Tobacco Fleet; the Twentieth-Century Economy; Literacy and Education in Scotland.

★ A comprehensive book review section with essays on new publications of general interest and specialised reviews of recent work.

★ An annual *Register of Research* which lists the interests of individuals engaged in serious research in this field.

★ A list of annual publications of both books and articles.

The Society also publishes an annual *Newsletter* with a diary of forthcoming events, conferences and seminars of interest to members. The *Newsletter* in addition provides a focus for correspondence relating to the Society's activities and development.

Among ESHSS's most successful activities are its conferences which are normally held twice a year in different centres throughout Scotland. At each meeting a particular topic is explored in depth with formal lectures combining with panel discussions and workshop sessions. Recent conferences have focused on Women in Scottish Society, Business Elites, Urban History and Unemployment in the Twentieth Century.

In September, 1987, the Society organised its first Residential Conference at the University of Aberdeen on the Society and Economy of the North of Scotland, 1700 to the Present, with sessions on Government and Crofting; Famine; Migration and Emigration; Landlords.

If you are interested in Scottish history or economic and social history and want to keep abreast of developments in the field your modest membership fee will be a worthwhile investment. Applications for membership and further information should be addressed to ESHSS, Department of History, University of Strathclyde, McCance Building, 16 Richmond Street, Glasgow G1 1XQ, Scotland.

# Contributors

*Callum G. Brown*
Lecturer in History, University of Strathclyde

*R.H. Campbell*
Professor Emeritus of Economic History, University of Stirling

*Tony Clarke*
Senior Lecturer in Sociology, Paisley College of Technology

*T.M. Devine*
Professor of History, University of Strathclyde

*Tony Dickson*
Professor of Sociology, Glasgow College of Technology

*W. Hamish Fraser*
Senior Lecturer in History and Dean of the Faculty of Arts and Social Studies, University of Strathclyde

*Malcolm Gray*
Formerly Reader in Economic History, University of Aberdeen

*R.A. Houston*
Lecturer in Modern History, University of St. Andrews

*Allan Macinnes*
Lecturer in Scottish History, University of Glasgow

*Rosalind Mitchison*
Emeritus Professor of Social History, University of Edinburgh

*Alexander Murdoch*
Research Worker, Edinburgh

*Stana Nenadic*
Lecturer in Economic and Social History, University of Edinburgh

*Richard B. Sher*
Associate Professor of History and Associate Dean, New Jersey Institute of Technology, U.S.A.

*J.H. Treble*
Senior Lecturer in Economic and Social History, University of·
Strathclyde

*Christoper A. Whatley*
Lecturer in Economic History, University of Dundee

*Donald J. Withrington*
Senior Lecturer in History, University of Aberdeen

# Illustrations

# Contents

# Introduction

## T.M. Devine

It has become fashionable in recent years for historians of English society in the eighteenth century to argue that economic growth and social change were much slower and more protracted than was suggested in some classic accounts of the Industrial Revolution. The process of modernisation in England was more evolutionary than revolutionary. Already by c.1700 the industrial, trade and urban sectors were well developed and both structural and economic advance in agriculture was very widespread. Growth in this view was cumulative, relatively modest and undramatic. The pattern currently delineated by English social and economic historians is of a society transformed over a very long period by a gradual process of evolution punctuated by phases of more rapid change.[1]

The studies assembled in this volume suggest that the Scottish route to modernisation differed fundamentally from the English. By the middle decades of the nineteenth century both economies were viewed as integral parts of 'the Workshop of the World', twin pioneers of the new industrial society, with remarkably high proportions of their occupied populations employed in manufacturing and living in cities and towns. But Scotland achieved that position over a much shorter period of time than England. From the later eighteenth century the break with the past seems to have been sharper and more decisive north of the Border and the consequent social transformation more disruptive and, in some cases, more traumatic for large sections of the Scottish people. This book, therefore, offers a case-study of a society exposed to the full impact of rapid economic diversification, occurring at an earlier period than any other in Europe. At the same time it provides a distinctive contrast to the more familiar story of English social change during the Industrial Revolution. It is very apparent that the Scottish experience in such key areas as demographic growth, urbanisation and agrarian change was so different from England's that any uncritical attempt to combine the two in an analysis of *British* social change at this time runs grave risk of fundamentally distorting the historical process. This book aims to establish the uniqueness of the Scottish route towards an industrial society.

This is not to suggest that before the middle decades of the eighteenth century Scottish society was inert and static. Nor is it to argue that the old

1

world was swiftly transformed within a few decades. Recent work on a number of themes for the period before c.1760 has shown such views to be untenable.[2] The commercialisation of agriculture was advancing in some regions, urban growth was vigorous and mercantile activity extending both at home and overseas. In a few areas in the Lowlands farm organisation was becoming more recognisably 'modern' with larger units of production under the control of single individuals who were committed to servicing the needs of the market. The dynamism of the 'early modern town' in Scotland has also been demonstrated in recently published research.[3]

However, by the standards of England, one of the most advanced economies in western Europe in the seventeenth century, Scotland was still poor and backward in material terms. Crises of mortality provoked by famine occurred as late as the 1690s in Scotland but had disappeared from England as early as the 1620s. Mortality rates were also much higher in Scotland than in England before 1760. This helps to explain why Scottish population increase in the later eighteenth century seems to have been more associated with a sharp fall in death rates rather than (as in England) with a significant rise in fertility.[4] In addition, the structures of the two societies reflected their respective stages of economic and social development. In most of England, a three-tier rural social system of landlords, tenants farmers and landless wage labourers was already in place. But before c. 1760 there were few entirely landless groups in the Scottish countryside. Rural tradesmen normally had a patch of land, much of the agricultural labour force was recruited from cottar families and even 'landless' farm servants were often born into a cottar household and some aspired to the possession of a smallholding during their lifetime. On the very eve of the great movement to agrarian reorganisation the vast majority of rural dwellers in Scotland depended to a greater or lesser extent on access to land to make ends meet.[5] In essence, therefore, this was still a peasant society which bore a closer similarity to some countries in mainland Europe than to its closest neighbour to the south. Certainly, the commercial element within the rural economy was not only significant but was expanding. However, one recent estimate suggests that in the early eighteenth century only about a quarter of all Scottish farmers were producing whole-heartedly for the market.[6]

There was a clear contrast also in the scale of urban development. Throughout the period before 1760 urban expansion in Scotland proceeded apace but as late as c.1700 an estimated 5 per cent of the national population lived in towns of 10,000 inhabitants or more compared to 14 per cent in England and Wales.[7] This difference partly reflected the much greater commercialisation of English society. In the seventeenth century Scottish overseas trade was less diverse than England's with exports dominated by unprocessed or partly processed primary products and imports by luxuries, manufactures and essential raw materials such as timber and, in years of harvest shortage, grain. In the eighteenth century increasing market activity penetrated the framework of the rural economy more effectively as urban growth intensified and the production of linen and other textiles in the countryside brought many more into the nexus of commercial exchange. But, relative to England, Scotland was still laggard. One telling indicator of this was the very late survival of the 'archaic' controls and regulations associated with traditional societies where the market enclave was relatively weak. The regulation of bread prices and artisan wages lingered on in Scotland into the period of the Napoleonic Wars. This partly explains why, in the later eighteenth century, the incidence of meal rioting in periods of high grain prices was much less common than in England. Intervention either by local authorities or the judiciary until c.1800 cushioned the impact of market forces. On the other hand, when these controls were finally rejected in the early nineteenth century, the effect was more disruptive and helped to fuel the social tensions which intensified in Scotland in the postwar years.[8]

It would be wrong to suggest that Scotland had caught up with England by the end of the period covered by this volume. By 1830 Scottish society was still much poorer and the industrial sector less developed than that of her southern neighbour. But the similarities by that date had become significantly more apparent than the differences. The overall social structure of Scotland was now more akin to England's than to that of other societies in western Europe. This could not have happened other than through a rapid process of social transformation. In simple terms, Scotland by 1830 was a different kind of society to that of 1760.

The precise meaning of this statement requires clarification. It is not suggested in the studies which follow that all major links were severed between the old and the new worlds. Most Scots by 1830 still lived and worked in a rural environment as their forefathers had done. The position of the traditional governing class of the society, the great landowners, was not undermined in this period and may actually have been temporarily strengthened.[9] Traditional religious affiliations were disturbed but religion remained a vital element in the social life.[10] The process of industrialisation was also far from complete in 1830. The great late nineteenth-century staples of coal, iron, engineering and shipbuilding were all underdeveloped. Fast industrial expansion was primarily concentrated in the textiles of linen, cotton and wool before 1830, and the metal manufactures, the giants of the later period, only managed to achieve a modest rate of growth.[11] However, too much stress on the continuities obscures the real significance of the series of social changes which took place in the decades covered by this volume. These produced alterations in the social fabric, not simply at the margins as in the past, but in the structure of society. The way of life of entire social groups was irreversibly changed.

It is true that as late as 1821 as many as two Scots in three still worked on the farm, the croft, in the country village and the small town but the conditions under which they lived were quite different from those of their forebears. By 1830 in the Lowlands most of the agricultural population had become landless employees whose lives were just as much subject to the new pressures of labour discipline, enhanced productivity and cyclical unemployment as those occupied in the burgeoning industries.[12] In the western Highlands a 'peasant' society was indeed maintained but it was quite different from that which existed before the mid-eighteenth century. Indeed, social change in this region was probably more traumatic and cataclysmic than anywhere else in Scotland as the Highlands moved from tribalism to capitalism over less than two generations.[13] The communal farming townships were dissolved by c.1820 and replaced by the system of individual croft holdings whose inhabitants worked to service the requirements of external markets for fish, kelp, whisky, military manpower and cattle. Customary relationships and traditional connections between clan elites and followers swiftly disintegrated as the entire fabric of society was recast in response to landlord demands, ideological fashion and, above all, the overwhelming force of market pressures.

Like everywhere else in western Europe, Scottish population rose in the eighteenth century and growth was not only sustained but accelerated in the nineteenth century. But arguably more significant than actual increase was the redistribution of the population because this was also an important demonstration of the structural changes underway in society. Recent research on comparative urban development in Europe suggests that the rate of urban growth in Scotland at this time was the fastest of any region either in Britain or the Continent.[14] By 1850, Scotland was second only to England and Wales in a 'league table' of 'urbanised societies' but that was a position which had been achieved over a much shorter time scale than the rest of mainland Britain. Urban growth at such a speed suggests a remarkably high level of labour mobility because the towns grew primarily through  inward migration. In many areas of Ireland, rural France and Germany before 1830, substantial proportions of the population often lived and died in the same parish. This was not the case in most areas of Lowland Scotland. Population mobility was already extensive before the mid-eighteenth century but became even more common later as befitted the pace of economic and social change. Land consolidation, the proletarianisation of the agricultural population and rapid urban growth combined to stimulate a very high level of internal permanent and temporary migration and emigration.[15]

There were also profound changes in Scotland's occupational structure though precise evaluation of its scale and extent is impossible at this stage of research. Nevertheless, it is obvious that jobs in manufacturing and services grew at a much faster rate than those in agriculture.[16] In linen, Scotland's staple manufacture in the mid-eighteenth century, output doubled every twenty or twenty-five years between c.1730 and 1800. The average annual yards stamped for sale in 1728-31 were 3,488,232 but had grown to 30,723,707 by 1818-32. The Borders woollen industry also experienced precocious expansion with, for instance, annual wool consumption in the town of Galashiels alone increasing from 17,000 lbs. in 1774 to 500,000 lbs. in 1825. The growth of the cotton industry in the west of Scotland was even more spectacular than either linen or wool though this is the sector least amenable to long-run statistical analysis. But it was because of the combined effect of the huge increase in all these forms of textile production that in 1830 there were around 78,000 handloom weavers in Scotland, the biggest single group of workers in manufacturing in the country and more than three times as many as there had been in the 1760s.

It is possible to argue that the textile industries formed the strategic presence in the Scottish economy for much of this period but it is equally important to stress that gains in production and productivity were spread across a whole range of other economic activities in both manufacturing and agriculture. Commerce, clothing, food and drink processing, domestic service, building, quarrying, milling, baking, brewing and distilling, paper-making, and professional services all made crucial contributions to the development of greater diversity in non-agrarian employment. These tasks were not usually carried out in the factory, which is often taken as the classic symbol of the new age. Technical change, the substitution of machinery for human effort, was mainly confined to some of the textile and metal industries. In consequence, the typical working environment for most Scots remained the land, the workshop and the home rather than the large complex employing several hundred people. But by 1830 the routine in the 'traditional' workplace had also altered. Work patterns were more regular and supervision had become more effective with the overt intention of boosting levels of labour productivity. Most tasks in Scotland by 1830 were still based directly on human effort but they were now organised in a more systematic and disciplined fashion than before.[17]

By 1830, therefore, market forces were dominant and affected the lives of all communities whether they lived in the remote Hebrides or in the centres of large towns. It was over the period of this volume that the commercialisation of Scottish society occurred. The majority of the Scottish people now depended on selling their labour power in the market. The welfare of entire social groups no longer derived from what could be grown on subsistence plots of land but rather on demand for industrial and agricultural labour. This, in turn, was shaped by labour supply and general economic conditions. In Scotland, demographic forces seem to have been a decisive influence on the labour market and so on the living standards of the people.[18]

Scottish population growth was distinctive in being relatively modest in the second half of the eighteenth century before increasing rapidly thereafter. The *actual* rate of growth (i.e. less out-migration) at 0.6 per cent per annum between c.1755 and 1801 was about half that of England's and about one third of Ireland's in the same period.[19] This was also a phase of considerable economic diversification with a consequent release of new employment opportunities. Real wages in many occupations between the 1760s and the 1790s therefore began to rise because, although the labour supply was expanding, it was probably not doing so at the same rate as the economy's new demands for more labour power.[20] The buoyancy of the labour market, the absence of structural unemployment and the gains achieved by several groups in living standards had very significant results. This was also a period of structural change in Scottish society, notably in the acceleration of the existing trend to tenancy consolidation and the removal of cottar holdings in the rural Lowlands. The favourable economic circumstances and the fact that local labour markets were not glutted by too rapid increases in actual population growth eased the process of social transformation and helped to remove the possibilities of major agrarian unrest.

On the other hand, by the early nineteenth century the actual rate of population growth doubled (partly because of Irish immigration) and, in the three decades from 1801 to 1831, achieved levels never again reached for the remainder of the nineteenth century. The age of optimism and relative amelioration came to an end and, especially after the end of the Napoleonic Wars, social antagonisms intensified.[21] It would, of course, be too simple to explain the postwar crisis solely in terms of the demographic variable. But there was considerable evidence of the emergence of a surplus of labour in the western Highlands and Islands and in some of the larger towns by the 1810s and 1820s.[22] The plight of the Irish poor in the cities, the agony of the handloom weavers and the acute destitution of the 'redundant' inhabitants of crofting society were all in part derived from the fact that the labour supply in the country as a whole was now increasing at a much faster rate than the creation of new employment opportunities. There were simply too many hands for the available work. Industrialisation helped to save Scotland from an Irish-type Malthusian catastrophe but economic growth was not yet strong enough to prevent structural unemployment and the regime of low and fluctuating wages which was its inevitable accompaniment.

In the postwar period the demobilisation of soldiers and sailors accentuated the emerging problems of labour surplus. In some years, such as 1816-18, 1825 and 1836, cyclical trade depression caused massive urban distress and maximised insecurity. The problems were aggravated by a new rigour in the application of the Scottish Poor Law and by the crumbling of traditional paternalistic controls on bread prices and artisan wages.[23] In this harsh world social divisions began to harden and the lines of class awareness became stronger and more coherent. The 'Radical War' of 1820 was primarily inspired by the deep tensions which now existed in this rapidly changing society and the conflict between the interests of different groups which were an integral part of the birth process of the new economic order.[24]

## NOTES

1. N.F.R. Crafts, *British Economic Growth during the Industrial Revolution* (Oxford, 1985); M.Berg, *The Age of Manufactures, 1700-1820* (London, 1985), ch.1; P.K. O'Brien and C.Keyder, *Economic Growth in Britain and France, 1780-1914* (London, 1976); P.H.Lindert, 'English Occupations, 1670-1811', *Journal of Economic History*, xl (4), 1980.

2. For summaries and analysis of recent research on the late seventeenth and early eighteenth-century economy see, T.M.Devine, 'The Union of 1707 and Scottish Development', *Scottish Economic and Social History*, 5 (1985), pp. 23-40 and T.C.Smout, 'Where had the Scottish economy got to by 1776 ?' in Istvan Hont and Michael Ignatieff, *Wealth and Income* (Cambridge, 1983), pp. 45-72.

3. M.Lynch (ed.), *The Early Modern Town in Scotland* (London, 1986).

4. Chapter 1 below.

5. Chapter 3 below.

6. R.A.Dodgshon, *Land and Society in Early Scotland* (Oxford, 1981).

7. Chapter 2 below.

8. Chapter 13 below.

9. Chapter 5 below.

10. Chapter 8 below.

11. The economic history of this period is covered in R.H.Campbell, *Scotland since 1707* (Edinburgh, 1985 ed.); H.Hamilton, *The Industrial Revolution in Scotland* (Oxford, 1932); B.Lenman, *An Economic History of Modern Scotland, 1660-1976* (London, 1977); T.C.Smout, *A History of the Scottish People, 1560-1830* (London, 1969); S.G.E.Lythe and J.Butt, *An Economic History of Scotland, 1100-1939* (Glasgow, 1975); A.Slaven, *The Development of the West of Scotland, 1750-1960* (London, 1975).

12. Chapter 3 below.

13. Chapter 4 below.

14. Chapter 2 below.

15. Chapter 1 below.
16. Chapter 11 below.
17. *Ibid.*
18. Chapter 10 below.
19. N.L.Tranter, *Population and Society, 1750-1940* (London, 1985), p. 36.
20. Chapter 9 below.
21. Chapters 7,10,12,13-14 below.
22. T.M.Devine, *The Great Highland Famine: Hunger, Emigration and the Scottish Highlands in the Nineteenth Century* (Edinburgh, 1988); N.Murray, *The Scottish Handloom Weavers, 1790-1850* (Edinburgh, 1978), chs. 2, 4-5.
23. Chapters 12 and 13 below.
24. Chapter 14 below.

CHAPTER 1

# The Demographic Regime

## R.A. Houston

## Introduction

Between 1760 and 1850 Scotland's economy and society were transformed. From a poor, rural country on the fringes of Europe, Scotland was catapulted by industrial development, agrarian improvement, and the growth and redistribution of population into an urbanised, industrialised and wealthy nation of world importance. The process was still incomplete in 1830, but many of the distinctive features of modern Scottish society which were being created in this century, notably the concentration of population in large towns and in the central Lowlands, were intimately associated with the sustained and rapid increase in numbers. This chapter outlines the nature of this process and examines the reasons behind it.

The importance of population trends to many features of economic and social life in the past was recognised by contemporaries such as a Thomas Malthus and has occupied historians for many years. Regrettably, the sources for Scottish demographic history are poor in both quality and quantity during this period, meaning that attempts to understand the process of population change in the early years of the Industrial Revolution are fraught with uncertainty. Shortcomings in the documentation make it hard to be certain about what caused population to grow, but it is possible to establish a plausible picture which sits reasonably comfortably with the limited material available. Two small steps can be taken to help the analysis. First, a comparative approach has been adopted since this enables us to establish the bounds of possibility and to distinguish those features of Scotland's demographic history which were special from those common to other European countries. At the same time, historical demography is far more developed as a field of study in England, France and Scandinavia than it is in Scotland. Methods, results and explanations derived from literature on the populations of these countries will help to clarify Scotland's experience. Second, the chronological bounds of this chapter have been stretched, partly because of the need to establish the context for population developments during the early Industrial

9

Revolution and partly to make use of the more extensive and reliable demographic figures which become available during the 1850s and 1860s.[1] A similar approach is adopted in the next chapter on Urbanisation, a theme which also requires the kind of precise quantification only available by the middle decades of the nineteenth century.

## Sources

In twentieth-century Britain demographic analysis is based on reliable, compulsory registration of births, marriages and deaths coupled with national censuses of population held once a decade. For historical demographers of later eighteenth and early nineteenth-century Scotland the position is very different. The first national census was conducted in 1801 though the amount of information which was recorded in that and the other five early nineteenth-century censuses was much inferior to what is offered in those from 1861 on. Civil registration of vital events was not initiated in Scotland until 1855, nearly two decades after England and 120 years after Denmark and Norway. In the absence of such documentation, the historian must often rely on sources which were not compiled for statistical purposes and which are therefore open to omissions and inaccuracy. These sources include local investigations into the size and structure of populations, such as lists of tax payers, communicants and those liable for military service. The only national survey before 1801 was carried out by the Reverend Alexander Webster in 1755, stimulated partly by personal interest, partly by government concern and partly as an actuarial exercise associated with a pension scheme for the dependents of parish clergy. In addition, the *Statistical Account of Scotland* complied by Sir John Sinclair from the returns of parish ministers during the early 1790s contains demographic information of varying reliability and comprehensiveness. Patterns of internal migration can be determined by using testimonials of moral and religious acceptability issued to movers by the Kirk, estate papers of hirings and leasings which give the place of last residence, and apprentice records. Population turnover can be crudely quantified by comparing successive listings of inhabitants or by contrasting expected rates of natural increase with observed populations of parishes or counties. Emigration estimates are based on customs officials' investigations into the muster rolls which skippers had to furnish under the Passenger Acts, along with records from places of destination. All can be supplemented by literary evidence.

Most important of these imperfect sources are parish registers of ecclesiastical ceremonies — baptisms, marriages and burials — on which historical demographers rely for many of the statistics required to build up a picture of the demographic regime. These sorts of documents have been used extensively and successfully to reconstruct population patterns for England from the sixteenth century and France from the later seventeenth century. Two techniques have been employed. Aggregative analysis involves comparing totals of baptisms, marriages and burials over a given time period in order to determine trends in crude fertility and mortality rates. More sophisticated but much more time-consuming is family reconstitution which builds up the genealogies of hundreds of families by linking named individuals in the registers. This technique allows analysis of important components such as infant mortality, age at marriage and the fertility of married women. In both quality and quantity of parish registration Scotland lagged behind her European neighbours, which means that detailed and reliable demographic analysis is not possible on any scale for Scotland. Advocates of civil registration vilified the accuracy and comprehensiveness of Scotland's parochial registers, calling them patchy, defective and all but useless as a record of actual demographic events. [2]

To a large extent this condemnation was deserved. Some vital events were not recorded at all while others were erratically and often seriously under-registered. Registration of deaths is particularly poor, with many infant deaths never written down by the parish clerk. Many parishes did not keep regular baptism and marriage registers: only 99 of 850 parishes which made returns to the census authorities in 1801 did so, and fewer still kept burial records. Marriage registers sometimes only record proclamations of banns and are thus records of *intention* to wed. Starting in 1551, the Scottish church had made frequent attempts to ensure that baptisms, marriages and burials were properly recorded but failed for four principal reasons.

Firstly, people had to pay to use the services of the established church and to have a christening or marriage or burial recorded in the official register. Charges were not exorbitant but were a sufficient disincentive for poorer people to register. A tax on registration introduced for a short time in 1783 had a serious impact on the number of events recorded, especially the registration of infant burials, and highlights the detrimental effect of cost. Secondly, developing religious pluralism in eighteenth and nineteenth-century Scotland reduced the comprehensiveness of registration. Few parish registers survive for the Catholic Highlands even at the end of the eighteenth century, and the Lowlands saw a fragmentation of Protestantism into a variety of camps, beginning in 1690 with the Presbyterian-Episcopalian split, passing through the secession of 1733 and the creation of a 'Relief Church' in 1761, and culminating in 1843 with the famous 'Disruption' which saw the establishment of the Free Church of Scotland. Protestant dissenters might be reluctant to use the services of an official Presbyterian minister and their vital events could escape registration. And those who had fallen foul of the church by producing a bastard child or who had failed to meet the standards of religious knowledge required to receive the services of the established minister could have the rites of baptism and marriage performed by an official of another denomination. 'Irregular' marriage did not require a clergyman. Thirdly, many Scottish parishes were very large both in area and population, meaning either that it was difficult to reach the church or that there were too many parishioners for the authorities to scrutinise. Urban growth exacerbated these problems during our period: St Cuthbert's, Edinburgh had roughly 30,000 people living in it by the end of the eighteenth century. Gaps in registration occasioned by changes of parish clerk are common. Finally, the Scottish law of marriage remained archaic until 1855 unlike England where Hardwicke's 1753 Marriage Act established only one legally binding form of wedlock. In Scotland there were four different but equally firm ways of creating a union, of which marriage in church by the official minister was only one.[3]

For all these reasons, the registration of vital events was far from complete: for example, Turnbull estimated in 1854 that only one birth in three was registered in Glasgow. Whatever the accuracy of this statement the shortcomings in parish registers are clear and the implication is that the demographic measures for our period fall a long way short of total accuracy. Only after 1855 does civil registration provide us with a firm statistical foundation.

## Components of Population Change

The growth, stagnation or decay of any population depends directly on the relative levels of fertility and mortality, and indirectly on nuptiality and the volume of migration. Scotland, along with most other European countries, experienced a sustained and unprecedented growth in population between 1750 and 1850 which was the result of a complex interaction between birth rates, death rates, marriage rates and net migration. Historians have devoted considerable effort to discovering the reasons for this 'modern rise of population': was it caused principally by growing fertility as in England or declining mortality as in Sweden, and if so what brought about the rise in birth rates or the fall in death rates?[4]

Scotland's population in 1755 numbered some 1.25 million, 1.6 million by 1801 and 2.6 million in 1841. In the first half-century the annual rate of growth was about 0.6 per cent (just over half that obtaining in England) compared with 1.2 per cent in the subsequent five decades: only slightly behind that of England. These rates are modest by the standards of third world countries in the twentieth century and were eclipsed by Ireland's 2.1 per cent, 1791-1821.

Yet population was at best stagnant during the century before 1750 and the increase which began in the eighteenth century was sustained until well into the twentieth century. Population increased more quickly in some decades than others: between 1811 and 1821 the rate was nearly 1.6 per cent a year. And some regions grew more rapidly than others, notably the Western Isles. Mull and the Outer Hebrides saw an 80 per cent increase between 1755 and 1811 while the population of Tiree trebled in the years 1755 to 1831.

Defects in the evidence make it very difficult to be certain about the reasons for population increase and the contrasts in growth patterns within Britain. Scotland in the 1850s and 1860s possessed crude birth and death rates which were in almost all respects identical to those of England, though marital fertility was higher than in both France and England. Household size and structure were both similar and stable, influenced more by enduring cultural values than by economic, social or demographic change. The sex ratio was slightly more biased towards women than in England, but the age-distribution of the population was virtually homogeneous across mainland Britain: 37 per cent of Scotland's people were aged fourteen or under in 1841 while 4 per cent were sixty-five or older. Population structure may not always have been so close, and superficially similar structures do not mean that the mechanisms behind change were also identical. In fact, the dynamics of growth seem to have been very different in the later eighteenth and early nineteenth centuries, as the following estimates of the basic components of population trends show:

*Crude Birth and Death Rates per Thousand Population in Scotland, England and France, 1755/6, c.1791, 1861*

|         | C B R | | | C D R | | |
|---------|----------|---------|--------|----------|---------|--------|
|         | Scotland | England | France | Scotland | England | France |
| 1755/6  | 41       | 33      | 41     | 38       | 26      | 36     |
| c.1791  | 35       | 39      | 37     | 24       | 26      | 31     |
| 1861    | 35       | 36      | 27     | 22       | 21      | 23     |

What these rates suggest is that Scotland had what might be called a 'high-pressure' demographic regime in the mid-eighteenth century: high births rates were cancelled out by swingeing mortality. If they are correct, expectation of life at birth in mid-eighteenth century Scotland must have been of the order of twenty-six or twenty-seven (based on stable population theory and the use of model life tables), while in England it was anything up to ten years or 30 per cent better. Work in progress suggests that this scenario may be too extreme and that life expectancy may be closer to thirty years. In the 1790s both countries had an expectation of life at birth in the late thirties. If these estimates are true, Scotland resembled France much more than her nearest neighbour.

Fertility fell in the second half of the eighteenth century, as it did in France (though marital fertility was probably higher in Scotland throughout), but this was more than offset by a spectacular improvement in the chances of survival, an amelioration in life expectancy at birth of roughly one third in less than four decades: similar in pace to France where twenty-eight years was the average life expectancy at birth until the 1780s and the Scottish/English level of the last decade of the eighteenth century was not achieved until the 1830s. We must exercise some caution here since the eighteenth-century Scottish figures are subject to a possibly large but unquantifiable margin of error. The mid-eighteenth-century figure may be too pessimistic about life expectancy and/ or that of the 1790s too optimistic. The apparent reduction in fertility may also be overstated during this period since the age structure of the population in Webster's census of 1755 is a rather 'old' one which suggests low fertility. Yet, even if the mortality of the early eighteenth century is exaggerated, or that of the 1790s underestimated, there is still a substantial improvement in life expectancy between the middle of the eighteenth century and the middle of the nineteenth which must be explained.

**Mortality**

In late twentieth-century Britain half of all deaths in a given year take place among those aged eighty and above. Mortality in infancy and childhood accounts for approximately 2 per cent of deaths. The mortality regime of the later eighteenth and early nineteenth centuries was very different. Estimates of age-specific mortality are extremely tentative for this period, but the overall profile and trend seem clear. A fifth to a quarter of all babies born alive in mid-eighteenth-century Scotland died before their first birthday, though this had fallen to a sixth by the 1790s and to one eighth in 1855. The causes of mortality were also very different from today, deadly infections being the most common killers. The final distinguishing feature of seventeenth-century mortality is that it continued to display marked fluctuations in intensity with 'crisis' years in which deaths climbed to double their normal level. The stabilisation of this crisis mortality in the eighteenth century was, according to Flinn and others, the most important reason for sustained population growth since the natural surplus of births over deaths which had always existed was allowed to continue unabated for longer periods than had ever been possible in the seventeenth century. Care is required here, because the important factor is not the prevalence of peaks in mortality, but the *underlying* death rate which may be relatively unaffected by the more spectacular but short-lived and often localised crises. Yet mortality certainly declined and we must try to explain why.[5]

Early modern Scotland shared with most other countries in Europe a susceptibility to famine. Death from starvation on any scale was almost unknown in England after 1623 but persisted in France and Highland Scotland into the eighteenth century (albeit at a subdued level), in Ireland until the 1840s and in Finland as late as 1865. Primitive, inflexible agricultural techniques meant that many of the peasantry risked being pushed below the margins of subsistence and that climatic accidents could bring about short-ages, high prices and even starvation. The last serious national famine ravaged Scotland during the 1690s, killing off perhaps one person in seven. During the eighteenth century, subsistence crises were much rarer and more localised: the shortages of 1782-3 were, for example, largely confined to the Highlands and Islands and involved few deaths. Indeed, from the 1690s onwards starvation played only a minor role in Scotland's demographic history. There are many examples of misery and want even in the nineteenth century, but people did not starve to death in any numbers. The conquest of famine can be put down to improved provision of ordinary poor relief, special emergency relief measures, developments in transport and marketing, economic growth which created the income to buy in more food from abroad and, from the 1770s, rapid agricultural improvements and the introduction in the Highlands of the potato.

Scotland's population was better fed in the later eighteenth century than a century before. Historians usually assume that as people become better nourished they become less susceptible to morbid diseases. Improved nutri-tion may indeed have helped to prevent men, women and children from dying of certain infections such as tuberculosis, pneumonia and some gastro-intestinal diseases which debilitate through diarrhoea, but there is no clear evidence of a general connection between malnutrition and enhanced likeli-hood of dying from diseases. Typhus and starvation, which tend to occur together, may, for example, arise from the same causes but be otherwise unrelated. If falling mortality from disease was important to the improvements in life expectancy we must explain it either by the increasing effectiveness of medical intervention, or better hygiene, or autonomous changes in the relationship between microbes and their hosts.

Plague had disappeared from Scotland in the 1640s, but other killer diseases continued, of which smallpox was the most significant. Smallpox was one of the most common causes of death in the eighteenth century, accounting for a sixth of all mortality in Kilmarnock between 1728 and 1764, and for a fifth of deaths among those under ten years in Glasgow during the last two decades of the eighteenth century. Yet medical developments were beginning to make headway against smallpox. Inoculation was used in some parts of Scotland from the mid-eighteenth century, but it was the discovery of vaccination by Jenner in 1798 and its rapid adoption under the auspices of the

Church and of the College of Surgeons in Edinburgh which made the most significant inroads into smallpox mortality. Between 1805 and 1812 only 2-3 per cent of all child deaths in Glasgow were attributed to smallpox.

Human intervention was highly effective in this case and vaccination may, in theory, have accounted for up to a half of the early nineteenth century fall in mortality. However, children saved from smallpox might succumb to other diseases such as measles, a negligible cause of mortality in the middle of the eighteenth century but one which accounted for 10 per cent of deaths, 1807-12. And the 1830s and 1840s saw the arrival of cholera epidemics from Europe (producing considerable public alarm but relatively few deaths), along with renewed waves of typhus, both of which preyed particularly on the inhabitants of the overcrowded cities of the central Lowlands. Lurking in the background was a spectrum of air-, animal-, insect- and water-borne infections such as influenza, scarlet fever, whooping cough, dysentery and typhoid. Most of these diseases were poorly understood: against them there was no effective precaution and no cure. Many were not eradicated until much later in the nineteenth or twentieth century by changes in medical care, building, sanitation and personal hygiene.

With the exception of smallpox vaccination, it is debatable whether developments in medical care contributed to the decline in mortality during the later eighteenth and early nineteenth centuries. Scottish medicine was among the best in Europe though its accessibility and effectiveness were still limited and medical intervention could be positively pernicious if the patient was subjected to the usual regime of purges, bleedings and blisters. Rising real wages from the end of the eighteenth century made changes of clothing and the washing of garments and persons more common. The urban environment in the eighteenth century began to be improved marginally in ways which might in theory have reduced the spread of disease. Civic authorities made some progress in improving water supplies and in cleaning up the streets of Edinburgh, said to be the dirtiest town in Britain during the early eighteenth century. On balance, however, the growing concentration of people in towns tended to make them less salubrious, especially between 1810 and 1830, and it was not until after 1850 that significant improvements were made in the urban environment.

Human action had also played a part in the conquest of famine. Yet changes in mortality may have resulted from developments wholly independent of these interventions. Put simply, men, women and (to a lesser extent) children may have developed a growing immunity to certain diseases which reduced their morbidity. At least part of the improvement in life expectancy may have been the product of wholly autonomous changes in the nature of micro-organisms which made them less virulent, or of a new accommodation between microbes and men which increased human resistance to infectious disease. It is impossible to quantify the importance of this independent factor but it must have been significant in the later eighteenth century since the major improvement in, say, deaths from typhus came well before medical developments could have played any part.

## Nuptiality and Fertility

Historians have usually assigned to changes in mortality the principal role in explaining the rise of population in later eighteenth-century Scotland. They tend, in consequence, to discount the importance of fertility, arguing that it changed too slowly to be of much importance to demographic expansion. Changes in mortality were undoubtedly important but we should not automatically credit all population growth between the 1750s and 1850s to improvements in life expectancy. Empirical research has shown that in England fertility increase accounts for three-quarters of the acceleration in population growth during the eighteenth century. Lack of reliable parish registers and civil registration makes the sort of sophisticated statistical investigation recently conducted into English population impossible for Scotland, but we can build up a tentative picture of fertility and the ways in which it changed.

Over most of north-western Europe, the vast majority of children were born within wedlock. In 1861 9 per cent of all births were illegitimate in Scotland: higher than England's 7 per cent but equal to Denmark and lower than Austria's 11 per cent. Higher bastardy levels in Scotland may be accounted for partly by disagreements over the definition of marriage, but there are further distinctive features. Most obvious is the pronounced regional variation in illegitimacy not paralleled in England. The western Border counties and north-eastern Scotland had the highest levels, possibly because parental supervision of courtship was weak and because single women could support themselves more easily in these areas, possibly because of the relative strength of the Church's moral discipline in different areas. The differences are striking. Women in their twenties who lived in Banff were five times more likely to have a bastard than those in Ross, and teenagers were twenty times more susceptible. Levels in earlier periods were lower, about 4 per cent over Scotland as a whole between 1660 and 1770, though the under-registration of illegitimate births was probably substantial. The parish register of Blair Atholl in Perthshire records thirteen bastard children between 1775 and 1779 but the Kirk Session minutes (which record offences against the church's precepts, including sexual immorality) mention thirty-two. Kilmarnock in the 1750s had an illegitimacy ratio of 2 per cent, Cathcart in Renfrewshire 8 per cent during the 1770s and 1780s, Blair Atholl 5 per cent between 1775 and 1779, Portpartrick (Wigtownshire) 8 per cent in the mid-1830s. Regional variations were similarly pronounced in the eighteenth century: the level in the central Lowlands averaged 3 per cent up to the 1760s but for Caithness it was 8 per cent and around 1770 south-west Scotland's illegitimacy ratio shot up to 12 per cent. Illegitimacy may have risen slightly during the later eighteenth and early nineteenth centuries, but the resulting contribution to any rise in total fertility was very small.[6]

The low levels of illegitimate fertility mean that we must concentrate on fertility within marriage. We have no reliable figures on the frequency with which married women in Scotland produced children at different stages of their lives before the middle of the nineteenth century, but it probably did not alter very much during our period. We know almost nothing about changes in Scottish breast-feeding practices which might influence marital fertility in the same way as it did in eighteenth and nineteenth-century Europe. Until the later nineteenth century there was no widespread use of modern contraceptive techniques which would permit birth *control* as we understand it. Men and women could *limit* completed family size but only by spacing births through the use of abstinence, *coitus interruptus* and prolonged breast feeding. However, if they wished to have a sex life, couples could not make an effective decision to stop childbearing completely before the woman's fertile span ended naturally in the early to mid forties.

Lack of modern contraceptive techniques, stable age-specific marital fertility and low bastardy levels mean that the age at which women first married is crucial to an understanding of overall fertility changes. Women can only conceive between the ages of approximately fifteen and forty-five, and thus have thirty years of possible childbearing if they marry at puberty. The age at which women first marry thus has a powerful influence on fertility: if early, fertility will be high (*ceteris paribus*), but the longer the delay between puberty and marriage, the lower will be fertility. Changes in age at first marriage for women must therefore influence fertility trends. If the age falls, then more of a woman's reproductive span can be used, the average length of a generation will be shortened and fertility will rise; the reverse will be the case if women begin to marry later.

In Scotland, and indeed all north-western Europe, marriage occurred long after puberty and usually in the mid-twenties. In 1861 the mean age at first marriage for women was twenty-five, and what evidence we have from a few dozen cases in one Lowland parish (Kilmarnock) in the mid-eighteenth century suggests a figure of a twenty-four for urban areas and twenty-six for rural at this time. Marriage came earlier for women in towns because superior industrial employment opportunities meant that they could, with their husbands, set up independent households more easily than in the rural Lowlands where farm tenancies or labouring jobs were less readily accessible. Trends in marriage age during the decades between the 1750s and 1850s are vital to an understanding of population growth.

Regrettably, demographic figures for the later eighteenth century are poor. Some idea of trends in age at first marriage can be gained for the early decades of the nineteenth century from the 1855 civil registration. Those who reported the death of a married woman to the civil authorities in 1855 were asked, among other things, to provide her age at death and the date of birth of all her children. Given that the interval between marriage and first birth was relatively constant at just over one year, the average age at first marriage can be calculated from the mean age of mother at first birth. Tentative figures derived from this source suggest that the age at which women first married was stable between the 1780s and 1810s. During the 1820s average age at first marriage for women was approximately twenty-six falling slightly to twenty-five in the early 1850s.

Further evidence of stable fertility in the first two decades of the nineteenth century is provided by the age structure of the population in the 1821 census. Periods of rising fertility produce populations with a large proportion of young people. England provides an excellent example since rapid increases in fertility created an 1821 age structure with 48 per cent of the population aged fourteen or less. In Scotland the figure of 38 per cent reveals that fertility had not risen nearly as much in the preceding years as in England.

These trends in age at first marriage may not have applied to the Highland zones. Anecdotal remarks by clergy and visitors to the Highlands point to a much lower age at marriage there in the eighteenth century. This may have been true of the Western Islands but it does not square with a partial family reconstitution of Laggan (Invernessshire) between 1775 and 1811 which found that women normally married at twenty-six to twenty-eight. Using the same information from death registration in 1855 as for the Lowlands, in the 1810s and 1820s the likely age at first marriage in the shires of Inverness and Ross was twenty-eight or twenty-nine. Population pressure in the Highlands may have encouraged later marriage from the end of the eighteenth century in an effort to balance people with resources. This late marriage for women created a powerful constraint on fertility. Men were usually two or three years older than their spouses throughout our period, but males are unimportant to fertility trends unless, for whatever reason, there are so few that women cannot find marriage partners. These circumstances were not applicable to Scotland at the time of the Industrial Revolution.

Also central to an understanding of fertility is the proportion of women who never married before the end of their childbearing span. In this respect Scotland and England were very different. Female celibacy in Scotland was double that of England at the time of the 1861 census: 20 per cent of Scottish women had not married by age fifty compared with 10 per cent in England. Between the mid-eighteenth century and 1861 English celibacy barely exceeded 10 per cent and sometimes fell to half that figure. Between c.1740 and c.1790 approximately 20-25 per cent of Scottish women had never been married by their mid-forties in a sample of Lowland burial registers, and the Statistical Account points towards levels of 15-20 per cent in the early 1790s over the country as a whole. These high and rather stable levels match those of nineteenth-century Ireland and must have exerted a powerful constraint on total fertility. The figures suggest a slight fall in celibacy in the late eighteenth century which would have allowed total fertility to rise, but we cannot rely too heavily upon them. As with illegitimacy, any changes were slight and the impact on trends in fertility minimal.

### Redistribution, Emigration and Turnover

Population growth between the 1750s and the 1850s altered certain demographic structures and accelerated others with a long history. Most important among the continuities was the presence in both rural and urban areas of a substantial volume of population mobility. For single people, brief employment terms of six to twelve months and desire to improve working conditions or find a marriage partner made mobility a common experience. Farmers too might have to move fairly frequently since most rented their land on short leases. At the same time, the structure of landowning and landholding made subdivision difficult in the Lowlands and indeed the trend was towards larger and fewer farms with the result that people had to accept a lower status occupation in the community (cottar, servant or labourer instead of tenant farmer), or move to another farm, or pull up roots and head for the towns in periods of population growth. The proletarianisation of many rural dwellers and the growth in non-agricultural occupations made mobility increasingly common, especially in the Lowlands.

The substantial proportions of the population of rural France and Germany who were born, lived and died in the same parish were never matched in Scotland: two thirds of the families listed for the village of Kippen in Stirlingshire in1789 were not resident there in 1793. The steady, often long-distance movement of young adult males apprenticed to craftsmen and tradesmen in Edinburgh and the other major, established cities was contracting in the later eighteenth century as the institution of apprenticeship declined and as intervening opportunities opened up in other growing towns. Other types of mobility remained frequent. In the household of the earl of Leven and Melville in Fife between 1754 and 1793, 83 per cent of female servants (single people employed by the year or half-year for keep and a small wage in cash and kind) and 68 per cent of males stayed less than one year; 97 per cent of females and 90 per cent of men-servants remained four years or less. Most rural mobility was over short distances: families who settled in twenty-five planned villages in north-east Scotland between 1740 and 1850 had mostly come from less than twenty miles away. In the growing towns, most workers rented their accommodation and movement within cities was similarly frequent. Population turnover was rapid and concentrated in those stages of the life-cycle between puberty, when young men and women first went into service outside their parental household, and marriage, when they set their own family unit.[7]

The same is true of the growing volume of seasonal migration. Movement of Highlanders to the arable areas of the eastern Lowlands had existed in the seventeenth century, but the volume of movement accelerated during the eighteenth century. There were two main reasons for this. First, and most important, the growing pressure of population on resources in the Highlands and Islands. On Tiree the average population per farm 'toun' increased from fifty-six in 1768 to eighty-two in 1792, and it is scarcely surprising that as early as 1771 the duke of Argyll described the island as 'over-peopled'. From the middle of the eighteenth century, observers of Highland society remarked on the subdivision of landholdings and their tiny size, describing the tenantry as 'the most beggarly wretches' imaginable.[8] The Edinburgh newspaper *Caledonian Mercury* carried a story in September 1799 about the many Highland harvest workers driven into Edinburgh and the Lothians by misery at home and the hope of work.

Second, the Lowlands provided employments on a scale not available in the Highlands with the result that both permanent and seasonal migration became common. Shearing corn was the most significant agricultural employment but the growth of towns in the early nineteenth century also created opportunities for domestic service and industrial work, especially for females. Most Highland families had at least one member involved in temporary migration by the 1840s, ensuring a degree of income flexibility which eased impoverishment and helped to slow down depopulation. In coastal areas kelping, cattle raising, fishing and the advent of the potato also alleviated the worst effects of over-population, though when employments did eventually contract, the problem was made even worse. Finally, on the Highland margin in Perthshire, Argyll and eastern Inverness rural domestic industry (notably woollen and linen spinning) supplemented income.

Despite the presence of factors which did help the balance between population and resources in the less economically developed northern and western zones, an increasing number of Highlanders uprooted themselves permanently and moved to the Lowlands. Most of this movement was 'voluntary'. Forcible evictions were comparatively rare until the second quarter of the nineteenth century (Sutherland in the 1800s and 1810s is an exception), and indeed many landowners tried to prevent migration south and overseas. In 1755 the central belt of Scotland, which now contains nine-tenths of the population, contained 37 per cent of her people. By 1821 this had risen to 47 per cent, all achieved at the expense of the northern parts whose share fell from 51 per cent to 41 per cent and has declined steadily ever since. Permanent migrants from the Highlands moved principally into the towns of the western central Lowlands. One in ten of Greenock's inhabitants was Highland-born in 1741 but by 1791 nearly one in three.

Urban growth was by far the most significant aspect of redistribution during our period. Some 9 per cent of Scotland's people lived in towns of 10,000 or more inhabitants in 1750 compared with 17 per cent by 1800, a rate of growth much faster than that of contemporary England (17 per cent and 20 per cent respectively) and indeed more rapid than that of any other European country except Poland which started from an extremely low level of 1 per cent in 1750. Urban growth accounts for a large proportion of total increase in population. Between 1755 and the early 1790s the growth of the Edinburgh/ Leith complex formed 86 per cent of the total increase in population experienced by the Lothians. Nearly all the biggest towns of the mid-nineteenth century were long-established burghs and had already been among the largest in the early eighteenth century. Scotland had five cities of 10,000 inhabitants or more in 1750 and just eight in 1800 compared with England's twenty-one and forty-four respectively. New, large towns were unusual, though the factory town of Catrine is an exception. The most important established centres were Edinburgh, Glasgow, Aberdeen, Dundee, Perth and Greenock but the most rapid growth occurred in the manufacturing towns such as Paisley which had 7,000 inhabitants in 1755, 31,000 in 1801 and 47,000 as early as 1821. Most of Paisley's expansion was fed by rural immigrants from Ayrshire and Renfrewshire. Glasgow too surged from 32,000 during the 1750s to 147,000 in 1821; by 1841 it held a tenth of the population and the distinction of being the least salubrious environment in Scotland. There were a number of planned communities such as New Lanark, Inveraray and Tobermory, none of them notable success stories in terms of growth rates.[9]

Localised movement in rural areas did little directly to alter the distribution of population. Movement from Highlands to Lowlands or from rural to urban living, on the other hand, did create changes in the demographic complexion of Scotland. It was from this sort of movement that Scotland's emigrants often sprang, though motivation ranged from the bulk departure of poor Highlanders for Canada to that of skilled Lowlanders seeking to better themselves in the Americas. Some Lowlanders were affected by changes in landlord priorities: farms increased in size and decreased in number, the opportunities to become a tenant farmer contracted and new labour force requirements reduced the number of sub-tenants. Social and economic changes in both Highlands and Lowlands therefore encouraged movement both within Scotland and overseas.

Migration is difficult to quantify since systematic sources covering the whole of Scotland are unknown before the nineteenth century. One estimate puts the departing Scots at 1 per cent of the population between 1763 and 1775, another suggests that in the last third of the eighteenth century emigration accounted for a sixth or a seventh of the natural increase. The volume of emigration was probably much lower before 1850 than after. Rates of emigration were certainly higher than in contemporary England though nowhere near Ireland's outpouring of the 1840s. Between 1871 and 1880 5 per cent of the natural increase in England's population was creamed off by out-migration, compared with 20 per cent for Scotland and 145 per cent for Ireland, differentials which seem to have been broadly replicated in earlier decades.

The traffic in people was not exclusively out of Scotland. Living standards and opportunities might be limited in Scotland compared with England or the New World, but they were still better than in Ireland. The volume of Irish immigration increased noticably after c.1780 attracted by optimism about the growth of industrial employment and buoyant real wages in Scotland, driven by pessimism about troubled political and economic conditions in their homeland. The 1841 census revealed the presence of 125,000 Irish-born living in Scotland, and 19 per cent of Dundee's people were natives of that country in 1861.


**Conclusion**


The tone of this chapter has been deliberately cautious, since material on the structures of, and changes in, fertility and mortality before the middle of the nineteenth century is at best sketchy and at worst inconsistent. Much research remains to be done not only on purely demographic dimensions, but also on social and cultural aspects such as geographical mobility, marriage formation and the role of women in work and family. The most important force behind Scotland's growing population between c.1750 and c.1860 was a fall in mortality. Fertility had its part to play but because changes in illegitimacy, fertility within marriage and celibacy were very small, the principal mechanism was the rise and fall in age at first marriage for women. Population rose slowly from 1700 to 1750 as Scotland recovered from the appalling mortality of the 1690s. Between c.1750 and c.1820 total fertility was probably stable. The decades between c.1750 and c.1800 saw a substantial improvement in life expectancy which produced the fastest rates of growth witnessed in either the eighteenth or nineteenth century. After c.1820 mortality levels improved only slowly but fertility rose until c.1870. The fall in mortality during our period has not been equalled in its rapidity since, though it was not until the late nineteenth century that the first contraceptive revolution produced the most fundamental change in historical fertility levels, allowing an unprecedented combination of falling age at first marriage and declining fertility.

The consequences of population growth and redistribution for Scotland's economy and society were considerable. Urbanisation created strains on educational resources, poor relief provisions, health care and public order. Yet, in the society as a whole, the ratio of dependent to productive members of the population remained relatively favourable compared with England where by 1821 more than half the population were either too old or too young to be net producers of wealth. Scotland avoided the worst effects of over-population evident in Ireland in the second quarter of the nineteenth century, and indeed joined with England as the first country to experience an Industrial Revolution. Population growth helped to create an industrial labour force, while willingness to move produced the necessary population redistribution for urban and industrial production. Relatively slow rates of population increase in the second half of the eighteenth century coupled with rising real wages in Scotland may have eased the transition to an industrialised society for a country which was still much poorer than England. Perhaps the most significant conclusion to draw from demographic developments between c.1750 and c.1850 is that the different regimes and the diverse mechanisms of change in Scotland and England were both equally compatible with the onset of economic change.

## NOTES

I should like to thank Michael Anderson, Tom Devine, Rowy Mitchison, Christopher Smout and Tony Wrigley for comments on earlier drafts of this chapter.

1. Unless otherwise stated, all material in this chapter is drawn from M.Flinn (ed.), *Scottish Population History from the Seventeenth Century to the 1930s* (Cambridge, 1977) and N.L.Tranter, *Population and Society, 1750-1940* (London, 1985). The latter contains a useful bibliography. There are now rather dated summaries of population

structures and trends in certain general texts on Scotland, including T.C. Smout, *A History of the Scottish People, 1560-1830* (Glasgow, 1972), pp. 240-60 and S.G.E. Lythe and J. Butt, *An Economic History of Scotland, 1110-1939* (Glasgow, 1975), pp. 87-107. Statistics on, and interpretations of, England and Continental Europe are to be found in E.A. Wrigley and R.S. Schofield, *The Population History of England, 1541-1871: A Reconstruction* (London, 1981); E.A. Wrigley, 'The growth of population in eighteenth-century England: a conundrum resolved', *Past and Present*, 98 (1983), pp. 121-50; E.A. Wrigley, 'The fall of marital fertility in nineteenth-century France: exemplar or exception?', *European Journal of Population*, 1 (1985), pp. 31-60 and 141-77; J. Mokyr and C. O'Grada, 'New developments in Irish population history, 1700-1850', *Economic History Review*, 37 (1984), pp. 473-88; M. Anderson, 'British population, 1700-1950', in F.M.L. Thompson (ed.) *The Cambridge Social History of Britain* (Cambridge, 1988); M. Anderson, *Population Change in North-western Europe, 1750-1850* (London, 1988).

2. W.B. Turnbull, *Memoranda of the State of the Parochial Registers of Scotland* (Edinburgh, 1854); G. Seton, *Sketch of the History and Imperfect Condition of the Parochial Registers of Births, Deaths and Marriages in Scotland* (Edinburgh, 1854).

3. T.C. Smout, 'Scottish marriage, regular and irregular, 1500-1940', in R.B. Outhwaite (ed.), *Marriage and Society* (London, 1981), pp. 204-36. The splintering of ecclesiastical registration which has made sophisticated demographic research so difficult in Scotland has had a similar effect in Holland.

4. T. McKeown, *The Modern Rise of Population* (London, 1976); R. Floud and D. McCloskey (eds.), *The Economic History of Britain since 1700*, vol.1 (Cambridge, 1981); G. Mackenroth, *Bevölkerungslehre* (Berlin, 1953); Wrigley and Schofield, *Population History of England*.

5. M.W. Flinn, *The European Demographic System, 1500-1820* (London, 1981).

6. L. Leneman, 'The study of illegitimacy in Kirk Session records: two eighteenth-century Perthshire parishes', *Local Population Studies*, 31 (1983), pp. 29-33; L. Leneman and R. Mitchison, 'Scottish illegitimacy ratios in the early modern period', *Economic History Review*, 40 (1987), pp. 41-63.

7. R.A. Houston, 'Geographical mobility in Scotland, 1652-1811: the evidence of testimonials', *Journal of Historical Geography*, 11 (1985), pp. 379-94; R.A. Houston, '"Frequent flitting": geographical mobility and social structure in mid-nineteenth-century Greenlaw', *Scottish Studies*, (1985), pp. 31-47; A.A. Lovett, I.D. Whyte and K.A. Whyte, 'Poisson regression analysis and migration fields: the example of the apprenticeship records of Edinburgh in the seventeenth and eighteenth centuries', *Transactions of the Institute of British Geographers*, new series 10 (1985), pp. 317-32; T.M. Devine, 'Temporary migration and the Scottish Highlands in the nineteenth century', *Economic History Review*, 32 (1979), pp. 344-59; T.M. Devine (ed.), *Farm Servants and Labour in Scotland, 1770-1914* (Edinburgh, 1984); T.M. Devine, 'Highland migration to Lowland Scotland, 1760-1860', *Scottish Historical Review*, 63 (1983), pp. 137-49; M. Gray, 'Scottish emigration: the social impact of agricultural change in the rural Lowlands, 1775-1875', *Perspectives in American History*, 7 (1973), pp. 95-174; M. Gray, 'Migration in the rural Lowlands of Scotland, 1750-

1850', in T.M. Devine and D. Dickson (eds.), *Ireland and Scotland, 1600-1850 (Edinburgh,* 1983), pp. 104-17; J. Bumsted, *The People's Clearance, 1770-1815* (Edinburgh, 1982); I. Levitt and T.C. Smout, *The State of the Scottish Working-class in 1843* (Edinburgh, 1979), pp. 236-58; T.C. Smout, *A Century of the Scottish People, 1830-1950* (Glasgow, 1986), pp. 58-69.

8. R.A. Dodgshon, *Land and Society in Early Scotland* (Oxford, 1981), p. 292.

9. J. de Vries, *Patterns of European Urbanisation, 1500-1800* (London, 1984), pp. 29, 39.

# CHAPTER 2

# *Urbanisation*

## T.M. Devine

---

### The Process of Urbanisation

Town growth in the period covered by this volume forms a bridge between the old world of rural Scotland and the urbanised society of the later nineteenth century and modern times. In 1830 urban development had still some way to go before it began to ebb. But its acceleration from the middle decades of the eighteenth century had been dramatic and is perhaps only underestimated through knowledge of the continued expansion which was to occur later in the nineteenth century. While historians recognise the scale and speed of town growth between 1760 and 1830, they differ in their interpretation of its significance. One writer claims that as early as 1800, 'Scotland was well on the way to becoming an urban society'. Yet another can assert that as late as 1820, '... the farm and the village were still not replaced as the typical social environment in which a man spent his life'.[1]

In part the disagreement derives from different definitions of what constitutes a 'town'. Some authorities regard a population of 1,000 as the minimum size while others prefer a threshold of 5,000 or even 10,000. But the dispute is also caused by the absence, until recently, of a comparative perspective. The extent to which Scotland was an 'urbanised society' by 1830 depends not on absolute measures alone but on the proportion of the population living in large towns relative to patterns in other European societies. New work by Jan de Vries on European urbanisation since the sixteenth century enables the Scottish experience for the first time to be examined in an international context and its significance evaluated against standards of comparison drawn from the example of several continental societies.[2] The de Vries team collected data from sixteen European 'territories' over the period 1500 to 1850 in order to measure the proportion of total population in each area at fifty-year intervals who lived in towns with over 10,000 inhabitants. Complete precision in all aspects of such an ambitious project is obviously impossible. The reliability of the data varies significantly over time and between different countries. For instance, as far as Scotland is concerned, there is real difficulty in establishing

the *size* of the national population before c.1700, even before any attempt can
be made to estimate the *proportion* living in an urbanised environment. Yet
the figures can indicate the general direction of urbanisation over the long run
and are useful for determining significant differences between countries. The
data are also most solid for the period after 1750 which is the primary focus
of the present discussion.

Table 1 makes fascinating reading for a Scottish social historian. The
numerical data confirm the conventional view that in the seventeenth century
and in the early part of the eighteenth, Scotland was a predominantly rural
society. In a league of 'urbanised societies' (as measured by the percentage of
total population inhabiting towns of 10,000 or over), Scotland was eleventh

*Table 1. Percentage of Total Population in Western European Territories Living in
Towns with over 10,000 Inhabitants, 1600-1850*

|                   | 1600 | 1650 | 1700 | 1750 | 1800 | 1850 |
|-------------------|------|------|------|------|------|------|
| Scotland          | 3.0  | 3.5  | 5.3  | 9.2  | 17.3 | 32.0 |
| Scandinavia       | 1.4  | 2.4  | 4.0  | 4.6  | 4.6  | 5.8  |
| England and Wales | 5.8  | 8.8  | 13.3 | 16.7 | 20.3 | 40.8 |
| Ireland           | 0    | 0.9  | 3.4  | 5.0  | 7.0  | 10.2 |
| Netherlands       | 24.3 | 31.7 | 33.6 | 30.5 | 28.8 | 29.5 |
| Belgium           | 18.8 | 20.8 | 23.9 | 19.6 | 18.9 | 20.5 |
| Germany           | 4.1  | 4.4  | 4.8  | 5.6  | 5.5  | 10.8 |
| France            | 5.9  | 7.2  | 9.2  | 9.1  | 8.8  | 14.5 |
| Switzerland       | 2.5  | 2.2  | 3.3  | 4.6  | 3.7  | 7.7  |
| N. Italy          | 16.6 | 14.3 | 13.6 | 14.2 | 14.3 |      |
| Central Italy     | 12.5 | 14.2 | 14.3 | 14.5 | 13.6 | 20.3 |
| Southern Italy    | 14.9 | 13.5 | 12.2 | 13.8 | 15.3 |      |
| Spain             | 11.4 | 9.5  | 9.0  | 8.6  | 11.1 | 17.3 |
| Portugal          | 14.1 | 16.6 | 11.5 | 9.1  | 8.7  | 13.2 |
| Austria-Bohemia   | 2.1  | 2.4  | 3.9  | 5.2  | 5.2  | 6.7  |
| Poland            | 0.4  | 0.7  | 0.5  | 1.0  | 2.5  | 9.3  |

*Source:*    After J. de Vries, *European Urbanisation, 1500-1800* (London, 1984),
pp. 39-48.

out of sixteen in both 1600 and 1650 and was still only tenth in 1700. The
distribution of her population was more like that of Ireland, the Scandinavian
countries, Spain, Austria and Poland than of such advanced economies as
England and the Low Countries. On the other hand, it has to be remembered
that the threshold of 10,000 significantly underestimates the absolute size of
the real urban enclave in Scotland before 1750. In the seventeenth century, for
instance, there was considerable town development, not only through the

expansion of the major burghs of Glasgow and Edinburgh, but in the rise of the salt and coal centres around the Forth estuary. The dynamism of the early modern town has been further clarified by recent research.[3] Yet even recognition of the fact that there was more Scottish urban growth before 1750 than Table 1 implies does not entirely invalidate the proposition that the country was one of the least 'urbanised' in Western Europe in the seventeenth century.

From that period, however, the data reveal a dramatically different pattern and indicate an explosive increase in the numbers in Scotland living in large towns. By the 1750s, Scotland was seventh in the league table of 'urbanised societies', fourth in 1800 and second only to England and Wales by 1850.Less than ten per cent of Scots lived in towns with 10,000 inhabitants or above in 1750 but almost one third did so in 1850. In the long-run perspective of historical development a change of this magnitude represented a decisive break with the past. Plainly a new social order was in the process of formation. By 1800, according to Table 1, Scotland was already one of the five most urbanised societies in western Europe, alongside England and Wales, the Netherlands, Belgium and northern Italy. But it had achieved this position only in the previous few decades. The Netherlands, Belgium and northern Italy were already highly urbanised two centuries before and town development there did not intensify in the period after 1750. Similarly, there is no evidence of any other territory on the continent (apart from Poland which started from a much lower base) experiencing such a rapid rate of urban expansion as Scotland between 1750 and 1850. The Scottish pattern was exceptional also in relation to England and Wales. Throughout the two and a half centuries after 1600, the tabulation suggests that a higher proportion of the population in the south lived in large towns than north of the Border. But, equally, it is clear that the gap between the two countries, which had been enormous in the early eighteenth century, narrowed very rapidly after that. Table 2 confirms that though England was still the more urbanised society, the Scottish rate of urban growth in the later eighteenth century was significantly

*Table 2. Percentage Increase in Urban Population (as defined in Table 1) from Previous Date. Scotland, England and Wales.*

|  | 1600 | 1650 | 1700 | 1750 | 1800 |
|---|---|---|---|---|---|
| Scotland | - | 17 | 51 | 124 | 132 |
| England and Wales | - | 94 | 45 | 42 | 83 |

higher. Until 1800 the English pattern seems to have been more one of a continuous and protracted process of steadily intensifying urban development. Town expansion in Scotland on this evidence was altogether more

1. Glasgow from the south, c. 1760. A provincial port town with a population of about 32,000.

abrupt and swift and was therefore more likely to inflict much greater strain and pressure on urban social relationships, amenity and sanitation.

The scale and speed of urban growth in this period is confirmed in Table 3 which employs a different and probably more meaningful measure of 'urbanism', namely the percentage of total population in towns with populations of *5,000* and over. The rates of town expansion achieved in Scotland between the censuses of 1801 and 1831 were the fastest of any period in the nineteenth century and raised the proportion of the population in towns of over 5,000 inhabitants from about one fifth to nearly one third of the Scottish total. At the end of the period covered by this volume most Scots still lived in quasi-urban

*Table 3. Urbanised Proportion of Scottish Population, 1801-1901*

|  | Percentage of Total Population in centres of 5,000 or over | Percentage Increase over previous decade |
|---|---|---|
| 1801 | 21 | 29.4 |
| 1811 | 24 | 31.7 |
| 1821 | 27.5 | 31.7 |
| 1831 | 31.2 | 28.2 |
| 1841 | 32.7 | 16.2 |
| 1851 | 35.9 | 17.3 |
| 1861 | 39.4 | 16.2 |
| 1871 | 44.4 | 23.6 |
| 1881 | 48.9 | 12.8 |
| 1891 | 53.5 | 17.6 |
| 1901 | 57.6 | 19.7 |

*Source*: M. W. Flinn (ed.), *Scottish Population History from the 17th Century to the 1930s* (Cambridge, 1977), p. 313.

settlements, in country villages, and in farm steadings. But the growing urban areas had now become the strategic presence in the society and economy of Scotland. The towns were no longer adjuncts to an overwhelmingly rural social order but had become the dynamic centres of economic change. The lives of the country population were themselves altered fundamentally by the needs of the teeming cities for food and raw materials and the impact which these requirements had on the social structure and stability of countless rural communities in the Highlands and Lowlands.

## The Bases of Urban Growth

Why Scotland should experience such a precocious rate of urban growth is a question which requires detailed consideration since its consequences for the long-run development of Scottish society were so profound. The essential foundation, though not the principal direct cause, was the revolution in agriculture which occurred in parallel with town and city expansion. Urbanisation could not have taken place without a substantial increase in food production to sustain the needs of those who did not cultivate their own food supplies. At the same time, agrarian productivity had to improve in order to release a growing proportion of the population for non-agricultural tasks in towns and cities. Later in the nineteenth century, industrialisation in Scotland allowed manufactured products to be exchanged for imported foods, and at that point the relevance of the indigenous system of food production became less critical. However, for much of the period of this analysis, the urban masses mainly relied on grain, milk, potatoes and meat supplied from Scottish farms. They were fed through a rise in both the production and productivity of agriculture achieved by a reorganisation in farm structure, a more effective deployment of labour and higher yields derived from improved fallowing, the sowing of root crops and the adoption of new rotation systems.[4] No authoritative measures exist of the precise rate of increase in food production but it must have been very substantial. One knowledgeable contemporary, for example, took the view that from the 1750s to the 1820s the output of corn and vegetables had doubled in Scotland while that of animal foods multiplied sixfold.[5] Grain prices rose significantly after c.1780 and especially during the Napoleonic Wars. Yet, though this did stimulate some social discontent in the form of meal riots, price inflation also tended to encourage innovation in better agricultural practices which in the long run continued to sustain urban expansion. It was vital that this response should take place. If it had not, town growth might have been hampered by growing social unrest and diversion of too much of the society's resources to current consumption and away from investment in residential construction and the urban infrastructure.

Agrarian change was a necessary precondition for urbanisation but the process of agricultural reform also contributed directly to town growth at two other levels. First, the increasing orientation of agriculture towards the market further stimulated the function of urban areas as centres of exchange. There was a greater need than before for the commercial, legal and financial facilities which concentrated in towns. Perth, Ayr, Haddington, Dumfries, Stirling and several other towns owed much of their expansion in this period to the increasing requirements for their services from the commercialised agricultural systems of their hinterlands. Regional specialisation in agrarian production also enhanced the need for growing centres of exchange. Inverness, for example, expanded on the basis of its crucial role as the sheep and wool mart of the Highlands as that area became a great specialist centre of pastoral husbandry in the first half of the nineteenth century. Secondly, the prosperity of Scottish agriculture during the Napoleonic Wars boosted the incomes of tenant farmers and inflated the rent rolls of many landowners. The increase in the purchasing power of these classes had major implications for urban growth because it resulted in rising demand for the products of town consumer and luxury industries, and for more and better urban services in education, in leisure and in the provision of fashionable accommodation.[6]

Yet agrarian improvement was the necessary condition for Scottish urbanisation rather than its principal determinant. Towns which acted mainly as exchange and service centres for rural hinterlands expanded only relatively modestly, at a rate which was only slightly more than the national rate of natural increase.[7] Moreover, the rise in population which occurred in all western European societies from the later eighteenth century encouraged food producers throughout the continent to increase their output to cope with enhanced demand. The nature of the Scottish Agricultural Revolution may have been distinctive but agrarian improvement was too common in Europe at this time to provide the basic explanation for Scotland's exceptional pace of urban development.[8] It is more likely that Scottish town expansion was a direct consequence of Scotland's equally remarkable rate of general economic growth between 1760 and 1830. The Industrial Revolution before 1830 was mainly confined to mainland Britain and it is hardly a coincidence that in this same period urbanisation occurred more vigorously in England and Scotland than in any other European country. Scottish industrialisation and Scottish urban growth were both results of the same economic forces: '...non-agrarian occupations do not absolutely demand location in an urban environment but they certainly favour it, as offering prompt access to concentrations of producers, distributors and consumers'.[9]

This process had two interlinked aspects. The first was commercial in origin. In the eighteenth century, Scotland was in a superb geographical position to take advantage of the changing direction of international trade towards the Atlantic world. This momentous alteration in transcontinental commerce was a highly dynamic factor in port development along the whole western coast of Europe from Cork to Cadiz. Scotland was virtually at the crossroads of the new system and the Clyde ports grew rapidly to become the great tobacco emporia of the United Kingdom until diversifying later into the importation of sugar and cotton.[10] It was no coincidence that in the later eighteenth century four of the five fastest-growing towns in Scotland were in the Clyde basin.[11] Commercial success was bound to foster urban expansion.

2. Glasgow c. 1835. The city's population had climbed to over 274,000 and Glasgow was the fastest-growing town of its size in western Europe. *Mitchell Library, Glasgow.*

The carriage and merchandising of goods in bulk were all highly labour-intensive in this period and demanded large concentrations of labour. Considerable investment was also needed to build up the complex infrastructure of trade: warehouses, ports, industries, merchants' mansions, banks, exchanges, inns and coffee houses. Greenock may be taken as the archetypal port town of the western Lowlands: It mushroomed in size from a population of 2000 in 1700 to 17,500 in 1801 and 27,500 by 1831. By that date Greenock had become one of the six largest towns in Scotland. Irish trade, coastal commerce and continuing economic connections with Europe also stimulated port development along both the east and west coasts.

But, in the long run, the expansion of manufacturing industry was even more critical for urbanisation than the stimulus derived from international and interregional commerce. Of the thirteen largest towns in early nineteenth-century Scotland, five at least trebled their population size between c.1750 and 1821. In addition to Greenock these were Glasgow (from 31,700 to 147,000), Paisley (6,800 to 47,000),Kilmarnock (4,400 to 12,700) and Falkirk (3,900 to 11,500). Greenock apart, the inhabitants of all these towns mainly depended either directly or indirectly on manufacturing industry. It was the larger industrial towns and the constellation of smaller urban areas with which they were associated which set the pace of Scottish urbanisation. It is important to emphasise, of course, that industry did not necessarily or inevitably generate large-scale urban expansion in the short run. As late as the 1830s, for instance, around two-thirds of Scotland's handloom weavers of cotton, linen and woollen cloth lived in country villages or small towns.[12] The water-powered cotton-spinning factories of the last quarter of the eighteenth century were more often to be found in rural settlements such as Catrine, New Lanark or Deanston than in the cities. Throughout the period under consideration both coal-mining and pig-iron manufacture were also located in small towns and country villages. The continued presence of industry in a variety of forms in the countryside helps to explain why a majority of the Scottish people still lived outside large urban areas by 1830.

Yet, in the long run there were obvious advantages in industrial concentration in towns.[13] Manufacturers were able to gain from 'external economies': firms saved the costs of providing accommodation and other facilities for their workers from their own resources; they were guaranteed access to a huge pool of labour and transport costs between sources of supply, finishing trades and repair shops could be markedly reduced or virtually eliminated by the close proximity of complementary economic activities. These advantages built up a dynamic for urban expansion even before 1800. Thereafter the new technology of steam propulsion and conspicuous progress in transport developments through the construction of canals and roads steadily intensified the forces making for urban concentration. In cotton-spinning, and eventually in other textile industries, steam power encouraged industrial settlements on the coalfields and removed the one major obstacle which had previous constricted the expansion of manufacturing in the larger towns. Glasgow provides the most dramatic case of the pattern of change.[14] In 1795 the city had eleven cotton-spinning complexes, but rural Renfrewshire had twelve. The fundamental need to have secure access to water power obviously diluted Glasgow's other attractions as a centre of textile industrial production. However, steam-based technology was rapidly adopted after 1800 and concentration accelerated on an enormous scale in the city and its immediate environs. By 1839 there were 192 cotton mills in Scotland employing 31,000 workers. All but seventeen were located in Renfrew and Lanark and ninety-eight were in or near Glasgow. In Paisley, or its vicinity, there was a further great network of forty factories employing almost 5000 workers. A similar process of intensifying convergence evolved over a longer time-scale in the Border wool towns of Hawick and Galashiels and the linen centres of the eastern Lowlands: '...there emerged a strong urban concentration — Dundee specialised in heavy flax and tow fabrics, Arbroath was the seat of the canvas trade, Forfar and Brechin produced heavy linens such as osnaburghs and northern Fife specialised in finer linens and bleached goods'.[15] Before 1830 textile manufacturing was the principal motor of this process of agglomeration. Up till then, for example, it was the cotton centres of Glasgow and its suburbs and Renfrewshire which grew most rapidly in the western Lowlands. Only thereafter, and especially from the 1840s, did intensive urban development spread from them to the coal and iron towns of Coatbridge, Airdrie and Wishaw in north Lanarkshire.

## The Urban Structure

Despite fast urban growth there remained considerable continuity between the old world and the new. The four major cities of the early nineteenth century, Edinburgh, Glasgow, Aberdeen and Dundee, were also the biggest Scottish burghs of the seventeenth century, although of course they had experienced substantial changes in size, occupational structure and economic specialisation over that period. Again, the thirteen largest Scottish towns of the early eighteenth century were the same, with only one or two exceptions, as those of 1830. The biggest urban areas, therefore, were all ancient places and the traditional county and regional capitals also continued to play a role whether as centres of administration, local government or as markets for prosperous agricultural hinterlands. But by 1830, the Scottish urban system had also developed some characteristic features typical of the new era.

First, urbanisation was mainly concentrated in the narrow belt of land in the western and eastern Lowlands. Between 1801 and 1841 never less than 83 per cent of the entire Scottish urban population (defined as those inhabiting towns of 5000 or more) lived in this region. Within the area there was heavy concentration in Glasgow and Edinburgh where, as early as 1800, 60 per cent of Scottish urban dwellers resided. This remarkable pattern had implications for the demographic structure of Scottish society because population concentration on such a scale could not have taken place without considerable redistribution of people over a relatively short period of time. Thus, whereas the percentage of total Scottish population in the central Lowlands rose from 37 per cent to 47 per cent of the whole between c.1750 and 1821, it fell from 51 per cent to 41 per cent in northern Scotland and remained roughly static at 11 per cent in the southern region of the country over the same period. The modern population profile of Scotland was beginning to take shape. Within the urbanising zone the fastest growth among the largest towns was in the west, with four towns in that area at least trebling in population. Paisley expanded more than six times, Greenock more than five, and Glasgow grew four-fold.

Second, there was wide diversity within the urban structure. Any attempt at neat categorisation of Scottish towns is bound to be arbitrary, but it is important that the effort should be made because differences in size, economic composition and employment opportunities had fundamentally varying effects on the health, living standards, education, religious practice and the class relationships of urban dwellers which are considered in detail in later chapters of this volume. It is necessary at least to emphasise that there was such a diversity of urban experience that generalisations about the impact of urban expansion on Scottish society at this time must be made with great care. In very broad terms, most Scottish towns fitted into three categories: first, the four major cities; second, industrial towns; third, local capitals in historic sites which performed marketing and service functions for their immediate neighbourhoods. In addition, there was a miscellany of other urban settlements including the fishing ports of the Fife and Moray coast, the old coal and salt burghs of the Forth estuary and the new inland spas of Bridge of Allan, Peebles and Strathpeffer. Of these groups, the industrial staple towns and some of the cities were most likely to suffer the adverse consequences of expansion which are often associated with urbanisation at this time. Such places as Paisley, Falkirk, Kilmarnock and Hawick grew swiftly, and their mainly working-class inhabitants were usually heavily concentrated in one or two industries which were often geared to overseas markets and hence were vulnerable to the changes in demand for international commodities. The ordinary people of

3. Princes Street, Edinburgh, c. 1825. Already known for its shops and as a busy fashionable thoroughfare, Princes Street shows the physical gulf between the Old and New Towns of Edinburgh, as well as differences in style of architecture and planning. *National Galleries of Scotland.*

these towns endured great suffering in the serious commercial depressions of 1816-17, 1825 and 1836-7. In relative terms, at least, those who dwelt in the regional centres were better placed. Their typically moderate rate of population growth ensured that the existing organisation of sewage and waste disposal was not so easily overwhelmed as elsewhere, though it must be stressed that sanitary problems were a familiar feature of all Scottish towns, whatever their size, at this time.[16] In addition, their occupational structure was more diverse than that of the staple towns and, because the economy of such centres primarily depended on their service function to surrounding rural areas, they were less vulnerable to the social crises provoked by cyclical unemployment. Again, however, distinctions should not be drawn too neatly because some towns of this type, such as Perth, for instance, had a considerable industrial presence and could not be entirely insulated from the ebb and flow of external demand for manufactured goods. The differences between centres like this and the staple towns were sometimes of degree rather than kind.[17]

The main contrasts in the occupational structure of Scotland's four cities are best studied from Tables 4(a) and 4(b).[18] One similarity, however, is worth emphasising initially. The dominance of textile employment, except in the case of Edinburgh, is very obvious from the tabulation, and underscores the point made earlier in this chapter about the essential importance of cotton, linen and, to a lesser extent, woollen manufacture in Scotland's first phase of urbanisation. The relative stability and balance of Edinburgh's economic base is also apparent. The majority of the employed population worked in small-scale consumer industries many of which depended on demand from a middle and upper class clientele. Domestic service was far and away the largest employer of female labour. This occupational pattern reflected Edinburgh's metropolitan status, the significant numbers of salaried professionals in the city who represented a large pool of demand for services and luxury consumer goods and the major functions of the capital in the areas of law, banking and education. Poverty and destitution were endemic in certain parts of the city, notably in the Old Town and elsewhere, but the ordinary people of the capital were less likely to experience the full horrors of cyclical unemployment on the same scale as their counterparts in Dundee and Glasgow.

Aberdeen, though smaller, was closest to Edinburgh in occupational structure. It performed the same key legal, educational and financial services for the north-east region as Edinburgh did for the whole of Scotland. The proportion of professionals in the employed population was second only to Edinburgh and there was also a significantly high number of domestic servants. On the other hand, there was extensive textile employment and, alone among the major cities, Aberdeen had a significant proportion of males occupied in fishing. By and large, the city possessed a relatively balanced occupational structure and by the standards of other large towns experienced a moderate rate of growth before 1830. Not surprisingly, therefore, it was spared some of the worst of the social problems which afflicted Glasgow and Dundee.

*Table 4(a): Occupational Structure in the Scottish Cities, 1841*

| Percentage of Workforce in: | Glasgow | Edinburgh | Dundee | Aberdeen |
|---|---|---|---|---|
| Printing & Publishing | 1.12 | 3.88 | 0.56 | 0.91 |
| Engineering, Toolmaking and Metals | 7.17 | 6.07 | 5.59 | 6.32 |
| Shipbuilding | 0.35 | 0.17 | 1.14 | 1.24 |
| Coachbuilding | 0.40 | 0.92 | 0.21 | 0.34 |
| Building | 5.84 | 5.73 | 6.05 | 5.99 |
| Furniture & Woodmaking | 1.06 | 2.73 | 0.77 | 0.87 |
| Chemicals | 1.22 | 0.24 | 0.19 | 0.37 |
| Food, Drink & Tobacco | 5.24 | 8.31 | 5.27 | 4.66 |
| Textiles & Clothing | 37.56 | 13.04 | 50.54 | 34.68 |
| Other Manufacturing | 2.90 | 3.02 | 1.29 | 3.18 |
| General Labouring | 8.40 | 3.69 | 3.84 | 6.87 |

*Source:* Census of 1841 (*Parliamentary Papers,* 1844, XXVII) and R. Rodger, 'Employment, Wages and Poverty in the Scottish Cities, 1841-1914', Appendix 1, in George Gordon (ed.), *Perspectives of the Scottish City* (Aberdeen, 1985).
Note that occupational classification in the 1841 census is questionable and imprecise. The precise figures presented here are unlikely to be wholly accurate; they provide an impression of overall structures rather than an exact measurement of them.

*Table 4 (b): Occupational Structures in the Scottish Cities, 1841 By Sector (Percentage of Total Workforce).*

| | Professional | | Domestic | | Commercial | | Industrial | | Agricuture & Fishing | |
|---|---|---|---|---|---|---|---|---|---|---|
| | M | F | M | F | M | F | M | F | M | F |
| Glasgow (and suburbs) | 4.53 | 0.57 | 2.03 | 31.60 | 15.09 | 2.87 | 73.92 | 64.59 | 4.43 | 0.37 |
| Edinburgh (and suburbs) | 13.34 | 1.93 | 6.53 | 70.36 | 14.10 | 2.71 | 63.26 | 23.61 | 2.77 | 1.39 |
| Dundee | 4.98 | 0.88 | 1.95 | 27.30 | 13.70 | 2.79 | 76.57 | 68.65 | 2.80 | 0.38 |
| Aberdeen | 6.46 | 2.24 | 4.05 | 40.37 | 14.57 | 2.44 | 68.71 | 53.98 | 6.21 | 0.97 |

*Source:* As for Table 4(a).

Glasgow and Dundee were alike in their heavy dependence on textile employment, the speed of their growth in the nineteenth century (though Dundee grew most rapidly from the 1830s and 1840s) and the relative weakness of the professional element in their occupational structures. It was these two cities which suffered very severe problems of health, sanitation and poverty. In the short term, and especially before 1840, Glasgow's difficulties attracted most attention. In the long run, however, Dundee appeared even more vulnerable. Over half of its employed population were engaged in textiles alone and increasingly these were low-paid females occupied in the heavy linen and jute industries. Already by 1841, the urban economy of Dundee had become dangerously lop-sided.

## Migration and Urbanisation

Not all towns in this period grew by migration. But those which experienced a rate of increase substantially greater than the national rate of natural population growth had to do so. Unfortunately, it is not possible to say much in precise terms about migration to towns in Scotland before the publication of the 1851 census which first printed the birthplaces of the population. Reliance on data extracted from this source in this analysis exaggerates the scale of Irish immigration, which was less for the period before 1830 than for that after the Great Famine. Otherwise the patterns recorded in 1851 are unlikely to drastically misrepresent trends in earlier decades.

Several points are worthy of comment. Migration was obviously very extensive. Of the ten principal Scottish towns in 1851, only 47 per cent of their inhabitants had been born in them. The majority of the migrants were young adults, more concentrated in the marriageable and child-bearing age groups than were the native inhabitants. High migration because of its age composition was therefore likely to fuel natural increase in the urban areas. Of those born in Dundee in 1851, only 37 per cent were aged 20 and over, whereas 70 per cent of the migrants to the city were in that age group. The overwhelming majority of migrants had only travelled short distances. Most new Aberdonians, for instance, were from the north-east counties; the largest number of Greenock's Highland immigrants came from localities in the vicinity of the town in the neighbouring southern Highlands. During the 1820s, burial records show that one-third of those buried in Dundee who were not natives of the city had been born in the city's county of Angus, and most of the rest came from the surrounding east coast areas.[19] The big towns, as Table 5 indicates, all had population catchment areas which were usually in their immediate regions.

Long-distance migration (again as revealed in Table 5) was surprisingly

4. St. Andrew's R.C. Cathedral, Glasgow. Built in 1816, this impressive structure symbolised the new Catholic presence in the west of Scotland in the early nineteenth century as a result of increased Irish immigration.

slight. In the main, only the largest centres, such as Glasgow and Edinburgh, had apparently the capacity to attract many people over long distances. Despite Scottish myth, which sometimes portrays the Highlands as being emptied to furnish labour for the large towns, permanent migration to the south from the north-west in this period was relatively limited and most of those who left tended to make for such western towns as Glasgow, Paisley and Greenock. As late as 1851, however, only around 5 per cent of Glasgow's population were born in the Highlands, and the majority of these came from the southern districts adjacent to the Lowlands rather than from the crofting region of the far west. The inhabitants of that area clearly preferred

*Table 5: Birthplaces of the Residents of Glasgow, Paisley and Edinburgh (Percentages), 1851.*

| | Far North | High- lands | North- East | W.Low- lands | E.Low- lands | Borders | Ireland | Rest of G.B.& overseas | Same City |
|---|---|---|---|---|---|---|---|---|---|
| Glasgow | 0.3 | 5.2 | 0.8 | 16.9 | 9.7 | 1.8 | 8.2 | 3.1 | 44.1 |
| Paisley | - | 2.9 | 0.2 | 17.9 | 3.4 | 0.6 | 12.7 | 1.4 | 60.9 |
| Edinburgh | 2.0 | 2.4 | 2.2 | 4.8 | 20.8 | 5.5 | 6.5 | 5.9 | 50.3 |

*Source:* 1851 Census, *Parliamentary Papers,* 1852-3, LXXXVIII, Pt. II; Flinn (ed.), *Scottish Population History*, p. 462.

transatlantic emigration to permanent movement to the cities. Temporary migration to the Lowlands was, however, much more extensive and important.[20]

Highland movement was dwarfed by Irish migration which accelerated from Ulster and eastern Connaught in the 1810s and 1820s due to the difficulties there of the native linen manufacture and the quicker and cheaper access to the Clyde ports afforded by the new steamships. The Irish immigrants of this period were both Catholic and Protestant and it was the transfer of traditional sectarian animosities to Scotland as much as native Scottish prejudice which provoked religious and social bitterness in the wake of this movement. In 1851, after the even greater immigration of the Great Famine, 7 per cent of the total Scottish population were Irish-born, more than twice that of England. But this bald figure underestimates the Irish influence on Scottish urban expansion. J.E. Handley, rightly stresses that those of Irish extraction should be included in the count as well as the Irish-born.[21] Handley's revised estimates would suggest that in 1841 almost a quarter of the people of the western Lowlands were of Irish extraction. Moreover, Irish immigration tended to concentrate on specific urban areas, and global figures conceal the impact of the distribution. Thus 44,000 of Glasgow's population in 1841, or 16 per cent of the total of 274,000, were Irish-born. But if Handley is correct, it would mean that around one in three of the city's inhabitants were of Irish descent at that date.

No single factor was decisive in explaining the increasing scale of rural-urban migration within Scotland. There was undoubtedly a distinctive urban pull: 'urbanisation meant more jobs, a wider diversity of social contacts and infinitely greater colour and excitement in the lives of the masses'.[22] Higher wages than were usual in the rural economy and a greater range of employment opportunities helped to hasten migration to towns *in the later eighteenth century* to such an extent that Scottish farmers in the zones where urban growth concentrated were forced to raise wages to retain labour. Even after the Napoleonic Wars, when urban demand for labour slackened, and clear signs emerged of a labour surplus in some of the cities, the towns still retained their allure. The poor health record of the large towns did not deter migrants, and indeed there is evidence that urban crises of mortality were sometimes followed by 'replenishment migration'. The fact that the overwhelming majority of newcomers to the towns came from adjacent districts was itself confirmation of the importance of the 'pull' factor.[23]

The close proximity between the source of migrants and the host towns facilitated migration. The urban areas were near and familiar. Migration did not mean that all contact with the native rural community was lost. There was much seasonal and temporary migration, and a connection could be retained with kinfolk who normally lived short distances away. Many of the migrants to the cities already had some experience of town life. One of the biggest migrant streams was that which linked different *urban* areas: not all or even the majority of new arrivals were the rural innocents of legend. It should not be forgotten either that extensive migration was not unique to the era of urbanisation. As was shown in Chapter 1, mobility over short distances was common in pre-industrial Scotland long before the late eighteenth century. Again, the apparent obstacles to rural-urban migration were often more apparent than real. A crude contrast is occasionally drawn between the radical change in life-style enforced upon peasant cultivators who moved to factory employment in the cities. But this stereotype did not necessarily apply to the majority of migrants. Most townspeople before 1830 worked outside the factory, in workshops, homes and in the open air. There were, therefore, often important continuities between rural and urban employments, especially when it is remembered that before 1760 the spinning and weaving of textiles was so extensive in Lowland Scotland that most country families must have had some members with experience of such industrial labour. The migrant could also ease the process of urban assimilation by lodging with kinfolk or with family friends from the same locality. Movement from country to town was in this way facilitated both by the previous experience of the migrants themselves and the strategies they adopted to adjust to a new life.

The most controversial aspect of migration at this time is the question of how far people were 'forced' off the land into towns as the process of agrarian reorganisation gathered pace from the later eighteenth century.[24] The numbers with either a legal or customary right to land in Lowland Scotland did decline rapidly after c.1780 as main tenancies were consolidated and subtenancies eliminated when rationalisation quickened. On the other hand, in the short run at least, the creation of the modern agrarian structure (through the construction of farmhouses, roads, fencing and dykes and the adoption of the new rotation crops of sown grasses and turnips, seemed to require more rather than less labour than the old system. The new ploughs were certainly labour-saving and labour productivity increased as work organisation was improved, but most farm tasks remained unmechanised and there was an overall increase in demand for labour as production of foods and raw materials intensified. In addition, textile and other manufactures expanded in the country villages and small towns. There was therefore often less need for dispossessed cottars with craft skills to move to the big cities to make a living. Rather, surviving wage data for the later eighteenth century, when agrarian reorganisation accelerated, suggest that rural employers were forced to offer increasing wages in order to compete with their urban counterparts. In that period, therefore, it would seem that many migrants from the country, far from being forced off the land, were being lured to the towns by the positive attractions of higher wages and a greater range of employment opportunities.

Yet, there were indeed fundamental links between rural-urban migration in Scotland and the social changes initiated by the Agricultural Revolution, even if they were more subtle than is sometimes suggested. The creation of a landless labour force did not necessarily cause people to leave their rural environment but it did facilitate it. Peasant farmers are notoriously reluctant to give up their holdings. As Pierre Goubert has written, 'No peasant willingly surrenders land, be it only half a furrow'. Landless wage labourers are, however, much more mobile. They survive through selling their labour power in the market and they cannot fall back on scraping a living from a smallholding, no matter how meagre. Again, outside the south-east Lowlands, Fife and some other districts, most regular farm workers in Lowland Scotland were unmarried male and female servants, hired on six-monthly contracts. At marriage, many were forced to move to alternative employments. They were a highly mobile group and one option among several for them was movement to the towns. All the local studies demonstrate a great haemorrhage from farm service at 23 to 25, the average age at marriage in Scotland at this time.

In the final analysis, however, the main momentum was probably generated by the acceleration in Scottish population growth, which occurred from the early nineteenth century, and the social effect that this had in country areas, as well as agrarian reorganisation in itself. As was shown in Chapter 1, Scottish demographic expansion in the later eighteenth century was unusually moderate by the standards prevailing in Ireland, England and several continental societies. Between 1755 and 1801, the annual rate of increase was only about 0.6 per cent. From 1801 and 1811, however, this doubled to 1.2 per cent and increased again to 1.6 per cent per annum from 1811 to 1821. Such a rate of growth might well have swamped rural labour markets and the problem

5. Gorbals main street, Glasgow, c. 1828. Originally intended as the core of a middle-class residential suburb, the village of Gorbals, on the south bank of the Clyde, began to deteriorate into into one of the most notorious slums towards the end of this period.

would have been aggravated by the great demobilisation of soldiers and sailors after the Napoleonic Wars. Though farmers had a need for more hands, the demand for labour was not increasing at anything like the pace of population growth, especially as agricultural income and hence employment opportunities contracted with the slump in grain prices after the Napoleonic Wars. One might realistically have anticipated, therefore, a huge expansion in structural unemployment in rural districts. This did happen in the western Highlands but not in the Lowlands. This was partly a result of the expulsive force of the Scottish structure of engagement for farm service. Both single and married servants in Scotland lived on the farm. Their accommodation was provided as part of their contract of employment. For many, to be unemployed, to fail to gain a 'fee' at the biennial feeing markets, meant not simply to be without work but also to be without a home. In the later eighteenth century, it became a major principle of Scottish improving policy that only the population essential for proper cultivation should be retained permanently on the land. Accommodation in and around the farm was strictly limited thereafter to the specific labour needs of the farmer. Cottages surplus to these requirements were pulled down and the building of new accommodation strictly controlled. This inevitably became a mechanism for channelling excess labour off the land, especially when it is remembered that the able-bodied unemployed had no legal right to be relieved under the Scottish Poor Law, even if occasional assistance was sometimes provided in several areas. The combination of this system, a natural and accelerating rise in population and only slowly growing or stagnant employment opportunities in agriculture after 1812-1813, helped to ensure an increasing movement of people from country to town. In the 1810s and 1820s Scotland had a growing problem of structural unemployment. But it did not concentrate in the Lowland agricultural sector and was mainly confined to the large towns, the western Highlands and the communities of industrial workers (and especially handloom weavers) in the countryside. Some of its effects will be considered in the final section of this chapter.

**The Urban Problem**

The speed of Scottish urban expansion did not have a significant impact on mortality rates until the second and third decades of the nineteenth century. The larger towns were mainly free of epidemic fevers from 1790 to 1815 but these diseases (mainly typhus) reappeared at recurrent intervals between 1817-20, 1826-7 and 1836-7. Scotland also experienced its first major cholera attack, which claimed 10,000 victims, in 1831-2. Interpretation of mortality statistics for any period in the first half of the nineteenth century is hazardous. But the careful enumerations carried out by some local doctors leave little doubt that the urban environment was steadily becoming more lethal. In Edinburgh, where conditions were by no means the worst of the larger towns, the death-rate which had fallen to 25 per 1000 in 1810-19, climbed to 26.2 in the following decade and reached 29 between 1830 and 1839.[25] So marked was the general rise in urban mortality rates that students of Scottish demographic history can demonstrate that they explain why *national* death rates also began to move upwards after a sustained decline in earlier decades.[26] There could be no more telling or ominous illustration of the new significance of the large towns in Scottish life. By the 1830s and 1840s some were approaching a social crisis of unprecedented proportions. Meaningful efforts at reform rather than temporary palliatives were not even contemplated until the 1840s. Not before the second half of the nineteenth century were some of the worst aspects of the urban problem effectively tackled.[27]

Urban growth brought major health problems throughout Britain, but both available statistical evidence and contemporary comment suggest that conditions were worse in Scotland than England. As Edwin Chadwick concluded in his *Sanitary Report* of 1842: 'There is evidence to prove that the mortality from fever is greater in Glasgow, Edinburgh and Dundee than in the most crowded towns in England'.[28] The influences which promoted environmental decline in cities in the first half of the nineteenth century have been chronicled in detail by a number of historians and there is no need to explore them at great length here.[29] They included, *inter alia*, the absence of effective sanitation; the Scottish tradition of accommodating people in high-built tenements, courts and wynds; little or no street cleansing in poor neighbourhoods; inadequate supplies of uncontaminated water; the inertia of unreformed municipal authorities; medical ignorance of the causes and nature of the major killer diseases; and ideologies which blamed poverty and squalor on weakness of character rather than environmental constraints. These and other factors ensured that rising urban death-rates did not begin to come under effective control until the 1850s. But most were common to both England and Scotland and cannot in themselves explain the peculiarly bad conditions in several of the Scottish cities. To do that, distinctively Scottish influences must be considered.

Some are already obvious from previous discussion. Scottish urbanisation proceeded at a faster pace than probably anywhere else in Western Europe between 1760 and 1830 and the rate of growth simply overwhelmed the primitive contemporary structures of sanitation and amenity in a huge rising tide of humanity. Much of Glasgow's notoriety as the unhealthiest city in Britain at this time stemmed from the simple fact that it was growing more swiftly than any other British city of its size, adding a staggering 5,000 every year to its population in the 1820s. It must also be remembered that the larger Scottish towns, especially those in the western Lowlands and Dundee, played host to migrants from Ireland and parts of the Highlands, two of the poorest societies in the British Isles. The Irish, in particular, often arrived in a semi-destitute condition, concentrated in the poorest quarters of towns, were more vulnerable to the diseases of the city and inevitably aggravated pressure on accommodation and amenity.

But the familiar plight of the Irish was but a part of a more general and deeper social problem in early nineteenth-century Scotland. The rapid indus-trialisation of the society was partially due to the fact that Scottish labour costs were lower than England's.[30] This, in turn, was a reflection of the relative poverty of the country, a poverty which, as another chapter in this volume demonstrates, persisted throughout this period.[31] Many thousands in the booming towns of Scotland eked out an existence close to the margins of destitution, a condition aggravated by the fact that the able-bodied unem-ployed had no legal right to relief within the terms of the Scottish Poor Law.[32] One calculation, for instance, suggests that in 1834 about half of Scotland's handloom weavers, a very large occupational group, fell below the primary poverty line as defined by late nineteenth-century social analysts.[33] In addi-tion, all the large towns had large numbers of casual labourers who worked in the varied urban tasks of fetching, carrying and construction. James Cleland estimated that almost one quarter of Glasgow's labour force in 1831 were casual workers.[34] They endured a regime of very poor wages, broken time and employment which fluctuated throughout the year. Groups such as these had little economic power to create market demand for decent housing.[35] Instead they were accommodated cheaply in the old centres of the cities, notably the Old Town in Edinburgh and the High Street-Gallowgate area of Glasgow, through existing buildings being subdivided and their backcourts filled in with additional dwellings. Housing conditions in such areas were appalling simply because many had no alternative but to accept them.

The connection between poverty and urban mortality was vividly demon-strated during the three great industrial recessions of 1816-18, 1825 and 1836. It was these rather than poor sanitation as such which precipitated the first upswing in urban death-rates in Scottish cities in the nineteenth century. Significantly, fever was much rarer in the early years of the century despite the fact that then too sanitary provision was very inadequate. Typhus only became a major killer in the crisis years of profound economic difficulty following the Napoleonic Wars. All three depressions were followed by savage epidemics in 1816-18, 1827-8 and 1837-9 which drove up mortality rates in all the larger towns. Poverty and destitution were obviously as lethal as inadequate sewage

6. Fiddler's Close, High Street, Glasgow, c.1840. Conditions deteriorated in central localities such as this most rapidly where eighteenth-century buildings of the type illustrated were sub-divided to accommodate huge numbers of migrants from rural areas. *Mitchell Library, Glasgow.*

and poor housing. This was not the result of urbanism *per se* but the inevitable consequence of a general imbalance between population and employment opportunities in Scotland in the two decades before 1830. It was an imbalance which only began to be reduced in the second phase of industrialisation when iron, coal and engineering expanded from the middle decades of the nineteenth century. Industrial expansion and its offspring, urbanisation, significantly increased the volume and range of jobs down to 1830 but not at the rate required to provide regular and decent employment for the constantly rising numbers of people entering the labour market. Economic change and industrial growth saved Scotland from the demographic horrors experienced in Ireland in the 1840s but were not yet vigorous or extensive enough to prevent social suffering on a large scale in the growing towns.

NOTES

1. Anthony Slaven, *The Development of the West of Scotland, 1750-1960* (London, 1975), p.145; T.C. Smout, *A History of the Scottish People, 1560-1830* (London, 1969), p. 260.

2. Jan de Vries, *European Urbanisation, 1500-1800* (London, 1987).

3. Michael Lynch (ed.), *The Early Modern Town in Scotland* (London, 1987).

4. See Chapter 3.

5. George Robertson, *Rural Recollections* (Irvine, 1829), p. 352.

6. L.J. Saunders, *Scottish Democracy 1815-40: the Social and Intellectual Background* (Edinburgh, 1950), pp. 79-96.

7. M.W. Flinn (ed.), *Scottish Population History from the Seventeenth Century to the 1930s* (Cambridge, 1977), p. 313.

8. On this point see T.M. Devine, 'Social Responses to Agrarian Modernisation: the Lowland and Highland Clearances in Scotland, 1500-1850', in R.A. Houston and I.D. Whyte (eds.), *Scottish Society, 1600-1800* (Cambridge, 1988).

9. P.J. Corfield, *The Impact of English Towns 1700-1800* (Oxford, 1982), p. 94.

10. T.M. Devine, *The Tobacco Lords: A Study of the Tobacco Merchants of Glasgow and their Trading Activities, 1740-90* (Edinburgh, 1975); L.E. Cochran, *Scottish Trade with Ireland in the Eighteenth Century* (Edinburgh, 1985).

11. Glasgow, Greenock, Paisley and Kilmarnock.

12. N. Murray, *The Scottish Handloom Weavers 1790-1850: A Social History* (Edinburgh, 1978), pp. 1-9.

13. J. Docherty, 'Urbanisation, Capital Accumulation and Class Struggle in Scotland, 1750-1914', in G. Whittington and I.D. Whyte (eds.), *An Historical Geography of Scotland* (London, 1983), pp. 244-5.

14. A. Gibb, *Glasgow: the Making of a City* (London, 1983), pp. 91-3.

15. Ian H. Adams, *The Making of Urban Scotland* (London, 1978), pp. 90-3; C. Gulvin, *The Tweedmakers* (Newton Abbot, 1973).

16. See, for example, S. Wood, *The Shaping of 19th Century Aberdeenshire* (Stevenage, 1985), ch. 2.

17. The whole issue of the smaller towns is well covered in Saunders, *Scottish Democracy*, pp. 145-160. See chapter 3 of this volume for an examination of village development.

18. This paragraph is mainly based on R. Rodger, 'Employment, Wages and

Poverty in the Scottish Cities, 1841-1914', in G. Gordon (ed.), *Perspectives of the Scottish City* (Aberdeen, 1985), pp. 25-63.

19. Flinn (ed.), *Scottish Population History*, p. 467.

20. T.M. Devine, 'Highland Migration to Lowland Scotland, 1760-1860', *Scottish Historical Review*, 63 (1983) pp. 137-49; T.M. Devine, *The Great Highland Famine: Hunger, Emigration and the Scottish Highlands in the Nineteenth Century* (Edinburgh, 1988), chs. 6, 8, 9-11; C.W.J. Withers, *Highland Communities in Dundee and Perth, 1787-1891* (Dundee, 1986).

21. James Handley, *The Irish in Scotland, 1798-1845* (Cork, 1943). A more recent analysis of Irish immigration to Britain (including Scotland) in this period is contained in R. Swift and S. Gilley (eds.), *The Irish in the Victorian City* (London, 1985).

22. A.S. Wohl, *Endangered Lives: Public Health in Victorian Britain* (London, 1983), p. 80.

23. This paragraph and the remainder of this section are based on: T.M. Devine (ed.), *Farm Servants and Labour in Lowland Scotland, 1770-1914* (Edinburgh, 1984); T.M. Devine, 'Social Stability and Agrarian Change in the Eastern Lowlands of Scotland, 1910-40', *Social History*, 3, no. 3 (October, 1978), pp. 331-46; M. Gray, 'Scottish Emigration: the Social Impact of Agrarian Change in the Rural Lowlands, 1775-1875', *Perspectives in American History*, VII (1973); M. Gray, 'Migration in the Rural Lowlands of Scotland, 1750-1850', in T.M. Devine and D. Dickson (eds.), *Ireland and Scotland, 1600-1850* (Edinburgh, 1983); Brenda Collins, 'Irish Emigration to Dundee and Paisley during the first half of the Nineteenth Century', in J.M. Goldstrom and L.A. Clarkson (eds.), *Irish Population, Economy and Society* (Oxford, 1981).

24. See Chapter 3 for a more detailed consideration of the social impact of agrarian change.

25. James Stark, *Inquiry into some points of the Sanitary State of Edinburgh* (Edinburgh, 1847).

26. Flinn (ed.), *Scottish Population History*, p. 19.

27. E. Gauldie, *Cruel Habitations* (London, 1974).

28. M.W. Flinn (ed.), E. Chadwick, *Report on the Sanitary Condition of the Labouring Population of Great Britain, 1842* (Edinburgh, 1965).

29. The interested reader should consult the following, *inter alia*: J.H.F. Brotherston, *Observations on the Early Public Health Movement in Scotland* (London, 1952); S.D. Chapman (ed.), *The History of Working Class Housing* (Newton Abbot, 1977); R.J. Morris, *Cholera, 1832* (London, 1976); Gauldie, *Cruel Habitations;* Wohl, *Endangered Lives.*

30. R.H. Campbell, *The Rise and Fall of Scottish Industry, 1707-1939* (Edinburgh, 1980).

31. See Chapter 10.

32. See Chapter 12.

33. Murray, *Scottish Handloom Weavers*, pp. 84-114.

34. James Cleland, *Enumeration of the Inhabitants of the City of Glasgow* (Glasgow, 1832), p. 231.

35. J.H. Treble, *Urban Poverty in Britain* (London, 1979), pp. 55-80.

# CHAPTER 3

# The Social Impact of Agrarian Change in the Rural Lowlands

## Malcolm Gray

### Society in the Old Ferm-Touns

The rural Lowlands of the eighteenth century inherited a social structure largely formed within the ferm-touns that lay over the arable land, sometimes in continuous array, sometimes scattered. In Fife, the Lothians and Berwickshire some of these were large enough to be described as villages but in other parts they were tiny units, seldom containing more than twenty families. Yet nearly all contained still smaller sub-groups, forming an internal hierarchy and a balance of specialised occupations. Tradesmen with a partial specialisation — such as weavers, tailors, wrights or shoemakers — were spread thinly through the touns rather than congregated in villages. And agricultural work was based on elaborate definitions of function and social position.[1]

Power and position within the touns lay mainly with the tenants who rented the land, often under leasehold terms, from owners taking no personal part in its working. In a belt running from Fife south-west to Ayrshire owner-occupiers were also to be found in some numbers. Such tenants and owners stood apart from other members of the toun but, comparing one with the other, they were often of very varied standing. Sometimes one tenant would hold a whole toun but often there were several to share and, among them, one or two might stand out in the amount of land they held as compared with their fellows.

Individual holdings were generally greater in the South-East than they were further north and west. In fact, this area contained a considerable group of husbandmen in comfortable independence; the 100- or even 150-acre holding was by no means unusual.

In the North-East, at the other extreme in the size of its holdings, even a successful husbandman would probably have little more than fifty acres. The North-East, too, had great numbers of very small holdings that can only have given the most precarious living. Such smaller units were probably less common in the South but they were everywhere a definite feature of the rural scene. Nowhere could it be said that truly large holdings predominated.

Even the smallest of the independent farmers required some help in the working of their land and the primary occupiers of the land were greatly outnumbered by the lesser folk whom they employed whole- or part-time. The duties and rights of these dependents were variously defined from place to place and from one person to the next, and they might go by varying generic names. On the whole, however, they fell into broad groups, composed of families or individuals in roughly similar condition.

Firstly, there were the families who held their small fragments of land by sub-tenure. Sometimes sub-tenancy told only of how they held their land and not of fuller dependency. But generally it meant inferior status with a range of duties to be performed for the main tenant. These sub-let portions might well be ploughed by the letting tenant or occupying small owner while rights of grazing along with the primary tenant's stock might also be included. In return, sub-tenants, often referred to as cottars, would provide a number of days' service in the year and possibly add to this some days of work to be paid according to day-labour terms. Cottars of this type sometimes lived in separate cot-touns but usually they would form part of the mixed community headed by the tenants or small owners. The tradesmen, often to be found within a toun, would hold small portions of land much as the cottars.

The second group consisted of servants, men or women engaged over periods of six months or a year at a time to give full-time service to the one employer. Married servants, who were numerous in the South-East, were paid in kind not in money, and the use of some land was normally included. They may in part be regarded as small-holders and indeed might be referred to as cottars or cottagers, but their position was substantially different from the cottars with the obligation to provide only a limited number of days' labour. Full-time service was for them a lifelong position, eased by the slight independence of having small pieces of land to cultivate as their own. In many parts of the country, however, including particularly the South-West and the North-East, most servants were unmarried, living within the farmer's household and eating in the farm kitchen. They were landless and, for the period of engagement, were bound in service to the one master. At the end of the six months' engagement they might seek a new master or perhaps, if he were willing, continue with the old. Yet they were not as helpless as might appear. Often they came of cottar families and on marriage might set up as had their parents. Sub-tenants, cottars and servants formed a seamless group, in which, through life, the child of a cottar bound to give service for some days in the year, yet with that precious if insecure title to land, would move into full-time service for a period before marrying and returning finally to the cottar position.

Distinctions of function and status were firm and, at any one time, clear. But families were not locked permanently in unchanging positions. Some holders

7. Woodhead, an early eighteenth-century farm, with accommodation for people and animals in the same building. *National Library of Scotland.*

of land would be bettering themselves, perhaps by adding to an existing holding, perhaps by taking over a new and bigger place. Sometimes a man who had been one among several tenants in a toun would take it over in its entirety. The tendency, particularly where there were market opportunities, was towards such enlargement. But one man's improvement often meant another's, or perhaps several others', failure. There must have been a lot of downward pressure on the less thriving tenants. Both consolidation of land and loss of a tenancy could well mean physical movement from one farm to the other, even from one estate or parish to the other. While mobility within the tenant class was considerable, upwards movement from lesser status to full tenancy was possible but probably infrequent. And the assumption of the responsibilities of the tenant without very much capital could well lead to quick failure and descent. On the whole it seems that families were quite firmly and almost permanently positioned within one or other of the two main strata. Differences of status were moderated by the fact that nearly all families, great and small, had some hold on the land. There were comparatively few who would not find themselves at some time in their lives with at least a fragment of land to cultivate as their own.

Every agricultural community had these various social elements but the balance varied: as between tenants of land and owner-occupiers; between greater farmers, lesser farmers and those at intermediate points on the minutely graduated scale of farm size; between tenants and owners as a whole and the lesser people; between sub-tenants, cottars and servants. In fact, even by the early eighteenth century, the internal social structuring of the touns was becoming increasingly diverse. The range of size of tenant holdings was extending as truly commercial agriculture took hold through the South-East and in the coastal areas further north. Holdings of 200 acres and more with one tenant in full and untrammelled charge were beginning to emerge. Yet it was still the family farm of less than 100 acres and the scores of even tinier holdings that predominated. And, whatever the developments and diversities among the tenants, they remained a well-defined group distinct from the lesser folk. In most parts sub-tenants, cottars and servants together formed a clear majority of the rural population. Only in part of the western Lowlands and along the more mountainous edges of the Lowland plain were they outnumbered by tenants.

The numerical predominance of families in dependent position is to be explained not only by the labour requirements of agriculture, great as these were, but also by the system in which even the greater tenants had to provide labour for their landlords. Where labour services still existed, as was common, the tenants' stated duties might be spread so as to rest on the cottars standing in for their immediate superiors. Much labour, too, was required for the gathering of fuel, and this too became a duty imposed by landlord on tenant and often passed on to the cottar or servant.

The primary occupiers of land — whether tenants or owners — made their way as individuals, gaining or losing position in personal struggle. In fact, they had much of the freedom of the farmer as it came to be understood in the nineteenth century. It is true that the tenants had often to pay heavy rents, in kind and in labour as well as in money. But these were well-defined and accepted as part of an implicit contract, often stated in the terms of a lease; even if there was no lease, tenants enjoyed a large degree of *de facto* security. The sections of land that made up the individual holding might be scattered but they usually had well-defined boundaries, sometimes designated in estate plans and not altered from year to year. The occupiers were responsible as individuals for the cultivation of their lands, used the produce as they wished after the payment of rent, took the profits and accepted the losses. Stock was individually owned, although, as we shall see, grazing was subject to common control and numbers of beasts might be limited. The farmer, too, had his own implements although if he did not own a full plough-team, as was common, he might be forced to share in the use of a plough. It is possible that a few of the farms may have been, in the fullest sense, joint enterprises worked co-operatively as single units with the subsequent sharing of the produce in fixed proportions.

In any case, farmers, whatever their degree of individual freedom, had also to operate as part of a community with mutual obligations involving their agricultural work. Land was cultivated in long sinuous strips in which, because of the mode of ploughing, the soil was piled high on a central ridge while the divisions were hollowed into troughs on furrows. Primarily this was a system of drainage but sometimes — not always — adjacent strips would be worked by different tenants. The mingling of tenant holdings — and sometimes of units of ownership — tended to keep tenants to uniform cropping schemes. They would generally hold most of their infield land scattered between the various sections or breaks which were the units in a communally arranged scheme of intensive cropping. The outfield was the subject of common control to an even greater extent. Each year different portions of the whole area would be brought under the plough while other sections would fall out of cultivation after a few years of continuous cultivation. Individual holdings had to be fitted into the pattern of ground to be broken in, to be held in crop or to be returned to pasture. Further, the practice of allowing animals to graze within a confined section of the field just before it was broken in drew the individual's flocks and herds into a common grazing pattern. Grazing was also regulated as to the access given to stubble fields after harvesting, which consequently had to be done within commonly arranged times. Most touns had access to a common grazing which was never cultivated but on which individuals were allowed only a limited number of beasts.

## The Process of Change

In settlements of the old type land had been assigned so as to give most families at least a scrap of ground for personal use, while controls imposed elements of a protective regime. By the end of the eighteenth century, however, restraints were collapsing, at least as they affected the most successful tenants, to be replaced by basically simpler forms of organisation which gave more power to individual tenants, less to the subordinates who were now being formed into a more homogeneous workforce. The final result was the farm separated from its neighbours, in which the tenant —or it might be the owner-occupier — reigned supreme, with only the terms of a lease to impose possible restraint. The consequences over the whole range of farm occupations were profound.[2]

The main roots of change lay in the tendency, visible at least as early as the seventeenth century, for a comparatively few thrusting individuals to take a larger share of the land. The number of touns held in single tenancy was tending to increase, while in other cases one or two tenants might take the dominant position within a shared farm. Even where a toun was still in

8. High Cross, an 'improved' early nineteenth-century farm house showing a rising standard of comfort and more spacious accommodation. This was a small tenant farm typical of those in parts of the western Lowlands and much less grandiose than those of the Lothians. *Mitchell Library, Glasgow.*

multiple tenancy the greater occupiers might well gather their scattered sections of land to form larger contiguous areas under individual control. There might then be enclosure and virtual separation of at least part of an individual holding. In fact the emergence of dominating individual tenants saw their gradual withdrawal from the forms of common action and the abandonment of the implied restraints. More and more the individual farmer of substance was becoming the master on his land. This was particularly so in the management of pasture arrangements, the core of the common procedures of the toun. When the individual had a sufficiency of consolidated strips to form viable enclosures, he might then sow the grasses that would give him superior grazing for his animals, and so common grazing practices would be eroded, a tendency that would be hastened when landlords felt that the rough grazing of the muir would be better divided into separate units each under individual control.

The re-arrangement of the ferm-toun did not stop at the coalescence of small holdings of scattered sections into large compact units or at the erosion of the practices that held together the various ranks. Concurrently, cottars and sub-tenants were being deprived of their land, helping to turn the old mixed community into a simple place of work in which employer confronted employee with no intermediate positions.

Changes, of course, were seldom wholesale or sudden. The rural order was transformed by the penetration toun by toun, and often only partially within the toun, by units of a new type. By 1800, however the areas of early, if gradual, improvement were firmly established in the minds of contemporaries as well-defined sectors of improved agriculture, with large farms in impressive array. Such were the counties of Berwick, Roxburgh and East Lothian, together with more isolated sections of the central and eastern Lowlands and coastal areas further north. Yet, as late as the end of the eighteenth century, even in such areas, the changes implicit in modernisation had some way to go. Extensive residues of small holdings could be found almost everywhere, and even where sub-tenancies had vanished there remained tiny holdings clustered in cot-touns. And away from the improved areas the older forms of social organisation might remain dominant and largely intact although interspersed with units of newer type.

The first two or three decades of the nineteenth century saw the new type of farm sweep into every corner of the arable Lowlands. Change in the areas that had been slow to take up the new farms was all the faster once started on a general scale. The appropriate styles for the improvement of agriculture, tested long and well where change had begun early, were relatively easy to apply in the laggard districts, and sometimes the migration of experienced farmers from the South-East helped to fire the process of reform.

The essential physical structure of the farm was now the same everywhere. Variations there were in typical size and agricultural purpose, but certain features stand out as essential and distinguishing characteristics of the new Lowland farming. The working unit was a compact block of land under individual control and without any form of common attached. Rotation crops covered nearly all the farm land and the grazing animals were fitted within the rotational system. Farm buildings — farm-house, steading and possibly cottages — were contained within the farm bounds and would house all of the full-time work force. A ferm-toun, or farm as it was now more usually called, was still a community.

The nature of this community was in part determined by the efforts of the tenant or owner, now strengthened in power, to shape a labour force that would be just sufficient to perform necessary farm tasks in the forms of agriculture that might be fitted to the tradition, the soil, the climate and the market potential of the particular place. Thus, a farmer would not brook the apparent waste of land broken up to make small subset holdings; at the same time he needed a labour force completely under his control through the whole working day over the succession of days and seasons. The removal of sub-tenants and cottars and even small tenants holding direct of the landlord left the employer with an enlarged force of workers whom he could engage for the traditional six-monthly or yearly terms as full-time servants.

Society within the farms was also shaped by wider forces. Particularly important were changes in farm size — a matter determined largely by estate policy. The greater the size of the typical farm, the less likely it was that the landless worker could ever acquire a place of his own; and the greater would be the numerical predominance in society of the virtually landless. As the eighteenth century wore on, the long-running tendency towards the formation of larger holdings quickened into a more positive drive. The advantages of the large farm, in terms of productivity, were frequently proclaimed although some lairds were held back by social considerations and by difficulties of finding appropriate tenants. By the end of the century reports were accumulating from all parts of the country of holdings thrown together to make more sizeable farms; often touns with multiple tenants would be consolidated into the one unit with one tenant. Yet the fact that the reports were so widespread serves to conceal vital differences in the pace and thoroughness of the process from place to place. Big and clear variations in the final results of rearrangement emerge and the social structure becomes markedly different from one region to the other.

The victory of the large farm was most complete in the South-East and particularly in East Lothian. Here the farm of 200 up to 600 acres of arable, which would employ at the very least five full-time workers, became entirely dominant even in terms of the number of units. Still more, of course, did it rule in terms of the total land held. Wage-earners outnumbered by ten to one independent holders of land. The other south-eastern counties of Berwick and Roxburgh also established sectors of large-scale farming. Elsewhere in Scotland smaller farms held their position better. North of the Forth the block of more easterly counties — Fife, Perth and Angus — had many substantial farms but these were more than balanced by greater numbers of smaller size. On the whole the further north one goes on the eastern side of the country, the more noticeable in the mix was the smallish farm. In the western part of the Central Belt and southwards through Ayrshire and Galloway, farming, modernised in terms of technique, had been consolidated within holdings much on the old scale. Here the family farm — the unit of 50 to 150 acres — continued to prevail.

The region with most distinctive social characteristics was the North-East, comprising the counties of Kincardine, Aberdeen and Banff. In this area there was a farming ladder rising from the tiny to the large holding with great numbers available at the lowest levels. One feature was the great predominance of units at the lowest level of independent farming — one-pair-horse or one-plough farms. Even so, wage-earners continued to outnumber independent farmers by almost three to one. The opportunities of these wage-earners

9. A group of cottages for farm workers forming a square in front of the factor's house. Farm servants in Scotland lived in the steading and so, as is shown here, could not escape the supervision of their employers even during leisure hours. *Scottish Ethnological Archive, National Museums of Scotland.*

were the greater because of the growth in the number of crofts, holdings too small for fully independent farming. These might provide the first step for a few servants aspiring to independence. The expansion in the number of crofts was made possible because the area, very unusually, had at the end of the eighteenth century a reserve of potentially cultivable land waiting to be brought under the plough. Landlords, to secure the clearance and improvement of land, placed settlers on the bare hillsides and moorlands. No common was created or sustained and each man's section became a minuscule unit worked under the standard rotations of the full-scale farm. The crofts were to become as numerous as in total were independent farms, and in a sense crofters replaced the cottars of earlier times; indeed many crofters may have been resettled cottars and their way of life continued to be much the same. They would work part-time for the greater farmers not because of formal obligation but because of the pressure of need. Their womenfolk were particularly important as farmworkers. Like the cottar families of old, too, crofting households provided many of the youngsters needed as full-time servants.

Deliberate measures of re-organisation interacted always with underlying population trends. Probably through the whole period from 1760 to 1830 the rural areas were producing a positive rate of natural increase. This might be partially concealed by out-migration and was in any case fairly weak before 1800, but after the turn of the century the rate climbed to give increases of between 10 and 20 per cent per decade. At the same time, except in the North-East, the number of tenant holdings was almost certainly decreasing, sub-tenancies were being swept away, and numbers of full-time employees were being rigorously limited to the requirement for efficient cultivation. Yet few were reduced to a landless condition alleviated by limited spells of employ-ment. Apparently some increase in full-time employment combined with the tenden:y for considerable numbers to move to the towns and so to ease the pressures that might have produced a pool of semi-employed or casual labourers.

### The Social Outcome: A Balance of Change and Tradition

The main result of re-organisation was to place males — whether heads of families or unmarried youths — more firmly in the ranks either of employers or self-employed on the one hand, or of wage-earners on the other. Only in the North-East was there still to be found any significant number combining the working of a holding with labour for wages. Yet this simple classification may serve to obscure the variety of conditions within the main groups; apparently fine distinctions might in fact be very important for the individual's perception of his place.[3]

The farmer, whether owner or tenant, certainly considered himself as entirely distinct in social standing from the lesser folk, some of whom he might employ. But he also had a place within a hierarchy of his own kind, determined by the scale on which he farmed. The difference between the greater and lesser farmers had been greatly extended by the selective process of consolidation in large units. This was by no means a distinction between tenant and owner-occupier. Tenants had just as much pride of position, and some in their ranks might have 600 acres of good arable land, might indeed employ twenty full-time workers, while providing housing for their families within the farm bounds. At the other end of the scale were tenants, or even owners, struggling to make an independent livelihood, say with forty marginal acres on a cold upland edge. The majority of farms, of course, lay somewhere between the extremes, in manifold variations of scale, but with the balance of numbers falling towards the upper or the lower limits according to the particular locality.

Whatever the scale of farming, a growing gulf was evident in the relations between the farmer and his workers. Social behaviour more and more emphasised this division. The master would now take his meals in the parlour while the workers fed in the kitchen; only in Ayrshire, apparently, did a rough sociability between the ranks continue to prevail. The division thus signalised in modes of living was the more serious where the enlargement of farms had removed the intermediate grades in the farming ladder and where the wage-earner could not hope for any elevation from his existing position. So it was, most markedly, in the South-East and to a diminishing but still serious degree in the midland areas. In the western part of the Central Belt a wage-earning group of relatively limited numbers was composed to a significant extent of farmers' sons with every hope of inheriting an independent position. In the North-East the large number of crofts and small farms gave a limited hope to the servant of some advancement.

As small-holders providing part-time labour were squeezed out of the system, the solid base of Lowland agriculture had come to be its long-hire workers, servants so-called. Everywhere they formed a major, and in many places with their families a numerically predominant, social group. In many ways they appear as a single type, living on the farms and hired for either six months or a year at a time. Yet within the general terms of a uniform hiring arrangement there were differences from one individual to the next and from one district to the other.

Firstly, there were well-recognised differences in individual standing. Even within the intimate group on the one farm there might be an intricate hierarchy of places on a social scale. These derived largely from the nature of farm work as now pursued. Improved farming came to be based very largely on horse-work. This implied specialisation both because of the high degree of trained skill involved and because horses, being expensive to maintain, had to be used to their full capacity; if a horse was idle it was not paying its way. Thus there was formed a hierarchy of workers with the horse-man at its head, followed by cattle-men and orra-men with varied duties. Further, the slow acquisition of skill implied a grading among horsemen according to experience and aptitude. Men were placed by employers in graded positions, paid according to placement and entrapped in a system of deferential procedures followed through all their daily lives.

This hierarchy within the farm was partly a differentiation based on age and experience, in which the individual might move from one position to the other. Much more important were more deeply-rooted differences that might determine continuing distinctions in the way of life.

One powerful influence was the availability of cottages for married men. In fact the servants' housing, always provided on the farm, might be any one of three types. In some parts of the country the bulk of the permanent labour force

10. A harvest scene, Midlothian, c.1800, depicting the large number of labourers required to cut and stack the grain, the importance of women in the harvesting process and the provision of food and drink as part of the wage reward. *Scottish Ethnological Archive, National Museums of Scotland.*

would be housed in cottages to be occupied by whole families. Such a system was the common way of housing the workers on the farms of the South-East, and the slightly less common way in the counties of Fife, Perth and Forfar, immediately to the north. But in these midland areas was to be found a second mode of housing — the bothy. This was a system mainly found on large farms in which a number of unmarried male servants would be placed within a single large apartment, there to sleep and to cook for themselves from the materials provided as part of the wage. In the western counties from Stirling through to Renfrew and Ayr and also in the extreme South-West but most of all in the North-East a third type of arrangement predominated, also for the unmarried who in this case might include women. Men and women would feed in the farm kitchen and the sleeping accommodation would be in small apartments wherever they might be fitted in around the steading. Often, for example, a mere unheated loft above the stable would be the sole living quarters afforded the individual.

These distinctions in the modes of housing tied into even more important differences in the typical course of a servant's life. Where cottages were plentiful the servant would probably have started life in a farm cottage. As a boy and still unmarried he might well be engaged for full-time service but for this period he would 'live in' rather than be placed in a cottage. Then, on marriage, he would graduate to the full position of cottager, possibly in one of a row of cottages attached to the farm. He would continue to be paid largely in kind, with an allowance of meal and milk, but he might be granted a fraction of an acre to plant with potatoes and possibly grazing for a cow. The areas of good cottage provision were often areas with few holdings of smaller size. The chances, therefore, of the man coming of a servant's family moving on to occupy land himself were remote; the alternative to life as a virtually landless wage-earner was to remove entirely from the agricultural sector, and with the population tending to increase beyond the available places in agriculture many must have done so. In any case, a man was not immutably stuck with the one master or on the one farm and there was extensive and frequent movement of whole families from one place to the other.

On the other hand, where cottages were scarce the unmarried servants who then predominated necessarily had family origins beyond the farms themselves. Where crofts were numerous they provided a likely source from which boys would come to start their careers as servants. But in other situations it was only through migration from areas well supplied with cottages that the necessary quota of boy entrants was found. Engagement for full-time service at the age of thirteen or fourteen did not settle the ultimate pattern of a boy's life. On marriage, perhaps ten years on, there was often little chance of obtaining a cottage from which to pursue the life of a fee'd servant, whatever the skill and position that had been acquired in earlier years. The common great hope was to acquire 'a place of his own' in the form of a small holding. And, where small farms were numerous, a croft might further lead to an independent farming position. But only a small minority was so fortunate and even a croft was often, particularly in the early years of marriage, unattainable. Servants starting under the kitchen or bothy systems might be pushed to the position of day labourers finding a precarious livelihood from a rented house — or more likely a single room — in one of the villages which had grown even as agriculture was reformed. Or they might make a more definite and final migration to a distant town. Some even chose to stay on among the unmarried men on the farm, their wives and children being lodged, generally in rented apartments, in nearby villages.

Agricultural work was based increasingly on year-round labour but it was still necessary to engage additional workers for specific tasks, such as harvesting or weeding and thinning in the turnip fields, at certain seasons. Much of this seasonal, or part-time, labour was female. Sometimes women workers were found in the families of the male servants; indeed in the South-East it was often a condition of occupying a farm cottage to provide such help. But many came from more distant sources. Some women came to work on a seasonal contract, particularly from the West Highlands; some came from families where the main source of income was industrial, for example from the villages with large concentrations of weavers; some came from nearby crofts. In fact, the role of women was even wider than the supply of labour needed in the busy seasons. It had for long been customary for the farmer to engage girls and women for continuous service on the same general terms as were the males. Some of these would work in the house at the tasks normal in any large household, but often enough they also had to work in the fields at the most physically demanding and demeaning tasks. Where they could not participate was in the skilled work of the horsemen. In all, Lowland agriculture was to continue to depend heavily on female help through the nineteenth century. Males engaged in seasonal work mainly at harvest time, being either migrants from the Highlands or from Ireland, or crofters. But with so many diverse sources there was no tendency for a distinct group to form in which the main source of income would be casual or seasonal farm work.

While relationships were evolving within the farms, the occupations connected with farming and with supply of services to the rural population were multiplying and thus creating a more complex society, beyond the farm bounds although still in a rural context. The result was the growth of villages of a larger size than had previously been usual in Scotland. Craftsmen of an older type such as weavers, shoemakers, wrights and tailors withdrew from the ferm-touns where once they had followed their trades and concentrated at points where they could reach larger populations, thus forming the cores of generally growing villages. To occupations of the older sort were added trades increased in numbers, or created by the decline in the self-sufficiency of the ferm-toun and by growing technical complexity. General merchants, established with true shops, were taking the place of the chapmen who had moved around the country and at the same time increased the variety of wares sold across the counter. Blacksmiths had more and more to do and specialist baking appeared as a new trade.

Another force behind village growth was the congregation of workers engaged in industries catering for wide markets. Such industry, exemplified best of all by the massing of linen weavers, tended to give villages a more purely industrial complexion. Perhaps they should no longer be termed rural, particularly in the more westerly parts of the Central Belt and in parts of Fife and Angus where they grew individually large and grouped to form major concentrations of population.

The growth of such settlements was helped, but scarcely caused, by the efforts of many landlords to create 'planned villages'. Planning of this type began early in the eighteenth century but the instances were relatively few and scattered before 1760, and most of the foundations fall into the period from

11. Coupar Angus from the Dundee Road, showing sowing and harrowing taking place in the foreground. The horse-teams provided the vital motive and haulage power of the new farming and most tasks remained highly labour-intensive. *Scottish Ethnological Archive, National Museums of Scotland.*

1770 to 1820. Particularly numerous were those grouped within the belt of country running from Buchan to Speyside. A landlord in making a plan to stimulate village growth might be thinking in terms of the resettlement of families displaced by his agrarian reforms but would also hope for an increase of income from rents and feu-duties. All depended, of course, on finding some means by which income would be generated by the villagers, and this meant something more than the provision of services for the local population. Spinning, weaving, distilling and fishing were the obvious industries able to sustain a population of some size. The essential plan would be very simple, no more than the laying out of feus in some regular pattern and the provision of access roads. But to this might be added some investment, say in a mill, a harbour or a bleach-field, while some safeguard was provided by the extensive lots for subsistence cultivation that were often attached to building sites.

These plans met with very mixed success. While there might be a positive effort to create work, the forces that determined whether a village was to grow and flourish were beyond the control of any landlord. Access to markets, the forging of industrial links, the availability of capital, local traditions of skill, position on main transport routes — all had a bearing. Successful survivors, then, might mesh with a locally flourishing industry, such as distilling or fishing in the North-East, or textiles in Fife, Angus and the western part of the Central Belt. A planned village might become merely one settlement among others which were unplanned and there might be little to distinguish it. Or success might be due to position at a junction or intersection of main routes. Some, too, flourished as servicing centres where there was a sufficient surrounding population and no effective rivals within reach. Many of these forces were tending to bring together populations that had no direct involvement in agricultural processes. Only a scattering of day labourers, some families of servants living at a distance on the farms, and womenfolk seeking jobs were employed in agriculture. The majority of the villagers worked as individual craftsmen or traders in small businesses, or as outworkers under the orders of merchants in the larger centres.

In spite of the growth of villages, the solid core of rural society and indeed the bulk of the rural population was still on the farms. Relationships within them had changed. They had been stripped of all but the full-time workers essential to the running of the farm, with or without their families, and each was now dominated by a single master. But many of the traditional features had endured. Most farmers were still tenants, generally with nineteen-year leases. The long-hire of servants, the quartering of the full-time workers on the farm, and payments in kind continued as widespread customs with significant effect upon social relationships. The great variety that was to be found from place to place was also within a traditional mould. Differences in the scale of farming typical of the various localities had widened but they had long been present in more limited form. And local peculiarities in the terms of engagement for servants also had long historical roots. So much had changed, yet so much remained the same. Above all, the distinctiveness of Scottish social arrangements was sustained.

NOTES

1. Information on eighteenth-century social structure has to be gathered mainly from works of larger scope, but see particularly: R.A. Dodgshon, *Land and Society in Early Scotland* (Oxford, 1981), Ch.7; R.A. Dodgshon, 'The origins of traditional field systems' in M.L. Parry and T.R. Slater (eds.), *The Making of the Scottish Countryside* (London, 1980), pp. 69-92; R.A. Dodgshon, 'The Removal of Runrig in Roxburghshire, 1680-1766', *Scottish Studies,* 16, 1972, pp. 121-37; M.Gray, 'Farm Workers in North-East Scotland', in T.M. Devine (ed.), *Farm Servants and Labour in Lowland Scotland, 1770-1914* (Edinburgh, 1984), pp. 10-28; M.Gray, 'North-East Agriculture and the Labour Force, 1790-1875', in A.A. MacLaren (ed.), *Social Class in Scotland: Past and Present* (Edinburgh, 1976), pp. 86-91; A.Orr, 'Farm Servants and Farm

Labour in the Forth Valley and South-East Lowlands', in Devine (ed.), *Farm Servants*, pp. 29-54; T.C. Smout, *A History of the Scottish People, 1560-1830* (London, 1969), Chs.V, XIII; I.D. Whyte, *Agriculture and Society in Seventeenth Century Scotland* (Edinburgh, 1979), Chs. 3, 6; I.D. Whyte, 'Continuity and Change in a Scottish Farming Community', *Agricultural History Review*, 32, 1984, pp. 160-6; I.D. Whyte and K.A. Whyte, 'Some Aspects of Rural Society in Seventeenth Century Lowland Scotland', in T.M. Devine and D. Dickson (eds.) *Ireland and Scotland, 1600-1850* (Edinburgh, 1983), pp. 32-45; H. Hamilton, *An Economic History of Scotland in the Eighteenth Century* (Oxford, 1963), pp. 46-54.

2. On the processes of change see: Dodgshon, 'The Removal of Runrig', pp. 121-37; A. Geddes, 'The Changing Landscape of the Lothians, 1600-1800, as revealed in Old estate Plans', *Scottish Geographical Magazine*, 54, no. 3, (1938), pp. 129-34; Gray, 'Farm Workers', pp. 12-6; Gray, 'North-East Agriculture', pp. 91-5; M.Gray, 'Scottish Emigration: The Social Impact of Agrarian Change on the Rural Lowlands, 1775-1875', in *Perspectives in American History,* VIII (1973), pp.112-44; G. Kay, 'The Landscape of Improvement', *Scottish Geographical Magazine,* 78, (1962), pp. 100-11; J.H.G. Lebon, 'The Progress of Enclosure in the Western Lowlands', *Scottish Geographical Magazine* 62, (1946), pp. 100-10; J.H.G. Lebon, 'The Face of the Countryside in Central Ayrshire during the Eighteenth and Nineteenth Centuries', *Scottish Geographical Magazine,* 62 (1946), pp. 7-15; B.M.W. Third, 'Changing Landscape and Social Structure in the Scottish Lowlands as revealed by Eighteenth Century Estate Plans', *Scottish Geographical Magazine,* 71 (1955), pp. 83-93; B.M.W. Third, 'The Significance of Scottish Estate Plans and Associated Documents', *Scottish Studies,* I (1957), pp. 39-64.

3. For the following section see: Ian Carter, *Farm Life in North-East Scotland* (Edinburgh, 1979), Chs 4, 5; T.M. Devine, 'Social Stability in the Eastern Lowlands of Scotland during the Agricultural Revolution, 1780-1840', in T.M. Devine (ed.), *Lairds and Improvement in the Scotland of the Enlightenment* (Dundee, 1979), pp. 59-70; T.M. Devine, ' Scottish Farm Service in the Agricultural Revolution', in Devine (ed.), *Farm Servants',* pp. 1-8; Gray, 'Farm Workers', pp.16-23; Gray, 'Scottish Emigration', pp.132-74 Gray, 'North-East Agriculture', pp. 95-101; L.J. Saunders, *Scottish Democracy, 1815-1840* (Edinburgh, 1950), Pt.I.

# CHAPTER 4

# Scottish Gaeldom: The First Phase of Clearance

## Allan I. Macinnes

## Introduction

The removal and relocation of population, emotively but not inaccurately depicted as Clearances, was not a uniquely Highland far less an exclusively Scottish phenomenon. Clearance was an integral aspect of the transition from a traditionalist to a capitalist environment accompanying industrialisation and the commercialisation of agriculture; a process which accelerated in the British Isles during the eighteenth century, spread to the rest of Europe and North America in the nineteenth and continues in the wake of colonialism to shape economic development in the Third World — especially Latin America, central and southern Africa — to the present day.[1] Because land was the main basis of wealth in pre-industrialised society, its apropriation and exploitation for the benefit of a ruling elite was of fundamental cultural as well as social significance, particularly if, as in the case of Scottish Gaeldom from the mid-eighteenth to the early nineteenth centuries, changes in land tenure and agricultural techniques entailed not only the abandonment of communal and co-operative farming, but the deliberate subordination of the balanced use of landed resources and manpower to the prevailing demands of the market and British imperial expansion.

## The Cultural Issue.

In essence, the cultural issue of Clearance within Scottish Gaeldom evolved around the traditionalist and legalist concepts of heritage. The traditionalist concept *duthchas*, translatable as heritable trusteeship, obliged chiefs and leading gentry as the clan elite to ensure security of possession throughout the territorial bounds settled by their kinsmen and local associates. The legalist concept of *oighreachd,* translatable as heritable title, allowed chiefs and leading gentry to reorientate the management of their estates to suit their own commercial interests as landed proprietors rather than as patrons and protectors of their clansmen.

The first phase of Clearance, which actually commenced prior to the Forty-Five, not only gathered momentum from the quashing of Jacobite political pretensions and the denigration of traditional clan values in the wake of Culloden, but marked the triumph of the legalist concept of heritage. Commencing with the phasing out of the tacksmen — the lesser gentry who acted as intermediaries between the clan elite and their followers — on the Argyll estates from the 1730s and concluding in the recessionary aftermath of the Napoleonic Wars during the 1820s, the gradual but inexorable reorientation of estates towards the market at the expense of clanship throughout Scottish Gaeldom can be viewed as a single cultural entity as well as a distinctive phase of management. Accordingly, the first phase of Clearance was characterised by the virtual elimination of the traditional township, the *bàile*, as the basic unit of land settlement and management within Scottish Gaeldom. Traditional townships — in effect multiple-tenant, communal farms managed by tacksmen — were broken up by chiefs and leading gentry intent on exploiting the marketable commodities of their estates to subsidise their political and social assimilation into British landed circles. The creation of the crofting community of individual arable smallholdings sharing common pasture to exploit kelp, fishing and quarrying — and to meet imperial demands for soldiers and sailors — was no less integral to this first phase of Clearance that the advent of the large single-tenant farm to exploit black cattle or sheep .

In assessing the triumph of the legalist over the traditionalist concept of heritage, three particular factors worked in favour of chiefs and leading gentry fulfilling their aspirations as landed proprietors. First, law, and especially land law within an agrarian economy, worked to the benefit of the propertied classes. Secondly, the improving spirit of the age — the prevailing Whig concept that material and cultural progress through the acquisition and exploitation of property entailed the replacement of customary by commercial relationships — identified the eradication of clanship in the aftermath of the Forty-Five with the 'civilising' of Scottish Gaeldom.[2] Thirdly, and perhaps most critically, customary relationships within the clans were generally becoming commercialised in the century before Culloden as attested negatively by the criticisms Gaelic poets directed against absenteeism, accumulation of debts and rent-raising on the part of chiefs and leading gentry and, more positively, by the expansion of landownership through the intermediary of wadsets, or mortgages, which enabled lesser gentry to acquire heritable title to lands formerly held in tack in return for advancing monies to members of the clan elite indebted by prolonged sojourns at Edinburgh, the Court at London or even Paris.[3] Gaelic society, therefore, was neither unprepared nor unreceptive to change by the Forty-Five, albeit the dynamic push towards commercialism within Scottish Gaeldom had to await the radical transformation of marketing opportunities consequent on British industrialisation in the later eighteenth century.

The essential significance of the Jacobite defeat at Culloden lay not so much in the repressive reprisals of central government as in the escape from traditionalist expectations afforded to chiefs and leading gentry. The demise of clanship was accomplished neither by proscribing the wearing of tartan nor by scrapping anachronistic judicial institutions and military services, the punitive measures promoted by central government in the erroneous belief that the personal obligations of clanship could be abolished by legislation. The demise of clanship was instead accomplished by chiefs and leading gentry — regardless of political affiliations as Jacobites or adherents of the House of Hanover — wholeheartedly embracing the Whig concept of progress and deliberately subordinating, if not throwing over, their personal obligations as patrons and protectors.

That the occupiers of the soil adhered tenaciously to the traditionalist concept of *duthchas* long after clanship had been abrogated by the conduct of chiefs and leading gentry is testimony more to the cultural disorientation rather than outright cultural alienation occasioned by the first phase of Clearance. Unlike contemporaneous Irish Gaels who were able to direct polemical attacks against the alien English forces of government, the land-owning classes and the established church, Scottish Gaels seem prisoners of their own culture, thoroughly perplexed, demoralised and disorientated by the process of anglicisation effected by the assimilation of the clan elite into the British establishment. The criticisms of the poets — still the main outlets for public opinion within Scottish Gaeldom — were usually expressed deferentially through misplaced strictures against factors, legal agents, tacksmen, incoming tenant-farmers and even sheep. On the rare occasions when landlords were indicated as instigators of Clearance, citations were depersonalised, the amorphous 'they' being held responsible.[4]

## The Debate on Clearance

Having subsequently been coloured by oral tradition and folk memory, the process of Clearance within Scottish Gaeldom cannot be disentangled from its cultural setting. However, the ongoing and often highly charged debate on the removal and relocation of the Gael, which manifests a prevailing tendency to condemn or condone the conduct of the clan elite, has arguably worked against clarification of why and how Clearance was implemented in the late eighteenth and early nineteenth centuries.

Apologists for the Gaels as victims of Clearance, though laudably redress-

12 Dunrobin Castle, Sutherland. A conspicuously triumphal monument to Clearance.

ing the historical imbalance that has worked in favour of the clan elite as im-
provers, tend to take their lead from the poets of the first phase, in being long
in heroic rhetoric but short in critical appraisal.[5] The picture of a contented
society broken up by alien forces wholly underestimates the cultural tensions
within the clans prior to the Forty-Five provoked by the commercialising of
customary relations by chiefs and leading gentry. Migration to the American
colonies, as to Lowland cities, was underway in advance of, though undoubtedly augmented by, tenurial change from the 1730s and can primarily be
attributed to population growth, itself a product of economic advance and
social stability consequent on the growing pacification of the Highlands and
the marked decline in militarism from the later seventeenth century, Jacobitism notwithstanding. Seasonal migration to the Lowlands in search of gainful
employment was already becoming an accepted facet of life in Argyllshire by
the 1740s.[6]

Apologists for the Gaels tend also to discount the depressing effect of the
Highland climate on enterprise. This was not just a matter of incessant rainfall,
high winds and snap frosts delaying sowing and prolonging harvests. The
relative failure of erstwhile clansmen to respond positively to commercialism
was testimony to a mentality shaped by an ingrained sense of defeatism after
the Forty-Five, such defeatism being compounded by evangelical missionary
endeavours in the later eighteenth and early nineteenth centuries which, by
propagating the message that life was a 'glen of tears' to anchor cultural

disorientation, placed emphasis on individual salvation rather than collective action to resist Clearance. Above all, though apologists for the Gaels in contrast to the poets are not averse to personalised criticisms of chiefs and leading gentry, too often these criticisms are impressionistic and anecdotal because of a wilful disregard for records of estate management. As a corollary, despite having brought the crofters into the mainstream of Highland history, there is a pronounced reluctance to admit that the creation of the crofting community, by underwriting the imbalanced use of land, made further Clearance inevitable in response to market demand.[7]

Conversely, the interpretation favoured by apologists for Clearance stresses that the removal and relocation of people consequent on the break-up of the traditional townships was essentially the product of objective demographic and economic factors, notably the presence of too many people on marginal land. Because there were few available or ancillary reserves to sustain a capitalist environment within Scottish Gaeldom, chiefs and leading gentry, however regrettable their conduct in abrogating trusteeship and however remiss their failure as landlords to provide adequate incentives and security for their tenantry to carry through improvements, had little alternative but to promote Clearance.[8] Yet, the break-up of traditional townships, the raising of rents and the introduction of sheep-farming were not just irritants in the changing commercial relationship between the clan elite and their erstwhile followers, but were above all subjective acts of estate management in the same way that crofting communities were erected as congested districts and allowed to degenerate into rural ghettos. The marked rise of population within Scottish Gaeldom, of the order of 54 per cent between 1755 and 1831 (from about a quarter of a million to about 350,000) exclusive of migration overseas or to the Lowlands, was by no means spread uniformly throughout the region, far less within shires and parishes as enumeration districts. In the islands, primarily due to the creation of labour-retentive crofting communities, population growth was as much as 75 per cent in the fifty years prior to 1811. In mainland Highland districts, natural increases in population were more markedly offset by differing levels of out-migration. Where traditional townships were given over to labour-shedding sheep-farming, around a third of the parishes had experienced a net loss of population by the 1790s.[9]

Not withstanding the subjective nature of managerial decisions to remove and relocate, some apologists for Clearance exhibit an uncritical acceptance of improving propaganda which sets the worst of traditionalist farming against the best of commercialised agriculture.[10] Yet, the more discerning of contemporaneous commentators, notwithstanding their vested interests in questioning the Whig concept of progress, considered that the commercialisation of agriculture within Scottish Gaeldom should take account of existing landed and human resources as well as market demands and that the fashionable pursuit of improvement must offset projected financial benefits against immediate social costs.[11]

In the Highlands, as in the Lowlands, traditional farming placed emphasis on crops grown not for their high but for their persistent and resilient yields. Apologists for Clearance have tended, perhaps, to overplay the recurrence of harvest failure which, apart from the mortality crises generated by endemic death in the late 1690s, the early 1740s and in 1782-3, was essentially localised and occasional. Conversely, the pastoral emphasis of farming allied to the purchasing power afforded by the relative buoyancy of the droving trade, arguably made traditional townships in the Highlands less vulnerable than their Lowland counterparts to fluctuations in grain supplies. Moreover, the relatively primitive technology of the Gael was not only consistent with agriculture as a labour-intensive pursuit, but was not lacking in ingenuity — notably the use of the foot-plough, the *caschrom*, in conjunction with lazy bed cultivation (sandwiches of soil and seaweed) — to break in land unsuitable for horse-drawn ploughs.

In areas where traditional townships were but gradually phased out in the late eighteenth and early nineteenth centuries, the tenantry on diverse estates throughout Scottish Gaeldom were not inattentive to the use of lime, marl and shelly sand to enrich the soil. But, a general shortage of readily available timber and high tariffs on the coastal carriage of coal meant widespread reliance on peat as the primary source of fuel. Its extraction and supply, a time-consuming and onerous task, compounded the lack of systematic labour rhythms which, in turn, inhibited the productive redeployment of labour from agriculture into manufacturing and quarrying. As evident from the innovatory cultivation of pease, turnips, grasses and even flax as well as the ubiquitous potato by the 1790s, tenantry on the remaining traditional townships were not unaware of the advantages of crop rotation. Exemplary enclosures and drainage were in evidence on large single-tenant farms. But, erstwhile clansmen were discouraged from attempting improvements to lands and buildings by the lack of capital and insecurity of tenure consequent on the heightening of rents and the shortening of leases.[12]

More tellingly, the major growth point in the Highland economy from the late seventeenth century was the droving trade in black cattle, based on unimproved pastoral farming, the rearing rather than the breeding of beasts able to travel on the hoof to Lowland markets and thence to English pastures. The phenomenal growth of London as Europe's largest city, imperial expansion protected by a Royal Navy fed on salt beef, and the spread of industrial towns and villages in northern England and central Scotland, ensured the demand for black cattle continued on an upward spiral throughout the eighteenth century.[13]

Notwithstanding that droving was firmly established as a major growth point for the Scottish economy by the mid-eighteenth century, commentators well able to differentiate between improving propaganda and substantive economic development have tended to paint a picture of clanship as static and lacking in indigenous enterprise prior to the Forty-Five, a picture which tends to rationalise Clearance as a clash between the productive and social use of land, the profit motive dictating the success of the former.[14] Gaelic society, even outwith the clan elite, was not devoid of enterprise or lacking in indigenous commercial impetus prior to Clearance. The profits realised by droving served to raise proprietary expectations, encouraging chiefs and leading gentry to promote land reclamation and innovative land use. The commencement of kelp manufacture in the Western Isles during the 1730s was complemented in the following decade by the introduction of the potato. Timber, slate and lime quarrying, lead and coal mining were simultaneously exploited in diverse Highland localities. The introduction of Lowland breeds of sheep from the 1760s was but a further aspect of innovative management in the reorientation of estates towards the market..

Droving, moreover, served to stimulate consumerism among the clans as evident from the ledgers of exiled Gaels who established merchant houses in Glasgow and Edinburgh, and conducted a vigorous tramping trade throughout Scottish Gaeldom during the first half of the eighteenth century, their principal contacts being tacksmen and shopkeepers. At the same time, enterprising clan gentry in the Western Isles were developing a shipping trade with Glasgow, Ireland and occasionally Holland, exchanging coarse cloth, hides and skins for grain, consumer durables and luxuries. Contacts established with merchant houses in Aberdeen and Peterhead as well as Glasgow led after the Forty-Five to a few gentry either side of the Minch becoming involved in the commercial pursuit of herring, cod and ling fishing and also the extraction of oil from basking sharks. Contacts of shopkeepers as well as the gentry with merchant houses in Lowland towns and cities sustained the weaving of plaid and subsequently of linen yarn as commercial activities, not just in peripheral Highland areas in the shires of Aberdeen and Perth but also in Badenoch and Tiree.

Probably the most sophisticated commercial development, arising initially from mercantile contacts in the Clyde ports and Ireland but expanding through native enterprise, was the interlocking network of companies that made up the marketing portfolio of the Campbells of Ardchattan and their family associates on Glen Etive from the outset of the eighteenth century through the first phase of Clearance. Their portfolio of commercial ventures

13. Kelp manufacturing. A messy, onerous and precarious operation. The principal commodity promoting the creation of the crofting community in the Western Isles. *Scottish Ethnological Archive, National Museums of Scotland.*

covered droving, debt recovery, the extraction of timber, importing meal and tobacco, coal mining and leasing iron works. From their base in the Lorn district of Argyllshire, their trading operations extended from Caithness to the Perthshire Highlands, expansion being particularly noted prior to the Forty-Five in the Lochaber area where they imported meal and tobacco in association with merchants at Fort William/Maryburgh, a developing commercial centre as well as a garrison town. There, local merchants, in association with neighbouring chiefs and gentry, were engaged in various commercial activities ranging from smuggling contraband wines and spirits to legitimate trading with the West Indies. Indeed, the Camerons of Lochiel, who had been dabbling in the New Jersey land market in association with Bristol merchants from the late seventeenth century, had secured an interest in a Jamaican plantation by the 1730s.[15]

Such indicators of commercial growth notwithstanding, the relative dearth of towns and the practice of chiefs, leading gentry and tacksmen to negotiate contracts for black cattle and other saleable commodities, meant that the tenantry in the traditional townships had but limited experience of marketing. Smuggling continued to provide an outlet for community participation in commercial activity. Although the smuggling of contraband goods on the western seaboard was curtailed severely following the Revestment Act of 1765, which brought the Isle of Man within the financial oversight of the

Treasury, Ireland remained a clandestine source of salt for curing fish and meat while the illicit distilling and distribution of malt whisky for Lowland markets was pursued with varying degrees of enthusiasm and commitment throughout the Highlands in the later eighteenth century. At the same time, the seasonal migration of youths and single adults to the Lowlands to engage in harvesting, herring bussing, wood cutting and stripping of barks for tanneries provided the systematic work experience of hired labour for underemployed Gaels and furthered fashionable consumerism as well as bilingualism.[16] Accordingly, it may be suggested that the commercial impetus within Scottish Gaeldom on the threshold of Clearance was not so much undeveloped as underdeveloped.[17]

## Static Expansion

While commercial activity outwith as within Scottish Gaeldom was heavily dependent on advances of credit, the economy of the Highlands and Islands undoubtedly lacked the depth and diversity manifest in the Lowlands. Experience of marketing commodities and labour was much less diffused. Anticipated profits from droving — an inherently speculative trade tied to the capacity of the drover to gauge the market profitably — served to underwrite absenteeism and subsidise the assimilation of the clan elite into the British establishment. Because opportunities for rent-raising were restricted by the tradition of long leases to tacksmen, the clan elite's exploitation of extractive industries provided an alternative means of servicing debts occasioned by southern sojourns. Despite their colonial ventures, the accumulated debts of the Camerons of Lochiel when their estates were forfeited after the Forty-Five were six times their annual rental — by no means an exceptional sum within Scottish Gaeldom. Although indebtedness was an accepted characteristic of the Anglo-Scottish landed classes, likewise the tendency to use profits accruing from marketable commodities to sustain conspicuous expenditure, the financing of the clan elite's social aspirations commenced from a weaker economic base than the rest of the British establishment. This was a situation highlighted by the surveying of estates which accorded special attention to landscaping and the siting of mansion houses, not to the search for or the creation of diverse employment opportunities to complement the commercialisation of agriculture. Indeed, the surveying of Highland estates, a spin-off from the road-building programme for the military containment of Jacobitism, was implemented less as a prelude to improvement as to wholescale Clearance.

At the same time, the profitability of droving, which had encouraged the clan elite to push up rents whenever leases were renewed, had accustomed the tenantry within traditional townships to offset rent increases, together with their consumer expenditure, against anticipated earnings from the marketing of black cattle on their behalf by the tacksmen. As a result, their lifestyles were not geared to the handling of money or negotiating commercial contracts with the clan elite or their agents. Hence. the failure of the drovers to assess the profitability of black cattle, as occurred in 1772, 1776, 1782, 1793 and 1803, occasioned periodic financial crises in estate management which furthered the accumulation of debts on the part of the clan élite and of rent arrears on the part of their clansmen.

The consequence threat of enforced bankruptcy for the former expedited the removal and relocation of the latter. While the clan elite were undoubtedly able to exploit their followers' attachment to the concept of *duthchas* as well as their relative unfamiliarity with commercial negotiations to enforce downward social mobility by which traditional farmers became crofters, farm servants and day labourers, erstwhile clansmen were not necessarily passive victims of Clearance. Emigration to America — notably to Northern Carolina and subsequently Nova Scotia — had the character of a community movement led by tacksmen whose managerial function was usurped by Clearance. The concept of *duthchas* was not inflexible either socially or territorially. That personal services or boon work should be only gradually phased out during the first phase of Clearance certainly points to the continuing difficulty of adjusting from customary to commercial relationships within Scottish Gaeldom. Yet, wage regulation had been abandoned throughout the Highlands and Islands by the 1790s, when the cost of hiring labour was generally reputed to have doubled from the 1760s — as much a comment on the improved bargaining position of the Gael as on his or her marked reluctance to undertake farm service or day labour. Not only were diverse opportunities for employment being opened up by the fishing (inshore rather than deep sea), quarrying and distilling, but seasonal migration and the attractive rates for piecework in manufacturing kelp and cutting timber made single men reluctant to commit themselves to a year's hire as farm servants. Farm service as well as day labouring tended to be undertaken by married men, resulting in the expansion of cottars' holdings, notwithstanding the break-up of traditional townships. In return, the retention of cottars on single-tenant farms as well as within the crofting community compounded the tendency towards early marriage, a not insignificant contributant to the phenomenal growth of population within Scottish Gaeldom in the latter eighteenth and early nineteenth centuries.

The first phase of Clearance can be deemed to have aggravated rather than solved the problem of static expansion within Scottish Gaeldom, a problem common in the pre-industrialised world whereby the agricultural base comes to support more people without necessarily generating any appreciable increase in income.[18] For the increased commercialism stimulated by droving was matched by the rapid increase in population, primarily attributable to improved dietary prospects following the introduction of the potato from the 1740s; survival rates being subsequently boosted by widespread inoculation against smallpox. Because the extension of the cultivable zone was a finite process, agricultural productivity tended to be outstripped by population pressure, occasioning a downward spiral in living standards generally which could only be prised open by imaginative estate management that allied balanced land use to the productive diversification of non-agricultural employment. Repeated calls for investment in quays, harbours, sawmills, tanneries and woollen manufactories remained largely unanswered between 1760 and 1830. Imaginative estate management does not appear to have been a sustained feature of Scottish Gaeldom during the first phase of Clearance, whether on the part of the clan elite or, indeed, of interventionist agencies intent on expediting assimilation with the Lowlands through exemplary improvement.

Genuine efforts at agricultural improvement and commercial diversification were attempted at various stages on diverse estates, particularly by clan gentry who had accumulated capital from professional careers in law, trade, banking or imperial service, civil as well as military. But, the first phase of Clearance is littered with well-intentioned projects never brought to fruition. Thus, the transformation of the fishing industry in the Sound of Harris, initiated by Alexander MacLeod after purchasing the island estate from his chief in 1778 with monies accrued from a profitable career with the East India Company, was terminated by his death in 1790. His son, Alexander, preferred to retain a lucrative civil post in India. Undoubtedly, the accumulation of debts by members of the clan elite lacking extraneous sources of income was a plausable deterrent to sustained investment prior to 1770, when the passage of the Entail Act enabled landlords to pass on to their heirs three-quarters of expenditure incurred through estate improvement. Though no longer obliged to wadset, which had necessitated the mortgaging and consequently the alienation of rents, the opening up of the land market through enforced sales and bankruptcies by the outset of the nineteenth century — a trend notably accelerated when the economic boom generated by the Napoleonic Wars collapsed after 1815 — hardly suggests more imaginative or financially sound estate management.[19]

The most notable difference in estate management with the Lowlands was the relative dearth of planned villages within Scottish Gaeldom — no more than forty, less than a third of the Scottish total by 1830 — to serve as local

14. An example of landlord enterprise in the later eighteenth-century Highland herring fishery. Kenneth Mackenzie's structure at Torridon, Wester Ross contained a curing house and storage facilities for salt and nets.

market centres offering diverse employment (textiles, fishing and distilling) and providing ready reservoirs of day labour to complement farm service on single-tenant farms. Although poor overland communications undoubtedly retarded such commercial diversification, this factor was arguably of greater significance not on the threshold of Clearance when population levels in both regions were not inequitable, but from the 1780s when industrialisation began to concentrate on the central belt. The first phase of industrialisation, associated with textiles in Scotland, largely bypassed the Highlands. Like much of contemporary Ireland, as indeed the Third World in the present day, having been denied a balanced transition from an agrarian to an industrial society Scottish Gaeldom was obliged to disgorge surplus labour from rural townships directly to cities as urban concentration quickened with the rapid expansion of heavy industries from the 1830s.

The promotion of the planned village, though much vaunted, was also much discredited by the Commissioners for the Annexed Estates and subsequently the British Fisheries Society whose production of improving blueprints was in inverse ratio to their implementation of exemplary ventures.

Though the annexation of thirteen Jacobite estates was effected by 1752, the Commissioners' efforts at commercial diversification lasted no more than fourteen years from 1760, being bedeviled by bureaucratic inertia, rigid Treasury control over expenditure and deficient capitalisation resulting in a diminishing annual sum to implement improvements. The initial reluctance of the tenantry to accept the forfeiture of the clan elite was not ameliorated by their own displacement to accommodate demobbed soldiers and sailors on the conclusion of the Seven Years' War. From 1763 the agency's role was primarily that of an imperial compensatory service. By the time of the full-scale restoration of the disinherited in 1784, who atoned for the regrettable lapses of their predecessors into Jacobitism by promoting recruitment for the American Wars of Independence, the annexed estates were financially dilapidated. Although central government was not directly involved in management, the operation of the British Fisheries Society within Scottish Gaeldom in the four decades after 1786 was attended by not dissimilar problems of attenuated decision-making and financial control from London. Concentration of investment in a few villages, not necessarily the best fishing locations, where monies tended to be tied up in fixed assets such as buildings rather than advanced as working capital for boats and tackle, was not a policy geared to secure fulsome co-operation from the clan elite or stimulate wholesale participation from erstwhile clansmen.[20]


## A Model for Clearance

Before rushing precipitously into a general condemnation of estate management, it must be stressed that few reliable case studies have yet been published on Clearance within Scottish Gaeldom.[21] The linking of extensive records of estate management to those of ownership, bankruptcy and legal sequestrations, a task of quantitative analysis that can be expedited by the new technology for data processing, will serve two qualitative purposes — to build up a reliable corpus of case-studies and provide a thorough examination of the relationsip between land-use and enterprise during the first phase of Clearance. In the meantime, a model can be constructed for the break-up of the traditional township to explain how the *bàile* gave way to the single tenant farm and the crofting community.[22]

Although piecemeal tenurial tinkering had occurred on several estates in the course of commercialising customary relationships, the first general reform which set the pattern for ending the *bàile* as the basic unit of management as well as cultivation (fig.i) and led to the virtual elimination of the traditional township during the first phase of Clearance was initiated in

Morvern in 1737, as in Mull and Tiree, by John Campbell, second Duke of Argyll. Determined to sustain his political and social standing as a Whig grandee, the Duke deemed a temporary recession in droving sufficient grounds for eliminating the tacksmen in order to monopolise all rents levied on his estates. The mechanism for change was competitive bidding, the commercial exploitation of *duthchas,* setting tacksmen against clansmen to secure the lease for each township. If the tacksman offered a higher bid, he was obliged to become a tenant farmer, clansmen being retained only as cottars or farm servants. If the clansmen outbid him, they remained traditional farmers but were deprived of the tacksman's managerial and marketing expertise. In the event, three-quarters of the townships became single-tenant farms (fig. ii). Although bidding at renewal of leases was subsequently modified to take account of commercial patronage, the upswing in droving encouraged over-bidding by both tacksmen and tenantry, their desire to retain their heritage impairing their livelihood.

Recourse to competitive bidding, moreover, opened the way for enterprising gentry from other clans as well as Lowland farmers to secure townships for the commercial farming of sheep, the introduction of such breeds as the Border black-face from the 1760s giving way to the Cheviot from the 1790s — breeds which were less hardy than the native Highland but were of greater carcass weight and yielded greater quantities of wool. Because the stocking of a sheep-farm was capital-intensive — the business being dominated by graziers with flocks of at least 600 — and because the needs of the new breeds for diversity of pasture and winter grazing were deemed incompatible with the retention of black cattle and traditional townships, single-tenant farms tended to expand and be consolidated (fig iii). At the same time, landlords were determined to retain a large labour pool, not least on account of the establishment kudos attached to the provision of recruits for the army and navy. In addition to the Black Watch (operative from 1740), twenty-three regiments of the line and twenty-six of fencibles, in excess of 48,300 men were recruited from Scottish Gaeldom following the outbreak of the Seven Years' War in 1756 until the conclusion of the Napoleonic Wars in 1815.[23] This was a testimony both to rising population levels and to congestion within surviving multiple-farms where the high yield from marginal land afforded by the potato cultivated in lazy beds led to the abandonment of conventional strip farming (runrig) and the creation of individual smallholdings in the crofting community.

In interior districts, erstwhile clansmen struggled to sustain a livelihood by club-farming sheep and became increasingly dependent on supplementary income from illicit distilling and seasonal migration unless they found employment in a few localities in quarrying which relegated agriculture to an

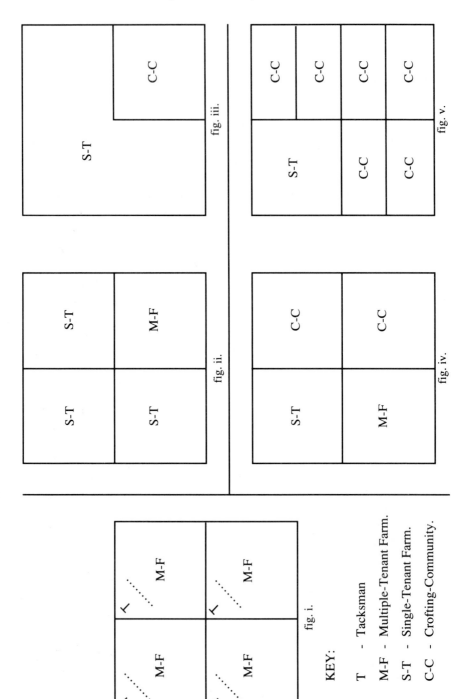

fig. iii.

fig. v.

fig. ii.

fig. iv.

fig. i.

KEY:

T - Tacksman

M-F - Multiple-Tenant Farm.

S-T - Single-Tenant Farm.

C-C - Crofting-Community.

ancillary pursuit. The bulk of erstwhile clansmen removed from interior glens and straths were relocated in congested coastal districts, some to exploit inshore fishing — made a more attractive proposition by bounties offered for catching and curing herring from 1786 as by the relaxation of the outrageous salt laws from 1796 — but the majority on the western seaboard became engaged in the manufacture of kelp, a commodity noted for its volatile prices which nonetheless continued on an upward spiral when the American Wars of Independence restricted supplies of wood-ash and the Napoleonic Wars deprived the chemical industry of barilla (fig. iv). Indeed, on the Western Isles, although single-tenant farms had evolved to exploit the black cattle trade but had not necessarily progressed to sheep-farming, kelping became the main economic pursuit, which confirmed the ancillary nature of agriculture within the crofting community (fig.v). By reserving proprietary control over the manufacture and marketing of kelp, landlords in the islands made extortionate profits which were used primarily to promote conspicuous expenditure; tacksmen, where retained, served merely to collect rent and parcel out smallholdings. The limited summer season for collecting and converting seaweed into kelp led to the retention of enormous labour pools not just of crofters but also of cottars and squatters. Because earnings from kelp had to be offset against rising rents and purchases of meal to supplement a potato diet, conditions within the crofting community were driven below subsistence by rampant subdivision which created a vulnerable and fragile economy.

## Conclusion

A distinctive historical perspective emerges from this model for the first phase of Clearance during which Scottish Gaeldom, as a net exporter of man-power and raw materials, became an internal colony rather than a beneficiary of empire like the industrialised Lowlands. In the first place, because the process of relocation and removal tended to be gradual, usually spread out over several generations, the much-vaunted Clearances effected between 1807 and 1820 on behalf of Elizabeth Gordon, Countess of Sutherland, should not be regarded as typical. Capitalised from monies generated in the English Midlands on the Bridgewater estates of her husband George Gower, Marquis of Stafford, Clearance in Sutherland did not lead to sustained commercial diversification, however, despite accomplishing the profitable introduction of sheep-farming, the creation of a transport infrastructure and the sumptuous erection of Dunrobin Castle.

Secondly, although families left Scottish Gaeldom prior to the expiry of leases because they were unable to meet high rents, and although pronounced

15. Lazy-bed cultivation. Sandwiches of soil and seaweed producing high yields of potatoes from marginal lands facilitated rampant subdivision within the crofting community. *Scottish Ethnological Archive, National Museums of Scotland.*

upward movement in commodity prices tempted landlords to abrogate leases by legal chicanery, removal and relocation were linked umbilically to competitive bidding for the renewal of leases. Thus the 'rage for emigration' in the later eighteenth century can be deemed voluntary only to the extent that relatively affluent tacksmen and tenantry were not prepared to accept downward social mobility and depression of their living standards when freehold land was on offer in America.[24] The combined efforts of government and landlords to retain a reservoir of manpower, which led to the Passenger Vessels Act of 1803 pushing up the costs of overseas passages under the guise of improving medical and dietry provision, served merely as a temporary check to emigration and encouraged tenantry to move to the Lowlands to escape the congestion of the crofting community. The associated promotion of Commissions for roads, bridges and canals, though timescale and costs of construction soon outstripped the development potential of the Great Glen as an arterial route for commerce, offered no more than temporary outdoor relief for the underemployed Gael.

Thirdly, the fragility and vulnerability of the crofting community to market forces was exposed by economic recession in the aftermath of the Napoleonic Wars. Indeed, not only did cattle prices fall markedly, but the main props of crofting collapsed during the 1820s. Inshore fishing was undermined by the contrary nature of the herring shoals. The combined impact of cheaper organic imports and the mass production of inorganic substitutes occasioned the terminal decline of kelping. Crofters' supplementary earnings were critically impaired by central government tightening up its policing of illicit distilling while scaling down its programme of canal, road and bridge building. Seasonal migrants to the Lowlands faced competition from Irish labour taking advantage of cheap steamer fares between Belfast Lough and the Clyde, although such temporary out-migration from the Highlands persisted and became more diverse in the course of the nineteenth century. Thrown back on their dependence on the potato, the crofting community became subject to localised famines of increasing frequency and duration. The growing view in official as in landed circles that the crofting community housed a redundant population was to usher in a second phase of Clearance characterised by the wholesale switch to sheep-farming accompanied by the piecemeal conversion and sale of estates for recreational use as deer forests.[25]

## NOTES

1. A wide-ranging historical perspective for the transition from a traditionalist to a capitalist environment is provided by E.L. Jones and S.J. Woolf (eds.), *Agrarian Change and Economic Development* (London, 1974). M. Turner, *Enclosures in Britain, 1750-1830* (London, 1984) provides a useful survey of the British dimension, while F.E. Huggett, *The Land Question and European Society* (London, 1975) ranges from Ireland to Russia. Probably the most readable Marxist analysis is E. Kamenka and R.S. Neale, (eds.), *Feudalism, Capitalism and Beyond* (London, 1975).

2. National Library of Scotland (hereafter N.L.S.), Some Remarks on t' Highland Clans and Methods proposed for civilizing them, Adv. MS 16.1.14. A. L: (ed.), *The Highlands of Scotland in 1750* (Edinburgh, 1898).

3. A.I. Macinnes, 'The Impact of the Civil Wars and Interregnum: Political Disruption and Social Change within Scottish Gaeldom', in R. Mitchison and P. Roebuck (eds.), *Economy and Society in Scotland and Ireland, 1500-1939* (Edinburgh, 1988), pp. 58-69.

4. Cf. 'Aoir Dhomhnaill Friseil' (Satire of Donald Fraser), 'Oran Fir Ghriminis' (Song to the Goodman of Griminish) and 'Oran Do Na Fogarraich' (Song to the Fugitives), in W. Matheson (ed.) *The Songs of John MacCodrum* (Scottish Gaelic Texts Society, 1938), pp. 52-5, 132-41, 196-203. Also 'Cumha Coire A' Cheathaich' (Lament for Misty Corrie) and 'Oran nam Balgairean' (Song to the Foxes) in A. MacLeod (ed.), *The Songs of Duncan Ban Macintyre* (Scottish Gaelic Text Society, 2nd edn., 1978), pp. 174-83, 346-9.

5. I. Grimble, *The World of Rob Donn* (Edinburgh, 1979). J. Prebble, *The Highland Clearances* (London, 1963).

6. N.L.S., Highlands and Islands, 'Description of emigration from Strathdean to Georgia, 1735', MS 9854, fos. 221-3. Scottish Record Office (hereafter S.R.O.), Campbell of Stonefield MSS, G.D. 14/17; S.R.O., Lord MacDonald MSS, G.D. 221/104. J.P. Maclean, *An Historical Account of the Settlements of Scotch Highlanders in America Prior to the peace of 1783* (Baltimore, 1878, reprinted 1978), pp. 102-87.

7. J. Hunter, *The Making of the Crofting Community* (Edinburgh, 1976).

8. D. Turnock, *Patterns of Highland Development* (London, 1970). E. Richards, *A History of the Highland Clearances,* 2 vols. (London, 1982 and 1985).

9. J. Gray (ed.), *Scottish Population Statistics* (Scottish History Society, Edinburgh,1952). There are no definite figures for population growth or movement within Scottish Gaeldom between 1755 and 1831. Prior to 1801, census returns from parishes were not always accurate and after that date census returns at the outset of each decade were based on the shires. Although the shires of Argyll, Bute, Inverness, Ross and Sutherland can be deemed wholly within the Highlands and Islands, Cromarty and much of Caithness can be considered Lowland, while extensive Highland districts can variously be identified within the predominantly Lowland shires of Nairn, Moray, Banff, Aberdeen, Angus, Perth, Stirling and Dumbarton.

10. M.I. Adam, 'Eighteenth Century Highland Landlords and the Poverty Problem', *Scottish Historical Review,* XIX (1921-22), pp. 1-20. M.M.Leigh, *The Crofting Problem, 1780-1883* (Edinburgh, 1929). A.J. Youngson, *After the Forty-Five* (Edinburgh, 1973).

11. M.M. McKay (ed.), *The Rev. Dr. John Walker's Report on the Hebrides of 1764 and 1771* (Edinburgh, 1980). (T.Douglas) Earl of Selkirk, *Observations on the Present State of the Highlands of Scotland* (Edinburgh, 2nd edn., 1806). T.Telford, 'Survey and Reports of the Coasts and Central Highlands of Scotland in Autumn of 1802', in *Reports of the Select Committee on the Survey of the Central Highlands of Scotland* ( Parliamentary Papers, 1802-3,IV).

12. Material drawn from D.J. Withrington and I.R. Grant (eds.), *The Statistical Account of Scotland, 1791-99 edited by Sir John Sinclair,* 20 vols. (reprinted Wakefield, 1973-83) based on a sample survey of the following 37 parishes: Archattan & Muckairn, Ardnamurchan, Craignish, Kilbrandon & Kilchattan, Kilfinan, North Knapdale, South Knapdale, Morvern, Strachur & Strachlachlan, *Argyll* vol. VIII; Dull, Fortingall, Kenmore, Killin, Weem, *North & West Perthshire* vol. XII; Crathie & Braemar, Glenmuick, Tulloch & Glengairn, Strathdon, *Kincardinshire & South-West Aberdeenshire* vol. XIV; Alvie, Glenelg, Kilmalie, Kilmanivaig, Kincardine, Kingussie & Inch, Lochbroom, Laggan, *Inverness-shire, Ross & Cromarty* vol. XVII; Assynt, Durness, Edderachylis, Farr, Reay, Tongue, *Sutherland & Caithness* vol. XVIII; Harris, Lismore & Appin, Small Isles, North Uist, Tiree & Coll, *Western Isles* vol. XX (Hereafter SAS sample survey).

13. A.R.B. Haldane, *The Drove Roads of Scotland* (Newton Abbot, 1973), pp. 20-67.

14. M.Gray, *The Highland Economy, 1750-1850* (Edinburgh, 1957, reprinted 1976). T.C. Smout, *A History of the Scottish People, 1560-1830* (2nd edn. London, 1970), pp. 332-60.

15. Strathclyde Regional Archives (hereafter S.R.A.), Mitchells Johnston,

'MacLeod Family papers', T-MJ 377, section 1/1-3. S.R.A., Burgh of Glasgow, Registered Deeds, B 10, section 15/3617. N.L.S., Cameron of Fassifern Papers, Acc. 9174, nos. 13,14,15 & 29. *National Register of Archives (Scotland)*, no. 934, Lt-Col. Robert Campbell-Preston. W.Mackay (ed.), *The Letter-Book of Bailie John Steuart of Inverness, 1715-52* (Scottish History Society, Edinburgh, 1915). A. Morrison, 'Harris Estate Papers, 1724-54', *Transactions of the Gaelic Society of Inverness*, XLV (1967-68), pp. 33-97.

16. For a fuller treatment of illicit distilling and seasonal migration, see two seminal articles by T.M. Devine, 'The rise and fall of illicit whisky-making in northern Scotland, c. 1780-1840', *Scottish Historical Review*, LIV (1975), pp. 155-77 and 'Highland Migration to Lowland Scotland, 1760-1860', *Scottish Historical Review* LXII (1983), pp. 137-49.

17. R. Mitchison, 'The Highland Clearances', *Scottish Economic & Social History*, 1 (1981), pp. 4-24.

18. Jones and Woolf (eds.), *Agrarian Change and Economic Development*, pp. 1-21. W. Abel, *Agricultural fluctuations in Europe* (London, 1980), pp. 197-260.

19. SAS sample survey. C. Fraser-Mackintosh, *Antiquarian Notes*, 2nd ser. (Inverness, 1897).

20. A.M. Smith, *Jacobite Estates of the Forty-Five* (Edinburgh, 1982). J. Dunlop, *The British Fisheries Society, 1786-1893* (Edinburgh, 1978).

21. The most substantial case study is that of E. Richards, *The Leviathan of Wealth* (1973), on the Sutherland Clearances. P. Gaskell, *Morvern Transformed* (1980), though ranging over two centuries of estate management, concentrates on Clearance in the nineteenth century. I.R.M. Mowat, *Easter Ross, 1750-1850* (Edinburgh, 1981) offers informative insights into Clearance on the Lowland peripheries, though lacking the detailed perspective afforded by V. Gaffney, *The Lordship of Strathavon* (Third Spalding Club, Aberdeen, 1960). L. Leneman, *Living in Atholl 1685-1785* (Edinburgh, 1986), through dealing lucidly with the break-up of Gaelic society, does not follow through fully on Clearance.

22. This model for the first phase of Clearance has been constructed from the following estate records: S.R.O., Clanranald Papers, 'Tacks', G.D. 201, section 2/6-68. S.R.O., Fraser-Mackintosh Collection, 'MacDonnell of Glengarry', G.D. 128, section 65/12. S.R.O., Breadalbane collection, 'Robert Robertson's Report on Nether Lorn, 1796', R.H.P. 972/5. M.M. Mcarthur (ed.), *Survey of Lochtayside, 1769* (Scottish History Society, Edinburgh, 1936). R.J. Adam (ed.), *John Home's Survey of Assynt* (Scottish History Society, Edinburgh, 1960). E.R. Cregeen (ed.), *Argyll Estate Instructions, 1771-1805* (Scottish History Society, Edinburgh, 1964). R.J. Adam (ed.), *Papers on Sutherland Estate Management, 1802-16*, 2 vols. (Scottish History Society, Edinburgh, 1972). J.G. Michie (ed.), *The Records of Invercauld, 1547-1828* (New Spalding Club, Aberdeen, 1901). R.C. MacLeod (ed.), *The Book of Dunvegan*, II (Third Spalding Club, Aberdeen, 1939).

23. J. Browne, *A History of the Highlands and the Highland Clans*, IV (Glasgow, 1832), pp. 133-384.

24. S.R.O., Airlie Papers, G.D. 16, section 34/355. S.R.O., Seafield MSS, G.D. 248, box 52/1. N.L.S., Highland Society of Scotland Papers, Adv. MS 72.2.15, fos. 443-

5. N.L.S., Melville Papers, MS 1053, fos. 104-9. N.L.S. Lee Papers, MS 3431, fos. 177-83. M.I. Adam, 'The Highland Emigration in 1770', *Scottish Historical Review*, XVI (1918-19), pp. 280-93 and 'The causes of the Highland Emigrations of 1783-1803', *Scottish Historical Review* XVII (1919-20), pp. 73-89. J.M. Bumsted, *The People's Clearance, 1770-1815* (Edinburgh, 1982).

25. R. Somers, *Letters from the Highlands* (Inverness, 1848, reprinted 1977) provides a perceptive critique of contemporaneous attitudes once the second phase of Clearance was underway.

# CHAPTER 5

# The Landed Classes

## R.H. Campbell

The advantages of the ownership of land have often been so many and so varied that, as one faded, another increased to take its place. So it was in Scotland between 1760 and 1830, with the result that the social standing of the landowners survived through many changes and challenges in society generally and within their own ranks. To think of the landowners as one group is confusing. Their power and influence varied, most evidently because of differences in the scale of ownership. For that reason the starting point for many investigations of the place of landowners in Scottish society between 1760 and 1830 is the pioneering work of Loretta Timperley, which gives precision to any discussion of the distribution of landholding.[1] The great landowners, defined as those with valued rent of over £2,000 Scots, had half the total of this agrarian wealth in 1770. They were to be found mainly in the south and east. In 1770 about one-third or more of the valued rent was held by the great landowners in the counties of Dumfries, East Lothian, Roxburgh, Selkirk, and in the Highland exception of Sutherland, and almost half or more in Aberdeen, Angus, Berwick, Bute, West Lothian, Moray, Nairn, Orkney and Wigtown; on the other hand (apart from the exceptional cases of Kinross and Shetland, which had no great landowners) they had only over 9 per cent in Stirling and under 25 per cent in Dunbarton and Clackmannan. Conversely, the small proprietors, defined as those with less than £100 Scots valued rent, held larger proportions of the land in the centre and west, though the total amount they held was obviously less. In 1770 they controlled over 10 per cent of the valued rent in Ayr, Clackmannan, Dunbarton, Kinross, Lanark and Stirling. (Shetland cannot easily be included because of its different system of udal tenure.) Since the size and land values of counties varied greatly, the absolute number of landowners who held only a small proportion of the land could be large and so have a considerable influence on the social structure of an area, especially if they were concentrated in a few parishes. In some of the western and central counties, above all in Ayrshire and Lanarkshire, where the small landowners had higher shares of the valued rent, their absolute numbers were large and they were also a high proportion of all landowners.

| Country | Total Small Landowners | Percentage of all Landowners |
| --- | --- | --- |
| Ayrshire | 762 | 89.6 |
| Clackmannan | 41 | 68.3 |
| Dunbarton | 178 | 91.0 |
| Kinross | 4 | 96.3 |
| Lanark | 838 | 93.7 |
| Stirling | 568 | 92.4 |

One significant change noted in Dr. Timperley's work is that the larger proprietors consolidated their position in the years under consideration, especially in those areas where the small proprietors had been most evident earlier. The move towards the consolidation of the larger holdings was not without qualification. The first was the continued presence of larger numbers of the small proprietors in those counties which had, or were near, major centres of urban growth. In Lanarkshire, including Glasgow, the small proprietors rose from 785 in 1770 to 1,096 in 1814; in Midlothian, including Edinburgh, the increase was from 419 to 569; in Renfrewshire from 178 to 300. Second, in the Borders, where tight control by the larger landowners remained, the attractiveness of property, and its proximity to Edinburgh, led to slight increases in the total number of landowners, with the increase distributed among all groups. Such qualifications had local significance and did not affect the general conclusions that, even during the years of major social change at the turn of the eighteenth and nineteenth centuries, the large proprietors still dominated the pattern of landownership in Scotland, and that many were acquiring more land. The great were becoming greater; the years of disposal on a large scale had yet to come.

The persistence of a commitment to the expansion and consolidation of landholding, and to a patriarchial conception of its ownership, is confirmed by the amount of land which continued to be entailed into the nineteenth century. The tenacity of the practice is striking since from an early stage it had been subject to criticism, which increased in the nineteenth century. Kames, Smith and others had objected to the practice, which was examined and largely condemned by a Select Committee in the 1820s.[2] Some of the relaxation of its strictness which took place was only permissive and no facility to disentail was available until 1848. Even the provision of the Act of 1770, which allowed a proportion of the expenditure on improvments to be charged to subsequent heirs, was hedged by so many restrictions that it is unlikely to have been as effective as historians have suggested. The defects and criticism make the increase in the number of entails from the 1760s particularly notable. Well over two-thirds of the deeds in the Register of Tailzies in 1830 were recorded after 1760, about twenty-five annually in the early nineteenth century. Not all deeds were separate entails by different landowners. Larger properties were entailed in stages; some deeds were amendments to earlier ones, and not all proved subsequently to be completely valid, though they were offset by others which were not registered, or the registration of which was delayed, but which operated in practice as though they were. To calculate the extent of the land entailed with any accuracy is impossible. Various estimates have been made, but the amount was great enough to provide confirmation of the landowners' determination to perpetuate and protect their succession.

The secure position of the landed proprietors from 1760 to 1830, especially of the larger among them, was challenged from both economic and political changes from the later eighteenth century, but was less radically affected than might have been expected.

The economic challenge was to the relative economic standing of the landowners in the community and came from the growing wealth of those engaged in trade and industry; it is a challenge which historians often accept unwittingly by the attention they give to the emergence of the new industrial structure from the late eighteenth century. The consequence has been that examination of rural society has often been confined to problem areas in the Highlands, the continued importance of the rural way of life in the industrialising Lowlands being neglected. Even by 1830 Scotland was still a rural country; the growth of the heavy industries which were to transform the conditions of life for most Scots had hardly begun.[3] The challenge of the new industries to the relative economic position of the landowners is more evident in retrospect when hindsight reveals the long-term significance of some of the changes in the economic structure which were only beginning by 1830. The fault into which many historians can fall is to attribute a greater degree of change than is evident in any quantitive measures that are available and to accord an earlier recognition of the emergence of an industrial society than is warranted.[4] Before 1830 the economic challenge to the standing of the landowners was only a threat, its nature portrayed vividly by John Galt, writing in 1821, with all the acuteness which places *The Annals of the Parish* among the finest studies of social change in Scotland in the fifty years after 1760.

Whatever their fears for the future, the early changes in the economic structure in the late eighteenth century strengthened the economic position of many landowners. Some were resentful of the invasion of their old privacy, as were more of their successors in the nineteenth century, but most regarded the new industrial activities as providing them with an additional source of revenue to exploit, by gaining new rents and royalties or by direct industrial participation, especially in exploiting their own landed resources, without the same degree of risk which had proved a disaster to many of the landowners of the earlier eighteenth century.[5]

Though for many landowners agricultural rents were their only source of income, and made a large contribution to the income of those who had other sources, the economic position of the landowners became more secure when the emergence of the industrial economy gave agriculture new and assured opportunities. In the longrun the ability to export industrial products and raw materials ensured that adequate foodstuffs and raw materials could be imported, but in the early stages of industrialisation, the prosperity of agriculture was crucial for the prosperity of industry as well, as good harvests ensured a healthier balance of payments and easier credit conditions. This critically important position of the landowners in the early stages of industrialisation needs to be stressed to indicate that behind any challenge from the new industry, which led in due course to the submergence of his economic interests, the landowner remained in a strong economic position, both relative and absolute, in these early phases of industrialisation before 1830. That economic reality lay behind his political and social power.

The second challenge concerns the political standing of the landowners, which had long depended on the possession of land, even from before the union of parliaments.

The privileges of political power remained similarly based, though in a different form, throughout the eighteenth century. The system was extremely complex. Detailed knowledge of the intricacy of its operation is not necessary to be able to appreciate its social significance.[6] The qualifications to vote lay with those who enjoyed the *dominium directum,* or the superiority of the land, and not the *dominium utile,* or the possession and use of the land. It was possible for landowners to retain the superiority, even when disposing of land, and to split and convey rights of superiority to others in ways which provided them with the qualifications to vote. By such methods the electorate remained small — 2,500 in the later eighteenth century[7] — and under the firm control of the landowners. The parliamentary union probably made matters worse. It did not specify the franchise or electoral procedure but left them as they were; the major difference was the lessening or removal of parliamentary or legal control. Even after it was given jurisdiction in 1743, the Court of Session failed to exercise its authority effectively. The opportunities for electoral manipulation were therefore considerable in the later eighteenth century. With the help of astute lawyers the landowners could rig the elections. The electorate in the Scottish counties was so small that the addition of a few votes under the control of one landowner could determine the outcome. The forty-

16. Culzean Castle, Ayrshire, rebuilt and extended according to the design of Robert Adam in the later eighteenth century. Rental revenue had to rise to support the splendour of these dwellings of the aristocracy while the magnificence of the buildings themselves symbolised the continuity of the social and political power of the landed class. *National Trust for Scotland.*

five MPs and the sixteen peers were more influential than their numbers would suggest, particularly at times of narrow parliamentary majorities. Since many of those who sat in parliament owed their place to the manipulation of the franchise by the landowners, they were often ready to act at their behest, and the landowners in turn at the behest of those who offered the greatest degree of patronage. The political ring was complete.

The economic potential of the land was less important for political authority than its possession. Social and political standing could still be retained even when the economic basis was uncertain, or when it had vanished, as in the Highlands. The need for economic strength lay in the possibility that without such economic strength there was the likelihood that the possession of the all-important landed property might be put at risk, especially if, as was so often the case, new and heavier demands were made upon it by the landowner and his family. The possession of property was the way to social prestige and to political power, but its economic potential was necessary if that social prestige was to be perpetuated. Those landowners who were able to add to their economic resources, either by exploiting the new possibilities of agriculture or by direct industrial development, were placed in a more secure position than those who had no such prospects.

Some of the challenges to the political power of the landowners in the later eighteenth century must be interpreted in this context. One was the action which followed the suppression of the Jacobites after the middle of the century. Some of the measures, though much recognised and stressed by subsequent commentators, were of less practical importance in a large part of Scotland. The strategic necessity for wardholding or military tenure had long since passed in much of Scotland and was fading even in the Highlands before the defeat of Jacobitism gave the impetus to its final removal. Of more general importance was the problem of the perpetuation of heritable jurisdictions and hereditary judicial offices.[8] They were anomalous in the Lowlands, where they contrasted sharply with the growth of a central system of justice. The abolition of heritable offices — an estimate of about 200 such hereditary offices has been deemed to be too low — was indicative of the final and formal removal of a traditional power from the landowners, but the retention of their power informally is evident in the continued influence of the landowners on the appointments which were made. It became more restricted when the death of the 3rd Duke of Argyll in 1761 marked the end of tight political control by a great landowner. His first successor of comparable influence was Henry Dundas after becoming Lord Advocate in 1775. Though Dundas was able to be judged, at least by his rhetoric, as continuing to lend support to the established landed proprietors, his assumption of the political mantle which no one had worn effectively since the death of Argyll, was a significant change in itself.[9] With the advent of Dundas, Scotland was no longer managed by a great, but by a small landowner, who was chiefly a lawyer. Previously, Lord Milton, comparable both professionally and socially with Dundas, could not have wielded such power independent of Argyll.[10] It is also significant that the basis of the landowners' advocacy of their favourites changed in the later eighteenth century from undiluted personal interest to supporting the claims of local or community interest. Even then they were not always successful. In 1799 the Duke of Buccleuch placed Sir Walter Scott as second choice as sheriff of Selkirk, but he was appointed none the less.

The moves towards political reform in the years at the turn of the century were more comprehensive challenges to the political power of the landowners, but they too were still limited. The second generation of those who analysed the nature of society so acutely — Dugald Stewart being the most influential — set limits to their proposals for reform.[11] Even the Scottish Whigs who advocated reform were ready to exploit existing procedures and create fictitious votes when they had the opportunity to do so. The criticisms of the old system recognised that the landed interest could no longer be considered the only one which mattered; other interests were rising to challenge them. But those with economic power could always join the way of exploiting the old system. It is not surprising that, when reform did come in 1832 — whatever popular basis it may have had — it did not remove the possibility of electoral malpractice through the manufacture of property qualifications, though due to poor drafting as much as to deliberate design. The political power of the landed interest was no longer intact; it was crumbling, but to the end of the period considered by the present volume it was still great.

The social significance of many of these electoral practices have not been recognised adequately. They seem so foreign to modern political thought that some historians, especially those of an older generation, whose moral perceptions were more frequently applied in historical analysis than is the custom among their descendants, found them so embarrassing that they ignored them or roundly condemned them.[12] More recently, historians have suggested that the practices are unimportant in the general history of Scottish society.[13]

Apologising sheepishly for the practices or ignoring them are reflections of the standards and attitudes of later society, and in consequence they underestimate the way in which it was accepted that landed proprietors should dominate political and social life. The privileged position of property, which generally meant land until well into the nineteenth century, frequently went unchallenged: both by intellectual critics and by many of those whose substantial economic position and power might have encouraged them to do so.

17. Saloon at Culzean Castle, showing the elegance and refinement of eighteenth-century aristocratic life. *National Trust for Scotland.*

A source of criticism lay in the rich intellectual life of Scotland in the late eighteenth century, but it remained potential. Adam Smith's views were representative when he commented on the 'sacred rights of property', and for him it had a central role in the subordination of some members of society to others; more to the point, John Millar thought property was 'the great source of distinction among individuals'.[14] The great thinkers of the late eighteenth century did not translate their analysis into proposals to abolish or annul the possession of property which was the origin of rank, not even when they criticised some of its aspects; it was accepted, and so their analysis lent support to the civil means of its maintenance.

The way in which those who achieved distinction through acquiring wealth were rarely content until they added landed status to their wealth as the means of entry to social and political power, confirmed Smith's well-known dictum that successful merchants were anxious to become country gentlemen. T.M. Devine's detailed analysis of the moves of the Glasgow colonial merchants to become landed proprietors in the late eighteenth and early nineteenth centuries shows the change. Why they made the move is more difficult to determine.

Prof. Devine rightly suggests that 'any attempt to erect these (reasons) into a hierarchical order of importance is doomed to failure'.[15] Many of those who made the above move increased the economic potential of their estates; they were responsible for planned villages; they even built up industrial enterprises in the process of doing so. There are differences of opinion on how important or effective these efforts may have been. Adam Smith was certainly too extreme and sweeping in trying to draw a sharp distinction between the success of the country gentleman and the merchant. It would not be easy to explain or justify the move on economic criteria alone; economically, most of those who acquired land would have been better advised not to do so, especially when it involved them in additional burdens and new forms of social expenditure. The possession of the estate had its unique attractions in the social and political power it offered. Whatever the motivation, the moves provide further confirmation that another group of potentially powerful critics of the landowners were using their economic power not to oppose but to join them. There could be no greater recognition of the social attractions of land ownership or guarantee of its continued security.

To apologise for the political activities of the landowners was more common a generation ago; to suggest that they are not of major significance in the general social history of the country is more common today. This more modern view fails to appreciate how the political interests and activities of landed proprietors were dependent on the resources of their estates and so affected the ways they were run and the lives of the people on them.

To consider the landed proprietors as one group when discussing the nature of the demands made on the estate and its ability to meet them is misleading. The dispersion of ownership was wide and all landowners were placing new demands on their estates, but the large and the small had their own distinct motivation, derived ultimately from different responses to the parliamentary union of 1707. Links with England, and their integrating influences, were not new but had the consequence, fraught with significance for the landowners, that the best, and in many ways the only, political life was to be realised on the larger scale of Westminster. The landowners needed substantial cash withdrawals from their estate to meet the demands of a new and exacting style of political and social living; if they had no resources other than their Scottish estates, a heavy burden fell on them. As a result many of the smaller proprietors could not follow such high political activity. While the parliamentary union opened new prospects for some, it closed them for others. For such proprietors the practical consequence was not that there was a little left for them to do; they found the expression of a new intellectual activity in the improvement of their estates.[16] The civic humanist case, that they sought virtue in these ways, is intellectually attractive but savours of a latter-day attempt to explain the motivation of a number of people in terms which they themselves would not have recognised or understood; it also fails to recognise the simple practical case for the improvement of the estates and one which had been accepted even before the intellectual changes of the eighteenth century which have given currency to the views of the civic humanists.

The desire to improve was generally adopted and applied, but it is subject to many interpretations and each has different social consequences. Improvement could mean an attempt to raise greater income; it could mean an attempt to provide the changes which would enable that increased income to be produced and maintained; it could mean experimental work which had limited economic benefit other than what may have followed from a demonstration effect, though it could lead to disastrous emulation; lastly, it could lead many to incur expenditure to beautify their estates and upgrade them to the standards which were being encountered elsewhere. Many interpretations of the activities of the landowners in the eighteenth century assume that improvement often meant the provision of a stable long-term base for the prosperity of the landed proprietors; it could do the reverse by placing additional burdens on the estate rather than by providing the means of meeting new demands. For these reasons it is important to draw a distinction between the frequently used and misleading term 'improvement', with its various interpretations, which lasted over a long period, and the commercialisation of the estate, which was the marked feature of the activities of the landowners from 1760 to 1830. Commercialisation is the key to the most radical changes in the position of the landowners in this period because its success was a prerequisite for the application of the other conceptions of improvement, which would not have been economically possible otherwise, and its failure removed the economic support essential for the landed proprietors to be able to continue to exercise their traditional role in society. The extent to which commercialisation was possible varied, and it determined if it was possible to effect a successful transformation from an old to a new social structure. It must be placed at the centre of any account of the social position of the individual landowner or of landowners as a group in the period.

The extent to which commercialisation was possible depended on how the personal objectives of the proprietors could be met within the options opened by a range of external influences. The external conditions depended on achieving a balance between the economic potential of the estate and the demographic pressures on it, though influencing any effort to achieve a balance were the ingrained attitudes to change of the tenantry. At one extreme were those areas where any possibility of change was limited by the pressures exerted by a rising population on the limited potential of the land, notably in the Highlands and especially in the far north and west. By contrast, there were other areas in the Lowlands, where favourable natural conditions gave obvious opportunities for successful change to ways which supported a larger population, and where adjacent industrial development mitigated demographic pressure. The proximity of the new industrial areas was indeed crucial to the success of the landowner in turning his estate to more productive use through commercialisation, as the industrial areas provided the possibility of marketing products as well as providing injections of cash to the rural hinterland by offering work to temporary migrants as well as opportunities for permanent migration. The ability of a landowner to deal with the challenge of the late eighteenth and early nineteenth centuries, especially the challenge of demographic pressure, depended largely on the combination of the proximity of the estate to industrial areas and its physical capabilities. They were the fundamental factors which determined how far commercialisation was possible, if at all; the abilities and sympathies of the landowners were of secondary importance as, whatever they may have been, they could not take the place of adverse external conditions. It is for that reason that the opportunities of the rise in price in the Napoleonic Wars were so critical in facilitating commercialisation on estates, even on those in the Highlands where it was normally difficult if not impossible to achieve.[17]

These were the more obvious factors which determined the ease of transition to a new relationship between landlord and tenant; the attitude of the tenantry has been the more potent factor affecting many of the views of subsequent commentators. In one sense these later commentators are correct in their emphasis because the attitudes of the tenantry could impede the commercialisation of an estate, even when the locational and agricultural factors were favourable, and leave a festering sore for subsequent historians to contemplate. Redistribution of population was easier in the Lowlands. The adaptation of the tenantry took place, not without difficulty, but sufficiently smoothly for historians to be given less opportunity to observe it. That was the experience in much of the Lowlands and so has encouraged the growth of the belief in the beneficial consequences of the improving landlords in the Lowlands, who may be compared adversely with those in the Highlands. The comparison is misleading because the two are so different that the comparison is not of like with like.

The benefits of the external forces favouring commercialisation were confounded or confirmed by the nature of the personal objectives of the landowners. Most landowners had some desire to draw additional resources from their estates. Those who needed to do so most of all were those who adopted a more expensive style of living; for them there was little alternative, but similar motivation lay behind the activities of many smaller proprietors. They gained — in spite of not having the extensive resources of the larger proprietors — in that their desire to improve was more likely to be aimed at long-term economic stability and was less likely to be offset by substantial expenditure to maintain a more expensive style of living. The success of the commercialisation of the estate has then to be qualified if the objective was to provide an estate considered appropriate for a resident proprietor, even if residence on it was only intermittent. Decisions, not then wholly economic, could permanently weaken the estate's capacity for survival. Ostentatious expenditure was the most striking illustration. It was not confined to the period being considered, but the economic opportunities of the Napoleonic Wars provided resources for its easier attainment.

After 1760 the improvement of the policies and of the surrounding agriculture went hand in hand, but the great edifices which were built and their surroundings took priority.[18] The Duke of Buccleuch incorporated one of his largest farms into the policies at Dalkeith. In the 1770s the Duke of Gordon moved Fochabers to a new well-planned site to improve the amenities and the approach to Gordon Castle. Most striking of all, and leaving the most lasting legacy, were some of the great houses of the period, especially notable being the work of Robert Adam, in some cases building on activities of other more neglected members of his family, as at Mellerstain and Culzean, or by the Mylne family, as in the work of Robert at Cally and at Inveraray.[19] These were a few of the great examples, which were to leave their legacies to posterity, but the expenditure was general and, even on the lesser properties, a large part went on the house and policies. After 1770, when it became possible to place part of the expenditure on entailed estates as a charge on subsequent heirs of entail, a more widespread record is available. It shows the belief that an appropriate mansion had to be provided, and, though the farm buildings were also improved, they became the largest items of expenditure only after the mansion and the policies.[20]

As the commercialisation of the estate provided for a new way of life with its wider horizons, the proprietors came to distance themselves from many of their fellow Scots and so brought about some deep divisions in Scottish society and culture. The distancing of the great propietors had taken place before 1760, but the increased wealth of all proprietors through the commercialisation of their estates in the late eighteenth and early nineteenth centuries spread the division down the social scale. Increasingly, educational and ecclesiastical affiliations were with England. It is easy to regard the move as the consequence of the simple desire to gain the best financial reward through the exploitation of new social and political connections, but there are other aspects which place the changing social allegiances of the landed proprietors in a different light. Until the political challenge was more complete, well after 1830, the landowners saw their function and role in life as a political one,

18. Dining Room at Culzean Castle. *National Trust for Scotland.*

which had to be exercised in London. It is easy, but unfair, to be cynical about the feeling of social responsibility which led to the acceptance of this role. More fundamental, and stretching beyond the ranks of the landowners, was the belief that intellectually and culturally Scotland could not offer the wider horizon for the life of an educated and cultured gentleman. It led as a direct consequence to the need to speak and write in a language most easily understood by cultured society, and that was not to be found in Scotland for many. Those who remained in Scotland might still speak with a different accent but they wrote standard English. Those who moved south had to speak as well as write in the more widely understood form. An example of how any landowner who sought to make his mark on wider society was bound to be drawn away from Scotland is the case of Sir James Macdonald of Sleat, who, in a short life, which ended in Rome in 1766, impressed the giants of European culture, but made no mark on his own country.[21]

One social consequence of the indirect interest in their estates was the need to use agents extensively.[22] The Scottish landowners were no different from many elsewhere, but for those who were absent from their estates for long periods and sought to use them as a means of maintaining their political position, agents of sagacity and political perception were required, so helping the legal profession to assume an unusually influential position in Scottish society. It can then be suggested that the greater landowners who went to occupy a major political role in London became even more remote from their estates and that effective power was passed to others. Some care must be exercised in assuming too readily that the major political figures were remote. The Argylls lost their high political influence after the death of the 3rd Duke in 1761 but remained politically active thereafter and still had time for a detailed interest in their estates.[23] Other proprietors bombarded their agents with advice from afar. The great landowners may have been remote and anglicised in many ways but they did not attempt to divest themselves of their roots as many Irish landowners did. Even when not normally permanently resident in Scotland, they still retained a direct interest in affairs there.

The lesser proprietors, even when part of the political scene in London, had little independent political power, had to seek patronage as much as anyone, and had little to offer in return. Their political links were with local administration and not with events at a national level. Paradoxically for most Scots that made them more rather than less influential, because for most what took place at a national level was of no great interest or importance. In these conditions the way in which the possession of land gave parochial authority, or the position of a Justice of the Peace or a Commissioner of Supply, ensured a place in the community that mattered, and that was the parish. It was in ecclesiastical affairs that the potential for contention with the landowners was often most widespread and became more bitter at the end of the period being considered. Their responsibilities as heritors to provide church, manse and stipend guaranteed conflict between minister and landowner. It widened with calls to join with the kirk session in the provision of parochial education and the relief of the poor, and became wider still over the right to appoint the minister to the parish, the protracted dispute over patronage restored in 1712. The Crown had the right of appointment in a large proportion of parishes, and had its own interest in perpetuating the system, and the landowners sought to maintain their position both because of their general belief in the need to protect the rights of property and because they were able to intrude parish ministers more acceptable to them theologically and socially. It was a system which ensured resentment. It meant interference in parochial matters, and so in the lives of many, and it did so in a field where Scots were peculiarly sensitive to any external, and increasingly remote, intervention. The resentment led to increasing conflict which peaked in the decade before the Disruption of the Church of Scotland in 1843.

The commercialisation of the estates, which was carried out notably during the Napoleonic Wars, opened up new ways of life for the landed proprietors.

19. Ederslie House, Renfrewshire. Residence of Alexander Spiers, one of the wealthiest tobacco merchants in eighteenth-century Glasgow. The very rich among the urban elite commonly bought small landed estates but Spier's mansion, though impressive, hardly compares with the splendour of the residences of the aristocratic elite. *Royal Commission on the Ancient and Historical Monuments of Scotland.*

It gave them opportunities to strengthen their economic power even as the basis of their traditional social and political power was beginning to crumble. The balance between these forces making for change varied. Where commercialisation was successful, the landowners' social prestige and power remained, but rested increasingly on a firm economic foundation, which was itself to lose its relative strength and standing in the mid-nineteenth century as other forms of economic activity grew in a new industrial society.

NOTES

1. Loretta R. Timperley (ed.), *A Directory of Landownership in Scotland c.1770* (Scottish Record Society, new series, 5, Edinburgh, 1976); 'The Pattern of Landholding in Eighteenth- Century Scotland', in M.L. Parry and T.R. Slater (eds.), *The Making of the Scottish Countryside* (London, 1980), pp. 137-54.

2. Henry Home, Lord Kames, *Historical Law-Tracts* (Edinburgh, fourth edn., 1792), Tract III on Property, and *Sketches in the History of Man* (Edinburgh, second edn., 1778), pp. 435f. The improbability of Kames persuading the landed proprietors to change their ways was recognised by Lord Chancellor Hardwicke, who, though in sympathy with Kames' views, warned him: 'I fear your great Landed Men will cry out Murder, if an attempt should be made to restrain them further than we are restrained in England, where Perpetuities are so much abhorred' (Scottish Record Office [SRO]. GD 24/1/557. Abercairney MSS. Lord Hardwicke to Lord Kames, 21 October 1759); Adam Smith, *Lectures on Jurisprudence 1762-3*, i, 164-7 (R.L. Meek, D.D. Raphael, P.G. Stein, eds., Oxford, 1978); Reports of the Select Committee on Scottish Entails. British Parliamentary Papers (BPP). 1828. VII. 151 and 315. Two later reports are largely formal : BPP. 1829. III. 413 and 1833. XVI. 35. For general discussion, see P. Irvine, *Considerations on the Inexpediency of the Law of Entails in Scotland* (Edinburgh, 1822); Erskine D. Sandford, *A Treatise on the History and Law of Entails in Scotland* (Edinburgh, 1822). The SRO's copy of Samuel Shaw, *An Alphabetical Index of the Registered Entails in Scotland 1685 to 1784* (Edinburgh, 1784) has been updated in manuscript to 1833.

3. See chapters 1 and 2 above.

4. A useful assessment of how far the Scottish economy had developed at the beginning of the period under consideration is in T. C. Smout, 'Where had the Scottish economy got to by 1776?', in Istvan Hont and Michael Ignatieff, *Wealth and Income* (Cambridge, 1983), pp. 45-72.

5. A considerable literature, much of it consisting of detailed local studies, has appeared since a pioneering article by T.C. Smout, 'Scottish Landowners and Economic Growth, 1650-1850', *Scottish Journal of Political Economy*, 11 (1964), pp. 218-34. Examples of the activities of landowners in many fields are to be found in J.P. Shaw, *Water Power in Scotland 1550-1870* (Edinburgh, 1984).

6. An excellent exposition and evaluation of the topic is in William Ferguson, 'The

Electoral System in the Scottish Counties before 1832', in Stair Society, *Miscellany II* (ed. David Sellar, Edinburgh, 1984).

7. C.E. Adam (ed.), *View of the Political State of Scotland in 1788* (Edinburgh, 1887).

8. Ann E. Whetstone, *Scottish County Government in the Eighteenth and Nineteenth Centuries* (Edinburgh, 1981).

9. John Dwyer and Alexander Murdoch, 'Paradigms and Politics: Manners, Morals and the Rise of Henry Dundas, 1770-1784', in John Dwyer, Roger A. Mason and Alexander Murdoch (eds.), *New Perspectives on the Politics and Culture of Early Modern Scotland* (Edinburgh, n.d.), p. 243.

10. J.S. Shaw, *The Management of Scottish Society, 1707-1764* (Edinburgh, 1983).

11. For recent examinations of their reforming activities, see Biancamaria Fontana, *Rethinking the politics of commercial society: The Edinburgh Review 1802-1832* (Cambridge, 1985); Anand C. Chitnis, *The Scottish Enlightenment and Early Victorian English Society* (London, 1986).

12. P. Hume Brown, *History of Scotland* (1911 edn.), III, pp. 281- 4.

13. T.C. Smout, *A History of the Scottish People 1560-1830* (London, 1969), p. 218.

14. Adam Smith, *The Wealth of Nations* (1776) (Glasgow edn., Oxford, 1976), I.xi.c.27; John Millar, *The Origin of the Distinction of Ranks* (third end., London, 1779) reprinted in W.C. Lehmann, *John Millar of Glasgow, 1735-1801* (Cambridge, 1960), p.176.

15. T.M. Devine, 'Glasgow Colonial Merchants and Land, 1770-1815', in J.T. Ward and R.G. Wilson (eds.), *Land and Industry* (Newton Abbot, 1971), p. 219.

16. Much of the extensive discussion in this field is derived from J.G.A. Pocock, *The Machiavellian Moment: Florentine Political Thought and the Atlantic Republican Tradition* (Princeton, 1975); for a discussion in a Scottish context see Nicholas Phillipson, 'The Scottish Enlightenment', in Roy Porter and Mikulas Teich, *The Enlightenment in National Context* (Cambridge, 1981), pp. 19-40.

17. Recent work, which has stressed the earlier moves towards improvement in agricultural practices, has been accompanied by an increasing recognition that their widespread application came later than was often thought to be the case.

18. The collection of estate plans in the SRO shows these changes. RHP 9528 (1817) and RHP 9537 (1824) show the changes in the Buccleuch policies at Dalkeith. See I.H. Adams (ed.), *Descriptive List of Plans in the Scottish Record Office*, vols. 1 to 3 (HMSO, Edinburgh, 1966, 1970, 1974).

19. T.R. Slater, 'The Mansion and Policy', in Slater and Parry (eds.), *Scottish Countryside*, pp. 223-247; Ian G. Lindsay and Mary Cosh, *Inveraray and the Dukes of Argyll* (Edinburgh, 1973). A convenient source showing the extensive construction of this period is in the series of guides, *Exploring Scotland's Heritage*, published recently by the Royal Commission on the Ancient and Historical Monuments of Scotland.

20. Registers of Improvements on Entailed Estates in the records of Sheriff Courts.

21. 'Were you and I together Dear Smith we should shed Tears at present for the death of poor Sir James Macdonald. We could not possibly have suffered a greater

Loss than in that valuable young Man.' David Hume to Adam Smith, August 1766 in *The Correspondence of Adam Smith* (ed. E.C. Mossner and I.S. Ross, Oxford, 1977), p. 118.

22. Compare the different levels of activity discussed in John M. Simpson, 'Who Steered the Gravy Train?', in N.T. Phillipson and Rosalind Mitchison (eds.), *Scotland in the Age of Improvement* (Edinburgh, 1970), pp. 47-72, and Eric Richards, 'The Land Agent', in G.E. Mingay (ed.), *The Victorian Countryside* (London, 1981), 2, pp. 439-56. Agents conformed increasingly to the latter view of them and gained such a reputation that some of those with the highest reputation in England came from Scotland. David Spring, *The English Landed Estate in the Nineteenth Century* (Baltimore, 1963), p. 99.

23. E. Cregeen (ed.), *Argyll Estate Instructions 1771-1805* (Scottish History Society, Edinburgh, 1964). A significant comment was made by the Earl of Galloway, writing from London to his agent at Galloway House in Wigtownshire: 'Now Nish, tho you see I am an Economist about buying Trees, yet I must beg you to be extravagent in beautifying about Galloway House, all my children are so partial to it. I want to make it as pretty as possible and soon tho I shd. throw away a couple of hundred extraordinary'. SRO. GD 138/3/21/5. Galloway MSS. Earl of Galloway to James Nish, 4 December 1801.

# CHAPTER 6

# The Rise of the Urban Middle Class

## Stana Nenadic

By 1832 when the passing of the First Reform Act enfranchised most of the middle class, British society and economy had become increasingly dominated by towns; and the towns, in turn, were dominated by the middle classes. This chapter considers the evolution of the middle class in Scotland, its rise from a state of fragmented power and limited collective identity in the mid eighteenth century to great unity and influence by the third decade of the nineteenth century. It aims to do three things. First, to identify those groups who formed the middle class and to indicate the ways in which they differed from other social groups. The factors that gave rise to middle-class growth, in both absolute size and as a proportion of the population, are next considered. Finally, there is an exploration of the forces that contributed to the 'making of the middle class' that generated a sense of class identity or consciousness. Much of the discussion is tentative. Compared with the growing literature on the middle class, in England there is a deficiency of modern studies on the Scottish situation;[1] though this is compensated, in some respects, by accessible published contemporary sources.[2] But while it is not possible to explore the Scottish middle class other than within a British context — nor is it desirable since it was during this period that Scotland was socially integrated with England — there are a number of distinctly Scottish elements to be observed in the process of Scottish middle-class formation. The first is based in a particular pattern of town development, and the dominance of the Edinburgh and Glasgow central Lowland axis; a phenomenon of urban concentration not rivalled elsewhere in Britain. An array of institutions — in education, law and the Church — contributed to the formation of a particular indentity, as did the forms of culture and political development seen in Scotland.

## Who Were the Middle Class?

Defining the middle class invariably presents problems, since class boundaries are not fixed or tangible. Assuming a three-class model — in the historical

20. A wealthy middle-class Edinburgh family, showing all the signs of conspicuous domestic consumption, greet their dowdier country cousins. 'The Arrival of the Country Cousins' by Alexander Carse, c.1821. *Duke of Buccleuch, K.T.*

context not irreconcilable with the notion of polarisation — there is a basic difficulty in the blurring of distinctions between the upper and middle classes on the one hand and between the middle and working classes on the other. Important transitional groups — such as the gentry merchants, petty capitalists or the labour aristocracy — span the margins between classes, and within the middle class there were a number of subgroups. Classes are formed partly through the dynamics of material accumulation, and partly through the self-conscious evolution of an intellectual identity. They are defined primarily by economic function (usually represented by occupation) and income which determine status, authority and power; and can be identified within social groups as common patterns of work, lifestyle, organisation, thought and behaviour.[3] In some respects the groups who emerged in the eighteenth century to form the middle class were the first to articulate a modern class indentity. This was located in particular types of urban occupation and non-landed wealth, and in new ways of organising work, of which the most notable feature was the increasingly stark division between the place of work and place of home and leisure. Middle-class work is usually non-manual and involves the application of intellect and direction rather than practical skill or physical effort. It is associated with particular types of clothing that denote non-manual status, certain forms of behaviour, and high levels of training, though these characteristics were not rigid since a group like the craftsmen employers, who also engaged in manual though skilled work were an important element in the emerging middle class. Most middle-class men required to engage in work with a direct economic return to maintain an appropriate family lifestyle. This set them apart from the leisured upper class. It was increasingly expected, from about the 1780s, that women and children should not undertake paid work outside the home and should aspire to be leisured, which clearly set them apart from the working class. Some elements of family income and the incomes of independent women and older retired men were derived from accumulated investments; a pattern that was to intensify during the nineteenth century and again distinguishes the middle class from the working class. But most income was generated through direct participation in the workplace.

From the foregoing discussion, and with the knowledge that the usual mechanisms for identifying class are located in economic function related to types of income, it is possible to define a middle-class structure composed of four broad groupings — businessmen (profit makers), professionals (fees and stipends), employees (wage earners) and the independent leisured (investments and pensions). The first was by far the largest, about 80 per cent. of the middle class,[4] and consisted of the makers and sellers of goods and services, such as merchants, manufacturers, shopkeepers, craftsmen, bankers and distributors. In Glasgow and Edinburgh in the later eighteenth century (based on published directories which are a broad index of middle classness) about 80 per cent. in the former and 65 per cent. in the latter fell into this category. In small towns they were even more dominant, over 90 per cent. in Dunfermline, for instance. The professional group was much smaller, probably no more than 10 per cent. in the 1780's, though larger in some places, notably Edinburgh where 20 per cent. of directory entries were in this category. They were dominated by the ancient professions of law and church and the more recent and still emerging medical professions; each with a common experience in the Scottish system of university education. The professional institutions, in particular the law and the church, were autonomous within Scotland and professional men made a significant contribution to a distinct middle-class identity, especially in the capital. The rise of Edinburgh as a centre of literary culture and Whig intellectualism, exemplified by the influential *Edinburgh Review* (founded 1802), which had an impact on elite social 'tone' as well as business opportunities, owed much to the professions. Teachers can also be included in this category, though many urban teachers of the period were very different to the earlier university-trained parish schoolmasters, or later teachers in charitable and board schools, who were employees. Urban teachers were often businessmen, or women, engaged in the sale of education as a service or a form of leisure. Military officers, of whom there were significant numbers in Scottish towns during the periods of warfare and unrest from the 1780s to early 1820s, might also be included among professionals, though their incomes had a salary element and frequently included profits in the form of prize-money. Employees were a small group prior to the mid-nineteenth century, about 7 per cent[5] and located mainly in the ports and cities. They included officials concerned with taxation, customs and excise and local government administration, or were clerks in business and law. During most of the period the clerk was a transitory occupation composed mainly of young men training as either businessmen or lawyers. As a distinctive group of adult wage earners, clerks were a phenomenon of the late nineteenth century. Finally there were the leisured, no more than 3 per cent[6] of the middle class, composed of independent women and retired men with incomes from a range of passive investments in business, property or government securities. Retired and half-pay military officers and government officials on pensions or sinecures were also among the leisured. By comparison with businessmen the extent of the three other categories — professionals, employees and leisured — was relatively modest in the later eighteenth century; but they were involved in a process of relative expansion, which hastened in the nineteenth century.

This structure was not static; it changed over the period and varied between towns. From the middle-class perspective there were six town-types in Scotland. First the big cities of Edinburgh and Glasgow, distinct in size and wealth, economic complexity and social diversity. Here the middle class was large and prosperous and formed a significant proportion of the population, as is shown in the ratio of female servants to families (another common index of the middle class). In Edinburgh in 1792 there was one servant for every eight families, in Glasgow there was one in fourteen.[7] Towns like Aberdeen, Perth or Inverness were another type: substantial by Scottish standards, yet small when compared with Edinburgh and Glasgow. They had a mixed commercial economy, provided services for the locality and consequently supported a fairly large middle class; in Aberdeen, for instance, the ratio of female servants to families was one in sixteen. A third type were the industrial towns like Paisley, Falkirk and Dundee, where the middle class was relatively small; in Dundee there was only one female servant for every thirty-six families. There were small industrial towns like Kirkcaldy and Renfrew; and small county towns like Montrose, Dumfries or Cupar. As centres of consumption and leisure the latter supported a large middle class; in Dumfries, for instance, the ration of servants to families was one in ten. Finally there were the ports of the west coast like Greenock or Port Glasgow, with a substantial commercial middle class.

21. A street scene of 1795 depicting figures from polite Edinburgh society. The identity of the fashionable ladies is unknown; the men are, James Hume Rigg (banker); Isaac Grant, W.S. (Clerk to the Commissioners of Teinds); Archibald MacArthur Stewart (landowner); Hon. Capt. John Lesie (of the Foot Guards); Capt. William Weyss (M.P. for Fife). John Kay's *Original Portraits*, (Edinburgh, 1838).

As indicated above, a functional definition of class based on occupational titles is a useful approach to an initial understanding of urban society and urban social distinctions. But several reservations should be borne in mind when looking at the middle class in this period. For instance, the implications of a particular occupational term at the individual level could vary considerably within and between towns. The term 'merchant' is a good example. The most prosperous and powerful, those in overseas trade in a city like Glasgow, were major capitalists engaged in a range of economic activities. Other individuals might call themselves 'merchants' yet be living on the margins of poverty and conducting businesses of a very modest sort. Another problem is inherent in the simple fact that specific individuals did not always fit into one or another category. A characteristic of the early middle class was a tendency to pursue a variety of occupations during a lifetime, passing rapidly from one type of work to another as opportunities presented. This was seen in the case of Samuel Hunter, the Editor of the *Glasgow Herald* in the early nineteenth century who was a military surgeon and then a textile manufacturer before entering the expanding newspaper industry. Another Glasgow man, Robert Reid, was a clerk to a muslin maker, a manufacturer on his own account, then a shipping merchant and wholesale upholsterer; and finally retired from 'mercantile pursuits' to become an author.[8] Wealthy men in larger towns often derived investment income from a variety of sources, and in certain circumstances, particularly in the earlier part of the period and in smaller towns where there was limited scope for specialisation, individuals actively engaged in multiple occupations. As remarked by James Boswell on visiting St. Andrews in 1773: 'we observed two occupations united in the same person who had hung out two signposts. Upon one was "James Hood, White Iron Smith" ... upon another, "The Art of Fencing, Taught By James Hood"'.[9]

Despite variations between towns and within occupations; despite the tendency for job mobility and multiple employment, occupation is an important indicator of class mainly because it determined wealth which in turn conveyed status and power. In Scottish towns of the eighteenth and early nineteenth centuries the two areas with the highest capacity for personal wealth and the highest status and power were merchants in overseas trade and legal professionals. In Glasgow, a city that had risen on the development of trade with the Americas, the Virginia merchants were regarded by contemporaries in the mid-eighteenth century as a sort of aristocracy (the 'Tobacco Lords'), and through the nineteenth century the term 'merchant', rather than 'gentleman', which was usual in England, was employed as a catch-all title for middle-class respectability. In Edinburgh, the highest prestige was allocated to lawyers and advocates, a group allied to and in the service of the landed aristocracy. Other occupations could generate great wealth and consequent status, especially after the turn of the century; cotton manufacturers and iron masters are notable examples. In certain circumstances status was not material in base. Ministers, who were sometimes very wealthy but were also highly educated and associated with a powerful institution, the church, are an obvious case. In general, though, the status hierarchies of the middle class were dominated by overseas trade and the law.

## The Growth of the Middle Class

Towns had always supported a small middle class, distinct from the mass of the mainly rural working population and from the landed; though before 1760 this would not have called itself a class, nor was there a sense of collective identity either within or between towns. The economic growth of towns from the mid-eighteenth century stimulated a major expansion of the urban population. In 1750 about one eighth of the Scottish population was urban, living in towns of more than two thousand people; by 1831 it was over a third, of whom somewhere between 10-15 per cent in the earlier year rising to 20-25 per cent by the end of the period were middle class.[10] The main areas of middle-class growth were in commerce and distribution, a pattern that was to remain into the nineteenth century. The expansion of overseas trade generated opportunities for extensive wealth-making. But the growth of local domestic trade was equally significant, as shown by John Galt in his novel *The Provost*. In the dealings of Provost Pawkie, and of his relatives and associates, Galt indicates the opportunities that were available to local businessmen, men like Mr. Firlot the meal monger 'who had made a power of money a short time before by a cargo of corn that he had brought from Belfast'. Pawkie himself had been apprenticed to a tailor, though 'not so much for learning the tailoring, as to get an insight into the conformity between the traffic of the shop and the board'. He was a mercer and haberdasher, and kept a wine cellar, in addition to owning land and houses.

The expansion of trade throughout Britain and overseas gave rise to shipping and transport services and the business service sector — bankers, accountants and the commercial lawyers. It promoted a massive administrative, professional and military infrastructure, which drew in many Scots, often deployed in London or abroad. This was especially true of professionals who were trained through the universities in far greater numbers than could be absorbed within Scotland. Military service, colonial administration and migration to the plantation economies could produce men of considerable wealth who frequently returned to Scotland to invest their fortunes — men like Mr. Ceyenne, the millowner and former Virginia planter in Galt's *The Annals of the Parish*. Or they came home to enjoy retirement and the modest comforts of life in a country town like Cupar, of which it was stated: 'Gentlemen of the military profession, having spent their youth in the service of their country frequently fix their residence…in the decline of life'.[11] The advance of urban manufacturing from about 1800 presented opportunities and produced new groups like the cotton and iron masters. Industry sometimes formed a secondary element in a trading enterprise, giving rise to a group of powerful merchant-manufacturers. But most manufacturers evolved from more modest craft and shopkeeping backgrounds, or from the earlier rural linen industry.

The wealth of the landed, following advances in Scottish agriculture, enhanced some towns as centres of consumption and entertainment which also generated middle-class opportunities. The capital, Edinburgh, was an obvious case; but there were several lesser examples, such as Dumfries which by the 1790s had 'become remarkable as a provincial town for elegance, information and varied amusements. The gentry from the neighbouring coun-

22. An incident of electioneering violence, a common occurrence in the agitation for political reform, in the town of Kinghorn, Fife in 1795. There are working men (in long trousers) among the combatants, but both sides include individuals from the better-dressed middle classes (in knee breeches and hose). 'Freedom of Election', from John Kay's *Original Portraits* (Edinburgh, 1838).

try are thence often inclined either to prefer it as a place of residence or to pay it occasional visits'.[12] With rising demand for textiles, pottery, books, medicines and cosmetics, exotic foods and wine, shopkeeping became a major area of middle-class work. The impact of the modern shop, now separated from the process of manufacture, with goods displayed to entice the customer, was considerable. As social institutions, an architectural presence in the 'high street', and one of the first elements in the development of consumerism shops changed the nature of urban life. Barbers and hairdressers, hotel, lodgings and inn keepers, entertainers and teachers provided services in the towns. Doctors, lawyers and clergymen were also required in increasing numbers. Coaching developed to furnish the demand for business or leisure travel. While to satisfy the need for printed entertainment and information there was an expansion in newspapers and publishing.

The consequent growth of the middle class, in absolute size and as a relative proportion of the population, came partly through demographic processes within the group and partly through the upward or downward mobility of individuals from other social groups. Mortality was falling, family size was increasing as was the rate of marriage. In regenerating itself the institutions of family and marriage were significant. Sons were trained into the business or profession of their fathers, or else family contacts gave them access to other areas of opportunity. Marriage was a mechanism for reinforcing business networks and partnerships. Since most businesses were family-based, and women could inherit family property, it also played an important role in the creation and perpetuation of middle-class status. Again the example of Provost Pawkie is useful. Pawkie is able to launch his cloth shop with a legacy of three hundred pounds from his uncle. Soon after he marries the daughter of an innkeeper, who leaves the couple a 'nest egg'; and he has another legacy from his wife's uncle 'who made his money in foreign parts'.

Middle class growth was also founded in the capacity to absorb individuals from outwith the group through a flexible process of downward and upward mobility. Certain elements, inevitably those with the highest wealth and power, were recruited from the younger sons of lairds and aristocrats whose access to land was constrained by primogeniture. Legal professionals especially in Edinburgh had close links with the land. Indeed, their expansion from the later seventeenth century was primarily due to the needs of the landed who were involved in complex processes of agricultural consolidation and improvement, which were inevitably prone to litigation, or estate purchases and extensions.[13] Many men with a landed family background but no personal landholdings entered overseas trade as merchants or planters, though this was often transitory since with fortunes made they were able to purchase estates and return to a landed lifestyle, a pattern that was also seen among lawyers. The movement between the land and towns, which was paralleled by social interaction, was not, of course, exclusive to the rich. The phenomenon was widespread and it smoothed the evolutionary path of the middle class as a whole. It was an important element in the creation of links between town and countryside and cemented the influence of towns and cities in their rural hinterlands.

Upward mobility, the recruitment of individuals from the lower orders, was on an ever greater scale than recruitment from the landed, particularly into the crafts, nascent industry and shopkeeping. The movement from weaver to small master and petty capitalist, such as a yarn dealer or cotton master, was relatively easy (as was the return journey in years of cyclical downturn) and many took this route, notably David Dale who eventually achieved the status of one of the great merchant-manufacturers. Movement from itinerant salesman, with a pack of petty goods, to shopkeeper was also one of relatively easy stages for the young and enterprising with sufficient money for the initial investment. Once launched on an upward path, providing that ill health, family circumstances or bad luck did not conspire to disrupt the process, it was possible to experience an advance in fortunes. The capital requirements of most businesses in this period were modest, the opportunities were great and the earlier restric.ions on economic activity were falling fast. Social mobility was possible, and though few Scots rose from total obscurity to great wealth, there were sufficient examples of those who had to generate the myth of the 'self-made man'.[14] It was inevitable, however, that the dangers of a volatile and increasingly uncontrolled business environment — chicanery, over-extension, bad debts or a decline in trade — could also result in an equally rapid reversal of fortunes.

A system of higher education that was relatively open when compared with that of England, and a structure of parish schools not yet overwhelmed by urban growth, also provided an avenue of mobility for some, especially into the lesser clergy, the teaching profession and administration.[15] Once the individual was embarked on upward mobility through economic enterprise or in some cases through education, then the other mechanisms for attaining, retaining and enhancing status, and for proclaiming class membership, were brought into play. Such things as having the right friends and social contacts; belonging to appropriate institutions, church and voluntary societies; acquiring an education (informal, part-time higher education was available to a wide group through the Scottish universities); attracting the right clients to the business; making a good marriage for self and children; and having the family engage in suitable social activities.

## The 'Making' of the Middle Class

'Class' is a valid theoretical concept only where there is evidence of a sense of class consciousness, and an indication that because of this consciousness the class is engaged in activity that promotes its collective interests. It is not enough to identify a group who were neither the aristocracy and landed, nor rural workers and urban labourers and call them the middle 'class'. It is necessary also to understand the ways in which this group had a 'sense of class' — something that crossed the variations in economic function, wealth and urban situation — and demonstrate where, when and how this evolved.

In 1760 there was no tangible sense of class in Scotland. As in England, society was hierarchical and layered, the layers linked by economic interests and regional loyalties and the pervasive systems of paternalism and patronage. There was an urban interest, but this tended to bind all urban groups against the interests of the non-urban; and some elements of what were later to be

23. Displays of wealth and fashion through conspicuous consumption were aspects of middle-class identity that extended from the home (see Fig 20) to the last resting place. The socially exclusive Necropolis in Glasgow was modelled on the elegant Père Lachaise cemetery in Paris. *Mitchell Library, Glasgow.*

called the middle class, such as lawyers, were strongly identified with the landed. The absence of a sense of class is shown in commentaries like the *Statistical Account,* which was written by ministers in the 1780s. Here the language of 'ranks and orders' describes urban society,[16] though other transitional terms indicating wealth and associated behaviour are also used. In Edinburgh there is reference to 'people of quality and fashion' who are set apart from 'tradesmen…and people in humble and ordinary life'. In Kirkcaldy there are 'men of rank and fortune'. In Perth there are 'opulent inhabitants … [who live] genteely… [and are] of better rank'. In Montrose it is only 'proper company' who are allowed to attend the assemblies. In Glasgow social divisions are founded in 'rank and consequence'. But significantly it is Glasgow which also reveals an early manifestation of the term 'class', used in reference to educational provisions for the 'lower classes' and the 'higher classes'.

By the 1830s the language of class was well developed in Scotland, though the terminology of 'ranks and orders' had not vanished from smaller and non-industrial towns. The middle class had evolved a sense of identity and collective solidarity. This was articulated in contemporary literature and through the active pursuit of class interests, such as greater access to political power, which united most elements of this varied group. A number of factors had combined to 'make' the Scottish middle class. The first of these was geographical proximity and concentration in the towns and cities of the central Lowlands. The demographical pull of the Lowlands and the attractions of the big cities to the young and enterprising were well evident by 1760. As the urban economies developed, so did the parallel systems of physical communications — roads, canals and transport services — and printed communications, notably newspapers. These developments were clearly regarded as significant by contemporaries; of Edinburgh it was remarked: 'In 1763 there were two stagecoaches…which went to the port of Leith…and consumed a full hour upon the road. There were no other stagecoaches in Scotland, except one, which set out once a month for London, and it was from twelve to sixteen days upon the journey. In 1783 there were five or six stagecoaches to Leith… which ran it in fifteen minutes…. There are… stagecoaches, flies, and diligences to every considerable town in Scotland…[and]…to London there were no less than sixty stagecoaches monthly…and they reached the capital in four days'. Of newspapers, there were two in Edinburgh in 1763 and six by the early 1790s.[17]

The dynamics of a geographically concentrated population, in which personal contacts were increasingly easy and the mechanisms for disseminating information were being enhanced, are vital to the understanding of class. Within this context ideas, knowledge and an awareness of common interests or grievances could be articulated widely. Linked to geographical concentration was a sense of intellectual proximity. The movements and organisations of the Enlightenment — in its refined academic forms and more popular manifestations — contributed to a new and dynamic intellectual culture by the later decades of the eighteenth century. The flourishing clubs and societies — literary, scientific, professional — provided an arena for conviviality and contributed to a critique of the political and economic status quo which enhanced the sense of identity. The mood was essentially optimistic; there was faith in future progress. With an emphasis on intellectual improvement, rational inquiry and the positive use of time, this culture was distinct. When linked to a positive espousal of active Christian observance and the evolving notion of respectability, the intellectual identity of the middle class was further refined and differentiated from other groups.

Consumerism, the availability and display of material possessions, was stimulated by the rise of the middle class, and also contributed to the formation of class identity.[18] Nowhere is the evidence of this more striking than in changes in housing, in the possessions that are found in houses and in the ideas that houses represent. The development of the 'new town' in the later eighteenth century — Edinburgh was the British exemplar, though there were lesser versions in most towns — is vital to an understanding of the middle class. New town design, symmetrical and grid-like, articulated the desire for a new sort of orderliness to replace existing patterns of incoherent urban growth; it was a powerful metaphor for social order and control.[19] The 'new town' house allowed richer elements of the middle class to engage in consumerism and to physically separate themselves from the rest of urban society. Private and self-contained, removed from the business districts and with more space for the family, for servants and to accommodate possessions, such houses revolutionised patterns of domestic activity and recreation. The home, the central institution of the nineteenth-century middle class, was gradually created as the place of family and leisure, quite distinct from the place of work. In this distinction was the notion of 'separate spheres' — women should occupy a private, home-based sphere, men the public sphere of work.[20] Since the ability to maintain a non-working wife was an index of wealth and consequently of status, 'separate spheres' became a central and unifying aspect of middle-class values. It was the new type of home, and the kinds of social activity and relationships that the home allowed, which created the greatest distance between the  middle class and the rest of urban society. And though the change was not sudden, and many families could not afford 'new' houses and elaborate possessions or achieve the ideal of 'separate spheres', these were desired and emulated to the extent that resources allowed.

Towns provided opportunities which attracted the middle class but they also attracted the poor, and in growing numbers. This was a source of collective anxiety and heightened class awareness since the poor were a threat to property and possessions. As middle-class consumerism developed, so did the material distance between the classes and the sense of threat was enhanced. Anxiety is illustrated in contemporary newspapers whose reports of petty crimes against property were legion. It is shown in the considerable resources that were invested by the middle class, through local government or the church, in the construction of mechanisms to control the poor. It is also shown in the rise of voluntary societies in towns and cities from the 1780s. Institutions like subscription hospitals, missionary or benevolent societies were adaptive and democratic, a basic element in the formation of middle-class identity. They addressed a range of issues associated with the poverty, health and religious education of the urban working class. They directed charitable relief, tried to promote appropriate values and exercise control in an environment where population growth was outstripping the capacities of many official agencies.[21]

Other factors helped to form a sense of middle-class identity in Scotland. The desire for cultural assimilation with England was significant, demonstrated in the disdain of 'Scotticisms' and the pursuit of the English idiom in speech and literature among those with intellectual aspirations; or in the conscious revision of aspects of the past, such as Jacobitism, in a romantic and non-threatening form. But the vital factor, both evidence of and contributing to the rise of class, was conflict. Conflict took place in a number of arena, political and economic, both within and between the classes. The primary arena concerned access to urban institutional power and was particularly strong in those towns where rapid growth and economic change had effectively overthrown the rationale of existing systems of closed and self-perpetuating burgh government. The detailed patterns of this conflict varied since there was great variety in the structures of town councils, but all observed a common challenge to the status quo by rising groups from within the increasingly confident middle class. It was remarked of Glasgow, for instance, that 'some of the more ambitious wish for some more political consequence than they at present enjoy under the laws of the Scottish burghs; which they consider as confining the presentation of ministers and the power of election and offices to a few…. As they are getting rich this desire will increase.' [22] On some occasions the anger provoked by electoral restrictions and by the chicanery that typified much of local politics could result in physical violence, as occurred in Kinghorn, the Forth coast town, in 1796.[23] Challenge to the distribution of power within towns was mirrored by a growing dissatisfaction with the character of representation in national government and with the role of government in the political management of

24. St. Vincent Street at Blythswood Place, Glasgow, c.1828 depicts the separation of middle-class home and work. The foreground is dominated by new and private houses of the wealthy 'West End', while in the distance the older commercial and working-class districts are visible. *Mitchell Library, Glasgow.*

Scotland. These concerns peaked in the years of economic stress immediately following the end of the Napoleonic Wars, when pent-up anxieties about the cost of the wars and anger with a wartime income tax, which had fallen heavily on urban businessmen and favoured the landed (as did the new Corn Laws), were coupled to moral outrage at the conduct of the Prince Regent (then engaged in a divorce scandal) and his court. Anti-government demonstrations and petitions became a feature of urban life, and although there was an articulate pro-government lobby the loyal Tories who dominated the town councils found it increasingly difficult to sustain a credible opposition to the calls for change, particularly where it concerned the extension of the franchise to include the middle class and an increase in urban parliamentary representation. When constitutional reforms were eventually introduced in the 1830s the Scottish middle class was largely united in their support

A second area of conflict lay in the often ambiguous and shifting relationships between the middle class and the working class. The political aspirations of the middle class were, of course, soon matched by the aspirations of the labouring classes; aspirations given further impetus by the successes of the French Revolution. In certain periods there was a strong alliance between the reforming middle-class and working-class political leaders; during the 1780s and following the Napoleonic Wars, for instance. But economic tensions coupled to fears of working-class insurgency, with the inevitable threats that these posed to middle-class property and interests, generally conspired to undermine a sustained unity of political purpose during these years. This was especially evident in 1820, a year of economic uncertainty and high industrial unemployment, which saw the Battle of Bonnybridge, an abortive and ultimately tragic uprising of west of Scotland weavers and factory operatives seeking political change and an amelioration of their economic plight. Though eventually small in scale and at heart a response to economic exigency, the uprising was ruthlessly suppressed by the authorities; and following a few days of near hysterical anxiety in anticipation of revolution, provoked a massive reaction in support of law and order and against radical reform from within the middle class. Factory owners in Glasgow united to impose economic sanctions on their radical workforce, and middle-class volunteer regiments — including men who a year before had been vociferous in their attacks against the Government — were formed to police the streets and protect life and property.

The Scottish urban middle class sought political change in the years from 1760 to 1830, but not such as to threaten their economic ascendency. In this commitment lay the source of both intra-class unity and inter-class conflict. In combination with geographical proximity, consumerism and new forms of organisation; and the generation of a new intellectual identity based on optimism, the separation of home and work, the popular precepts of the enlightenment and evangelical religion, and distinct patterns of culture and language, these were the essential elements in the making of the middle class.

## NOTES

I am grateful to Elspeth Moodie and Rowy Mitchison for comments on an early draft of this chapter.

1. The best account is still to be found in T.C. Smout, *A History of the Scottish People 1560-1830* (London, 1969). Also of value are T. Dickson (ed.), *Scottish Capitalism: Class, State and Nation from before the Union to the Present* (London, 1980); B. Lenman, *Integration, Enlightenment and Industrialization; Scotland 1746-1832* (London, 1981); L.J. Saunders, *Scottish Democracy 1815-1840* (Edinburgh, 1950); R.J. Morris, 'The middle class and British towns and cities of the Industrial Revolution 1780-1870', in D. Fraser & A. Sutcliffe (eds.), *The Pursuit of Urban History* (London,1983). Useful religious, educational and cultural perspectives are given in, J.F. McCaffrey, 'Thomas Chalmers and Social Change', *Scottish Historical Review* 60 (1981), pp. 32-66; J.V. Smith, 'Manners, morals and mentalities: reflections on the

popular Enlightenment of early nineteenth century Scotland', in W.M. Humes & H.M. Paterson (eds.), *Scottish Culture and Scottish Education 1800-1980* (Edinburgh, 1983), pp. 25-54; J. Dwyer, R. Mason & A. Murdoch (eds.), *New Perspectives on the Politics and the Culture of Early Modern Scotland* (Edinburgh, 1982); A.J. Youngson, *The Making of Classical Edinburgh 1750-1840* (Edinburgh, 1966); A. Chitnis, *The Scottish Enlightenment: A Social History* (London, 1976); D. McElroy, *Scotland's Age of Improvement: A Survey of Eighteenth Century Literary Clubs and Societies* (Washington, 1969); C.W.J. Withers, 'Kirk, club and culture change; Highland societies and the urban Gaelic sub-culture in eighteenth century Scotland', *Social History* 10 (1985), pp. 171-192; I. Campbell (ed.), *Nineteenth-century Scottish Fiction* (Manchester, 1979). On business groups, see T.M. Devine, 'An eighteenth century business élite: Glasgow West Indian merchants 1740-1815', *Scottish Historical Review* 57 (1978) pp. 40-67; T. M. Devine, *The Tobacco Lords* (Edinburgh, 1975); T. Donnelly, 'The economic activities of the members of the Aberdeen Merchant Guild 1750-1799', *Scottish Economic and Social History* 1 (1981), pp. 25-41. Notable English studies include L. Davidoff & C. Hall, *Family Fortunes: Men and Women of the English Middle Class 1780-1850* (London, 1987); L.D. Schwarz, 'Social class and geography: the middle classes in London at the end of the eighteenth century', *Social History* 7 (1982), pp. 167-185; R.G. Wilson, *Gentlemen Merchants: the Merchant Community in Leeds 1700-1830* (Manchester, 1971).

2. See particularly Sir J. Sinclair (ed.), *The Statistical Account of Scotland,* 21 vols. (Edinburgh, 1791-9). Personal perspectives on Scottish society include J. Boswell, *The Journal of a Tour to the Hebrides with Samuel Johnson, LL.D* (London, 1785); H. Cockburn, *Memorials of His Time* (Edinburgh,1856). Novels, which were written by the middle class for a mainly middle-class readership are especially valuable for their social insights (date given is year of first publication; all but Lockhart are available in modern editions): J.G. Lockhart, *Peter's Letters to His Kinfolk* (Glasgow,1819); S. Ferrier, *Marriage* (Edinburgh, 1818) and *The Inheritance* (Edinburgh, 1824); J. Galt, *The Annals of the Parish* (1821), *The Entail* (1822) and *The Provost* (1822); Sir W. Scott, *Waverley* (Edinburgh, 1814).

3. This definition is based on a Weberian class model. For an historical perspective on the theory of class that is sensitive to the problems of middle-class interpretation, see the companion volumes R.S. Neale, *Class in English History 1680-1850* (Oxford, 1981) and R.S.Neale (ed.), *History and Class Essential Readings in Theory and Interpretation* (Oxford, 1983); also J. Raynor, *The Middle Class* (London,1969).

4. This broad estimate is derived from a sample analysis of *Williamson's Directory for the City of Edinburgh* (Edinburgh, 1774); *Jones's Directory for the City of Glasgow* (Glasgow, 1787); and the occupation listings for a number of smaller towns given in the *Statistical Account.*

5. *Ibid.*

6. *Ibid.*

7. Scottish Record Office, Edinburgh. M.S.E 326/6/27 Female Servant Tax 1791-2.

8. A. Phillips, *Glasgow's Herald* (Glasgow, 1982), p. 33; R. Reid, *Autobiography* (Glasgow, 1865), pp. 7-10.

9. Boswell, *Tour to the Hebrides.*

10. These percentages are a broad estimate of proportional growth derived from *Census of Scotland, 1831* (Edinburgh, 1832) and the sources cited in notes 4 and 7. See also H. Perkin, *The Origins of Modern English Society 1780-1880* (London, 1969), ch. 2 for the King (1688) and Colquhoun (1803) estimates.

11. *Statistical Account*, vol 17, p.170.

12. *Ibid.*, vol.5, p.143

13. N.T. Phillipson, 'The social structure of the Faculty of Advocates in Scotland 1661-1840', in A. Harding (ed.), *Law-making and Law-makers in British History* (1980), pp. 146-156.

14. See F. Crouzet, *The First Industrialists: the Problem of Origins* (Cambridge, 1985) which includes Scottish material.

15. W.M. Matthews, 'The origins and occupations of Glasgow students 1740-1839', *Past and Present* 33 (1966), pp. 74-94

16. A. Briggs, 'The language of ''Class'' in early nineteenth century England', in A. Briggs & J. Saville (eds.), *Essays in Labour History* (London, 1967), pp. 154-77 and reprinted in Neale, *History and Class.*

17. *Statistical Account*, vol.6, pp. 586-87, 592.

18. See N. McKendrick, J. Brewer & J.H. Plumb, *The Birth of a Consumer Society* (London, 1982).

19. This idea is explored in T. Markus (ed.), *Order in Space and Society* (Edinburgh, 1982).

20. L. Davidoff & C. Hall, 'The architecture of public and private life, English middle class society in a provincial town 1780-1850', in D. Fraser & A. Sutcliffe (eds.), *The Pursuit of Urban History* (London, 1983).

21. R.J. Morris, 'Voluntary societies and the British urban elite 1780-1850', *Historical Journal* 26 (1983), pp. 95-118

22. *Statistical Account*, vol. 5, p. 534.

23. See *A Series of Original Portraits and Caricature Etchings by the late John Kay, Miniature Painter, Edinburgh* (Edinburgh 1837-8), plate 137 which illustrates the issue of 'Freedom of Election'.

CHAPTER 7

# Literary and Learned Culture

## Alexander Murdoch and Richard B. Sher

The late eighteenth and early nineteenth centuries mark a notable period of Scottish cultural confidence and achievement, particularly in the fields of literature, history, philosophy, science, medicine and education. Yet Scottish culture during this era (as well as others) has often been seen as deeply divided. In the 1960s the literary historians David Craig and David Daiches each put forward a version of a thesis that defined the polite and popular cultures of this period as two distinct entities.[1] On one side, it was argued, stood the high culture of polished English poetry and prose, rational religion, genteel manners and amusements, empirical methodology and formal institutions such as universities and philosophical and scientific societies. On the other side stood the informal, largely oral, indigenous vernacular culture of the 'people', who expressed themselves in popular ballads, songs and poems like those of Robert Fergusson and Robert Burns in Scots and Alasdair MacMhaighstir Alasdair, Rob Donn Mackay and Dugald Buchanan in Scottish Gaelic.

Those who apply this 'two cultures' thesis to Scottish history offer various theories to explain it. The Marxist explanation emphasises class differences: polite culture is of and for the well-to-do, just as popular culture is of and for the people. The nationalist explanation stresses the tension between native and foreign (usually English) manners and mores, associating the former with popular culture and the latter with polite culture. Proponents of both these points of view generally exalt the popular over the polite, whereas a third alternative, associated chiefly with students of the Enlightenment, reverses that judgement by explaining differences between the two cultures in terms of a struggle between enlightenment and superstition, education and ignorance, tolerance and bigotry.

No matter how one attempts to explain it, this dualistic approach to Scottish culture requires qualification. We now know that Scots poets such as Robert Fergusson and Robert Burns had substantial links with English and Scottish literary culture.[2] Similarly, 'enlightened' and high-born eighteenth-century Scots often shared in 'popular' culture by speaking Scots and singing or even composing Scots poems and ballads. It was said that Highlanders spoke 'purer' English than Lowlanders, and virtually all the literati spoke English with broad Scottish accents. The gentry, clergy and men of letters could adopt national causes, as in their sometimes fervent campaigns for a Scots militia.[3] Class differences were often less pronounced in the eighteenth century than in England and other European countries. It was possible for a printer like William Smellie to establish a reputation among the learned and for a farmer's son like William Wilkie to try his hand at being a farmer, poet, clergyman and professor. Even if traditional claims for universal literacy and democratic parish education have been somewhat exaggerated,[4] Scottish literature and learning in this period cannot always be made to fit the model of two separate and distinct cultural worlds.

A look at the subject of language during this period reveals the complexity of the matter. This was the age in which Latin finally lost its hold over Scottish letters, becoming a secondary language even within the halls of academe. By 1750 the formidable Latin humanist tradition in Scotland, stretching from Boethius and Buchanan in centuries past to Thomas Ruddiman in the first half of the eighteenth century, was all but dead. It was also the age of the obvious decline of Gaelic and Scots. In the Lowlands Gaelic became a sign of backwardness if not barbarism: 'to be a Gaelic speaker marked one as "outside and below" in terms of culture and class'.[5] Yet the eighteenth century is considered the great age of Scottish Gaelic poetry, when lovely poems of romance, faith, joy, sadness and celebration of the land were produced by a variety of poets. If educated Lowlanders were deaf to these achievements, the reasons must be sought not only in their ignorance of Gaelic — which virtually none of them understood — but in their general preconceptions about Gaelic culture. It was not that Gaelic culture was considered inherently inferior or unpoetic; it was that its poetic genius was thought to be limited to the expression of primitive thoughts and emotions. Gaelic was compared to Homeric Greek as a raw, powerful tongue capable of little refinement but much passion and grandeur. Ancient epics were therefore expected from it by Lowland men of letters, who were eager to embrace James Macpherson's generally spurious Ossianic epics as authentic translations of old Scottish Gaelic works.

The relationship between English and Scots is more complex. There are those who consider Scots a regional dialect of English and those who, looking back to the late medieval and early modern period, point out that Scots was a language of particular depth and range, most powerfully displayed during this period in the poetry of Burns and Fergusson and the novels of Sir Walter Scott. The question has sometimes been seen as part of the larger debate over Scotland's cultural dualism. In the 1930s Edwin Muir argued in *Scott and*

*Scotland* that there was an inherent and crippling contradiction in the fact that so many Scots cultivated standard English in their writing and speaking but thought and felt in Scots. David Daiches has employed the term 'cultural schizophrenia' to represent the eighteenth-century manifestation of this phenomenon and has made a strong case for its being the prime reason for the failure of polite eighteenth-century Scots either to produce good English poetry themselves or to appreciate fully the excellent Scots and Gaelic poetry that was being produced under their very noses. The Aberdeenshire philosopher-poet James Beattie — patron of Scots poetry as well as author of an attack on ungainly 'Scotticisms' — has been described as a 'veritable Jekyll and Hyde on the question of Scots language'.[6] But must the tension over language that Beattie and other eighteenth-century Scots experienced be interpreted as a simple struggle between good and evil? Is it not possible to accept the reality of linguistic tension but judge it less harshly, seeing it as indicative not of a crippled culture but of a rich, multilingual one in which Scots (or Gaelic) would be considered appropriate for certain purposes, such as ordinary social exchange, whereas English would be considered appropriate for most other purposes and Latin might still be employed for certain formal functions?[7]

It is therefore not quite fair to accuse eighteenth-century Scots who wrote self-consciously polished English of pandering to the 'ruling classes' or assimilating themselves to a dominant English culture. As the new *lingua franca* of the age, English opened the door to a larger cultural world, just as it does in many non-English-speaking countries today. It represented a means rather than an end. By the mid-eighteenth century English had become the medium of a polite, urbane Scottish culture in the universities and cities of Edinburgh, Glasgow and Aberdeen. It flourished particularly among the professional classes of lawyers, clergymen, physicians and professors. Above all, it provided the linguistic and cultural foundation for the set of men known as 'literati'. More than merely literate, or learned, or the representatives of a certain social class, the Scottish literati belonged to that broad European movement now called the Enlightenment. They believed strongly in cultivating and promoting virtue, justice, science, improvement, religious tolerance, freedom of inquiry and polite manners. In this sense they were much like other groups of 'enlightened' men of letters elsewhere, such as the French *philosophes*. Their orientation was cosmopolitan — as illustrated by David Hume's famous declaration that he was 'a citizen of the world' — yet in certain circumstances they could be fierce British patriots and even staunch Scottish nationalists. The term 'Scottish Enlightenment' conveys the fundamental tension inherent in the movement, at once international and Scottish.

It was a creative tension that helped to generate impressive contributions to the republic of letters. As the literati grappled with the problem of defining their identities as inhabitants of a nation that was not a nation-state, they set out to make their marks indelibly. If English was to be the language of modern composition, they would learn to use it with a purity and skill that few English-men could match. If politeness was to be one of the hallmarks of enlightened civilisation, they would set the standards for polite composition in all fields of literature. If science and medicine were to be the keys to a new world of technological and social improvement, they would lead the way in those fields. If London was to be the centre of publishing and patronage, they would use their connections there to get themselves well read and well placed. It has sometimes been asked why we commonly hear of a Scottish Enlightenment but not of an English one, even though eighteenth-century England had its fair share of notable philosophers, scientists and literary figures. One fundamental reason is the sense of collective identity and purpose that existed among the Scottish literati, who were driven to succeed at least partly by the tension inherent in their situations.

An essay on the intellectual history of the Scottish Enlightenment would need to discuss the remarkable scholarly achievements of the Scottish literati during the last three-quarters of the eighteenth century: Francis Hutcheson, David Hume, Thomas Reid and Dugald Stewart in philosophy; William Robertson and Hume in history; William Cullen, Joseph Black and James Hutton in science and medicine; Adam Ferguson, Lord Kames and John Millar in social theory; Hugh Blair and George Campbell in rhetoric and belles lettres; Adam Smith in political economy; John Home in drama; and Henry Mackenzie in literature, to name just a few.[8] In an essay on the *social* history of literary and learned culture, however, it is necessary to focus on the equally extraordinary social world that the literati inhabited.[9] Several factors created an ideal atmosphere for 'enlightened' intellectual activity. As 'moderate literati' led by William Robertson gained control of the church and leading universities, Scotland entered an era in which the clerical establishment not only did nothing to block the ideas and publications of the Enlightenment (anti-Enlightenment sentiments voiced by 'orthodox' clergymen such as John Witherspoon being generally ineffective), but actually took a leading role in promoting the Enlightenment by means of the writing, teaching, preaching and political activity of its ministers.[10] Other traditional institutions, such as law and medicine, were also receptive to Enlightenment principles. The universities, especially those at Glasgow and Edinburgh, benefited from reforms that established a 'modern' system of lectures by specialised profes-sors, many of whom were selected by sympathetic patrons such as the 3rd Duke of Argyll and the 3rd Earl of Bute. Thus, by the 1750s institutional pressures of all kinds served to advance the Scottish Enlightenment, in contrast to the retarding effects they sometimes had on the Enlightenment elsewhere.

Economic and political factors also played a role. The great era of the Scottish Enlightenment, roughly from the 1750s to the 1780s, was a time of steady, if unspectacular, commercial development and agricultural improvement.[11] Coupled with the stable political situation that came into being soon after the suppression of the last Jacobite uprising in 1746, economic improvement was conducive to the spread of the Enlightenment. The atmosphere was relatively progressive and open, with less of the reactionary narrow-mindedness that was characteristic both of times of depression such as the 1690s and times of rapid economic growth and political turmoil such as occurred at the end of the eighteenth century.

The demographic and geographic situation encouraged the same result. For several decades after 1750 Scotland's major cities were large enough to foster a cosmopolitan, urbane culture, yet small and homogeneous enough (and in the case of Glasgow and Edinburgh, near enough to each other) to sustain an unusual degree of camaraderie and social cohesion among men of letters. The celebrated 'clubbability' of the Scottish literati was to a large extent a consequence of these circumstances, for in the three major cities it was no difficult thing for men with similar interests in a particular activity or branch of learning to gather together on a regular basis for conversation and refreshment. This was what happened in Edinburgh, for example, with the establishment of the Select Society as a polite debating club (1754), the Poker Club as a militia propaganda organisation (1762) and the Royal Society of Edinburgh as a forum for scholarly investigations (1783).[12] And it was what happened in Aberdeen when Thomas Reid, John Gregory, George Campbell and other local literati established in 1758 the remarkably productive Aberdeen Philosophical Society, or 'Wise Club'.[13]

Women rarely participated in the world of the Scottish Enlightenment. This state of affairs marks an obvious contrast with the French model, featuring gatherings of *philosophes* at salons run by women of taste and intellect. For all their concern with tolerance and freedom of inquiry, the Scottish literati generally showed little interest in admitting women to their company — let alone their ranks — where intellectual affairs were concerned. Only foreign women of established reputation, such as the English bluestocking Elizabeth Montagu, were accorded real respect as intellects. Yet if women were generally excluded from the formal institutions of the Scottish Enlightenment, their visibility and importance were gradually increasing. Questions dealing with women and marriage were among the most popular topics debated at the Select Society. John Millar's *Origin of the Distinction of Ranks* (1771) devoted its substantial opening chapter to the changing role of women in different stages of civilisation, and Dr. John Gregory's *A Father's Legacy to His Daughters* (1774) became one of the century's best-selling advice books.

25. Painting room of the Foulis Academy, Glasgow, showing Robert and Andrew Foulis giving instruction. Drawn by David Allan, who had been a student at the Academy. *Mitchell Library, Glasgow.*

As the century advanced, women began to appear at special chemistry lectures, and early in the nineteenth century the extraordinary Mary Somerville established herself as a mathematician and scientist of some renown.[14] It was, however, not mathematics and science but sentimental drama and fiction that did most to elevate the place of women in the life of the mind. The decisive event was the production late in 1756 of John Home's tragedy *Douglas*, which played off a 'masculine' theme of martial virtue against a 'feminine' one of maternal love and loss. It was said that Edinburgh ladies at tea parties swooned when reciting the pathetic lines of the unfortunate Lady Randolph, who dies grief-struck after the death of her long-lost son. Less well known is the fact that several young Scottish women were among the small group that read and criticised the play when it was circulating in manuscript form. In novels, newspaper articles and the celebrated literary magazines the *Mirror* (1779-80) and *Lounger* (1785-87), Henry Mackenzie and his circle combined the pathos of *Douglas* with the common-sensical and moralistic social commentary of Gregory's *A Father's Legacy to His Daughters*, forging an ethos of bourgeois domesticity and 'gentle sensibility' that has only recently begun to receive the critical attention it deserves.[15] By the nineteenth century Scottish women were contributing their own polite novels, such as Mary Brunton's *Discipline* (1814) and Susan Ferrier's *Marriage* (1818), and Mackenzie could remark in his *Anecdotes and Egotisms* that among the authors of the large number of books and articles being produced at Edinburgh in the mid-1820s were 'several ladies, most of whom are known or shrewdly guessed at; but, like the beauties of Spain, come out veiled'.

Novels and magazines attracted large audiences in part because a sizeable reading public had been nurtured by several popular periodicals. The most notable was the *Scots Magazine,* which from 1739 until 1817 was the chief monthly repository of information about local and national politics, foreign affairs, agricultural prices, publications, births, deaths and marriages. Along with a few newspapers such as the *Caledonian Mercury*, it was the central forum for debate on various kinds of social issues. It also contained original poetry, excerpts from recently published books and pamphlets and news of proceedings at the annual General Assembly of the Church of Scotland. Some of the articles were from English newspapers and magazines, but by and large the content of this periodical was Scottish enough to justify its name.

The *Scots Magazine* deliberately cultivated an impersonal editorial tone. How different were the new breed of Scottish literary magazines that began to appear in the early nineteenth century! The famous *Edinburgh Review* was written by men with a point of view.[16] In long review essays by the likes of Francis Jeffrey, Henry Cockburn and Henry Brougham, the *Edinburgh's* contributors explored social and intellectual issues with the same sharply critical eye. The Whiggish *Edinburgh* (established 1802) produced a Tory reaction in the form of *Blackwood's Magazine* (established 1817), which featured biting essays by 'Christopher North' (John Wilson). Both magazines reflected changes in Scottish literary and learned culture since the end of the eighteenth century. In particular, the French Revolution and the French wars, rapid economic development and inflation, and sustained population growth soon made the age of the Scottish Enlightenment seem peaceful, even innocent, by comparison. Politeness gave way to political realism. It is significant that the founders of the *Edinburgh Review* were mostly young lawyers who had suffered for their Whig beliefs during the repressive era of British backlash to the French Revolution. It is also significant that they were extremely well paid for their services, thanks to the liberal payment policy instituted by the *Edinburgh's* aggressive young publisher, Archibald Constable.

Political polarisation was not the only response to the social and economic changes affecting Scottish society at the turn of the century. For some, evangelical Christianity was the answer. For others, the best hope was science, which swept through society with a nearly evangelical fervour. For still others, the solution lay in the (often romanticised) Scottish past, which was brought to life so vividly in the historical novels of Sir Walter Scott, the popular tradition books of writers like Robert Chambers — author of *Traditions of Edinburgh* (1824) — and the handsome volumes of classic texts and manuscripts produced by nationalist book clubs like the Bannatyne and Maitland.[17]

One common denominator was that increasing numbers of people were expressing themselves in print on a growing range of subjects, and the audience for literature was rapidly expanding. General and specialised journals proliferated, as did all kinds of books and pamphlets produced by Scottish authors and publishers. 'At this present time,' commented Henry Mackenzie in 1824 in his *Anecdotes and Egotisms,* 'the literature of Edinburgh (like a great common taken into culture) is productive of a great many works, periodical and in volumes, which are bought and read with avidity'. The growing size and wealth and the emerging sense of identity of the urban middle class, as discussed by Dr. Nenadic in the preceding chapter of this volume, were largely responsible for the phenomenon Mackenzie described. Sales of fiction, for example, entered a new age following the publication of Sir Walter Scott's *Waverley* in 1814, and the market for fiction was to be found chiefly among the middle-class reading public — including middle-class women — with sufficient amounts of money and leisure time to spend on novels. Supplying the reading demands of the middle class, however, required an effective network of publishing and bookselling. It was necessary not only to produce enough books with appeal to large numbers of readers, but also to make those books available at prices that the ordinary book buyer could afford.

In the mid-eighteenth century Scottish publishing had been undertaken on a relatively small scale, although there is evidence that the trade was already reprinting English authors in quantity for sale within Scotland. Even at that early date those involved in publishing and bookselling were instrumental in furthering learning. In Edinburgh a succession of bookshops owned by Allan Ramsay, Gavin Hamilton, Alexander Kincaid and William Creech provided opportunities for men of letters to congregate and discuss the latest publications. The fact that most of these men gained prominence as magistrates (Kincaid and Creech both served as lord provosts) is but one indication of their social importance. A different sort of example of the broad impact of booksellers and publishers on Scottish culture is provided by Robert and Andrew Foulis of Glasgow. Encouraged by professors at the university to expand their business from bookselling to publishing, the brothers succeeded brilliantly. They then proceeded to establish an Academy of Fine Arts that offered education in painting, drawing and sculpture as well as (chiefly Continental) works of art for sale. Though important artists such as David

Allan and James Tassie were trained at the Foulis' Academy, it was never a commercial success, and by the time it closed in 1776 the family finances were in disarray.

Even for those less adventurous than the Foulis brothers the booktrade was fraught with risk and uncertainty. For much of the eighteenth century Scottish publishers were held in check by aggressive London firms that sought to control the trade (notwithstanding the fact that some of those London firms were run by men of Scottish birth, such as William Strahan and Andrew Millar). A breakthrough in relations occurred in a legal case of 1774, when the House of Lords overturned the London booksellers' claim to perpetual copyright and instituted the limited copyright system still in use today. The effect was to enable Scots to publish their own editions of popular works without fear of litigation by London booksellers.

At first Scottish booksellers benefited by producing cheap editions. Later the wealth generated by cheap publishing made possible a dramatic change in the relationship of Edinburgh and London as publishing centres. Sir Walter Scott's publisher Archibald Constable was in the forefront of this development, which dazzled contemporaries. 'One that has not examined into the matter would scarcely be able to believe how large a proportion of the classical works of English literature, published in our age, have made their first appearance on the counters of Edinburgh booksellers,' wrote Scott's son-in-law J.G. Lockhart in *Peter's Letters to His Kinfolk* (1819). Lockhart added in wonder, 'I do not know of any other instance, in the whole history of the world, of such a mart existing and flourishing in a place not the seat of government, or residence of a court, or centre of any very great political interest'.

*Titles Published Annually in Scotland*

| Year | Published Items |
| --- | --- |
| 1750s | 141 |
| 1760s | 157 |
| 1770s | 193 |
| 1780s | 167 |
| 1790s | 266 |
| 1801 | 265 |
| 1815 | 565 |

Note: The eighteenth-century figures are decade averages drawn from a search of the unfinished *Eighteenth-Century Short Title Catalogue* generated 28 April 1987 by Blaise Online Services, which is administered by the British Library's Department of Bibliographic Services. Figures for 1801 and 1815 are drawn from series 1, phase 1 of the *Nineteenth-Century Short Title Catalogue*, which is also still in progress.

Although current efforts to identify and collate surviving literature from this period are far from complete, preliminary data support Lockhart's claims. During the early years of the nineteenth century the Edinburgh-based Scottish publishing industry exhibited a vast increase in the production of books and pamphlets (see Table).

This development generated an atmosphere of boundless optimism in which large fortunes could be made and (as Scott and Constable learned to their dismay in 1825) quickly lost again if one's resources were over-extended when a financial crisis struck. The Scottish publishing industry survived such blows by continuing to specialise in the production of inexpensive books intended for mass consumption.

The expansion of the publishing industry in the early nineteenth century was accompanied by a further expansion of the reading public in two inter-related ways — downward, to include the lower ranks of middle-class and even working-class readers, and outward, to include readers in smaller towns and rural villages. The movement of printers and booksellers to market towns all over Scotland was indicative of these changes. In 1774 William Creech, Edinburgh's leading bookseller, complained that 'in every little town there is now a printing press. Cobblers have thrown away their awl, weavers have dismissed their shuttle, to commence printers'.[18] In reality it took some time for the trend that so alarmed Creech to become statistically significant. Of forty-one British towns known to have printed at least fifty items during the eighteenth century, only five — Edinburgh, Glasgow, Aberdeen, Perth and Paisley — were Scottish, and roughly 97 per cent of the items printed in those five towns were concentrated in the two largest. Indeed, Edinburgh, which ranked second only to London in the production of printed items, and Glasgow, which ranked fourth behind London, Edinburgh and Oxford, seem to have dominated eighteenth-century Scottish book and pamphlet printing even more completely than London dominated that trade in England.[19]

During the first half of the nineteenth century, however, almost every sizeable Lowland town came to have a press, and most of them had a newspaper. Sometimes bookbinding, papermaking and bookselling were practised along with printing and publishing. Sometimes bookselling was mixed with other endeavours, including selling stationery, household wares and textiles. Presses in towns like Stirling and Falkirk tended to specialise in cheap chapbooks of eight or sixteen pages, usually of songs or ballads, or in pamphlets of an evangelical Christian or even radical political nature. These items were frequently sold by 'chapmen' — country peddlers who offered these little works along with buttons, thread and other wares. By 1830 it became possible to print and publish books at prices low enough to increase significantly their availability to working people. Speaking of these times,

William Chambers observed in his memoirs that 'so far as the humble orders were concerned' it almost seemed 'as if the art of printing, through certain mechanical appliances — particularly the paper-making machine and the printing-machine — was only now effectually discovered'. In the wake of the popular publishing successes of William Chambers and his brother Robert came William Collins of Glasgow and Thomas Nelson of Edinburgh, both of whom rose from publishing and selling religious literature to running large publishing houses catering to the vast new popular reading market.

*The Encyclopedia Britannica* was one particularly ambitious Scottish publishing venture that spanned practically the entire period covered by this essay. It was founded in Edinburgh during the late 1760s by an engraver and a printer armed with the novel idea of combining in a single work the features of dictionaries and scholarly treatises. This plan was responsible for the *Britannica*'s peculiar organisation: after several pages of one- or two-line definitions, a reader would suddenly come upon a lengthy, comprehensive treatise on a general subject such as 'agriculture', 'anatomy', book-keeping', or 'law'. Many of these treatises were written by the *Britannica's* bright young editor, William Smellie, but more seem to have been drawn — with or without acknowledgement and compensation — from existing scholarly works. The anonymous article on 'moral philosophy', for example, was actually the gist of David Fordyce's *Elements of Moral Philosophy* (1754), which had first appeared in Dr. Dodsley's *Preceptor* (1748).

Compared to the great French *Encyclopédie,* the first edition of the *Encyclopedia Britannica* (1768-71) appears more factual and scientific (reflecting Smellie's own scientific orientation), less interpretive, original, critical and witty, as well as less voluminous. With the second edition that was completed in 1784, however, the number of volumes increased from three to ten, and this figure rose to eighteen by the time the third edition was finished in the 1790s.[20] By then sales had risen from their first-edition level of just over three thousand copies to about thirteen thousand copies. When interest seemed to wane in subsequent decades, due in part to competition from new rivals such as David Brewster's *Edinburgh Encyclopedia* (established 1808), the *Britannica* was rescued by Constable, who produced an impressive *Supplement* that featured learned dissertations by Dugald Stewart and John Playfair. After Constable's bankruptcy the copyright was obtained by the Edinburgh bookseller Adam Black, who continued to develop the enterprise. While other encyclopedias fell by the wayside, the *Britannica* perfected the modern idea of an encyclopedia as a repository of factual information that is periodically revised to keep up with the times.

As an instance of the popularisation of knowledge, the *Encyclopedia Britannica* was but one of many efforts to bridge the gap between learned and popular culture. In the early nineteenth century education was widely regarded as the primary means by which Scottish society could maintain equilibrium in the face of social dislocation. Recent scholarship has brought to life the 'popular enlightenment' of this era by focusing on three representative thinkers: George Miller of Dunbar, Samuel Brown of Haddington and Thomas Dick of Methven and Broughty Ferry.[21] The leading characteristic of their work was a blend of science and evangelical Christianity. Another characteristic was opposition to radical ideas and a profound belief in social order. George Miller's publications held up the 'refinement' and 'civility' of a good home for moral approval, in contrast to the 'vice', 'profligacy' and 'coarseness' of the tavern, the fair and the street. Appeal was made to the harmony of nature itself, as revealed in astronomy and the biological sciences. Similar lessons were taught to working men in the new mechanics' institutes being founded in many of the leading towns. Whig political economy reinforced these teachings with its emphasis on the need for self-reliance and discipline.[22] All these ideas were incorporated into the programme of the prolific evangelical reformer Thomas Chalmers, who sought through his writings and urban pastoral service to inculcate the values of self-reliance, social harmony, political conservatism and home-centred Christianity.[23]

As the 'popular enlightenment' gained momentum, academic and scholarly culture remained prominent. Early nineteenth-century Scotland continued to play a leading role in many of the fields for which it had been distinguished during the age of the Scottish Enlightenment, including moral philosophy, the natural sciences and medicine. Within the world of letters, however, there was a shift in intellectual leadership from clergymen and professors who wrote formal prose to novelists and essayists, many of whom came from the ranks of the legal profession. Sir Walter Scott and the contributors to the *Edinburgh Review* and *Blackwood's Magazine* set the tone. By the 1820s the new Scottish literary culture was in full bloom. In that decade John Galt published his charming novel of eighteenth-century rural life, *The Annals of the Parish,* and James Hogg produced his extraordinary exploration of the darker recesses of the psyche, *Confessions of a Justified Sinner.*

At the same time concerns were being voiced about the need to define and reinforce Scotland's cultural identity. In 1819 *Blackwood's Magazine* printed an anonymous article calling for a Scottish national monument on Edinburgh's Calton Hill as a symbol of Scotland's cultural achievements, particularly since the Union. Unless Edinburgh and Scotland remembered and sustained their accomplishments, it was argued, 'the city and the nation which have produced David Hume, and Adam Smith, and Robert Burns, and Henry Mackenzie, and Walter Scott, would cease to exist; and the traveller would repair to her classical scenes, as he now does to Venice or Ferrara, to lament

26. Unfinished National Monument on Calton Hill, Edinburgh. This attempt to build a replica of the Parthenon was the most obvious manifestation of the hope that Edinburgh would become the cultural centre of Britain, playing Athens to London's Rome. *City of Edinburgh Museums and Art Galleries.*

the decay of human genius which follows the union of independent states'. London would play the part of Rome and be the seat of fashion and political power, the writer conceded, but through peaceful competition within the empire 'Edinburgh might become another Athens, in which the arts and the sciences flourished, and established a dominion over the minds of men more permanent than even that which the Roman arms were able to effect'. By continuing to develop as a centre of literary and learned culture, in other words, Edinburgh could transcend Scotland's political and economic weakness and establish a lasting identity for itself and for Scotland.

The monument on Calton Hill represented a dream that lives on to this day as a lasting tribute to Scottish literary and learned culture of the late eighteenth and early nineteenth centuries. Yet there is also symbolism in the fact that the monument was never completed. As the pace of demographic and social change continued to quicken, it became increasingly difficult to contain cultural change within the structure of traditional Scottish society. There was a growing sensitivity to the insufficiency of Enlightenment values for solving nineteenth-century social problems. In this new age, conflict and competition would become more prevalent than improvement and politeness.

In the end all roads lead to Walter Scott. More than any other nineteenth-century figure, it was he who brought together the various strands and paradoxes discussed in this essay. By mastering the presentation of vibrant (if somewhat bastardised) Scots dialogue in the context of urbane English novels with universal appeal, he found a way to resolve the linguistic tension between Scots and English as well as the broader cultural tension between the 'popular' and the 'polite'. Scott appreciated both the Enlightenment and the counter-Enlightenment; he could evoke enthusiasm for the writings of the literati as well as sympathy for an old Covenanter like Davie Deans in *Heart of Midlothian*. He could be, at turns, a hard-headed rationalist and an incurable romantic, a nineteenth-century Tory politico and an eighteenth-century man of letters standing high above the fray. His novels brought to life all classes with equal grace, recreating historical events like the Forty-Five and probing the inner workings of human nature. In addition to novels he wrote histories, biographies, essays and poems, participated in nationalist book clubs and contributed to periodicals and the *Encyclopedia Britannica*. The year of Scott's death, 1832, symbolised the end of an era in Scottish literary culture almost as much as in British politics.

## NOTES

The authors are grateful to John Dwyer, Warren McDougall, John Morris and the Reference Department of Edinburgh Central Public Library for their assistance and to Anand Chitnis and the History Seminar at Stirling University for an opportunity to discuss some of the points considered in this chapter.

1. D. Craig, *Scottish Literature and the Scottish People, 1680-1830* (London, 1961); D. Daiches, *The Paradox of Scottish Culture: The Eighteenth-Century Experience* (London, 1964).

2. C. McGuirk, *Robert Burns and the Sentimental Era* (Athens, Ga., 1985); F.W. Freeman, *Robert Fergusson and the Scots Humanist Compromise* (Edinburgh, 1984); J. MacQueen, *The Enlightenment and Scottish Literature: Poetry and Progress* (Edinburgh, 1982).

3. J. Robertson, *The Scottish Enlightenment and the Militia Issue* (Edinburgh, 1985).

4. R.A. Houston, *Scottish Literacy and the Scottish Identity: Illiteracy and Society in Scotland and Northern England, 1600-1800* (Cambridge, 1985).

5. C.W.J. Withers, 'Kirk, Club and Culture Change: Gaelic Chapels, Highland Societies and the Urban Gaelic Subculture in Eighteenth-Century Scotland', *Social History*, 10 (1985), pp. 171-92, and *Gaelic in Scotland, 1698-1981* (Edinburgh, 1984); V.E. Durkacz, *The Decline of the Celtic Languages* (Edinburgh, 1983).

6. Freeman, *Robert Fergusson*, p. 6.

7. See, for example, James Kinsley's remarks in his essay 'Burns and the Peasantry 1785', *Proceedings of the British Academy*, 60 (1974), p. 138. The matter is further complicated by Henry Mackenzie's distinction between 'a pure classical *Scots* spoken by genteel people' and a coarser variety spoken by 'the lower orders of the people'. *The Anecdotes and Egotisms of Henry Mackenzie, 1745-1831*, (ed.), H.W. Thompson (London, 1927), p. 15.

8. See H. Trevor-Roper, 'The Scottish Enlightenment', *Studies on Voltaire and the Eighteenth Century*, 58 (London, 1967), pp. 1635-58; J. Rendall, *The Origins of the Scottish Enlightenment* (London, 1978); R.H. Campbell and A.S. Skinner (eds.), *The Origins and Nature of the Scottish Enlightenment* (Edinburgh, 1982); I. Hont and M. Ignatieff (eds.), *Wealth and Virtue: The Shaping of Political Economy in the Scottish Enlightenment* (Cambridge, 1983).

9. See N.T. Phillipson, 'The Scottish Enlightenment', in R. Porter and M. Teich (eds.), *The Enlightenment in National Context* (Cambridge, 1981), pp. 19-40, and 'Culture and Society in the Eighteenth-Century Province: The Case of Edinburgh and the Scottish Enlightenment', in L. Stone (ed.), *The University in Society*, 2 vols. (Princeton, 1974), vol. 2, pp. 407-48; R.L. Emerson, 'The Enlightenment and Social Structures', in P. Fritz and D. Williams (eds.), *City and Society in the Eighteenth Century* (Toronto, 1973), pp. 99-124; A. Chitnis, *The Scottish Enlightenment: A Social History* (London, 1976); C. Camic, *Experience and Enlightenment: Socialization for Cultural Change in Eighteenth-Century Scotland* (Chicago, 1983).

10. R.B. Sher, *Church and University in the Scottish Enlightenment: The Moderate Literati of Edinburgh* (Edinburgh and Princeton, 1985).

11. T.C. Smout, 'Where Had the Scottish Economy Got to by the Third Quarter of the Eighteenth Century?', in Hont and Ignatieff, *Wealth and Virtue,* pp. 45-72

12. D.D. McElroy, *Scotland's Age of Improvement: A Survey of Eighteenth-Century Literary Clubs and Societies* (Pullman, Wash., 1969).

13. S.A. Conrad, *Citizenship and Common Sense: The Problem of Authority in the Social Background and Social Philosophy of the Wise Club of Aberdeen* (New York, 1987).

14. R.K. Marshall, *Virgins and Viragos: A History of Women in Scotland from 1080 to 1980* (London, 1983), ch. 10; E.C. Patterson, *Mary Somerville, 1780-1872* (Oxford, 1979).

15. J. Dwyer, *Virtuous Discourse: Sensibility and Community in Late Eighteenth-Century Scotland* (Edinburgh, 1987).

16. J. Clive, *Scotch Reviewers: The Edinburgh Review, 1802-1815* (London, 1956); B. Fontana, *Rethinking the Politics of Commercial Society: The Edinburgh Review, 1802-1832* (Cambridge, 1985).

17. M. Ash, *The Strange Death of Scottish History* (Edinburgh, 1980).

18. Quoted in G. Walters, 'The Booksellers in 1759 and 1774: The Battle for Literary Property', *The Library,* 5th series, 29 (1974), p. 308.

19. These observations are based on data in C.J. Mitchell, 'Provincial Printing in Eighteenth-Century Britain', *Publishing History,* 21 (1987), pp. 5-24.

20. H. Kogan, *The Great EB: The Story of the Encyclopedia Britannica* (Chicago, 1958).

21. J.V. Smith, 'Manners, Morals and Mentalities: Reflections on the Popular Enlightenment of Early Nineteenth-Century Scotland', in W.M. Humes and H.M. Paterson (eds.), *Scottish Culture and Scottish Education, 1800-1980* (Edinburgh, 1983), pp. 25-54, and 'Reason, Revelation and Reform: Thomas Dick of Methven and the "Improvement of Society by the Diffusion of Knowledge"', *History of Education,* 12 (1983), pp. 255-70.

22. A. Tyrrell, 'Political Economy, Whiggism and the Education of Working-Class Adults in Scotland, 1817-40', *Scottish Historical Review,* 48 (1969), pp. 151-65.

23. S.J. Brown, *Thomas Chalmers and the Godly Commonwealth in Scotland* (Oxford, 1982).

CHAPTER 8
# Religion and Social Change

## Callum G. Brown

---

I

Religion was a crucial ingredient in popular responses to the economic and social transformation which unfolded in Scotland in the late eighteenth and early nineteenth centuries. With the church the focus of community organisation and local government, the changes wrought by agricultural improvement, industrialisation and urban growth provoked enormous turbulence in ecclesiastical affairs and popular religion. During this period, and indeed until late in the nineteenth century, religion provided the vocabulary by which many of the people expressed their values, aspirations and grievances in the midst of upheaval.

The religious changes in Scotland were part of wider patterns.[1] The Enlightenment, the American Revolution and the French Revolution spread ideas of religious liberty and liberty from religion. The rise of commercial and industrial capitalism fomented social division, heterogeneity, and new social tensions. Population growth and movement stimulated the breakdown of parochial structures and older forms of community relations based round the parish church, and propelled people into cities where ties with religion might dissolve. Three overall trends were at work: *religious polarisation* between churches on the one hand and secularist ideas (non-belief) on the other; *religious pluralisation*, with adherence to state churches receding as competing denominations grew; and *religious alienation* induced by secularising trends like class division, improving education and the *anomie* of city life.

In some countries polarisation dominated. In post-Revolutionary France there arose the great nineteenth-century contest between Catholicism and anti-clericalism. In other countries (like Germany and Holland) polarisation and pluralisation produced an exceptional segmentation of the population into sub-cultures centred around different churches and secularist or humanist traditions. In countries where secularism was less influential, the pluralisation (or multiplication) of churches dominated. The United States, with no state church, developed a powerful and ethnically-variegated religious culture

143

starting with the 'Great Awakenings' of the eighteenth and nineteenth centuries. In England, Wales, Scotland and Sweden, the struggle between state and dissenting churches (what was referred to south of the Tweed as 'church versus chapel') was exceptionally strong. But an additional, and in some places primary, conflict was Protestant versus Catholic, prevalent in Ireland, central and southern Scotland and, at various times, in the English north and north-west, the United States, southern France and southern and south-western Germany.

Whilst these conflicts did much to sustain popular adherence to churches, religious alienation became in the long term the most profound of the three overall trends. Secularisation and the decline of religion is a major theme in historians' treatment of nineteenth-century Britain (mostly England), centred on the alienation of the industrial working classes. Research in the 1950s stressed working-class exclusion from churches resulting from industrialisation.[2] In the 1960s and 1970s research pointed to the role of religion as 'the midwife of class' during the period 1760-1830. Nonconformist chapels of the urban middle classes became the cultural focus of their claims to recognition in national political life, and the base for trying to impose social control over unchurched plebeians. Marxist historians drew attention to how sections of the working class expressed — or misdirected — their 'chiliasm of despair' with early industrial oppression in their own Nonconformist and especially Methodist chapels rather than in political and industrial struggle. The social functionality of religion — the secular and almost irrational use made of it for group identity and psychological comfort during profound upheaval — came to account for its endurance through what historians of many hues agreed was the underlying secularisation of industrialising Britain.[3]

These approaches are starting to be challenged in Scotland as they have been in England and Wales.[4] New themes are emerging: the sheer popularity of religion amongst the working classes, proletarian dominance of most congregations, the plebeian self-creation of religious culture from the mid-eighteenth century onwards, and the long-term rise of church membership down to 1900. Whilst historians are becoming less willing to see religion solely as crude bourgeois control over an unwilling proletariat, differential religious affiliation within the working classes is starting to be explored. A picture is emerging of a rapidly-changing society in which religion continued to have an important place.

## II

In the middle of the eighteenth century, the religious map of Scotland was confused.[5] Presbyterianism was in a comfortable ascendancy, but its strength varied greatly from region to region. The centre of its power lay in the central and southern Lowlands which had been the focus of the covenanting struggles of the seventeenth century. A fierce loyalty to the presbyterian system had developed there amongst both urban tradesman and the rural peasantry, but further north support weakened under challenges from three opposing and interconnected traditions in Scottish religion: Catholicism, episcopacy and mediaeval Christian ritual (described by presbyterians as paganism). Apart from the Lowland area between the Tay and the Moray Firth, where episcopacy and Catholicism retained considerable strength due to the protection afforded by landed and titled gentry, the religious complexion of the north was unusually confused, with religious traditions and practices intermingling in a manner which makes it difficult for the historian — who is used to a system of well-defined denominations — to assign the people (or even many of the clergy) to any particular church.

The difficulty in defining the religious alignment of the people is not one confined to the the Highlands and the north. Though the Episcopal Church was given a degree of recognition by the Toleration Act of 1712, there had not yet emerged, as in England, a tradition of forming new churches out of ecclesiastical dispute. The Church of Scotland remained, as it had been in the seventeenth century, contestable territory for all religious groups except the Catholics, with dissension being contained within it. Even when dissenting groups were formed, they usually did not call themselves 'Churches' but 'Presbyteries' or 'Synods', thereby implying historic unity with the one and universal kirk they hoped to reclaim.

An issue that poses even greater difficulty is that of how 'religious' the people of mid-eighteenth-century Scotland were. The problem is one of concepts. The Church's role was not defined by 'membership' (largely a nineteenth-century innovation), but by its civil status. The kirk session was the local court for all manner of minor civil as well as religious offences (ranging from Sabbath desecration and fornication to assault, wife-beating and infanticide). It was the collector and distributor of poor relief and issued 'testimonials' to allow migrants to be received in other parishes. The parish school was designed to educate all children, and the kirkyard was usually the only place for burials. The parish church and parish state were virtually one and the same.

In such circumstances, church attendance was not usually compulsory except for miscreants and paupers. The kirk of 1650 to 1760 was a community venue, where worshippers came from all social backgrounds to meet friends, exchange gossip and conduct business. As the rural church performed virtually all civil functions — police, magistracy, education, tax collection, burials and many others — the only forms of religious 'alienation' were criminality, immorality or heresy. For people not overtly falling within those categories, non-churchgoing implied little about what later generations came to call their 'religious condition'. The concepts of irreligion and alienation, as developed by the Victorians and twentieth-century sociologists respectively, were themselves alien to the early-modern period, and it is only after 1750 in Scotland that parish ministers started to complain of non-churchgoing—initially amongst the gentry and aristocracy.

## III

Hence, the first sign of social change in the mid-eighteenth century was not irreligion but religious dissent.[6] Though the tradition of informal dissent lingered into the nineteenth century, with ministers, worshippers and entire congregations drifting between denominations, sharpened lines of ecclesiastical demarcation developed after 1750. The social and economic context in which presbyterian divisions were emerging was complex. The changing patterns of landownership and land use brought about by agricultural improvement were disrupting the organisation of parish government, poor relief, and the arrangements for providing the people with entry to the parish church for Sunday worship. In part, landownership was becoming more concentrated, but perhaps more importantly it was being *asserted* in new ways. The engrossing of commonties and the removal of small farmers and sub-tenants, together with the increased wealth which such improvement brought to the class of large landowners, emphasised the social and economic dominance of the elite in rural society.

A landowner introduced this into the parish church by erecting a special gallery — the 'laird's loft' — to accommodate himself and his family in elevated and spacious style. At the same time, landowners went to the local sheriff to claim their right to a proportion of the ground floor of the church equal to the proportion of their landholdings in the parish. In their appropriated area within the church, fixed pews were erected and allocated — most commonly to landowners' servants and tenant farmers, with any remaining 'sittings' being rented out to the highest bidders with the revenue passing to the poor fund. In the context of the eighteenth-century rise in population, the cost of renting a pew was increasing, and the proportion of the people able to obtain entry to Sunday worship was diminishing.

Ecclesiastical taxes exacerbated grievance. These were the 'teinds' (a tax on the agricultural rateable value of land from which came the minister's stipend, paid most often after the harvest in victual, or, as in Unst in Shetland, in a mixture of butter, ling, wool and lambs); compulsory 'donations' to the poor fund, which became larger as population rose and as landowners moved to town houses in Edinburgh or London; labour services on the manse and glebe; and a series of minor taxes including one on registration of births which, it was alleged, caused the people of Kintail in Wester Ross to defect to the Catholic Church. Social tension was expressed in other ways. A tradition had arisen since the Reformation for the precentor, who led singing in church, to read each line of a psalm so that the illiterate in the congregation could join in. This became less necessary after 1700 but remained a symbol of popular proprietorship of the kirk. For the landowning classes, however, it was an inelegant practice, a throwback to the seventeenth-century covenanters. Between the 1730s and the 1780s, many patrons and landowners instructed that 'reading the line' be abolished, fomenting considerable protest in many parish churches.

The most crucial grievance, though, was the use of patronage — the right belonging mainly to the class of large landowners, town councils, universities and others in positions of wealth and influence of 'presenting' (or selecting) a parish minister. This right had been abolished in 1690 as opposing the presbyterian principle of 'the call' (in which a congregation as a whole selected and signed an invitation to a minister), but was restored in 1712 by a Westminster parliament accustomed to such a system operating in the Church of England. It was only from about 1729 that the landowning class started to make selections more frequently, and to do so in the face of congregational opposition.

The clergy selected by patrons were invariably adherents of the 'Moderate' party which dominated the General Assembly of the Established Church from the 1750s until 1833. In caricature (the Rev. Alexander Carlyle of Inveresk being probably the best example), the Moderates rejected the harsh Calvinist heritage of severe church discipline, fiery didactic sermons and proscription of pursuits like dancing, heavy drinking and gambling. They favoured instead refinement and elegance, aping the taste and social pretensions of the English landed classes. But Moderates could attract supporters from a range of religious attitudes and social backgrounds, and ministers often drifted between the Moderate camp and that of its antithesis — the Evangelical party. At the General Assembly, loyalty to the Moderate 'party line' was exceptionally well-managed by the nexus of Edinburgh lawyers representing country (i.e. landowning) clients. Lawyers accounted for between 50 and 60 per cent of assembly commissioners (members) during the 1820s, and with the addition of Moderate clergy and landowning elders, the landed interest total came to as much as 80 per cent.

But in the country as a whole, Evangelicals were numerically dominant throughout all of our period, and indeed invariably controlled the local courts (presbyteries and synods) of the Church. Evangelicalism represented a greater puritanism in religious life — in part revitalising the covenanting heritage of the seventeenth century, and in part promoting the open, salvationist gospel characteristic of Methodism and the English-speaking Reformed Church on both sides of the Atlantic. The problem for Evangelicals, both laity and clergy, was that they were in social terms divided and intrinsically unstable: emanating from the rising urban middle classes, modernising rural peasantry, and industrial working-class congregations of small villages and larger towns. Moreover, at the General Assembly, Evangelical clergy could easily be persuaded of the efficacy of the Moderate line on many issues — most notably, on the potentially 'revolutionary' nature of Evangelical methods like open-air preaching during the French and Revolutionary Wars. Whilst the Evangelical and Moderate parties represented the extremes on the presbyterian continuum, they came to symbolise social fragmentation. The outlook of the Moderate party, favoured by the civil government, dominated in high circles, whilst Evangelicalism developed an association with the middle ranks and the working classes of urban and rural society.

For this reason, the selection of Moderate ministers by landowning patrons and by the Crown, which was patron in over a fifth of Scotland's parishes, created severe congregational protest. The people (and notably women) obstructed the induction of unwelcome ministers, barring entry to the church, leading to violent scenes on many occasions with cavalry being called in by a patron to lead the new minister into his pulpit. Patronage disputes reflected a variety of social tensions. In the Highlands, for instance, the disputed settlement of a parish minister often occurred at the same time as, and as a product of, landowners' clearance of the peasantry in preparing estates for sheep farming. During evictions in Assynt in Sutherland in 1813, a minister newly selected by the patron was driven out by the people, resulting in the summoning of a navy cutter and a detachment of militia. In burghs, where town councils were usually the church managers and patrons, patronage disputes became part of political contests involving aspiring artisan and middle-class groups: in Edinburgh during the so-called 'Drysdale Bustle' of the 1760s, and in a dispute at the Wynd Church in Glasgow in the same decade which led to the formation of three new congregations — two dissenting and one self-financing chapel-of-ease within the Church of Scotland. When a congregation was ruptured — whether because of patronage, singing reform, pew-renting or other reasons — so dissent emerged, adding to the national level of defection from the Church of Scotland.

IV

The varied social tensions produced geographical differences in the church structure. The suppression of the Highlands and Hebrides after the Jacobite Rebellion of 1745 continued a campaign originating earlier in the century to give the presbyterian Church of Scotland ascendancy over the recusant Catholics and episcopalians of the region.[7] Schools of the Scottish Society for the Propagation of Christian Knowledge assisted Lowland ministers, missionaries and locally-recruited catechists in trying to convert the peasantry from Gaelic language and 'heathenishe' religion and culture. Many of the ministers, though, were Moderates, selected by wealthy landowners, and were socially estranged from the middle and lower orders. At the same time, the erosion of land used in common, and the mixture of inducements, pestering and threats used to remove people of the middle and lower ranks to crofting townships, fishing communities, small industrial centres, the Lowlands or the New World, severely disturbed paternalistic relations and fomented a major religious divide between landowners and the booming peasant population.

Whilst the landowning class, their factors and servants tended to support (if not actually worship with) Moderate ministers of the Established Church, the religion of the people making livelihoods from elements of crofting, fishing, domestic or extractive industry underwent a revolution. Excited particularly by Lowland evangelical missionaries, the vast majority of peasant Gaels were turned during the second, third and fourth quarters of the eighteenth century from episcopal-Catholic-pagan religious culture to staunch presbyterianism. For both the prospering and poor in the Highlands and Hebrides, puritanical presbyteriansim in the mould being developed by Lowland dissenters became the core of a culture of oppression. As Evangelical ministers obtained parish charges (notably Aeneas Sage and Lachlan Mackenzie, who made Lochcarron a centre of religious interest between 1727 and 1821), many Moderate brethren were harried for ostentation, 'lukewarmness' in religion and immorality. Unpopular Moderate ministers in the Highlands, as in the Lowlands, were sometimes placed in a see-saw position of loyalty between peasant parishioners on the one hand and parsimonious heritors and patrons on the other who deprived the minister of a habitable manse and the people of a usable parish church. Sometimes Moderate ministers could attract the people's support in fighting the lairds; at other times, they could find opposing 'Separatist' groups of crofters meeting outside the doors of the church for worship conducted by lay leaders — the so-called 'Men' who were noted for religious visions and powers of prophecy. But except in the few places where Independency took root (mostly small towns like Thurso and Campbeltown, Inner Hebridean islands like Tiree, and in the northern isles of Orkney and Shetland, resulting from missionary work by the Haldane brothers in the late 1790s), dissent remained almost entirely informal. Despite the key work of southern missionaries, and despite the desperate shortage of accommodation in Highland parish churches, Lowland dissenting congregations were rarely established. The great Highland defection from the state church was to come after 1830.

27. Depictions of the Seceders are rare. This shows an early meeting (on 6th December 1733) of the entire Secession Presbytery at which the Rev. Ebenezer Erskine from Stirling (on the extreme right) was elected Moderator. Its initial support came mainly from the central counties, but by the 1760s its two elements, the Burghers and Antiburghers, were recruiting all over the central and southern Lowlands.

The church structure that developed in the non-urban Lowlands centred on the growth of the Associate Presbytery (popularly known as the Secession Church) and the Relief Presbytery (or Church) which came into being (in 1733 and 1761 respectively) directly as a result of the patronage issue. They adhered to presbyterian forms of church government and to presbyterian doctrine (as laid down in the Westminster Confession of Faith of 1643). The Relief Church had leanings towards Independency, and was liberal in offering communion, but the Seceders were extremely strict and centralised in their structure. The Secession suffered endemically from schism, giving rise to two separate synods (or churches) after 1747 (known popularly as the Burghers and Anti-burghers according to whether they agreed to take the Burgess Oath) ; these then split around 1800 into four groups with the prefixes 'New Licht' or 'Auld Licht' according to whether or not they accepted new evangelical views.

Such splits reflected change and differentiation within Lowland society.[8] Initially, in the 1740s and 1750s, the Seceders recruited mainly in central Scotland from existing 'praying societies' derived from covenanting hillside conventicles of the late seventeenth century. But recruitment expanded to all parts of the Lowlands. In the burghs, the Burghers and the Relief Church developed as the largest dissenting churches, becoming popular amongst the middle and higher echelons of the industrial and commercial population. They

were often wealthier and largely burgh-centred compared to the more numerous Antiburghers. Although the geography of Antiburgher growth is so far
poorly chronicled, it seems that it went in tandem with the spread and pace of
agricultural improvement, rising rapidly with animosity towards landowners
in south-eastern and central counties between the 1750s and 1780s — only to
stagnate as acrimony deflated and the people accepted changes to the land.
Between the 1790s and the 1830s, rural growth of the Secession moved
northwards into the counties between the Tay and the Moray Firth. Throughout, the Antiburghers were characterised as the poorest presbyterians, noted
for the 'rusticity' of their preachers and the broad Scots vernacular used in the
preaching. For example, in Hamilton in the early 1790s, the Antiburghers
were observed to be 'more widely dispersed' in the environs than the Relief
Church, 'the circumstances of the people less affluent, and the provision of the
clergyman more scanty'.[9]

However, in all three of those churches, recruitment amongst urban and
industrial workers dramatically increased in the 1790s. Urban dissent had first
emerged in the 1750s, '60s and '70s in the form of congregational independency favoured by many defecting Church of Scotland presbyterians of
the period. New textile manufacturers, their servants and their workers formed
small sects called the Glasites, the Scotch Baptists, the Old Scots Independ-
ents and the Bereans — many of which had originated amongst fishermen,
weavers and spinners in East Fife, Dundee and Perth. But by the 1780s, most
of those sects were in decline, and town inhabitants were being drawn in very
large numbers to the Burgher, Antiburgher and Relief Churches, attracted by
'New Licht' evangelicalism which, by emphasising open salvation, the
culture of prosperity and the need to separate church and state, drew the
majority of Seceders towards union in 1820 in the United Secession Church.

The emergence of presbyterian dissent represented the greatest institutionalised division in eighteenth-century Scottish society. By 1800, between
rarely less than a fifth and in some places as much as 70 per cent of the
population in Lowland parishes were members of dissenting churches (predominantly the Secession). The highest proportions were to be found in
industrialising communities, especially textile, metallurgical and mining
villages, and in agricultural parishes in areas where enclosures and improvement had proceeded the furthest. Whilst rural society changed at a fairly slow
pace over an extended period, the split in the congregation meeting in the
parish church marked a very sudden and swift rupture in the community
which, by 1826, suggested that 38 per cent of the Scottish people were
dissenters. In the towns, the sudden popularity of dissent in the decades around
1800 marked the transition from commercial to manufacturing society, and
the disintegration of traditional patterns of urban paternalism. As well as the

rise of presbyterian dissent, immigrants introduced non-presbyterian churches: Methodists from England, Catholics and episcopalians from Ireland. The overall result was that by the 1830s, less than half the churchgoing population of the two largest towns, Edinburgh and Glasgow, attended the Established Church of Scotland.

The Establishment-dissent split in a parish was by no means a simple one between different groups or classes in the social hierarchy, though between 1790 and 1814 Moderates linked the rise of evangelicalism with lower-class sympathy with revolutionary ideas. In small industrial communities — hand-loom-weaving and spinning towns, pit and metallurgical villages — the Secession and Relief Churches developed as vital focuses of group identity, alarming the elites in the wake of the French Revolution. Amongst the industrial population of Lochgelly in Fife in 1790, the Seceders outnumbered adherents of the Establishment by almost two to one, and whilst they obeyed civil government, 'They could, however,' the parish minister warned, 'be easily stirred up to sedition in matters of religion'.[10]

Radical political groups like the Friends of the People did include dissenters, and celebrated cases fostered criticism of their evangelical doctrines. But dissent was not revolutionary. It just had enormous appeal to social groups as diverse as the peasantry and the urban middle classes who were learning to live — many very successfully — by new economic rules in communities (often industrial) from which paternalistic relations based on the parish church had diminished or disappeared. In parishes where agriculture was the largest single economic activity, dissenting congregations tended to attract disproportionately large numbers of small and medium landowners, skilled tradesmen and skilled farm servants. Amongst migrants, dissent had fantastic recruiting success. It was reported in the mid-1790s that when 200 people arrived a few years earlier at Balfron in west Stirlingshire to staff the new print and bleach fields, the Relief and Burgher churches each 'immediately set up a tent for themselves, and have ever since been contending, with much animosity, for the honour of making proselytes'; as a result, nearly all the workers adhered to those denominations.[11]

City dissenting congregations also attracted skilled workers in large numbers. But urban worshippers, like urban social classes at large, were highly mobile both spatially and socially, often switching their church allegiance —'hearing sermon promiscuously' as the churches called it. Without the occupational unity of the sort found in a mill village, the opportunity arose in the mêlée of city life for migrants and inhabitants to slip from the churches' view.

V

There are fewer topics more open to differing interpretation in the social history of religion than the extent to which urbanisation and industrialisation fomented popular alienation from organised religion. On the one hand, there seems to be little doubt that urban growth centred on the emerging industrial economy of late eighteenth-century Scotland disrupted existing patterns of religious adherence. Church accommodation fell behind the needs of the population in nearly every parish in Scotland, and particularly so in the larger urban centres. In the city of Glasgow, the number of churches to population (a very crude indicator of accessibility to Sunday worship) had been improving from the mid-seventeenth to the mid-eighteenth centuries, but then started to deteriorate; in 1763 there were 1,769 inhabitants to every church, 2,200 in 1801 and 3,000 in 1821. Whilst this trend applied equally to rural areas (especially in the Highlands and Hebrides) as to cities, urban social structure heightened awareness of non-churchgoing.

One of the most important circumstances, and ultimately the mechanism which determined exclusion from the church, was the system of pew-renting.[12] This had existed in most burgh churches since the mid-seventeenth century, but it had traditionally been used to provide all social groups with access to community worship. Glasgow Town Council, for example, which owned and managed nearly all the Established churches in the city up to the 1810s, had until the 1780s allocated free church seats to the very poor, reserved large numbers of 'low-rented' seats (under 2/6d. *per annum*) for the 'lower classes of inhabitants', and set aside pews for the inmates of city pauper institutions. At the other end of the social scale, seats were allocated to university staff, students, the town council and members of the incorporated trades; some seats were owned by wealthy families, and some seats were rented to individuals by virtue of long-standing family tradition. Only after all these seats were distributed were the remainder rented out, often by 'roup' (auction).

This system of ensuring widespread access to urban parish churches broke down in most burghs around 1800. In Glasgow between 1782 and 1812, there were large and repeated rent increases as demand rose with population increase, and low-rented and *gratis* seats were removed or made available for renting to the highest bidder. The system spread across all denominations (with the partial exception of the Baptists) and to every part of the country in the late eighteenth century. This intrusion of 'free-market' economics into church life occasioned much of the non-churchgoing by unskilled and lower-paid workers. The need to pay seat rents six-monthly in advance exacerbated the financial difficulties of casual and seasonal workers. The Glasgow City Mission, in its first annual report of 1827, noted that a quarter of all the seats in the city's churches were empty, and identified the main cause as the high level of pew rents. But it also noted the need for fine clothes to attend church. The development of 'Sunday best' attire was one aspect of the unwelcoming atmosphere in churches felt by many of the lower working classes.

In a government report on levels of churchgoing made just after the end of our period in the mid-1830s, it was calculated by presbyterian investigators that 25 per cent of Glasgow's population and 23 per cent of Edinburgh's attended church, whilst 40 and 46 per cent respectively were 'in habit of attending'.[13] With few other statistics, it is difficult to ascertain whether patterns of urban and rural churchgoing diverged during this period. At a general level, religion played an important part in urban popular culture. Anti-Catholicism, for instance, was an ideology which bound all presbyterian ranks in Lowland towns.[14] In 1778, when the Catholic Relief Act was passed for England and Wales, a strenuous and successful campaign was started by Scottish town councils, city incorporations and presbyterian ministers of Establishment and dissent against a similar measure being prepared for Scotland. This led to the destruction of a Catholic chapel in Edinburgh and to a fast-day riot in Glasgow which wrecked the property of an English pottery owner. Giving relief to the Catholic faith was seen as 'highly prejudicial to the interest of the Protestant religion in Scotland, dangerous to our constitution, civil and religious, a direct violation of the treaty of union, inconsistent with the King's honour, and destructive to the peace and security of his best subjects'.[15] Despite the emergence of toleration amongst Protestant manufacturers and pit-owners who employed Catholics from the 1780s in Lanarkshire, Dunbartonshire, Renfrewshire and Ayrshire, sectarian feelings strengthened amongst skilled workers in the west of Scotland. Though approximately one-third of new arrivals from Ireland were Protestant (presbyterians, episcopalians and Methodists), it was the Catholic Irish who were identified as threatening the jobs and status of native Scots. By 1829, many ministers and skilled workers in the east of the country supported the Catholic Emancipation Act, but the objections of the Protestant working class of the west presaged an era of considerable sectarian unrest and discrimination in worker organisations.

Sectarianism apart, we need to be cautious about concluding that the working classes and the poor were social groups alienated from the churches. Skilled workers predominated in most congregations of Establishment and dissent, but unskilled workers, like labourers and carters, were under-represented amongst churchgoers. Yet, in the rapidly changing industrial and commercial economy of urban Scotland between 1780 and 1830, high levels of geographical, occupational and social mobility allowed and encouraged individuals to transfer between the non-churchgoers and the churchgoers. For the same reasons, the social composition of congregations tended to rise, sometimes very rapidly, leading to frequent rebuilding of churches to ever-more refined and expensive designs. As with the Wesleyan Methodists in England, the Seceders were by the 1810s replacing barn-like thatched meeting-houses with ornate stone churches, installing gas-lighting, and increasing ministers' stipends.

At the same time, there was constant and accelerating recruitment to the churches. Arguably, the majority of non-churchgoers were not long-standing unchurched, but in-migrants (well over half of urban dwellers) whose denominational attachment lapsed on arrival because of lack of money, urban status or space in a church. Migrants from distinctive ethnic or denominational backgrounds were relatively easy targets for recruiters: Highland Catholics, Irish Catholics and Highland presbyterians.[16] The problem was resources. The movement of first Highland and then Irish Catholics to the west-central Lowlands in search of industrial employment created severe logistical problems for a Church which, to all intents and purposes, did not exist in the region. In the 1770s, priests travelled from Perth and Edinburgh to minister to the twenty or so Catholics in Glasgow, and in the 1790s priests migrated with their Highland flocks to the city and its environs. The numbers of Catholics in Glasgow increased very rapidly: perhaps 60 in 1791, 2,300 in 1808 and 27,000 in 1831. By the end of the period, Catholics made up about 13 per cent of Glasgow's population with higher concentrations developing in nearby industrial districts like Old Kilpatrick, Renfrewshire and Monklands. Without an offical hierarchy, the Catholic Church found organisation and finance difficult. Priests were settled and chapel-schools started, but the task of erecting proper chapels was a slow process until after 1840.

Thus, it seems highly probable that there was a temporary (perhaps generational) lapsing or weakening of observance amongst many Catholics. On the one hand, Catholic migrants became strongly represented in unskilled and semi-skilled jobs, and through high levels of inter-marriage and, in many places, residential concentration, formed a group with a marked cultural identity. But it was not an entirely homogeneous group either socially or re-ligiously. The Church induced a social and ethnic hierarchy which assisted in the assimilation to the social values and ideals of industrial society. Pew rents were regarded as essential by the Scottish-born priests, who predominated during this period, to inculcate reverence for civic values; without them, Bishop Scott of Glasgow wrote to a Paisley priest in 1812, 'The Irish...never can be helped on the way to salvation'.[17] Fine clothes became a pre-requisite for many chapelgoers, matching their presbyterian neighbours, and priests encouraged the virtues of self-reliance and respectability. In this way, religious identity was maintained whilst cultural assimilation proceeded, with limited resources, amongst the Irish-born Catholic community.

28A & 28B. 'Before and after chapel built'. Unruly nineteenth-century street life is transformed when a ' low exhibition' is replaced by a church. Contemporaries placed religion beside 'secular' symbols of social reform; note that as well as improved behaviour and 'respectable' dress, the arrival of the church is accompanied by pavements, street lights and the repair of houses. *Scottish Ethnographic Archive, National Museums of Scotland.*

A very similar process occurred with migrating Highland presbyterians. From around 1770, special Gaelic congregations were started and churches built by middle-class Highlanders in Edinburgh, Glasgow and Aberdeen to cater for their poorer brethren arriving from the north-west. Whilst sustaining cultural and linguistic identity, these presbyterian congregations — like all others — were socially constructed to reflect the urban class structure. Elders and managers were drawn from merchants, manufacturers and skilled artisans, and it was through their use of the systems of congregational discipline and pew-renting that new migrants were socialised to the values and expected aspirations of the emerging industrial culture of the Lowlands.

For other migrants, coming over shorter distances, contact could be arranged with others (both laity and clergy) who had moved from the district. But the statutory system of 'testimonials' broke down in the demographic turbulence of the period, and large numbers of people moving from country to town were lost from the churches' view. With the population of a large city like Glasgow almost doubling every twenty years between 1780 and 1840, and that of smaller industrial towns in ten years or less, there was a need to develop effective methods of recruitment.

VI

The churches in urban society remained, as they had been in agrarian society, vital agencies of social stability and good order. Whilst the rural elites favoured Moderatism (and many Episcopacy), deprecated religious 'enthusiasm' (like revivals), and sought to worship with all ranks of their loyal parishioners, urban elites were increasingly excluding the 'unrespectable' from their congregations by charging high pew rents and by the development of more exclusive suburban congregations. Consequently, new urban 'agencies'[18] were developed to provide an 'outreach' into the alienated lower working classes and to recruit them for what might be called the churches' 'outer membership' — organisations in which rural migrants could be socialised into evangelical and civic culture and then encouraged to form their own self-financing congregations.

The first agency, and the one to remain the largest throughout modern history, was the Sunday school, popularised by Robert Raikes of Gloucester in the 1780s. By keeping child workers from running loose on the streets and fields on the Sabbath, and preventing them from burglarising worshippers' homes whilst attending church, the Sunday school attracted considerable attention from urban evangelicals. Initially using paid teachers, town councils sanctioned the establishment of 'Sabbath exercises' in Edinburgh, Aberdeen and Glasgow in 1786-7. In 1796-7, groups of dissenters again copied an

English idea for *gratis* Sunday schools, using volunteer teachers, and by the 1810s the Congregationalists were particularly active amongst working-class children in the larger towns. Whilst Moderate hostility to the movement checked growth during the Revolutionary and Napoleonic Wars, the Sabbath School Union for Scotland claimed by 1819 the affiliation of 567 schools with 39,000 scholars.

The Sunday school was followed by the development of other evangelical 'agencies'. Special churches were built for the working classes — whether on a territorial basis, or for groups like seamen. It was found that tract societies, which started operating in earnest in 1805-10, did not provide a 'follow-up' with the unchurched, and were superseded by 'visitation' or mission schemes where non-churchgoers were visited in their homes, urged to attend church, and encouraged to send their children to church day-school and Sunday school. The most famous early scheme was at St. John's Parish in the east end of Glasgow where in 1819 Thomas Chalmers initiated an experiment in replacing statutory poor-relief assessments and payments — which he regarded as undermining moral values — with voluntary donations dispensed parsimoniously after parochial visitation by elders and other helpers. Though the financial aspects of his experiment failed, the idea of 'aggressive visitation' became a central feature of urban evangelicalism in the nineteenth century. In 1824, one of Chalmers' admirers, David Nasmith, founded the Young Men's Society for Religious Improvement, and two years later the Glasgow City Mission; Nasmith exported his ideas to Dublin, London and overseas. At the very end of our period, in 1828-9, the temperance movement was imported from North America to Maryhill and Greenock from where a lawyer, John Dunlop, travelled Britain giving lectures on the evils of drink.

In this way, a machinery was being developed for evangelising the urban unchurched. The interdenominational and international character of the movement brought Scotland into the mainstream of Atlantic evangelicalism. From the earliest beginnings of *gratis* Sunday schools, English evangelicals like Charles Simeon and Rowland Hill were welcomed in Scottish pulpits. Equally, there was a great interchange with North America where the evangelical 'Great Awakenings' were inspirational to generations of Scottish presbyterian ministers. Religious revivals were not favoured by all evangelicals; there were many who, like Chalmers, were disturbed by evangelicalism's similarity with the libertarian ideas and methods (open-air assemblies, late-night meetings and tract distribution) associated with political radicals. But whilst Chalmers expressed fear of the 'brawny vigour' of the urban multitude, even his friends were becoming more disposed to encourage revivalism of the kind already seen amongst agricultural workers at Cambuslang and Kilsyth in 1742 and elsewhere in rural and village Scotland during this period.[19] By 1830, Chalmers' publisher, William Collins, was circulating a magazine which investigated the American revivals in search of the blueprint for manufacturing them in Scottish cities, but it was to be another thirty years before it could be tested.

## VII

In the eighty years after 1750, the religious map of Scotland underwent a radical transformation. Episcopacy was in severe decline in the northern half of the country, losing adherents from the lower ranks to presbyterianism (especially puritanical versions). Whilst the Scottish Episcopal Church became increasingly 'high church' in its liturgy, decoration and style, attracting probably a majority of the aristocracy and large landowners, there is much evidence that in-migrating 'low church' episcopalians from elsewhere in the British Isles (especially Ireland) found the Church doing comparatively little to accommodate industrial workers. For its part, presbyterianism was riven apart, with a third of Lowland Protestants joining the dissenting churches by 1830. Catholicism was growing again in the Lowlands as a result of Irish immigration, and though resources were slow to be provided during this period, native sectarianism helped to sustain Catholic cultural identity.

In addition, the process of religious pluralisation had given rise to a variety of smaller sects and churches. The most popular were products of schism from indigenous presbyterianism. Numerically most significant were the Congregationalist and Baptist churches, which developed strong localised support amongst disaffected presbyterians in the larger towns of the central Lowlands and in fishing communities in all parts of Scotland. The Methodist message proved popular, brought north initially by John Wesley and George Whitefield in the 1740s and 1750s, but the Methodist church was generally not. Native presbyterian churches were increasingly providing the same evangelical message, and with a few exceptions like the fishermen of Shetland, and migrant English and Irish workers in the vicinity of Glasgow and Airdrie, Methodist membership stayed very low (less than 1,400 in 1790 and under 4,000 forty years later).

Small sects of presbyterianism ebbed and flowed with the endemic schisms of the period. The Reformed Presbyterians, the descendants of the covenanters, recruited from patronage disputes, settling churches in many parts of the Lowlands (even as far west as Campbeltown), but suffered defections to the Secession and other churches. There were peculiar and still little-understood groups like the 'Lifters' and 'Non lifters' — small groups of Seceders who argued in the late eighteenth century over the precise point during the communion ceremony when the minister should raise the cup. The Scottish version of Joanna Southcote, Elspeth Simpson (Mrs Buchan), professed in the 1790s to be the 'woman clothed with the sun' (Revelation 12) who would preside over the end of the world; harried from parish to parish, the Buchanites (many recruited from the Relief Church) settled on a farm at Closeburn in Dumfriesshire where their numbers dwindled away. The social and economic turbulence of the period fomented a widespread though varied millenarianism — from the cathartic visions of Mrs Buchan, to the more regulated presbyterian version institutionalised in the Antiburghers' 'days of fast and humiliation'.

Even when religious enthusiasm was held in check, agricultural improvement and industrialisation had interacted with the rise of class consciousness to make religious values widely relevant. The values and culture of evangelicalism, in particular, were shared by merchants and miners, weavers and wrights, fishermen and farmers. At the same time, however, population growth coupled with the rise of class consciousness and the values of financial self-reliance and respectability, had made access to the ordinances of religion more difficult in both rural and urban districts, and created a large group who were alienated from the churches. Nevertheless, religious values and ideals did not become the sole preserve of the 'churched'. There remained a strong heritage of popular presbyterianism which laid the basis for sustained church recruitment in urban and industrial districts when the non-churchgoing population became, in the Victorian period, the target for the most aggressive proselytising of modern times.

## NOTES

1. H. McLeod, *Religion and the People of Western Europe, 1789-1970* (Oxford, 1981); R. Carwardine, *Trans-Atlantic Revivalism: Popular Evangelicalism in Britain and America, 1790-1865* (Westport, Connecticut and London, 1978).

2. E.R. Wickham, *Church and People in an Industiral City* (London, 1957); K.S. Inglis, *The Churches and the Working Classes in Victorian England* (London, 1963). A most important review of the whole debate, including Scotland, and providing an extensive bibliography, is H. McLeod, *Religion and the Working Class in Nineteenth-century Britain* (London. 1984).

3. H. Perkin, *The Origins of Modern English Society, 1780-1880* (London, 1969); A.D. Gilbert, *Religion and Society in Industrial England: Church, Chapel and Social Change, 1740-1914* (London and New York, 1976); A.D. Gilbert, *The Making of Post-Christian Britain: A History of the Secularization of Modern Society* (London and New York, 1980); E.P. Thompson, *The Making of the English Working Class* (Harmondsworth, 1968); and E. Hobsbawm, 'Religion and the rise of socialism', *Marxist Perspectives,* 1 (1978), pp. 14-33.

4. C.G. Brown, *The Social History of Religion in Scotland since 1730* (London, 1987), which covers many of the issues raised in this chapter; E.T. Davies, *Religion*

*in the Industrial Revolution in South Wales* (Cardiff, 1965); T.W. Laqueur, *Religion and Respectability: Sunday Schools and Working-Class Culture, 1780-1850* (New Haven, 1976); and C.G. Brown, 'Did urbanisation secularise Britain?', *Urban History Yearbook* 1988.

5. J. Mackay, *The Church in the Highlands, 563-1843* (London, 1914); A. Edgar, *Old Church Life in Scotland: Lectures on Kirk-Session and Presbytery Records* (Paisley and London, 1885 ); J. H.Gillespie, *Dundonald: A Contribution to Parochial History*, vol. 2 (Glasgow, 1939). On the issue of 'religiosity', see D.J. Withrington, 'Non-churchgoing, c.1750-c.1850: a preliminary study', *Records of the Scottish Church History Society*, xvii (1970); H.G. Graham, *The Social Life of Scotland in the Eighteenth Century* (London, 1901). See also M. Spufford, 'Can we can count the "godly" and the "conformable" in the seventeenth century?', *Journal of Ecclesiastical History*, 36 (1985).

6. For change in the parish, see J.M. McPherson, *The Kirk's Care of the Poor: With Special Reference to the North-east of Scotland* (Aberdeen, c. 1941); and J. Lindsay, *The Scottish Poor Law: Its Operation in the North-east from 1745 to 1845* (Ilfracombe, 1975). On party divisions in the Church of Scotland, see W.L. Mathieson, *Church and Reform in Scotland: A History from 1797-1843* (Glasgow, 1916); A.L. Drummond and J. Bulloch, *The Scottish Church 1688-1843: The Age of the Moderates* (Edinburgh, 1973); I.F. Maciver, 'The Evangelical Party and the Eldership in General Assemblies, 1820-1843', *Records of the Scottish Church History Society*, 20 (1980), pp. 1-29; and I.D.L. Clark, 'From protest to reaction: the Moderate régime in the Church of Scotland, 1752-1805', in N.T. Phillipson and R. Mitchison (eds.), *Scotland in the Age of Improvement* (Edinburgh, 1970), pp. 200-24. On popular religious protest, see K.J. Logue, *Popular Disturbances in Scotland 1780-1815* (Edinburgh, 1979); E. Richards, 'Patterns of Highland Discontent 1790-1860', in R. Quinault and J. Stevenson (eds.), *Popular Protest and Public Order* (London, 1974), pp. 75-114: R. Sher and A. Murdoch, 'Patronage and Party in the Church of Scotland, 1750-1800', in N. MacDougall (ed.), *Church, Politics and Society: Scotland, 1408-1929* (Edinburgh, 1983); R.B. Sher, 'Moderates, managers and popular politics in mid-eighteenth-century Edinburgh: the Drysdale "Bustle" of the 1760s', in J. Dwyer *et al* (eds.), *New Perspectives on the Politics and Culture of Early Modern Scotland* (Edinburgh, n.d.).

7. For religious change in the Highlands and Hebrides, see C.W.J. Withers, 'Education and Anglicisation: the policy of the SSPCK toward the Education of the Highlander, 1709-1825', *Scottish Studies*, 26 (1982), pp. 37-56; C.W.J. Withers, *Gaelic in Scotland 1698-1981* (Edinburgh, 1984); the very useful Chapter 3 in V.E. Durkacz, *The Decline of the Celtic Languages* (Edinburgh, 1983); J. Hunter, 'The emergence of the crofting community: the religious contribution 1798-1843', *Scottish Studies*, 18 (1974), pp. 95-116; J. Hunter, *The Making of the Crofting Community* (Edinburgh, 1976); and S. Bruce, 'Social change and collective behaviour: the revival in eighteenth-century Ross-shire', *British Journal of Sociology*, 34 (1983), pp. 554-72.

8. There is a dreadful paucity of research on Lowland religious schism and dissent during this period. Starting points include A.T.N. Muirhead, 'A Secession congregation in its community: the Stirling congregation of the Rev. Ebenezer Erskine, 1731-1754', *Records of the Scottish Church History Society*, xxii (1986), pp. 221-33; D.B.

Murray, 'The influence of John Glas', *Records of the Scottish Church History Society*, xxii (1984), pp. 45-56; and Brown, *Religion in Scotland*, pp. 23-44, 89-115. On religion and political radicalism, see H.W. Meikle, *Scotland and the French Revolution* (Edinburgh, 1912 and later reprints), especially pp. 194-213.

9. J. Sinclair (ed.), *The Statistical Account of Scotland*, 21 vols (Edinburgh 1791-99) 2, p. 202.

10. *Ibid.*, 1, p. 457.

11. *Ibid.*, 17 p. 534.

12. C.G. Brown, 'The costs of pew-renting: church management, church-going and social class in nineteenth-century Glasgow', *Journal of Ecclesiastical History*, 38, no. 3, July 1987.

13. Brown, *Religion in Scotland*, p. 83.

14. R.K. Donovan, 'Voices of distrust: the expression of anti-Catholic feeling in Scotland, 1778-1781', *Innes Review*, 30 (1979), pp. 62-76; I.A. Muirhead, 'Catholic emancipation: Scottish reactions in 1829' and 'Catholic emancipation in Scotland: the debate and the aftermath', both *Innes Review*, 24 (1973).

15. The motion at a public meeting in Glasgow, quoted in *Scots Magazine*, 41 (Feb. 1779), p. 107.

16. On the Catholic Church, see P.F. Anson, *The Catholic Church in Modern Scotland, 1560-1937* (London, 1937); P.F. Anson, *Underground Catholicism in Scotland, 1622-1878* (Montrose, 1970); J.E. Handley, *The Irish in Scotland, 1798-1845* (Cork, 1945); C. Johnson, *Developments in the Roman Catholic Church in Scotland, 1789-1829* (Edinburgh, 1983). On the presbyterian side, see C.W.J. Withers, 'Kirk, club and culture change: Gaelic chapels, Highland societies and the urban Gaelic subculture in eighteenth-century Scotland', *Social History*, 10 (1985), pp. 171-192.

17. Quoted in Johnson, *Catholic Church in Scotland*, p. 145.

18. For the development of evangelical agencies to 1830, see S. Mechie, T*he Church and Scottish Social Development, 1780-1870* (Oxford, 1960); C.G. Brown, 'The Sunday-school movement in Scotland, 1780-1914', *Records of the Scottish Church History Society*, 21 (1981), pp. 3-26; R.A. Cage and E.O.A. Checkland, 'Thomas Chalmers and urban poverty: the St. John's Parish experiment in Glasgow, 1819-1837', *Philosophical Journal*, 13 (1976), pp. 37-56; J.F. McCaffrey, 'Thomas Chalmers and social change ', *Scottish Historical Review*, 60 (1981), pp. 32-60; and, for the influence of Nasmith, C. Binfield, *George Williams and the Y.M.C.A.* (London, 1973).

19. On Lowland revivalism, see T.C. Smout, 'Born again at Cambuslang: new evidence on popular religion and literacy in eighteenth-century Scotland', *Past and Present*, 97 (1982), pp. 114-27; A. Fawcett, *The Cambuslang Revival: The Scottish Evangelical Revival of the Eighteenth Century* (London, 1971); and Carwardine, *Trans-Atlantic Revivalism.*

# CHAPTER 9

## *Schooling, Literacy and Society*

### Donald J. Withrington

From the mid-eighteenth century onwards there is a growing amount of information available on Scottish schooling, and it becomes increasingly possible
to make sensible and informed assessments of the extent and also of the calibre
of educational provision.

When the Scottish parochial schoolmasters met in and after 1749 to petition
Parliament for an increase in their stipends,[1] much diminished in value by
inflation, it became clear that, in the Lowlands at least, the centrepoint of
concern in educational discussion had shifted from the provision of schooling
to the questions of how to secure more stability in the teaching force (for there
was much movement from parish to parish in order to improve incomes,
however slightly), and how to ensure better styles and methods of teaching in
those appointed to the publicly-supported schools. In fact Parliament did not
enact any improvement in the schoolteachers' stipends, nor did it make any
parallel move to augment the stipends of ministers in the Established Church:
nonetheless, there are indications that in some areas (e.g. Wigtownshire,
Kirkcudbright)[2] the local landowners sympathised sufficiently with their
schoolmasters' plight to ensure that at least the legal minimum 100 merks
were paid regularly thereafter and frequently more than what was required by
law. There was, however, the opportunity for these school teachers to augment
their incomes even if stipend was not increased.

By the middle of the century new subjects, with a strongly vocational
emphasis, were gradually being introduced, firstly into burgh schools, then by
masters of initiative and ability into rural parochial schools.[3] They got the
support of heritors, magistrates and kirk sessions in doing so, and were often
given greater freedom to take in boarders, from elsewhere in Scotland, from
other parts of Britain and from overseas. Generally, parochial schoolmasters
were permitted to charge relatively high fees for such subjects as French or
geography or mensuration or geometry or navigation or book-keeping, and
these, together with substantial fees from boarders, gave the chance to add
considerably to otherwise meagre incomes.

What is also worth noting is that kirk sessions, at the same time, usually

163

insisted on maintaining at a very low level (or allowed only the most modest increases in ) the fees demanded for teaching the basic curriculum—reading, writing, arithmetic, Latin and church music. Inflation had actually reduced the real value of these fees but they were kept low in order to make schooling in these subjects as widely available as possible to all groups in the community. It was the able poor for whom the opportunity to learn Latin could be crucial, if they hoped to go to university and thus make their way in the world through one of the learned professions. In the course of the eighteenth century Latin had become much less important for the middle and upper classes whose careers did not generally depend on their attending the full degree course at university as regular or 'gowned' students; if they went to university in Scotland they could usually elect to take only those classes which they and their parents thought were properly useful and relevant to their intended employments.[4] It was at these groups that the new school subjects, and the adventurously modern courses at the new academies, were mainly aimed; it was for the able poor ( and not, as has been claimed, for the upper classes) that Latin was often preserved in later eighteenth-century parish schools, and for whom its disappearance was regretted elsewhere.[5] What we can discern, dimly at times before more and better evidence comes readily to hand in the 1790s with the publication of Sir John Sinclair's *Statistical Account*, is a wider diversity of schooling in the Lowlands in the decades after 1750—but also, and importantly, a much wider availability of schooling for all, whether at a modest or at a notably high academic level, at a considerable expense or remarkably cheap, in parish or burgh schools, in public or private academies, in subscription schools of all kinds, in private adventure schools for the refined education of the daughters of the lesser gentry and the socially-climbing merchants, or in those tucked away in the remoter corners of deeply rural parishes where young men on vacation from their college studies could teach the rudiments to the children of the lesser tenantry who farmed at considerable distance from the nearest parochial school.

## The Pattern in the Highlands

Surprisingly perhaps, there is actually more easily accessible evidence about schooling in the Highlands and Islands than in the Lowlands in mid-eighteenth century. Yet it has become customary (apart from in recent studies of the decline of the Gaelic language, and sometimes even there too)[6] virtually to write off the Highlands as all-but unschooled in the seventeenth and eighteenth centuries, even to claim that these areas would latterly depend almost entirely for what little schooling they could obtain on an outside agency

— namely, the Society in Scotland for the Propagation for Christian Knowledge. Here are two recent verdicts:[7]

> In the Highlands the main problem was simply that the 1696 Act had had little effect. Only in Argyll and in a few parishes along the western seaboard...had the act any real impact. (Withers, 1984)

> Schools were generally few and far between in the Highlands...even the Commissioners of Supply had failed to plant schools in 175 Highland parishes.... Through neglect, poverty, language and geography, the literacy of the Highlands lagged far behind the rest of Scotland until the late 19th century. (Houston, 1985)

The implications of both statements are seriously misleading. The evidence that is available to those who care to look for it runs strongly counter to these views. Houston in particular does his readers a grave disservice in retailing a gross misinterpretation of a comment made in 1758 by the SSPCK, that an extensive survey carried out in 1755 showed that there were 'no parochial schools in 175 parishes where Society's schools are erected'; in doing so he has unnecessarily perpetuated a crippling misunderstanding of Highland schooling which was quite specifically corrected some time ago.[8] In the 1750s and later the SSPCK defined 'parochial school' very narrowly, restricting the designation to a school whose master was paid at least the minimum stipend by heritors and tenants 'according to law'. Yet a parish might well have running through it a river or some other natural obstruction which meant hat it was not possible to provide widespread access to schooling on one site alone. In such a case (e.g. Monivaird in Perthshire) the legal stipend was therefore divided in two and the teachers so placed as to ensure the attendance of the greatest numbers of children. The Society declared that Monivaird had 'no parochial school', since no one master had 100 merks at least of stipend, and then threatened to withdraw its school for that reason. That heritors and tenants had here met the financial requirements made of them, that they had certainly obeyed the spirit of the law, that they had acted in order to maximise the opportunities for schooling in accordance with the Reformers' grand design to provide instruction for all, all this appears to have been lost on the SSPCK. Hence the need to be particularly careful in interpreting the Society's statement in 1758. As we shall see, there was much more schoolkeeping than has been assumed in the Highlands and Islands.

In fact, a good many of the original returns to the Society's enquiry of 1755 have survived, and there is pretty firm information there which relates to just over 200 parishes in twenty-three presbyteries. Many ministers did not bother to reply because they had no charity school and neither wished nor expected to have one.[9] Among the twenty-three presbyterial returns was one for Langholm, an entirely Lowland area in Dumfriesshire; while some 'mixed' Lowland-Highland presbyteries provided answers only for their more obviously Highland parishes, others sent in returns for all of theirs (for example, Alford, Auchterarder, Brechin, Fordoun, Fordyce, Forfar). Unfortunately we lack replies of any kind for ten Highland or Island presbyteries—Abertarff, Abernethy, Caithness, Kirkwall, Lochcarron, Nairn, Skye, Strathbogie, Uist, Weem; for some others only a few parish returns were sent or have survived (for example, only Durness, Farr and Tongue itself in the presbytery of Tongue). There are also pretty full replies from the presbyteries of Aberlour, Dornoch, Dumbarton, Dunkeld, Dunoon, Gairloch, Inverness, Kincardine O'Neil, Kintyre, Lorn and Mull, Cairston and North Isles in Orkney, and reports which cover all of Shetland. The extant returns for the Highlands and Islands form a good sample of parishes and represent a fine geographical spread.

If we use Withers' 'base-map' of parishes in the Gaeldom of that day to exclude the essentially Lowland parishes, and add in those for the Northern Isles, we are left with 105 parishes for our analysis.[10] Of these at least seventy-seven (73.3 per cent) had schools which were supported by landlords and tenants, whether or not they met the Society's too narrow definition of parochial schools; if we supplement the 1755 survey evidence from other sources (church records, estate papers, etc), then a total of eighty-eight parishes (83.8 per cent) had schools. This is a far cry indeed from the statement by Withers which was quoted earlier, and is in even sharper contrast to Houston's conclusion that schools were 'generally few and far between in the Highlands' in this period. Indeed, if we focus only on the mainland Highlands and the Inner Hebrides, then just over 80 per cent of parishes were providing their inhabitants with schooling of some kind, supported from public funds.

But we need not be content with these bare statistics: the 1755 returns, together with letters of the time sent to the SSPCK in Edinburgh, and further reports in 1760 and 1771-72 from visitors sent out by the Society, have a good deal more to tell us. There are many more instances where large Highland parishes, attempting to provide some schooling at least for widely-scattered populations, were not content to establish only one master at a legal salary.[11] Thus the united parish of Kilcalmonell and Kilberry in Kintyre reported 'five schools maintained by different heritors etc, and those at a much higher stent than what the law requires'; Kilmorie in Arran had '4 parochial schools situated at a convenient distance from one another'; in Kintyre again, in Killean and Kilchenzie, there was said to be 'no parochial school...but the tenants are in use to pay a stouck of Corn and some two stouks out of each merkland of old extent towards the support of their Schoolmasters' of whom there were 'three at the charge of the parish' as well as Society teacher. In the country part of Campbeltown parish—the town itself had a long-standing grammar school— there were small salaries for four district schools, each paid out of a common fund of contributions made by the tenants of those districts. In Walls in mainland Shetland the minister reported that ' I don't think there is one parochial school properly so called within the bounds of the Presbytery, that is a school with a legal standing salary. But in my parish I have several little schools in different corners supported by the voluntary contributions of the inhabitants'; and in Orkney, in the parish of Cross and Burness, similarly without a 'legal' parochial school, the minister wrote that in the more distant parts of the parish 'heritors and people gave encouragement to such as are usefull in the way of instructing the Poor who cannot be benefited by the Society's school'. The response from the presbytery of Gairloch noted that there were 'no parochial schools' in its bounds, but again it is wrong to assume that no schooling of any kind was available: the minister of Applecross, for instance, complained in his reply that 'the poor at a distance can not maintain their children at school' (but which school, and where?) and then went on to say that 'all the schools I see on this coast are of little service—few attend them at any time.'

Only Blair Atholl of all the parishes in the presbytery of Dunkeld has left us a response to the survey of 1755, but it is a highly informative one:[12]

> Within the parish there are no fewer than 7 schoolls at which were taught last winter and spring 250 schollars, viz at the parochiall schooll of Blair 50, at the Society's school at Petagown 52, at the schooll of Glengarry erected by the Factor on the forfeited estates of Strowan and Lochgary continued by the Exchequer 34, at the schooll of Glenerachty erected and continued in the same manner 35, at the schooll of Strathtummel the master of which gets no other encouragement than what he gets from the parents of his schollars 42, at the schooll of Glenfinder whose master is supported in the same manner 27 schollars, at the schooll of Bohespick supported in sd manner 10. Many of the schollars attending these by-schoolls are poor. I would therefore humbly propose that if the Society's funds will not admit of their giving salaries to such of the above schoollmasters as have no other subsistence but what they get from parents of their schollars, who are far from being in plentiful circumstance, they would at least order some supply in books for those poor schollars.

Not only do we find here evidence of a remarkable provision of schooling —with 250 at school and 3257 in the population in 1755, one in thirteen of the parish were being taught to read at least—the letter more than hints at criticism of SSPCK policies, which required it to support only a limited number of schools under direct Society management rather than to aid local initiatives and ensure greater continuity in schooling for a much larger number of children. This was not the only criticism of the Society's education policies in these mid-century records. In 1760 the moderator of the presbytery of

Gairloch wrote with some heat, in the name of that presbytery, to the clerk to the SSPCK in Edinburgh, William Ross:[13]

> We have before us a letter from the Protestant part of the parish of Glenelg desiring that we represent to you the hardship they are under for want of a proper school.... The necessaries of life are now so high that no man qualified for the teaching of youth can live by the salaries commonly granted by the Society—and the expense of education is such that very few of the people of better condition can afford to send their children to any great distance from themselves. The people of Glenelg, sensible of this and willing to do all the justice they are able to their children, have agreed among themselves, tho they can obtain no assistance from the Roman Catholics, who are by much the greatest part of the people of the Parish, to make up a sum not below eight pounds Sterling to help make a salary for a good sufficient schoolmaster, and to oblige themselves to continue said eight pounds yearly for seven years at least. And therefore beg the Honorable Society would add a sum not below ten pounds Sterling for the above space of seven years, more effectively to encourage such a school: for which they further oblige them to build a sufficient schoolhouse—for a shorter time they can neither get a schoolmaster to their satisfaction, nor think of being at the expense of building a schoolhouse... .

The parishioners were ready to provide as part-stipend a sum well beyond the minimum in law (in sterling 100 merks was roughly £5.11s) if the SSPCK would add a further £10. They believed that it needed the equivalent of 324 merks Scots, more than three legal salaries, to attract to Glenelg a 'good sufficient master'. Even so, the main issue was not the provision of schooling as such—as the Applecross minister had indicated five years earlier for that same area, teaching to some modest level was likely to be available in small schools serving the scattered communities of the region. What the Glenelg protestants wanted was a 'proper school'. The moderator's letter goes on to make their wishes more explicit, and is worth quoting at length:

> We cannot but agree with the honest People in wishing that your Plan of Schools was different from what it is, as we are persuaded that one good school would moderately speaking be greater use in the country than three of the present set of schools. As to the objection that your Schools are intended for the benefit of the poorer sort, you cannot, sir, but be sensible that the schools which are best for the children of the richer sort are likewise best for the poor. And where a school is so bad that it is not worth the richer people's while to send their children to it, the poor will reap little benefit by it. Besides that, the example of the richer sort is necessary to bring the poorer to send their children to school. We are therefore ready to join the honest people above in promising to you that the children of the poor shall have full justice done to them and make at least as good progress at such a school, as they can be supposed to do at any school in the present Establishment. And this being the case, and the People willing to contribute so heartily towards the encouragement of a schoolmaster, we presume the Honorable Society will judge it reasonable to

indulge them in a Schoolmaster who can teach Latin or anything else they incline to their children. And as to the objection that you are not empowered by the Constitution of your Society to have Latin etc taught in your schools, we humbly think, when you see from the above that the Spirit and Design of your Constitution is fully answered, that it would be an injury to imagine you capable of giving up the spirit and design of your Constitution for the letter of it. Besides it would be of the most pernicious consequences to discourage so laudable a spirit, as the Design must drop unless you support it.

Nothing in the SSPCK papers suggest that his letter had the slightest impact on the Edinburgh management of the Society. And, apparently, no account was taken elsewhere of similar attempts to erect and maintain grammar schools—and to pay over the odds for them, without financial help from the Society. In the Western Isles the parishes of South Uist, North Uist and Harris had pooled their stipends 'in erecting one good school instead of three trifling ones' and sited it in North Uist. At some point before 1760 two groups of Skye parishes (Kilmuir, Snizort and Portree; Bracadale and Duirinish) each combined to support a common school of quality, the former offering its master 300 merks in salary, the latter as much as 400 merks. When a survey of parishes was again made in 1770-71 the SSPCK visitor ignored the reasons behind these arrangements and merely noted that there was a parochial school in the parish in which it happened to be sited, and then entered 'no parochial school' in respect of the other contributing parishes![14]

In 1760, plans were afoot to have 'one great school at Pennigowan', with a master and a doctor able to teach Latin and Greek, to serve the two parishes of Mull and that of nearby Morven, and supported from the schoolmasters' stipends for all three. The visitors who reported this Mull proposal were sceptical about it, while showing some sympathy for these Highland parishes which—in their own terms and from their own knowledge and understanding of the locality—were trying to use public funds in the most advantageous way: the sticking point again was the visitors' interpretation of the function of parochial schools:[15]

> It were indeed much to be wished that some schools of this kind were instituted in different places of the Highlands but, although this scheme may answer very valuable purposes, yet it must bear hard on the common people, and can only serve those who can afford to send their children from them and pay board for them. By want of parochial schools the poor people must be left wholly destitute of their means of instruction.

Perhaps unknown to the two visitors, Hyndman and Dick, there were of course already 'schools of this kind' in the Highlands and Islands, and in the case of the projected school at Glenelg, 'full justice' was promised to be done at it for the children of the poor. Secondly, if the better off were able to send their children to a nearby school, keeping them at home or boarding them cheaply with kinsmen rather than sending them 'to Inveraray or any part of the Low Country, to be taught in a proper manner', then might not more money have been retained locally and used to fund more small elementary schools in the home parishes? Thirdly, as we have seen from the 1755 survey, many similar Highland parishes, if they had kept strictly to the rules for the legal establishment of parochial schools, would have greatly reduced the means of instruction for the poor in their localities: the value of a strictly legal establishment to the poor might be obvious enough in Lowland parishes where the only alternative to the cheap or free parish school might be expensive private schooling, but was the Lowland experience really relevant in this quite different situation?

The data we have for the later eighteenth century indicate that, apart from the Outer Hebrides and a very few mainland parishes where the poor inhabitants seem to have had only a meagre interest in educating their children, there was otherwise throughout the Highlands and Islands, and certainly in the Northern Isles, a deep concern to have children instructed by whatever means could be found, whether in publicly-supported parochial or other schools, in charity schools, or in schools paid for by the parents themselves. Much painstaking work remains to be done on education in the eighteenth-century Highlands, and on Lowland education too for that matter, before we can begin satisfactorily to answer some of the more difficult questions about it. Some better understanding of the actual provision of schooling, and of the impulses which inhibited or promoted it, is certainly a prerequisite. But, given the evidence we have been discussing, it is certainly unwise to be as dismissive of the educational efforts of Highland parishes as Dr. Houston has been, assuming that little or nothing could have been achieved from within and that everything must have depended, more rather than less, on the activities of outside agencies such as the SSPCK or the Gaelic societies.[16] That said, Dr. Houston has correctly reminded us recently that not all educational activity was to be found in school-groups taught in a fairly structured and formal way. Yet it seems to me that the family-tutoring to which he is mainly referring was generally confined to children who were too young or perhaps too unhealthy to be able to travel any distance to a school; save in the Northern Isles, and perhaps not always there, such home instruction was not expected to be a substitute for schooling. For all of Dr. Houston's doubts in the matter, school provision assuredly remains the best single indicator of education for literacy in the Scottish population. While we are on this point, however, we should add another feature of home life in presbyterian Scotland which forced schoolchildren to practise and perfect new reading skills learned elsewhere: the fact that it was still common in the eighteenth century for parents on Sundays to have their children read to them passages from the Bible; by all accounts this was a regular practice more often found in the rural Lowlands than in western Gaeldom, just as family tutoring was much more likely to be found in the Northern Isles than in the Western Isles. Such factors indeed, rather than lack of schooling as such, may help to account for the low levels of literacy which are reported from the Outer Hebrides.

## Perspectives in the 1790s

It is not until the 1790s, and the compilation of the *Statistical Account*, that we find another source which offers even better coverage of education, this time in Highlands and Lowlands alike. The continuing plight of ill-paid parochial schoolmasters brought renewed calls for legislation, not only to improve incomes but also to force landlords to provide more than one parochial school in large and populous parishes where a single school was entirely inadequate to meet the demand for cheap and accessible schooling. Some ministers wished to see the State act to extend school provision, not because schooling was lacking in their localities but because they wanted to offset or remove the influence of secular or dissenting schools, to ensure that the Established Church would regain its control of and rights of inspection over all schools in their parishes, as a direct means of countering the radicalism and the 'immorality' (that is, social or political irresponsibility) which were so closely associated in the 1790s with all non-Establishment groups and agencies.

But what can the *Account* tell us about schooling and literacy? Unfortunately it was rather late in the day when Sinclair added questions on education to the lists of queries which were sent out to his correspondents;[17] by then a good number of the earlier returns (1790-91) had already been prepared and sent in. And Sinclair gave little or no direction to the ministers, when he did add schooling as a topic, about those aspects which he thought they should highlight. Thus, for example, there was no specific request to report on levels of literacy. As a result, the *Account* offers a rather mixed bag of commentaries, sometimes too constrained and too narrowly-focused to be as helpful as they might otherwise have been. Having been asked about parish schooling, a number of ministers decided to enter information only about the parochial school and about the 'official' parochial master, leaving out entirely any discussion of other schools (which we can discover, from other sources, certainly existed in their parishes). Yet, even if it is more patchy and more anecdotal than might be wished, we can still glean much of value from the *Account*. In some areas of the country—for example, the bounds of one presbytery perhaps—the ministers appear to have agreed among themselves a particular style of response to Sinclair's enquiries, and they then often set down their information in such a way that it is easily possible to make some statistical analysis of the data.

In the county of Argyll, 11 out of 22 parishes included figures on school attendance (some, such as Campbeltown and Inveraray, cautious estimates) and we find that, in these 11 parishes, an average of at least 1 in 12.8 of the population was at school. Again, 21 out of 28 parishes in north and west Perthshire provided attendance figures, this time giving an average of as many as 1 in 8.2 at school. Only 6 parishes in the remainder of Perthshire gave details of school attendance—these show 1 in 12.3 at school, a proportion with which the ministers nonetheless seemed well satisfied. Three parishes in Midlothian and 6 in East Lothian similarly produced evidence of school attendance, of 1 in 11.2 in the former and 1 in 12.0 in the latter. We have this kind of information only for 3 parishes in Dunbartonshire—Luss, Roseneath and Row—and together they were schooling as many as 1 in 7.8 of their inhabitants. Of the town-parish of Dumbarton itself it was said, 'school fees are very low, so that any person has an opportunity of following any branch of learning'. Only one 'stray' return from the remoter Highlands quotes attendances: the parish of Glenelg could boast 1 in 10.7 of its population at school. In Stirlingshire, meanwhile, 5 parishes averaged 1 in 12.9 at school, and the ministers of 2 others had revealing comments to make about the educational attainments of their localities. Of St Ninian's, near Stirling, it was said:

> Some of our farmers (ie tenants, smallholders) have been favoured with a liberal education. A few of them have been instructed in the rudiments of the Latin tongue. Almost all of them have been taught writing and arithmetic, as well as to read the English language with understanding and ease... .

while the 'education and manners of our manufacturers' were very similar to the farmers'. The return for the upland parish of Campsie reminds us that education did not need to stop with the end of ordinary schooling: large numbers there went to night classes 'wholly made up of grown persons who attend for the purpose of writing, arithmetic, etc,' the implication being that they were building on reading skills learned earlier at school.[18]

Direct references to reading literacy are scattered throughout the contributions to Sinclair's survey, from many different parts of Scotland. While this information will need to be supplemented from other sources (such as the increasing number of Presbyterian visitation reports to be found in church records) before it is possible to attempt any precise assessment of schooling and its relation to the incidence of reading and writing literacy, the indications are clear that in many very different areas of the country, literacy in reading at least was very widespread. Readers of the *Account* must be struck by the matter-of-fact way in which high levels of literacy are reported—with no obvious indication of special pride in their achievement, more as a normal expectation which had been quietly fulfilled. A few examples must suffice. 'There is scarcely a child of 8 or 9 years of age that cannot read pretty distinctly' (Cleish, Kinross); 'besides, if their children can read English, write, and understand a little of arithmetic, they think them sufficiently well educated' (Inverchaolain, Argyll); I believe there is no native of this parish who has not been taught to read' (Bendochy, Perthshire); 'Scarcely any fail to put their children to school to learn English, writing and arithmetic' (Dalmeny, West Lothian); 'a common labourer earns enough to give his family an education; they are all taught to read and write, and many of them to keep accounts' (Walston, Lanarkshire); 'Fees:...reading alone 1s 6d or as it is commonly paid by the children of the labouring people who form the great proportion of the school, $1\frac{1}{2}$ d. per week' (Duddingston, Midlothian); 'All of the people can at least read the Bible: and the greatest part of the young men, whose parents could afford but little for their education, attend the schoolmaster in the winter evenings, who, for a small consideration, teaches them writing and the common rules of arithmetic, by which means they acquire good habits and become useful as farm and family servants' (Pencaitland, Midlothian); 'The language principally spoken in this parish is Gaelic. In the height of the parish, very few of the inhabitants understand any other language. But in the lower end of the parish, many of those being taught to read and write at school, can transact ordinary business in English' (Kiltarlity, Inverness-shire).[19]

The bulk of the reports in the *Account* say nothing directly about levels of literacy and do not give sufficient details of school rolls and school attendance to assess these with any accuracy. Nor is it likely to be a fruitful exercise to place against the quotations above others from the less well-favoured districts, where poverty or language restricted access to schools, where parents were more indifferent to their children's education, and so on. Poverty certainly did not always remove the possibility of being schooled—far from it; and language was no necessary barrier to learning to read. For instance, most inhabitants of the parish of Urray in Ross-shire were 'at pains to read the Gaelic New Testament and Psalm Book' while several could read the English Bible too.[20] There were Lowland parishes which felt themselves educationally deprived, and there were Highland parishes with remarkably well-educated and literate populations.

But the evidence from the 1790s should at the least save us from repeating those untenable generalisations which have characterised so much of the writing on Scottish schooling, either adulatory or damning: Scottish education did not 'emerge from the 18th century in good shape' nor was there 'general discontent' with it; and we should be very wary of assuming that there could be no substance at all in contemporary claims about the relatively high literacy rates which could be found in Scotland, for that again is clearly mistaken.[21]

For the 1790s, just as for the 1750s, historians must strain to make their interpretative best out of incomplete and sporadic data. But in the first three decades of the next century there appeared comprehensive and elaborate surveys, dealing directly and indeed exclusively with education, and so planned as to permit at least simple statistical analyses of the data they produced. We must now turn to the first of these, which was completed in 1818.[22]

## The 1818 Survey

Henry Brougham, in the aftermath of the Napoleonic Wars, and much troubled by the social and political disruptions of the time, had persuaded the House of Commons in 1818 to set up a Select Committee to investigate the provision that existed — or did not exist — for the education of the poor. The inquiry began with London, and was then extended to the remainder of England and Wales at the same time as the General Assembly was asked to organise replies from every Established parish minister in Scotland. The ministers were invited to describe the provision of schools, whether any special arrangements were made for the education of the poor, what endowments if any were available for the support of schools in which the poor were educated and whether or not their schooling was free, and to add any observations on how well or not, both formally and informally, the instruction of the poor in the locality was managed. *A Digest of Returns* was published in 1821, containing extracts from or précis accounts of the returns, with summary tables constructed from the information that had been gathered.

The clerk to the committee began with the English data with which he was more familiar and only then proceeded to prepare the digest for Scotland. In setting out the parochial returns for each Scottish county, the clerk used the same classifications as in the English section, 'endowed schools' and 'other institutions,' but refined this further in the summary table for each county into 'parochial schools' and 'unendowed day-schools'. When he prepared the final table, however, a listing by county for the whole of Scotland, we find still more refinement, with entries for 'parochial schools' and 'endowed schools' in one grouping, another for 'dames' schools' and 'ordinary endowed schools', and a third containing a column of entries under 'Sunday schools'. Faced with quite detailed responses relating to an educational structure with which he was unfamiliar, in the Scottish section, the clerk proceeded to make some very curious allocations under the various headings. He found especial difficulty in trying to define what was an 'endowed school', even when the category 'parochial school' had been established separately. Was a school properly 'endowed' only if it were established on a mortification, with a stated and secured salary being paid out of the accrued interest? In which category, and was it 'endowed', did one place a school not described by the minister as parochial, yet one in which a yearly stipend was paid by the heritors or by heritors and tenants, and was to all intents and purposes seemingly permanent? Should one classify as 'endowed' what is often described as a subscription school, formed under a trust deed and with accrued funds for its support — even if the greatest part of those funds were gathered (subscribed) year by year? In the end, and frequently for reasons that are not at all obvious from the data, very similar institutions were variously listed as 'endowed' and 'unendowed'. For example, if a minister described a side-school established under the 1803 act and himself called it a parochial school, then it was likely to be listed as a 'parochial school'; but if in another return the same kind of school, with salary paid out of the legal fund for schooling in that parish, were merely designated an additional school supported by the principal heritor or heritors, it often was categorised as 'endowed' or, if it were described in a way which hinted that it might not be secure or permanent, then it might well be entered as 'unendowed' and lumped in with all the small private adventure schools.

SSPCK schools, one would think, would not be a problem. Yet while they were generally entered as 'endowed schools', this was certainly not always so. And the clerk's treatment of the Scottish burgh schools — sometimes, and even more confusingly for him, described as academies (altogether different institutions from the English dissenting or private academies) — is bewildering; they are sometimes entered as 'parochial schools', sometimes as 'endowed schools', not infrequently even as 'unendowed schools'. Moreover, the burgh school often had independent or near-independent departments each of which was quite commonly described as a school (classical school, writing school, English school, mathematical school, etc). In the summary tables we find that such schools might be listed as one institution (for example, Dollar Academy with four distinct schools) or as several (virtually the same descriptions of the establishments at Dunbar and Haddington are entered respectively as two schools and one). Even more puzzling perhaps was the clerk's treatment of schools in Dunfermline. Here 'six schools supported partly by charitable endowment' are mysteriously categorised as 'parochial', yet schools noted as 'supported by public bodies' (and very likely to include the town council's burgh schools) are, almost unbelievably, allocated to the 'unendowed' list. Elsewhere if a minister wrote that he had two or three or four parochial schools, it was customary to record them as such: but when the minister of Holywood parish in Dumfriesshire wrote that he had 'three parochial teachers' rather than three parochial schools, that parish was credited with two 'parochial schools' and an 'endowed' one.

And there are other anomalies too: mistakes have been made in transferring figures from the extended digest to the summary tables; some glaring omissions from the tabulated information (including eighty private schools missed out in the return for Glasgow); and strange variations in practice in judging what figure to put in for descriptions such as 'a few other schools' or 'some men and women teach small schools' — usually given as three, but not always so, and sometimes ignored.

The tabulations therefore are constructed from dubiously-interpreted data, and are inconsistent and even obtuse in the categorisations employed. As they stand, they are likely to be very misleading — and are virtually unusable. Yet it is these same summary tables that have mainly been taken at face value by historians of education, while the original and dependable data in the digest have been ignored. It has been customary to quote the 'national' summary to show that the once proud, legally-supported, 'state' school system of Scotland was incapable any more of fulfilling its intended role, for the relevant table reveals that there were only 942 parochial schools teaching 54,161 pupils while 2222 private adventure schools (not counting dames' schools) taught 106,627. In particular, E.G. West has used the 1818 tables to argue the case that it was private-enterprise schooling which was mainly responsible in Scotland for the sheer extent and the marginally superior effectiveness of Scottish nineteenth-century education.[23] Not only is the basis for such a conclusion now thrown into very serious doubt, but, in E.G. West's own interpretation of another item in the summary — that 212 'endowed schools' in Scotland were teaching 10,177 pupils — he makes his own extraordinary error. Here he equates these with the richly-endowed and increasingly exclusive grammar and public schools of England, and assumes that they were used only by the wealthy upper and upper-middle classes in Scotland; in fact the schools which are entered under this heading in the Scottish tables were most often established on modest mortifications and were primarily intended, in most instances, for the free schooling of the parish poor.

The invaluable evidence in the *Digest,* not least in the quotations from the ministers' comments which are recorded there, is too good to pass by. To be properly useful for our present study, however, the statistical data needed to be reworked and new tables constructed according to some simple but apposite guidelines in framing the categories of schools. In the first instance, five headings were selected:

(i)  parochial/ burgh schools (that is, all schools which were set up under the acts of 1696 and 1803 and all 'official' burgh schools set up by town councils)

(ii) other publicly-funded schools (all schools other than those under (i) which had salaries paid by heritors and magistrates or had part-salaries and schoolhouses provided by them; and schools under trust-deeds which were directly controlled by the heritors or magistrates.)

(iii) schools supported out of mortifications, donations by others than heritors or magistrates, subscription schools set up under long-term or permanent trusts (unless the trustees were town councils and the schools were really the town schools differently organised).

(iv) schools supported by national or regional charitable organisations (for example, SSPCK, Royal Bounty, Edinburgh Gaelic Society, etc).

(v) private or adventure schools with no offical support, whose teachers were entirely dependent on fee-income from the parents of their scholars.

By the time the new summary tables were constructed from the individual parish returns, however, it seemed unnecessary (and historically misleading) to separate (ii) from (i), because the entries under (ii) were often hardly to be distinguished at all from 'parochial' or 'burgh' schools. They were schools intended for the behoof of the community as a whole, and they too could be judged to be 'publicly-funded' since the basis for their funding — from heritors' purses and from town council monies — was generally indistinguishable from that which supported the official public schools, and they were almost always set up in order to extend the community-based public schooling available to the whole inhabitants. The tables on the next page are based therefore on four categories — schools directly supported by heritors and burgh councils; schools supported from mortifications and donations; charitable society schools; and schools set up on adventure and for private gain.

Here we have a quite different picture from that represented in the summary tables prepared by the clerk to the Commons committee. Only half of the school population was being taught in private adventure schools, not the two-thirds usually quoted. And there were not twice as many pupils in private as in public schooling: only 40 per cent more if we compare the adventure school population with that for the parochial and burgh schools, only 20 per cent if we compare private schools with all the schools supported from funds which were intended to provide for the instruction of the community as a whole (heritors, magistrates, bequests) and were under community management. Only in the central-west region was a majority of the school population in private schools; indeed, two thirds of pupils did go to adventurers. In contrast, a majority of attenders in the Borders went to the public schools. In the Highlands alone was there substantial attendance in charity schools.

The proportions of the population at school in the various regions produce some surprises too. They were at their highest in the industrialising and

*People and Society in Scotland*

*Table 1(A): Numbers Attending Various Types of School*
        *(i) publicly funded              (ii) supported by gifts and bequests*
     *(iii) funded by charity societies   (iv) private, supported only by  fees*

| | Population in region | at school | Ratio in school | (i) | (ii) | (iii) | (iv) |
|---|---|---|---|---|---|---|---|
| Highlands | 445978 | 45231 | 9.86 | 15784 | 1301 | 12316 | 15830 |
| North-East | 335237 | 27952 | 11.99 | 11256 | 2698 | 1360 | 12638 |
| Fife, Lothians | 203903 | 22645 | 9.57 | 9714 | 2238 | 126 | 10567 |
| Central, West | 488475 | 64451 | 7.58 | 15754 | 4069 | 477 | 44151 |
| Borders | 194121 | 22750 | 8.53 | 12936 | 927 | 325 | 8562 |
| | 1667714 | 183029 | 9.11 | 65444 | 11233 | 14604 | 91748 |

*Table 1(B): Proportions  (%) of Pupils in Each Type of School*

| | (i) | (ii) | (iii) | (iv) |
|---|---|---|---|---|
| Highlands | 34.90 | 2.88 | 27.23 | 35.00 |
| North-East | 40.27 | 9.65 | 4.87 | 45.21 |
| Fife, Lothians | 42.90 | 9.88 | 0.56 | 46.67 |
| Central, West | 24.44 | 6.31 | 0.74 | 68.50 |
| Borders | 56.86 | 4.07 | 1.43 | 37.13 |
| | 35.76 | 6.14 | 7.98 | 50.13 |

*Note*: In the tables above the following counties are included in each region.

*Highlands*: Argyll, Bute, Perth, Nairn, Inverness, Ross & Cromarty, Sutherland, Caithness, Orkney, Shetland.
*North-East*: Angus, Kincardine, Aberdeen, Banff, Moray.
*Fife, Lothians*: Fife, East, Mid and West Lothian.
*Central, West*: Clackmannan, Kinross, Stirling, Dumbarton, Lanark, Renfrew, Ayr.
*Borders*: Berwick, Roxburgh, Selkirk, Peebles, Dumfries, Kircudbright, Wigtown.

urbanising districts of the central and western area, but were notably lower in the mainly agricultural counties of eastern Scotland; with the Highlands as well as the Borders occupying the middle ground. There was also, but not shown in the table, much variation in school attendance, county by county, the lowest being noted for Shetland and the highest for Lanarkshire including

Glasgow. Of 33 counties, 12 had fewer than one-tenth of their inhabitants at school, all of these (save West Lothian) in the Highlands and Islands and in the north-east; only 4 counties showed more than one-eighth at school–Argyll, Kinross, Kirkcudbright and Roxburgh. The average for the whole country was 1 in 9, no mean achievement; but that average covers up markedly low attendances in Inverness-shire (in the Ross-shire and Inverness-shire Isles generally), Caithness, and, rather surprisingly, in Banffshire, Aberdeenshire, Kincardine and Angus. These very considerable variations, their causes and effects, deserve further study on another occasion.

There was, then, in the bulk of Scotland a great deal of schooling being carried on. But were the poor getting their fair share of it? In fact, one question put to the ministers in 1818 was whether or not the poor in their parishes had 'sufficient means' of schooling. The question was ambiguous and in consequence received diverse answers. One large group thought that it referred to the availability or not of instruction, purely as a matter of geography (was the parochial school too distant from home to be easily attended?). Another concluded that the crucial issue was ability to pay fees, and there is much talk of the disincentive of poverty, about gallant efforts to educate children by parental frugality (even the selling of clothing), about the widespread use of parochial funds to pay the school fees of the poor.

The ministers' replies for the major cities are especially illuminating and strangely consistent: 'the poorer classes are abundantly provided with the means of education' (Aberdeen); 'All the poorer classes are within reach of some schools ...and willing to make considerable sacrifices to procure education for their families' (Dundee); 'Every child has easy access to any of the schools, either gratis or for a very small fee ... . The numerous schools which exist in the city afford ample means of instruction to the poor, of which they avail themselves' (Edinburgh); 'The poorer classes in the city have easy access either to gratis schools, or to others on paying a comparatively small fee to the teacher' (Glasgow). One or two more replies for new industrialising areas should be added: 'The means of education are accessible to the most indigent of the parish' (Port Glasgow); 'The means of education are so ample, that where children are not educated it must be from extreme regardlessness in themselves or gross negligence in their parents' (Gorbals); 'At present, on account of the stagnation of trade and other causes, many of the parents have been under the necessity of withdrawing their children from school, but this will be only temporary, and will cease when the cause is removed' (Wemyss, Fife).

But in remoter districts of the Highlands, and the Islands, the pattern was different. We need only to refer to Ross and Cromarty to exemplify this: 'The poor are very desirous of education, but the tenants residing at a distance from the parochial school are unable to derive any benefit from it' (Glenshiel); 'The situation of the parochial school does not afford the means of education for the poor' (Lochs, Lewis); 'The poorer classes, owing to the distance from the parochial school, and the great poverty of many of them, are deficient in the means of instruction' (Stornoway). But was the parochial the only school?

Some Highland parishes, however, sent in replies which showed that their means of education were 'sufficient' (Ardchattan and Muckairn, Argyll; Glenisla in Angus; Cromdale, Inverness-shire; Kintail, Ross-shire; Clyne and Kildonan in Sutherland) and several Isles ones too (Evie and Rendall, Firth and Stenness, and Hoy and Graemsay in Orkney; Uist in Shetland). Others wrote powerfully about lack of means, but sometimes without giving all the relevant information. Thus Inverchaolain in Argyll, which had as many as 1 in 5.2 of its young inhabitants actively learning, was said to have a parochial school which 'cannot afford the means of education to one-sixth of the children', a very high ratio in any case, but the report omitted to mention a second public school and an adventure school paid for by the tenants alone. The minister of Urquhart and Glenmoriston complained that 'from the local situation of the parochial school the means of education are deficient', yet he managed to omit to say that there were two side schools paid for by the heritors and tenants and also two SSPCK schools.

This emphasis on the parochial school is a noticeable feature of a good many returns from Highland ministers, heavy with the implication that the education of the poor depended on their having access to it; perhaps because the kirk session might pay fees for the poor there but not elsewhere, perhaps because it was only there that instruction in subjects beyond the elementary was possible at very cheap rates. In general, Lowland writers were less committed to the idea that the poor could only get reasonable access to education in publicly-supported schools, though many shared the concept that there should be sufficient public schooling for all in the parish, including the poor. To this attachment to one traditional policy was added another: that the only secure moral and religious training was to be had in public schooling under the direct supervision of the Established Church. In particular, the poor should not be forced to look for their education in private schools taught by non-believers or (even more dangerous perhaps) in schools taught by seceders or dissenters. The minister of Kinnellar in Aberdeenshire echoes a comment which we have met already in the *Statistical Account*: 'In too many parishes, proper encouragement is not given to that very useful class of men, the parochial schoolmasters...it affords opportunity to itinerant sectaries to set up schools, which in some cases have a very bad effect, both on the moral and the religious opinions of the rising generation'.

Here is one cause of Thomas Chalmers' plea for the improvement of the parochial school system and its extension into the large towns, published in 1819, as a counterweight to the political disorder and moral debasement he saw there.[24] Since an extended parochial system would naturally be under the inspection and supervision of the national church, the General Assembly was an enthusiastic advocate of more and better parish schooling of that kind. Indeed, in estimating the need for additional schools, Chalmers and his supporters tended to ignore or discount secular or dissenting establishments.

It was all but inevitable that the publication of the *Digest* of the returns from the 1818 survey would cause a stir, with its message — taken at face value — about the low state of the parochial school system in comparison with that of the private (including sectarian) schools. It was used to persuade the General Assembly to set up a new education committee, 'for increasing the means of education and religious instruction...particularly in the Highlands and Islands and in large and populous cities where, in these times, the children of the poor demand the most careful and deliberate action'. Yet, as we have seen, the cities and even the new conurbations reported in 1818 that they were well supplied with schooling. What was very upsetting to the Church, now beginning to come under the spell of Dr. Thomas Chalmers and his determination that renewal of the Church in the towns could only be achieved by injecting the community-led parochial tradition into them, was that the great majority of town schools were outside and beyond Church influence or supervision. As a result, the 1818 survey was used to shock the Church and its supporters into action, and the most was made of its bad news in order to force as swift a reaction as possible. The survey data were certainly a stimulus to an Inverness charitable school society to initiate its own reading-survey of the Highlands and Islands, and to report its saddening results in the pamphlet, *the Moral Statistics of the Highlands and Islands*, in 1826: in the north-west Highlands and the Hebrides, an estimated 70 per cent illiteracy; in the middle and northern mainland, 40 per cent illiteracy; in Perthshire and Argyll, 30 per cent; but in non-Gaelic speaking Orkney and Shetland, only 12 per cent.[25] But how reliable are these much quoted findings?

The number of replies to the Inverness society's questionnaire was surprisingly limited, and there are clear hints that some ministers may not have responded because they had good and sufficient schools in their parishes and would have no interest in applying for a charity school to the society. Yet the replies which did appear were nonetheless used, by extrapolation, to construct estimated results for the whole of the Highlands and Islands. It is possible, using the reworked data for the 1818 survey, to calculate the average school attendance for parishes which made returns to the Inverness questionnaire and similar averages for the remaining Highland parishes (which did not respond) county by county:

*Table 2: Proportion of Population at School, Highland Counties 1818.*

| County | Proportion of Population at School (1 in…) | | County |
|--------|---------------------|----------------|--------|
|        | *'Moral Stats'* parishes | Other parishes | |
| Argyll | 8.1 | 7.5 | 7.7 |
| Inverness | 15.7 | 11.3 | 13.8 |
| Nairn | 11.3 | 11.3 | 11.3 |
| Ross | 12.2 | 8.2 | 10.5 |
| Sutherland | 12.3 | 10.1 | 10.8 |
| Caithness | 11.8 | 11.9 | 11.8 |
| Orkney | 18.7 | 10.0 | 10.4 |
| Shetland | 31.9 | 14.1 | 16.9 |

All four Nairn ministers had responded, as did nearly all the Caithness ones. Elsewhere, however, this was not so. The table demonstrates that there was a marked difference in school attendance in many counties between sets of parishes which did or did not reply to the Inverness Society's circular. But, as has been noted, the compilers of the Inverness report imagined the returns they received to be entirely representative of their districts, and they constructed their final statistics accordingly. The result has been that the picture of Highland schooling they gave us is, almost certainly, much blacker than it could and should have been. And yet the *Moral Statistics* have been taken at face value and wearisomely used, for their own purposes, by contemporaries who for political and religious reasons found their 'message' very advantageous, and later by educational historians with or without particular axes to grind. Here is another source which needs to be used with much more care than it usually gets.

Many of its supporters were to weigh in on the Church's side. In 1827, in a well-known article on Scottish education, we find even Henry Cockburn agreeing that 'education is not nearly so much under the protection of the public authorities as it ought to be'.[26] However, Henry Brougham, who in 1818 had been very warmly in favour of legislation for an extension to the Scottish parochial system(and was preparing to press for the introduction of a Scottish-style parish schooling in England), was soon shifting his ground. Much to the Established Church's disgust, in the late 1820s and the early 1830s he was using the 1818 reports — for England and Wales, as well as for Scotland — to claim that educational deficiency was being quickly abated and would be best overcome by Parliament leaving the matter more or less alone. By the early 1830s the Liberals could not afford to upset their supporters among the dissenters. More than that, Brougham had been genuinely surprised and impressed by the remarkable response to educational need, shown by private schoolteachers, in filling the gaps.[27] While Chalmers and other evangelical churchmen were being fired anew into a furious commitment to the philosophy of 'state' schooling under the state church, so the new Liberal government after 1832 waned very markedly in enthusiasm for it. Meanwhile argument after argument used the 1818 summary tables and the *Moral Statistics* to point up the supposed educational deprivation of Scotland, at least in the Highlands and in the large towns. On 9 July 1834 an address to the House of Commons led to yet another questionnaire on schooling being sent out to the parish ministers. We shall move just outside our period to glance at this, because for the first time a government enquiry asked directly for information on literacy, 'a Return, showing how many children of each Sex in the Parish, under Five years of age, have been taught to read or are now learning to read; how many Children of each Sex, between Five and Fifteen years of age, have been taught to read or are learning to read; and how many of such Children have been taught to write or are now learning to write'.[28]

## The 1834 Survey

No report was written and presented to Parliament, only in due course an *Abstract of the Answers and Returns* with some very meagre remarks on the treatment of the statistics. While some parish returns were obviously wonderfully full and their ministers had gone to great pains to get the figures that were asked for, others were not. A few parishes made no returns at all; some gave only minimal information. Others did what they could in difficult circumstances (for example, in city centre parishes); many produced the information they had to hand and made little attempt to get any more (for example, sending in minimal figures for the parochial school, none on other schools in the parish). The compiler of the *Abstract* had done his best, using extrapolation ('the usual rules of proportion') to make a reasonable stab at producing sensible estimates where there were gaps. We can use the same grouping of counties as before to summarise the returns filled out in this way. The figures in brackets (Table 3, overleaf) show the proportions in the whole population (1 in...) who were attending, reading and writing.

But was extrapolation and the fairly frequent use of estimates likely to blur realities? It seemed worth checking Table 3 against another, using only complete or near complete answers to the queries, and then grouping them as before (Table 4). The two sets of figures, happily, show the same general trends. The main results are clear. By 1834, and perhaps much earlier, the

*Table 3: Learning to Read and Write, Scotland, 1834 (A)*

|  | Population | Largest Attendance (1834) | | Reading or learning to read | | Writing or learning to write | |
|---|---|---|---|---|---|---|---|
| Highlands, Islands | 554539 | 69642 | (7.96) | 81354 | (6.82) | 36681 | (15.12) |
| North-East | 431603 | 50353 | (8.57) | 70238 | (6.14) | 36961 | (11.68) |
| Fife, Lothians | 407670 | 62940 | (6.48) | 63195 | (6.45) | 32417 | (12.58) |
| Central, West | 725981 | 68374 | (10.62) | 99391 | (7.30) | 44571 | (16.29) |
| Borders | 245321 | 35489 | (6.91) | 38519 | (6.37) | 21743 | (11.28) |
|  | 2365114 | 284898 | (8.30) | 352697 | (6.71) | 172373 | (13.72) |

*Table 4: Learning to Read and Write, Scotland, 1834 (B)*

|  | Population | Largest Attendance (1834) | | Reading or learning to read | | Writing or learning to write | |
|---|---|---|---|---|---|---|---|
| Highlands, Islands | 203843 | 23311 | (8.74) | 33705 | (6.05) | 15347 | (13.28) |
| North-East | 101098 | 12231 | (8.27) | 20951 | (4.83) | 11196 | (9.03) |
| Fife, Lothians | 39845 | 5057 | (7.88) | 6482 | (6.15) | 3130 | (12.73) |
| Central, West | 193071 | 18015 | (10.72) | 33702 | (5.73) | 13505 | (14.30) |
| Borders | 55020 | 7163 | (7.68) | 10906 | (5.04) | 5585 | (9.85) |
|  | 592877 | 65777 | (9.01) | 105746 | (5.63) | 48763 | (12.16) |

provision of schooling was well up to the contemporary expectation which claimed that, if a country had 1 in 8 of its population at school, then it was meeting its educational responsibilities. These tables show that only in the Central, West region of Scotland was this not so. Yet the highest attendance figures in any one short period do not themselves tell us absolutely how many children were benefiting from schooling. There was seasonal attendance and regular-but-intermittent attendance to be accounted for too. With the figures for those reading and learning to read in the age-range 0-15 years in Table 4 we may well be close to the 'real' attendance ratio. And that proportion, of readers and would-be readers (1 in 5.63), is in line with what was judged to be the educational target of exceptionally well-provided countries, the 1 in 6 which was the Prussian ratio of schooled to total population.

In other words, towards the close of the period covered in this study, there can be little doubt that the machinery for producing a highly literate population in Scotland was well in place, and indeed had been so for some time. Such differences as there are in the tables we have for 1818 and 1834 highlight the fact that the provision of schools, attendance at school and the prospects for literacy in the Highlands and Islands improved considerably, and that there had been some decline, proportionately, in school attendance in the Central, West region while reading-literacy rates were nonetheless maintained. By 1834 ministers in some of the large towns, particularly in Glasgow, were anxious — even despairing — about the depravity of the population there, and assumed this to be closely connected to non-school-going and non-church-going. The awful truth was, however, that there was a high provision of schooling, just as there *was* a high provision of seats in churches. The problem was not one of provision, and in schooling it had not been so for some time in most places. School-age children in the poorer classes in the towns, however, were not going regularly to school, if at all in certain areas, and many of the lower orders of any age were not going to any of the abundance of churches that were available to them. When Chalmers led his crusade in the 1830s for greater support from the state for national schooling, under Established Church supervision, and also for church extension, it was a partisan campaign for and on behalf of the Established religion. He might argue for the need for more schools and for more churches (and his style of argument misled contemporaries just as it has, in later times, misled historians), but Chalmers and his coterie were, in effect, fighting a losing battle and fighting it with worn-out weapons. An empty place in a church would not be filled, as they imagined, just because it could be made cheap or free. The once dispossessed would actively need to want to fill it. And an available school place, cheap or free as it might be, would not be filled if parents no longer cared to send their children because the household depended on their earnings, or if mill-wages were preferable to learning (and even to the prospects of salvation), or if the children themselves saw little advantage in going. The next stage in the struggle to achieve universal education would be fought on new terrain.

## NOTES

1. *Scots Magazine*, xii (1750), pp. 289-292, 452, 488, 491, 596; see also *ibid.*, xlvi (1784), pp. 1-22, 163-64, and xlvii (1785), pp. 618-19 for later petitions and meetings for the same purpose.

2. James A. Russell, *Education in the Stewarty of Kirkcudbright, 1560-1970* (Newton Stewart, 1971) and *Education in Wigtownshire, 1560-1970* (Newton Stewart, 1971), *passim*.

3. See *Aberdeen Journal*, 20 Oct. 1760 — advertisement for a schoolmaster at Monymusk 'to teach English in the new way, and writing, Arithmetick, Book-Keeping, Surveying and other parts of Mathematicks, and Church-music; as also Latin to any who desire it'; *Glasgow Journal*, 3-10 May 1764 —advertisement for a school master at Cowal to teach 'the grounds of book-keeping, as well as English, writing, arithmetic and Latin', and an almost identical advertisement for the vacant schoolmastership of Kilbarchan, *ibid.*, 15-22 Nov. 1764. The Seafield Papers contain an intriguing and entertaining account of the filling of schoolmaster vacancies at Grantown and Abernethy in 1786-87: the superior school was to be at Grantown and the position there made more attractive by introducing extra income from boarding. On the general background to and development of these factors, see D.J. Withrington, 'Education and Society', in N.T. Phillipson and Rosalind Mitchison (eds.), *Scotland in the Age of Improvement* (Edinburgh, 1970), pp. 169-199.

4. *Ibid.*, p. 190: Principal John Chalmers of King's College and University in Old Aberdeen in January 1760 — '...there are many Students who know nothing of either Latin or Greek. Their plans and schemes for Life do not depend upon the knowledge of these Languages and yet by attending the other classes they may learn a great deal of useful Knowledge'.

5. Much is said on these points, directly and indirectly, in the parish ministers' contributions to Sir John Sinclair's *Statistical Account for Scotland,* often in relation to the inability of a parish to attract a graduate master because of the lowness of stipend and other remuneration: such comments are to be found well scattered throughout the country — see, for example, St Andrew's Lhanbryde in Moray in the new edition of the *Account* (Wakefield, 1982), xvi, pp. 642-4.

6. V.E. Durkacz, *The Decline of the Celtic Languages* (Edinburgh, 1983); C.W.J. Withers, *Gaelic in Scotland, 1698-1981* (Edinburgh, 1984).

7. *Ibid.*, p. 117; R.A. Houston, *Scottish Literacy and Scottish Identity: illiteracy and society in Scotland and Northern England, 1600-1800* (Cambridge, 1985), pp. 74, 82.

8. D.J. Withrington, 'The SPCK and Highland schools in mid-eighteenth century', in *Scot. Hist. Rev.*, xli (1962), pp. 89-99.

9. *Ibid.*, p. 93; SPCK Records, SRO, GD/95/80/3(3) — parish of Dunning, Perthshire.

10. Withers, *Gaelic in Scotland*, pp. 10-12.

11. Withrington, 'SPCK and Highland schools', pp. 91-3.

12. SRO, GD/95/80/8(1).

13. Withrington, 'SPCK and Highland schools', p. 97n; SRO, GD/95/14/254 (William Ross letters).

14 *Ibid.*

15. SRO, Church of Scotland, General Assembly records (CH/1): Mss report by Hyndman and Dick on visits to Society and Royal Bounty stations, 1760, p. 27.

16. Houston, *Scottish Literacy and Scottish Identity*, p. 113.

17. See the introduction to volume 1 (General), p. xxiii, of the new edition of the *Statistical Account.*

18. *Ibid.*, ix, p. 44 (Dumbarton), p. 261 (Campsie), pp. 583-84 (St Ninian's).

19. *Ibid.*, ii, p. 242 (Duddingston), p. 556 (Pencaitland), p. 729 (Dalmeny); viii, p.

166 (Inverchaolain); xi, p. 641 (Cleish); xii, p. 69 (Bendochy); vii, p. 605 (Walston); xvii, p. 189 (Kiltarlity).

20. *Ibid.*, xvii, p 682.

21. G.E. Davie, *The Democratic Intellect* (Edinburgh, 1961), p. xvii; James Scotland, *History of Scottish Education*, 2 vols. (London, 1969), i, p. 174; Houston, *Scottish Literacy and Scottish Identity, passim* (esp. pp. 1, 8).

22. *A Digest of Parochial Returns made to the Select Committee appointed to inquire into The Education of the Poor: session 1818* (London, 1821), p. iii: the parish returns are printed alphabetically by county; the summary table for Scotland as a whole is at pp. 224-25.

23. E.G. West, *Education and the Industrial Revolution* (London, 1975), pp.59-73.

24. Thomas Chalmers, *Considerations on the System of Parochial Schools in Scotland, and on the Advantage of Establishing them in Large Towns* (Edinburgh, 1819).

25. *Moral Statistics of the Highlands and Islands of Scotland, compiled from Returns received by the Inverness Society for the Education of the Poor in the Highlands, to which is prefixed a Report on the Past and Present State of Education in these Districts* (Inverness, 1826), p. 27.

26. *Edinburgh Review*, xlvi (1827), pp. 107-32 (see esp. 112).

27. D.J. Withrington, '*Scotland a Half Educated Nation* in 1834? Reliable critique or persuasive polemic ? ', in W.M. Humes and H.M. Paterson (eds.), *Scottish Culture and Scottish Education, 1800-1980* (Edinburgh, 1983), p. 59.

28. *Education Enquiry. Abstract of the Answers and Returns made pursuant to an Address of the House of Commons, dated 9th July 1834: Scotland.* (London, 1837), p. 3.

# CHAPTER 10

# The Standard of Living of the Working Class

## J.H. Treble

## The Standard of Living Debate in Britain

The question of whether or not the standard of living of the working class rose during the late eighteenth and early nineteenth centuries has long formed part of a wider historiographical discussion about the socio-economic consequences of those changes that we associate with the Industrial Revolution. The modern origins of that debate can be traced back to the fundamentally antagonistic interpretations of the 1790-1850 decades which were advanced by Clapham and J.L. Hammond in the late 1920s and early 1930s. Clapham's main objective was to remove the many ambiguities that arose from excessive reliance upon qualitative evidence by addressing the fundamental issue of how real wages moved over time. Employing Silberling's cost of living index and the Bowley-Wood wage data, he argued in favour of a substantial, albeit by no means uninterrupted, growth in the real income of industrial and agricultural workers for the period as a whole. In other words, industrialisation yielded material gains that the old economic order could never have generated. Hammond, on the other hand, devoted much of his reply to Clapham's thesis by painting a picture of a marked deterioration in the quality of working-class life as the pulse of agrarian and industrial capitalism quickened. The formative phase of the controversy was thus distinguished less by a direct collision between two adversaries arguing their respective cases upon the basis of a mutually agreed agenda and more by an evaluation of the condition of the working class from two quite distinct perspectives. The optimistic assessment of Clapham rested firmly upon measurement of the material rewards accruing to labour, the pessimistic case of Hammond upon what he regarded as the impoverishment of the social life and environment of the worker.

From the late 1940s onwards, however, those historians who have been preoccupied with this topic have largely succeeded in confining what threatened to be a thematically eclectic debate within much narrower parameters. Starting with Ashton's seminal article, the central concern of successive investigators has been with those key indicators that shed light upon the relationship between prices and money incomes. There are, of course, a few notable monographs, in particular Thompson's treatment of the cultural challenge that industrialisation posed to the traditional lifestyles of major sections of the English working class, that are lineal descendants of Hammond's qualitative approach; but such exceptions do not invalidate the general conclusion that the controversy has increasingly focused upon trends in real wages over time. Yet this shift to quantification, far from stilling debate, has merely intensified it. Optimistic and pessimistic schools of thought have remained in being, each trying to identify that point in time between 1790 and 1850 when working-class living standards moved unmistakably upwards. Thus in the acerbic exchanges between Hartwell (optimist) and Hobsbawm (pessimist), the former argued for a substantial improvement in real wages from the early 1820s onwards while the latter located the decisive turning-point virtually at the end of the period under discussion, in the mid-1840s. Alongside this kind of fundamental conflict has to be placed the vigorous argument which has emerged within the ranks of those who subscribe to the optimist thesis. Ashton, for instance, did much to cast doubts upon the roseate claims of Clapham by highlighting the unrepresentative nature, in terms of working-class consumption patterns, of the commodities that formed the basis of the Silberling price index, while Flinn and Lindert and Williamson have disagreed over the chronology and dimensions of real wage advance in nineteenth-century Britain.[1]

These fresh disagreements stem from five main sources. Firstly they have arisen from the fragmentary nature of much of the published price and wage data. Secondly they are the direct sequel to differences in the analytical tools that have been used to elucidate long-term trends in living standards. Thirdly, divergent conclusions have surfaced either as a result of individual historians employing different data from one another or from their willingness to accept, or their desire to modify, several of the price indexes that have been constructed for this period. Fourthly, interpretative conflicts have resulted from disputes over the geographical area that should be surveyed. Some writers have elected to explore the movement of real wages in Britain as a whole; others have restricted their fields of vision to England; and yet others have adopted the even more restricted perspective of an individual town, region or county. Finally, diverse verdicts upon the course of the real income of the working class have been delivered because of lack of agreement over the timespan to be examined.

The elements of controversy, however, that surround much of this new work should not obscure the overall significance of three distinct approaches to the question that have been followed in recent years. At one level Feinstein's study of real consumption *per capita* in Britain during the Industrial Revolution has presented us with a picture of virtual stagnation for each decade between 1760 and 1800, of the most modest improvement between 1801 and 1820, but of more buoyant growth thereafter. And although his results for 1760-1820 could conceal shifts in real consumption *per capita* not merely between classes but also within the working class itself, his overall assessment of that era was bleak: 'no worthwhile improvement in real consumption of goods and services per head (took place) during the first six decades of industrialisation'.[2] At another level Flinn and Von Tunzelmann, having pushed back the starting point of the classic debate about living standards in Britain from 1790-1800 to 1750, tried to delineate the course of change during the ensuing century. Flinn's main aim was to identify the secular trends in real wages by removing from his data those violent short-run fluctuations that were associated with poor harvests and/or the boom-slump phases of the conventional trade cycle. Arguing that real wages 'tended to change most at times when prices moved most rapidly or changed direction most decisively', he divided his period of study into four self-contained sub-periods.[3] Between 1750-4 and 1788-92 he found no evidence nationally of any improvement, a pattern that was repeated during the inflationary years of the Napoleonic Wars (1788-92 to 1809-15). Spectacular advances in real wages were, in fact, according to Flinn, overwhelmingly concentrated in his third sub-period (1809-15 to 1820-6) when relatively stable money wages accompanied by price deflation secured gains of 2.5 to 3 per cent per annum. Between 1820-6 and 1846-50 further gains were recorded, although, compared with the post-1809-15 surge, they were much more limited.

In a general chapter of this nature it is not, of course, possible to probe in detail Flinn's methodology. Nevertheless one vital point must be made, namely that these calculations 'of percentage changes (in real wages) between these 'quinquennial' turning points (1750-4, 1788-92, etc.) rely on the data on each series for the years averaged alone'.[4] In short, assumptions were made about the course of real wages in the intervening decades — for example, in the 1770s and 1830s — without the author submitting those assumptions to empirical investigation. It is precisely this gap that Von Tunzelmann's work has filled. By applying the technique of principal component analysis to — with but minor alterations — the same corpus of statistical material that was utilised by Flinn, he not only presented the reader with chronological profiles of the changing pattern of the standard of living for the entire century; he was also able to challenge the latter's findings in one major area. For while Von Tunzelmann conceded that there was evidence to support the thesis that real wages rose in the immediate post-Napoleonic War years, he concluded that Flinn overemphasised the importance of the ensuing decade by failing to separate fully short-run cyclical influences from the secular trend. Indeed, as a later publication confirmed, Von Tunzelmann placed the decisive phase for the upturn in real wages in Britain in the 1820s rather than a decade earlier. More recently Lindert and Williamson, traversing a different methodological path, have also identified the origins of a long-term ameliorative trend in the standard of living of the English working class in the post-1819 years, although they claimed a much higher rate of increase between 1820 and 1850 than either Flinn or Von Tunzelmann did for Britain as a whole.[5]

This last conclusion has obvious implications for this study of the Scottish experience. At first glance it suggests that the inclusion of Scottish wage data might have biased in a downward direction the standard of living in Britain primarily because, compared with England, Scotland remained a low-wage country throughout the 1750-1850 period. Bearing this point in mind, how important, for instance, is the fact that Hobsbawm's pessimistic essay was devoted to Britain, the optimistic contribution of Hartwell to England? Here the outside observer should tread warily since a mere reference to Britain should not lead him/her to believe that a weighting for lower returns to labour north of the Border had been automatically integrated into an assessment of the real wage experience of the British working class. Thus, while Hobsbawm's 1957 article was entitled the 'British standard of living', Scottish data were rarely deployed and the issue of English-Scottish wage differentials was completely ignored. On the other hand Flinn and Von Tunzelmann discuss at some length the low base from which Scottish wages started in 1750 and the narrowing of the gap between the rates of remuneration of Scottish and English workers that had taken place by late eighteenth and early nineteenth centuries. This finding produces a somewhat different perspective on the issue of bias to which I referred in the preceding sentences. For if wages differentials were narrowing, the incorporation of Scottish data in any evaluation of British living standards would have yielded a more, not less, favourable profile of the working-class's experience. Neither of these scholars, however, fully assimilated Scottish wages into their analyses, although in Von Tunzelmann's case, the omission of Scottish farm servants from his calculations was largely a product of the chronological gaps that existed in the published statistics.

Drawing attention to the existence of a distinctive Scottish pattern in the sphere of money wages inevitably raises another major issue. If the Scottish worker's wages were below those obtaining in England, was he/she also exposed to a different cost of living experience to that which was recorded in prices indexes based upon London data? Equally relevant, did the Scottish working class follow a different dietary regime to that which was regarded as the norm for the South of England? It is the existence of these kinds of problems in the regions of England as well as in Scotland that has led to the third approach to the subject of real wages which I want to discuss. For what unites this group of historians is its desire to elucidate living standards in a town or a region by constructing indexes that, as far as possible, reflect local prices and by relating those indexes to wages that were paid by local employers. The best of this work — Gourvish on Glasgow (1810-31), Neale on Bath (1780-1844) and Hunt and Botham on North Staffordshire (1750-92) — clearly demonstrates that in different parts of Britain the movement of real wages could run counter to the national trend.[6] Expressed in another form, indexes that draw too heavily upon London contract or wholesale prices are not necessarily a good guide to the experience of working people who lived in areas that were remote from Britain's capital city.

**The Sources for the Scottish Experience**

Against the backcloth of this historiographical survey it is now time to define how I propose to analyse the standard of living of the Scottish working class between 1760 and 1830. In the first place, because of the distinctive price history of the period, I have divided these decades into three component parts, starting with the gentle upward trend in prices that marked the years 1760 to 1792-3, continuing with the high inflationary pressures of the quarter of a century of war (1792-3 to 1814), and finishing with the post-1814 era when many consumer prices moved in a downwards direction. But since the ensuing analysis of the standard of living is very much dependent upon published data, it is vital to discuss the nature of the source materials that are to used. For money wages I have drawn heavily upon the work of other investigations, among them Hamilton, Duckham, Flinn, Gourvish, Murray, Fraser and above all Bowley and Wood. Particularly for the eighteenth century, however, when we are often provided with a mere handful of wage rates that relate to perhaps only a single year in a decade or to a single locality, interpretation of the chronology of change will be supplemented by reference to other sources. For the price indexes that I have employed to chart the pre-1792-3 pattern in the cost of living, I have relied upon Gilboy, Tucker and Hunt and Botham. In the case of the first two indexes I have recalculated their data so that 1790 equals 100, the base year for the Hunt and Botham index. But in relation to Scotland, a further point must be made about them. Gilboy's and Tucker's tables are open to exactly the type of criticism that I have already advanced. Both reflect London contract prices and both have a weighting for cereals which fails to do justice to the predominance of oatmeal in the Scottish diet. In addition while Gilboy ignores house rent, Tucker gives it a weighting of one-sixth of total consumer spending, which reflects the dearness of housing in London rather than the Scottish experience. Nevertheless until a Scottish cost of living index has been assembled for this timespan, these London-based sources must serve as benchmarks to measure Scottish trends supplemented by the Botham and Hunt Index. For the post-1793 era I have extended the Gilboy and Tucker series to 1815 and 1830 respectively, although in the latter instance minor changes have been made by its author in the weighting and composition of the basket of goods and services that formed its core. Finally, I propose to utilise the Gayer, Rostow and Schwartz (GRS) index of domestic commodity prices, an admittedly imperfect instrument since it excludes rent and potatoes from its remit, and such Scottish price data as have been published in recent years.

The real wage experiences of specific occupational groups, expressed in terms of these cost of living indexes, are to be found in Appendix Tables 2 to 7. Before, however, interpreting these data it is essential to inquire further into the raw materials upon which they have been constructed and to acknowledge their limitations. In the first place the chronological spread of money wage returns is remarkably uneven, with a few observations for the pre-1790 decades and a relative profusion of evidence from the 1800-1820 period. Furthermore, some of the statistics which have been employed to delineate national or regional trends in money wages in the pre-1790 era — for example the money wage columns in Table 2(A) — are built around a handful of observations that are themselves not always free from ambiguity. In relation to masons' and carpenters' earnings, for instance, we cannot be certain whether, for the pre-1760 period, a value has been attached to an 'in kind' component in the published materials. On the other hand Table 7(B), which is based upon Bowley's detailed assessment of the total earnings of all grades of adult male farm workers, poses a different interpretative problem. Although Bowley, in recognition of the massive role that 'in kind' payments assumed in the wage bargain struck between farmer and employee, attempted to translate all 'in kind' transfers into cash equivalents, the very existence of regional disparities in prices robs the ensuing calculations of absolute precision.

On the prices side of the equation, if all the relevant indexes move in the same direction, there remain important differences between them. Thus, while they succinctly capture major short-term peaks in the cost of living, they can on occasion differ in recording the timing of those peaks. The massive surges, for example, in prices that occurred at the turn, and at the beginning of the second decade, of the nineteenth century, took place, according to Gilboy, in 1799-1800 and 1811-2, but, according to Tucker and GRS, in 1800-1 and 1812-3. The existence of this lagged response has therefore to be borne in mind when the reader examines the tabulated changes in real wages between 1811 and 1813. Again the decline between 1790 and 1794 in the real value of the money component of unmarried ploughman's wages (Table 7(A)) and of the real wages of all grades of farm workers (Table 7(B)) that is highlighted by the Gilboy index owes everything to the fact that between these dates the Gilboy series recorded a substantial increase in the cost of living (26.3 per cent) compared with the more modest rises of Tucker and GRS. In more general terms all of these indexes tend to understate increases in the Scottish cost of living that undoubtedly occurred during those concentrated surges in the fiars price of oatmeal, largely because they underweighted this staple foodstuff of the Scottish working class. While, for instance, the fiars price of oatmeal in East Lothian rose by over 100 per cent, in Fife by almost 70 per cent, in Perthshire by virtually 60 percent and in Lanarkshire by around 85 per cent between 1760 and 1762, the Tucker and Botham/Hunt indexes recorded only the most minuscule shifts in the cost of living.[7] Finally, pursuing the theme of the appropriateness or otherwise of English indexes for measuring Scottish real wages, Gourvish has argued that for 1810-31 every series based upon London wholesale prices projects a more favourable picture of the real incomes of Glasgow's working class than his own indexes which reflect Glasgow retail prices.[8] For this reason Gourvish's price indexes have been incorporated into several of my tables, above all in those of workers in the Glasgow area, to provide what is a more meaningful assessment of living standards in the industrial capital of Scotland. Unfortunately, however, because of their limited chronological coverage they cannot be employed to tease out secular trends for our period as a whole. This drawback and the other deficiencies that have been mentioned mean that these tables must be supplemented by qualitative materials that shed light upon the direction and timing of changes in real wages. It is against this backcloth that we now turn to analyse the movement of real income in that period of gently rising prices which runs from 1760 through to 1792-3.

## Amelioration, 1760-c.1793

As has already been shown, the commonly accepted view among historians is that the standard of living of the British working class remained virtually stationary for the whole of this timespan. Given, therefore, that Scotland was, in *per capita* terms, a poorer country than its southern neighbour, the scope for a radical departure from the average experience of the British workers might appear to be very limited indeed. Yet the data at our disposal suggest otherwise. Table 7(B) which deals with the largest single source of male employment in eighteenth-century Scotland, presents a picture of substantial growth in the real income of agricultural workers in almost every region.

According to the Tucker and Gilboy indexes, the adult agricultural workforce in the Mid East, Mid West, South West and East Central regions experienced an improvement in their standard of living of between 40 and 50 per cent or more between 1760-70 and 1790. A more pessimistic picture emerges when the Botham/Hunt index is applied to the same money wage data, although even then the size of the increases remains impressive, with real wage advances of between 34 and 41 per cent being recorded. All three indexes display slow but still perceptible advances in the Lothians, the area most attuned to capitalist farming methods in eighteenth-century Scotland, and single out the South East as the region where, in percentage terms, the process of amelioration was most rapid.

Turning from agriculture to the skilled sector of the urban labour market, a similar pattern can be readily identified amongst Glasgow mechanics and machine makers (Table 4(A)) who secured an increase in their real income between 1777, a year of recession in the local economy, and 1793 of, at worst 52 (Gil) and, at best 58 (Tucker) per cent and amongst Edinburgh printers (Table 5) whose purchasing power rose between 1773, another period of depression, and 1791 by between 25 per cent according to the lowest, and 41 per cent according to the highest, estimates. In this latter case the trend was powerfully assisted by a 14 per cent increase in piece rate for book work in 1785. Outwardly the fortunes of Scottish masons and carpenters (Table 2 (A)) seems to follow a similar path, with substantial gains accruing to them between 1767-77 and 1791. Yet if we probe deeper into their history a more sombre conclusion starts to surface. Firstly, as Table 2(A) demonstrates, the real incomes of both groups were considerably higher in 1745-60 than during 1767-77. Indeed, the Gilboy — but not the Tucker — index shows that between 1745-60 and 1791 the scale of improvement in their standard of living was of the most modest proportions. Secondly, Table 2(B) which has been constructed upon the assumption that money wages remained constant between 1745-60 and 1767-77, points in the same direction. Thus, the Botham/Hunt index suggests that Scottish masons were more prosperous in the early 1750s and at our starting point in 1760 than in 1791 while the Gilboy index again yields, on an annual basis, relatively few gains between a base line drawn in 1760 and 1791. In other words, these data can be used to project a radically different interpretation of the craft worker's living standards to the more optimistic profile derived from studying the movement of Edinburgh printers' and Glasgow mechanics' real earnings between the 1770s and 1791. For this backward projection of our analysis of masons' and carpenters' real wages to 1760 suggests that the vast bulk of those gains which occurred after 1767-77 was overwhelmingly the result of a 'catching up' process, restoring the purchase power of money incomes which had been badly eroded in that decade to their 1750 or 1760 levels. And if this was true of these two occupations, can the historian, in the absence of runs of money wages, apply this concept of a post-1766 stationary state to other groups, Edinburgh compositors and Glasgow machine makers among them?[9]

Surveying the published evidence, qualitative as well as quantitative, as a whole, there are valid grounds for rejecting this bleak evaluation of the pre-1792-3 era and for arguing that the more optimistic portrayal of living standards which arises from our study of agricultural workers, mechanics and printers was much more typical of that ever-increasing segment of Scottish society which was dependent for its livelihood upon the cash economy. For one thing, as has been pointed out, we cannot be certain that the average figures for masons' and carpenters' wages during the 1745-60 period do not include an 'in-kind' element which had been transmuted into cash terms. If that is the case, their real wage figures for those years would have to be revised downwards. More important, it is possible to identify the existence of a positive trend which, although it cannot always be quantified, was reflected in other parts of the labour market as that market became tighter over time and started to undergo significant structural change. In this context two general factors tended to benefit the Scottish worker across a broad spectrum of trades. They were a much slower rate of population increase than occurred south of the Border and, compared with the English experience, a more concentrated process, in a chronological sense, of economic change. Since the demographic regime is described elsewhere in this collection, it suffices here to point out that Scotland's annual rate of population growth of 0.6 per cent during the years 1755-1801 was roughly 50 per cent below that which was recorded over the same timespan in England. It only required, therefore, a modest element of acceleration in a labour-intensive economy for the creation of conditions conducive to a rise in the living standards of working people, via a more buoyant labour market. That acceleration was forthcoming in the shape of Scotland's Agrarian and Industrial Revolutions which started somewhere around the late 1770s or early 1780s and the very swift pace of urban growth thereafter. And although by 1792-3 the transformation of the Scottish economy still had far to go, the scale of change in the preceding decade and a half had been significant, not marginal. Equally important, in this formative phase, its impact upon working-class real incomes was for the most part benign.

For one thing the scale and range of openings for skilled hands had started to expand by the late 1770s and early 1780s. At one level the historian can point to the evolution of new skills. By the 1780s cabinetmakers and chairmakers were quite distinct from the old craft of wright/joiner from which they had emerged. High-quality plasterers were also identified as a relatively recent addition to the craft elite in the building industry, while if bookbinding can clearly be listed as a pre-1780 occupation, its status was to be much enhanced thereafter as a result of greater regularity in employment and a substantial improvement in earnings.[10] Although, therefore, there were segments of the skilled labour market which by the 1790s were starting to be pressurised by the developing 'dishonourable' trades,[11] the balance that can be struck between gains and losses in the living standards of the craft workforce between 1760 and 1791-3 remained firmly in favour of amelioration. Nor was this an exclusively urban phenomenon. Sprott among others had drawn attention to an increase in the number of rural craftsmen and semi-skilled hands who were beneficiaries of the changing structure of Scottish farming.[12] Albeit on a lesser scale, an identical trend can also be discerned in certain parts of the unskilled labour market; for a careful study of the *Old Statistical Account (OSA)* reveals that between 1750-60 and the 1790s wage differentials between craft and unskilled hands tended to narrow. Last, but not least, evidence relating to textile workers, Scotland's largest industrial labour force, and salters and colliers (the two occupations that were associated with serfdom until the 1775 act weakened, and the 1799 statute repealed, a mode of securing labour that can be traced back to an earlier age), also points towards a rise in their living standards.

Durie's monograph on the linen industry and Murray's study of the condition of Scotland's handloom weavers provide much information upon the changing pattern of demand for textile workers in the post-1760 era. Thus, despite the existence of a well demarcated pattern of short-term fluctuations in the output of linen cloth throughout the 1730-1815 period, the secular trend was sharply upwards, with the early 1790s recording, in volume terms, a level of output almost two-thirds above that which was attained in 1760. This growth was accompanied by a parallel shift in the geographical distribution of output share. Whereas in 1760 weavers in Fife, Perthshire and Angus accounted for 57 per cent of total output, their share by 1790 had soared to 87.8 per cent. Conversely the share accruing to their counterparts in Lanarkshire and Renfrewshire moved in the opposite direction, falling from 27.1 per cent at the earlier date to 10 per cent in 1791. That shift was the product of the dynamic demand for cotton weavers in the West where cotton had replaced linen as the dominant fabric in little more than a decade. What was taking place during the 1780s, therefore, was a massive increase in the demand for all types of weavers — Murray has estimated an 80 per cent growth in their numbers during that decade —, an expansion in the full-time element of the labour force and enhanced opportunities for upward mobility in the labour market, all with positive consequences for the level of real earnings compared with mid-century. Weaving apart, linen spinning, a preserve of female labour, also brought fresh gains to agricultural workers' families from the 1760s onwards not merely in its traditional strongholds but also in such South-East Highland parishes as Moulin (Perthshire), primarily because employment outlets grew and working patterns became more regular over time.[13]

Finally, serfdom in the mining and salt industries was never linked with low rates of remuneration. Adam Smith, writing in the 1770s, was perhaps the most eminent contemporary observer who drew attention to the fact that the Scottish miner was much better rewarded than his colleague in the developing coalfields of North-East England. Indeed, pressure to scrap serfdom in the 1770s came not from the miners themselves, who skilfully used the system to underpin their position, but from the mineowners of the West, preoccupied with high labour costs. The evidence, however, strongly indicates that despite the 1775 Act, miners' real and money incomes continued to rise until, and indeed beyond, the early 1790s. Duckham has drawn attention to a secular growth in the demand for Scottish coal between 1780 and 1810, while Flinn concluded that between 1700 and 1790 the standard of living of the Scottish collier rose sharply. Retail prices in those decades increased by roughly one-third but hewers' wages doubled. Examining Flinn's table of hewers' daily rates, the inescapable conclusion is that most of those gains came in the post-1750 decades.[14]

Even if, therefore, a Scottish retail price index might temper the scale of the real wage rises which have been computed for agricultural workers, mechanics and printers, the reality of improvement seems indisputable not merely for these occupations but for most segments of the Scottish labour force that were integrated into the money economy. The slow but progressive erosion of wage differentials between lower-paid Scottish occupations and their English equivalents adds weight to this conclusion. In other words, Scottish workers, like their contemporaries in Lancashire and North Staffordshire, were for the most part beneficiaries of eighteenth-century economic growth.[15]

A major methodological problem, however, remains. How do we treat those parts of Scotland which by the 1790s had still not been fully assimilated into the market economy? The answer provided by those who are firmly committed to quantitative techniques is that the historian should ignore them because it is impossible to measure changes in the standard of living of a society which met many of its own needs without resort to the labour market. But in a Scottish context the problem cannot be left there if only because it affected a substantial geographical area. As late as 1790 this pattern of life can be discerned in the North-West and South-East Highlands, Caithness, the Northern Isles and parts of the North-East.

The approach, thereafter, that I intend to pursue here is to outline, in very broad terms, the changing nature of Highland society over the whole period 1760-1830 and to see whether any firm conclusions can be drawn. Three points can be made at the outset. First, in 1760 a peasant society was not exclusively a Highland or Northern phenomenon. On other hand by the 1790s in many areas and by 1830 almost everywhere outside the Highlands, that structure had been dismantled. Second, after 1760 there are indications that sections of Highland society were being offered the chance to benefit from the general development of a market economy in Central Scotland and England. The growth of bye-employments, the sustained rise in the price of black cattle, the development of inshore fishing and kelping were tangible signs of this process. Third, Highland society was not immune from structural change. The Clearances and the formation of crofting townships were salient features of this change in the North-West. In the South-East the conversion of small tenants into farm servants represented a different kind of discontinuity. But in the latter region those who moved into paid employment had, in the medium term, some prospect of improving their living standards, partly because they were working in an area marked by high rates of out-migration. In the North-West, however, the demographic factor placed a firm brake upon the scope for material advance, even during what has sometimes been called the age of optimism (1760-1815). Its retention of its people, the upward movement of land rents, the increasing use of the potato and the severity of recurrent subsistence crises mean that it is impossible to speak meaningfully about a rising standard of living in those decades. After 1815 when the kelp industry collapsed, the fishing industry encountered problems and bye-employments shrank, poverty emerges as the endemic feature of the North-West Highlands.

In a fundamental sense the North-West Highlands experience runs counter to the conventional interpretation of the 1790-1830 decades. Most historians who have researched this topic view the quarter of a century of the French Wars as a period when working-class living standards underwent relatively little change and the post-1815 years as one of advance, although the timing and scale of that advance have been the subject of vigorous disputation. Before, however, testing these verdicts against the statistical evidence assembled in the relevant Appendix Tables, certain comments must be made about the interpretation of those data. In the first place the chronologically scattered nature of the money wage returns prevents the construction of a time series, based upon an unbroken run of annual observations. When, therefore, we are perusing those tables we must be aware, for the pre- and post-1815 years, of the movement of the trade cycle and to note that figures which relate to years of recession (for example 1797, 1803, 1809, 1811-2, 1816, 1818-9, 1826) or of boom (1824-5, for instance) can lead to intense short-term fluctuations in money incomes and real wages. In addition, those concentrated surges in the cost of living to which I referred earlier can also trap the unwary into reaching misleading conclusions about the underlying trend in real earning unless allowance is made for the distorting effect of such peaks. Furthermore, while we can calculate the average annual rate of change in real income between two dates, we can not often determine whether that change was evenly spread over the intervening timespan or whether it was an extremely concentrated process. But the uneven chronological distribution of the money wage data poses a further problem. For almost all the listed categories of workers there are huge gaps in these observations for the 1790s and 1800s which make it impossible, on the basis of quantitative evidence alone, to discover how far the opening phase of the Napoleonic conflict reversed or sustained those positive influences that had operated in their favour in the pre-1792 era. Last but not least the vast majority of these Tables only delineate the pattern of movement in the standard of living of individual groups of workers for the post-1790 period. Conversely a mere handful of observations embrace both the pre- and post-1790 decades. In order, therefore, to secure even a limited comparison of how real wages moved between 1760-90 and 1790/3-1814, the historian is compelled to employ those data that have already been analysed for the earlier period — primarily agricultural workers, Edinburgh compositors and Glasgow machine makers — and to extend the analysis of these returns forward into wartime Scotland.

## Stagnation, 1793-1814

Bearing these points in mind, we can now examine the period of conflict and the ensuing decade and a half of peace in turn. During the French Wars it is clear that, with few exceptions, the money earnings and wage rates of outwardly disparate groups moved upwards, although the percentage rates of change varied enormously. The existence of such differences within, as well as between, occupations is, of course, important because of the light it sheds upon the nature of local labour markets. But in relation to living standards such disparities are significant in another sense. The extent to which any individual's standard of life improved or deteriorated during these years depended upon the degree to which his/her earnings grew faster or slower than the prevailing rate of inflation. And, as the appropriate cost of living indexes indicate, the inflationary pressures that were exerted, especially between 1799 and 1813, were of such impressive dimensions that they brought in their wake the spectre of falling real income.

Part, at least, of this conclusion is endorsed by several of those Tables whose base year is located somewhere between 1790 and 1793 and which possess real wage measurements for 1810 and/or 1814. For the 1790-3 to 1810 period the Gilboy cost of living index consistently produces the most favourable profile of the standard of living of all the relevant occupational groups. Even so the picture which emerges form this source for most industrial and construction workers is relatively bleak. Only Edinburgh's carpenters and Cupar's stonemasons achieved an annual average rate of growth in real earnings, calculated between these two dates, of around 1 per cent per annum. Elsewhere the gains were either marginal (Glasgow machine makers improved their living standards by less than 5 per cent over the period as a whole) or an actual decline in real wages had taken place. An even more lugubrious scenario is portrayed when money wages are deflated by Tucker's index. Apart from a barely perceptible rise in the living standards of Edinburgh's carpenters and Cupar's stonemasons, the real wages of every other group had fallen, often by substantial dimensions, by 1810. In the realm of agriculture, however, both indexes highlight a more benign trend. As Table 7(B) demonstrates, between 1790 and 1810, the real earnings of Scotland's agricultural workers moved upwards for every region where such trends can be assessed. Moreover, the scale of that increase in the South-Central, South-West, North-East and North regions exceeded 1 per cent per annum.

By 1814, when the Gilboy index is employed, a more general movement towards amelioration can be identified amongst most urban-based employees, although, Glasgow machine makers apart, almost all the relevant readings are taken from the construction trades. But in that sphere of economic activity every group, except Arbroath's stonemasons and those Glasgow labourers who in 1793 were in receipt of the highest daily rates of pay, had achieved an increase in their standards of living compared with two decades earlier. Nevertheless, only Glasgow stonemasons, who in 1793 belonged to the worst-remunerated section of this artisan group, had improved their real earnings by more than 1 per cent per annum. On the other hand, the Tucker index suggest that none of the various categories of urban workers was better placed in 1814 than in the opening years of the 1790s. And there are grounds for arguing that these last findings are closer to capturing the general urban situation than the modest improvements that the Gilboy data portray. For the favourable real wages results that are obtained by employing the latter index flow exclusively from the sharp fall in the cost of living that it charts between 1810 and 1814. By 1814 the Gilboy index was more than 20 points lower than the GRS index and almost 30 points lower than the Tucker index. If, however, we compare the percentage rates of change in all three of these cost of living indicators between 1810 and 1814 with the equivalent statistics for Gourvish's Indexes 1 (skilled workers) and 2 (unskilled hands) for the same timespan, it becomes clear the Tucker index most closely follows, and the Gilboy index most widely diverges from, the Glasgow experience during that quinquennium. While we cannot extrapolate Gourvish's indexes backwards in time to our 1790-3 base, this result strongly suggests that the scale of movement in real income between 1790-3 and 1814 was at best marginal for the industrial working class as a whole. But for the agricultural worker the outcome was more decisively in his favour.

Viewed from a longer perspective, the braking effects of the war years can also be illustrated for those occupations for which we possess money wage data in the pre-1790-3 world. Thus, while the real wages of Glasgow mechanics rose, according to the Gilboy index, by 79.5 per cent between 1777 and 1814, two-thirds of that rise was concentrated between 1777 and 1793. On the other hand the less favourable Tucker index points to a 58 per cent growth in the real earnings for the same occupational group between 1777 and 1793 and an actual fall in its standard of living from 1793 to 1814. Again agricultural workers in every region where the trend in their real earnings can be quantified made impressive gains between 1760-70 and 1810. But except in the South-West and North-East — and in the latter case the result for 1760-70 is highly suspect — around two-thirds of the increase in their real income had accrued by 1790. Finally, whereas both indexes point to an improvement in the standard of living of Edinburgh printers of around 40 per cent between 1773 and 1791, the returns for the War years display a level of of real earnings little removed from that which had been achieved in the early 1770s.[16]

Yet while the War years were distinguished by either a decline in, or a deceleration in the rate of growth of, the real incomes of almost all working-class groups, the raw data still leave unanswered one major question to which I have previously alluded. Was the opening phase of the conflict characterised by a continuation of the pre-1793 ameliorative trend and were the 1800s marked by an equally profound reversal of the process of improvement? There are, in fact, certain indirect indicators that can be used to support such a hypothesis. Thus, as Scottish farming in the 1790s and the early 1800s became more attuned to the pull of the market, the money wage component of farm servants' wages rose steeply. This trend was accompanied by an increase in their real income, as the rural labour market became over time more efficient and, in the medium term at least, tighter. In the manufacturing sector of the economy the growth of a factory-based cotton spinning industry was matched by a further expansion in the size of the handloom-weaving labour force. Between 1790 and 1800 this last group grew by over 25 per cent although that rate of growth was not initially inimical to their standard of living.[17] The coal industry was also continuing to expand its labour force in these years without depressing miners' incomes. According to Duckham, for instance, in the high-wage mining districts of Midlothian and the West miners improved their real earnings, compared with 1790-3, during 1796-8 and 1802-4.[18]

Shortly after the turn of the nineteenth century, however, the positive aspects of this structure had started to crumble. Prices surged ahead at a much faster rate than in the 1790s; the demographic variable, despite army recruitment, started to operate against the interests of many occupational groups; and the intensification of capitalist farming methods transferred to urban areas part of the rural able-bodied population that was not required for the smooth running of Scottish agriculture. Such urban in-migration helped in turn to swell an ever expanding pool of unskilled labour. But the difficulties confronting those situated in this segment of the labour market were compounded by the fate of weavers of plain fabrics. For while weavers' numbers continued to grow until 1820 (73 per cent higher in the latter year than in 1800), the long-term decline of the least skilled elements of that workforce had already started by 1808, although it was to be temporarily interrupted by a minor recovery in 1814-5 (Tables 3(A) and (B)). The interaction of these forces, allied to a higher rate of population growth, was, by the closing years of the Napoleonic conflict, exerting downward pressure upon money earnings of several un-skilled groups, increasing the size of the labour reserve in Scotland's larger towns, and extending the boundaries of urban seasonal and casual labour markets. While, therefore, judgement upon the amelioration hypothesis must be suspended in the light of the state of current knowledge, the validity of this immiseration thesis is, for the unskilled at least, vindicated by the extant data[19] Assessed overall, however, the experience of the Scottish working class between 1790-3 and 1814 conformed quite clearly to the English pattern, with no sign of a sustained advance in the living standards of most occupational groups and a deterioration in real wages of numerically significant elements among the unskilled.

**The Postwar Condition**

The task remains of analysing how far this situation altered in the post-1815 period when the economy was free from the constraints placed upon it by twenty-five years of conflict. In terms of the purchasing power of money wages there was at least one major influence operating in favour of the working class that had been conspicuously absent in the preceding quarter of a century, namely the inflationary pressures of 1799-1813 were reversed. Between 1814 and 1820 the Tucker index had registered a fall in the cost of living of around 15 per cent; by 1830 it was approximately one-third lower than sixteen years earlier. The GRS index moves in the same direction, high-lighting a decline of almost identical proportions for the period as a whole, although, unlike the Tucker index, two-thirds of this drop had been achieved by 1820. Nevertheless the scale of this deflationary movement has to be kept in perspective, for the cost of living in 1830 was still 18.7 (Tucker) to 16.8 (GRS) per cent higher than in 1790.

Scarcely surprisingly, with but few exceptions, those artisan occupations which are listed in the Appendix Tables were the principal beneficiaries of these changes. A few examples must suffice, using the Tucker index to deflate money wages since it is the only cost of living index that we possess which covers the entire post-1760 era. (For comparative purposes for the post-1790 years computations have also been made employing the GRS index.) Thus, by 1831 Glasgow machine makers were, in real terms, 42.9 per cent better off than in 1814, while between 1816 and 1831 Edinburgh's miscellaneous artisans and South of Scotland miners had increased their real earnings by 33.6 and 24.8 per cent respectively. If gains that were made in other areas of the skilled labour market were on a lesser scale, the strength of a trend that must have touched most members of the craft elite was undeniable. Yet these high percentage rates of growth must still be qualified in two important respects. First, they were for the most part secured after, not before, 1820. Second, because, according to the Tucker index, few of our tabulated crafts had managed to improve their real incomes during the Napoleonic wars, the scale of this post-1814 surge in living standards was in part a catching up exercise, reclaiming the ground that had been lost in the previous two decades. Some groups (Glasgow machine makers, plus 28.6 per cent and Edinburgh's miscellaneous artisans, plus 17.8 per cent) had by 1830 obtained gains which left them in a much better economic position than in the early 1790s.[20] Elsewhere, however, the increases that were recorded were either much more modest or, as with South of Scotland colliers, barely perceptible (see Appendix Tables).

But to the unskilled worker the post-1815 years brought little comfort, primarily because of the intensification of those adverse pressures that we have already described in relation to the early 1800s. Notwithstanding, for instance, a temporary improvement in the position of handloom weavers during the 1824-5 boom, the secular trend in their living standards, skilfully charted by Murray and presented in microcosmic form in Table 3(B), remained firmly downwards. Similarly, if the real wages of Glasgow's building labourers rose between 1814 and 1831, they were still as a group much poorer at the end of our period than four decades earlier (Table 2(E)). In this last case we know too little about the rewards of unskilled labour in other parts of Scotland to be able to generalise from the Glasgow experience. Nevertheless there are grounds for arguing that the persistence of a reserve army of labour in other major towns made it unlikely that the living standards of their unskilled workforce would have differed significantly from this Glasgow pattern. On the other hand, after 1810-14 the economic position of farm workers is more difficult to decipher because of the lack of hard data. For example, Bowley's index of Scottish agricultural workers' wages possesses a fundamental drawback: between 1814 and 1833-40 its course is determined by the imposition of 'English rates of change...on the Scottish pivot numbers'.[21] But given the fact that the mixed nature of much of Scottish agriculture meant that it adapted better to the post-1815 depression in wheat prices than its English counterpart, and given that Scotland's farmers did not hoard labour, it seems probable that Scottish farm servants would be less affected by the rigours of the post-1815 era. While, therefore, the cash component of the agricultural labourer's income declined after 1815 — by 1821-3 it was perhaps a quarter to one-third lower than its 1808-9 peak[22] — there were countervailing influences working in his favour, including the steep drop in the price of clothing upon which he spent at least part of his money income and the minor role that cash still assumed in many counties in the total wage package. In such circumstances the majority of farm servants were able to maintain their real incomes at or slightly below the level attained in 1810, although a significant setback took place in 1819-23 when the fortunes of Scottish farming reached its post-war nadir in the period under review. But that still left agricultural workers with a standard of living considerably above that which had obtained in 1790.[23]

Summing up, the historian can conclude that, contrary to the conventional interpretation of real wages in England, there is an extensive corpus of evidence which points to a rise in the real earnings of the bulk of the Scottish working class in contact with the market economy, between 1760 and early 1790s; that the Napoleonic Wars yielded few gains and several losses to the majority of employees in the manufacturing and construction industries; and that between 1815 and 1830 the skilled labour force benefited greatly from tumbling prices. Translated into comparative terms, between 1790 and 1830 the direction and chronology of shifts in the living standards of the Scottish and English working class moved closer together as wage differentials continued to narrow. Finally, viewed from a more extended perspective, real wages in almost every segment of the Scottish economy were considerably higher in 1830 than in 1760. Yet since poverty, in the basic sense of an income inadequate to maintain the physical efficiency of the family unit, was deeply entrenched in mid-eighteenth century Scottish society, the nature of this post-1760 advance requires to be more precisely defined. For the skilled it meant, by 1830, a more variegated diet, better clothing and the acquisition of a broader range of mass-produced consumer goods. But for the unskilled and sections of the emerging semi-skilled labour force gains were on a much more humble scale. Marginal improvement in diet and attire did not extend very far into other areas of consumer expenditure. For them improvement had meant approaching nearer to achieving 'mere subsistence' without breaking through the poverty line. In other words, if the data indicate that there was less poverty — in the sense that Booth and Rowntree defined that term in the late nineteenth century — in 1830 than in 1760, poverty itself still remained an endemic feature of Scottish society.[24]

## NOTES

1. The articles and books upon which this paragraph is based are listed below: J.H. Clapham, *An Economic History of Modern Britain*, vol. I (Cambridge, 1926). J.L.Hammond, 'The Industrial Revolution and Discontent', *Economic History Review*, 1st Series, Vol. II (1930). E.P. Thompson, *The Making of the English Working Class* (London, 1963). The Ashton, Hobsbawm and Hartwell articles are produced in A.J. Taylor (ed.), *The Standard of Living in Britain During the Industrial Revolution* (London, 1975).
M.W. Flinn, 'English Workers' Living Standards During the Industrial Revolution' and P.H. Lindert and J.G. Williamson, 'Reply to Michael Flinn', *Economic History Review*, 2nd. series, Vol. XXXVII (1984).

2. C.H. Feinstein, 'Capital Accumulation and the Industrial Revolution', in R. Floud and D. McCloskey (eds.), *The Economic History of Britain Since 1700*, vol. I (Cambridge, 1981) p. 136.

3. M.W. Flinn 'Trends in Real Wages, 1750-1850', *Economic History Review*, 2nd. Series, Vol. XXVII (1972), p. 397.

4. G.N. Von Tunzelmann, 'Trends in Real Wages 1750-1850, Revisited', *Economic History Review*, 2nd. Series, Vol. XXXII (1979). p. 34.

5. G.N. Von Tunzelmann, 'Technical Progress During the Industrial Revolution', in Floud and McCloskey (eds.), *Economic History*, p. 159; P.H. Lindert and J.G. Williamson, 'English Workers' Living Standards During the Industrial Revolution: A New Look', *Economic History Review*, 2nd. Series, Vol. XXXVI (1983).

6. The Neale article is reproduced in Taylor (ed.), *Standard of Living*; T.R. Gourvish, 'The Cost of Living in Glasgow in the Early Nineteenth Century', *Economic History Review*, 2nd. Series, Vol. XXV (1972); E.H. Hunt and F.W. Botham, 'Wages in Britain During the Industrial Revolution', *Economic History Review*, 2nd. Series, Vol. XL (1987).

7. My calculations of the changes in fiars price from the data collected M. Flinn *et al* (eds.), *Scottish Population History* (Cambridge, 1977), p. 495.

8. Gourvish, 'Cost of Living in Glasgow', pp. 74-8.

9. For the calculations upon which these paragraphs are based, see the appropriate Appendix Tables.

10. For a discussion of these points, see W.H. Fraser, *Conflict and Class: Scottish Workers 1700-1838* (Edinburgh, 1988), Chapter 2. I am very grateful to Hamish Fraser for access to some of the materials that he had collected for that project.

11. *Ibid.*

12. G Sprott, 'The Country Tradesman', in T.M. Devine (ed.), *Farm Servants and Labour in Lowland Scotland, 1770-1914* (Edinburgh,1984), pp. 146-9.

13. The points raised in this paragraph are based upon A.J. Durie, *The Scottish Linen Industry in the Eighteenth Century* (Edinburgh, 1979), pp. 23-5, 76-80; N. Murray, *The Scottish Hand Loom Weavers 1790- 1850* (Edinburgh, 1978), p. 73; M. Gray, Economic Welfare and Money Incomes in the Highlands, 1750-1850', *Scottish Journal of Political Economy*, vol 2 (1956), p. 56.

14. This paragraph is based upon C.A. Whatley, ' "The fettering bonds of brotherhood": combination and labour relations in the Scottish coal mining industry c. 1690-1775', *Social History*, Vol. 12 (1987); B.F. Duckham, *A History of the Scottish Coal Industry,* vol. I, 1700-1815, (Newton Abbot, 1970), p. 271; M.W. Flinn, *The History of the British Coal Industry*, vol. 2, 1700-1830 (Oxford, 1984), pp. 387-8, 390.

15. The North Staffordshire pattern of improvement has been outlined in Hunt and Botham, *art. cit*; for the rising standard of living of the Lancashire labourer, see E.W. Gilboy, 'The Cost of Living and Real Wages in Eighteenth Century England', in Taylor, *Standard of Living*, pp. 9-13.

16. The preceding paragraphs are based upon the data contained in the relevant Appendix Tables. For a discussion of Gourvish's Indexes 1 and 2, see Gourvish, *art.cit.* The thesis that real incomes experienced relatively small or no gains for the period of the French Wars as a whole is sustained in part by the returns contained in Table 6(B) (South of Scotland colliers) and Table 8 (miscellaneous artisans). If comparisons are made of real income trends amongst these groups between 1790 and 1816, the GRS index records in the former case a rise of 0.8 per cent for the period as a whole and in the latter instance, an improvement of considerably below 1 per cent per annum. The Tucker index in each case reveals a fall in living standards. 1816, of course, was a year of depression in the Scottish economy and, compared with 1814, could bias real income in a downwards direction. But, as other tables illustrate, this bias, produced by downward pressure upon money wages, could be offset by the scale of the drop in the cost of living between 1814 (which we have used as our terminal date elsewhere in this discussion) and 1816. Furthermore in the case of coalminers Table 6(A) shows that in the West of Scotland real and money incomes were under pressure from 1811 onwards, interrupted only briefly by a relative improvement in miners' living standards in 1815.

17. Murray, *Handloom Weavers*, pp. 23, 40-2.

18. Duckham, *Scottish Coal Industry*, pp. 277-8.

19. There are, of course, adverse factors that must be considered in relation to the amelioration thesis. They include, among others, the distorting effect of the War itself upon the markets and sources of raw materials and the sharp fall in the production of linen cloth in the late 1790s and early 1800s. In relation to the rural-urban migration thesis see T.M. Devine, 'Social stability and agrarian change in the eastern Lowlands of Scotland, 1810-1840', *Social History,* 3 (1978), pp. 331-346.

20. The post-1820 turning point for the artisan is strongly underlined by the data in Tables 2(C) and (D). If we ignore the massive, short-term impact of the 1824 building boom in Edinburgh, it is still clear that Edinburgh's carpenters and Cupar's stonema-

sons and carpenters had by 1826 secured a massive rise in their real income compared not merely with 1819-20 but also with 1790. Yet 1826 was a year of profound depression in the Scottish economy.

21. A.L. Bowley, "Agricultural Wages' (Part IV), *Journal of the Royal Statistical Society,* vol. 62 (1899).

22. On this point see R.A. Dodgshon, 'The Economics of Sheep Farming in the Southern Uplands during the Age of Improvement, 1750-1833', *Economic History Review,* xxix (1976), pp. 564-5; M. Gray, 'Scottish Emigration: the Social Impact of Agrarian Change in the Scottish Lowlands, 1775-1875', *Perspectives in American History,* vol. VII (1973), pp. 154-5.

23. In several counties, however, — for instance, Perthshire — the worker's family income was reduced after the early 1800s by the decline of linen spinning. Bye-employments in such areas became less plentiful over time.

24. For a discussion of poverty, assessed from this perspective, in the post-1830 era, see J.H. Treble, *Urban Poverty in Britain, 1830-1914,* (Batsford, 1979; Methuen paperback edition, 1983).

APPENDIX

*Note on Sources used in Constructing Tables*

Table 1 is derived from the following sources:

(a) Gilboy index and Tucker index have been calculated from their data in A.J. Taylor (ed.), *The Standard of Living in Britain during the Industrial Revolution* (London, 1975).

(b) The Botham and Hunt index has been taken from E.H. Hunt and F.W. Botham, 'Wages in Britain during the Industrial Revolution', *Economic History Review,* XL, No. 3 (August,1987).

(c) The Gayer, Rostow and Schwartz index has been calculated from their index of domestic commodities in B.R. Mitchell and P. Deane, *Abstract of British Historical Statistics* (Cambridge, 1962).

The abbreviations Gil., T., BH, and GRS have been used for these indexes in several of the following tables.

Tables 2(A) to (D).- the money wages used in these tables have been taken from A. Bowley, 'Wages in the Scottish Building Trade', *Journal of the Royal Statistical Society,* vol. 63 (1900). The only exception to that rule is the two tables of Glasgow masons' and building labourers' money wages which have utilised the relevant volume of the *OSA,* J. Cleland, *Statistical and Population Tables relative to the City of Glasgow* , 3rd. ed., (Glasgow, 1828) (p. 134 records for 1822 a rise of 10 to 15 per cent. in building workers' wages which I have incorporated here) and J. Cleland, *Enumeration of the Inhabitants of the City of Glasgow* , 2nd. ed., (Glasgow, 1832).

Table 2(E). has also been constructed from these last three sources.

Tables 3(A) and (B). I have taken money wage data from N. Murray, *The Scottish Handloom Weavers, 1790-1850* (Edinburgh, 1978). The Gourvish cost of living index is contained in T.R. Gourvish, 'The Cost of Living in Glasgow in the Early Nineteenth Century', *Economic History Review,* XXV (1972).

Tables 4(A) and (B). The money wage data have been taken from Gibson, *History of Glasgow* (Glasgow, 1777) for 1777, for 1793 and 1824 from Wood and Bowley, 'Time Wages in Engineering and Shipbuilding', *Journal of the Royal Statistical Society,* vol. 68 (1905), and for the remaining years from the same Cleland sources that were listed under Tables 2(A) to (D).

Table 5. The money wage data have been taken from Bowley and Wood's study of printers' wages, *Journal of the Royal Statistical Society,* vol. 62 (1899).

Table 6(A). The money wage data have been taken from B.F. Duckham, *A History of the Scottish Coal Industry,* vol. 1, 1700-1815 (Newton Abbot, 1970).

Tables 7(A) and (B). The money wage data have been taken from A. Bowley, Agricultural Wages — Scotland', *Journal of the Royal Statistical Society,* vol. 62 (1899).

TABLE 1

*Cost of Living Indexes*

(1790 = 100)

| Year | Gilboy | Tucker | Hunt and Botham | Gayer, Rostow and Schwartz |
|------|--------|--------|------------------|---------------------------|
| 1760 | 72.9 | 83.8 | 65.2 | |
| 1761 | 74.4 | 79.8 | 65.7 | |
| 1762 | 82.0 | 83.1 | 67.3 | |
| 1763 | 82.7 | 80.7 | 77.7 | |
| 1764 | 86.5 | 83.5 | 82.6 | |
| 1765 | 88.0 | 86.9 | 84.1 | |
| 1766 | 93.2 | 88.4 | 88.9 | |
| 1767 | 92.5 | 91.3 | 90.5 | |
| 1768 | 82.0 | 90.5 | 85.3 | |
| 1769 | 81.2 | 84.0 | 83.2 | |
| 1770 | 88.7 | 86.2 | 83.4 | |
| 1771 | 97.7 | 92.1 | 88.9 | |
| 1772 | 102.3 | 98.7 | 90.5 | |
| 1773 | 98.5 | 98.8 | 88.5 | |
| 1774 | 97.0 | 96.8 | 93.3 | |
| 1775 | 96.2 | 92.7 | 86.5 | |
| 1776 | 90.2 | 85.8 | 76.0 | |
| 1777 | 98.5 | 93.9 | 83.0 | |
| 1778 | 92.5 | 90.2 | 83.5 | |
| 1779 | 88.0 | 85.8 | 75.0 | |
| 1780 | 94.0 | 81.0 | 74.8 | |
| 1781 | 94.0 | 96.1 | 79.3 | |
| 1782 | 108.3 | 100.1 | 85.7 | |
| 1783 | 104.5 | 99.2 | 97.1 | |
| 1784 | 97.0 | 96.8 | 90.1 | |
| 1785 | 99.2 | 94.0 | 86.7 | |
| 1786 | 96.2 | 92.1 | 87.6 | |
| 1787 | 97.7 | 92.6 | 89.8 | |
| 1788 | 95.5 | 92.3 | 90.4 | |
| 1789 | 100.8 | 94.9 | 89.2 | |
| 1790 | 100.0 | 100.0 | 100.0 | 100.0 |
| 1791 | 98.5 | 97.2 | 98.0 | 97.0 |
| 1792 | 105.3 | 95.9 | 105.6 | 92.5 |

TABLE 1 contd.

| Year | Gilboy | Tucker | Hunt and Botham | Gayer, Rostow and Schwartz |
|------|--------|--------|-----------------|----------------------------|
| 1793 | 111.3 | 101.9 | | 105.2 |
| 1794 | 126.3 | 103.7 | | 110.6 |
| 1795 | 134.6 | 119.2 | | 130.4 |
| 1796 | 115.0 | 119.3 | | 133.0 |
| 1797 | 114.3 | 117.9 | | 115.7 |
| 1798 | 124.1 | 118.8 | | 115.0 |
| 1799 | 172.2 | 128.2 | | 137.7 |
| 1800 | 189.5 | 160.1 | | 179.8 |
| 1801 | 142.9 | 162.9 | | 185.6 |
| 1802 | 124.8 | 138.3 | | 140.4 |
| 1803 | 128.6 | 142.9 | | 138.2 |
| 1804 | 153.4 | 144.2 | | 137.4 |
| 1805 | 147.4 | 158.8 | | 153.3 |
| 1806 | 151.1 | 154.6 | | 151.4 |
| 1807 | 169.9 | 154.2 | | 147.3 |
| 1808 | 177.4 | 162.3 | | 162.2 |
| 1809 | 172.2 | 177.9 | | 176.6 |
| 1810 | 169.2 | 178.1 | | 176.2 |
| 1811 | 200.0 | 176.7 | | 171.3 |
| 1812 | 203.0 | 193.3 | | 197.7 |
| 1813 | 168.4 | 198.6 | | 198.7 |
| 1814 | 148.9 | 179.3 | | 170.5 |
| 1815 | 137.6 | 162.0 | | 143.1 |
| 1816 | | 157.7 | | 132.0 |
| 1817 | | 161.8 | | 151.3 |
| 1818 | | 163.4 | | 160.5 |
| 1819 | | 160.6 | | 149.7 |
| 1820 | | 151.2 | | 134.8 |
| 1821 | | 138.9 | | 113.0 |
| 1822 | | 124.8 | | 96.3 |
| 1823 | | 126.9 | | 111.4 |
| 1824 | | 128.9 | | 119.6 |
| 1825 | | 139.9 | | 133.8 |
| 1826 | | 134.5 | | 122.5 |
| 1827 | | 132.1 | | 121.9 |
| 1828 | | 127.9 | | 118.1 |
| 1829 | | 125.4 | | 118.0 |
| 1830 | | 118.7 | | 116.8 |

*People and Society in Scotland*

TABLE 2(A)

*Real Wages of Scottish Masons, 1730-1791*

(1791 = 100)

| Year | Money Wages | Gilboy | Tucker | Botham and Hunt |
|------|-------------|--------|--------|-----------------|
| | | Real wages expressed in terms of the following indexes: | | |
| 1730-45 | 50 | 70.2 | 71.2 | — |
| 1745-60 | 70 | 92.0 | 80.1 | — |
| 1767-77 | 70 | 74.0 | 74.1 | 79.5 |
| 1791 | 100 | 100.0 | 100.0 | 100.0 |

Real Wages of Scottish Carpenters, 1730-1791

(1791 =100)

| Year | Money Wages | Gilboy | Tucker | Botham and Hunt |
|------|-------------|--------|--------|-----------------|
| | | Real Wages expressed in terms of the following indexes : | | |
| 1730-45 | 50.0 | 70.2 | 71.2 | — |
| 1745-60 | 66.7 | 87.6 | 76.3 | — |
| 1767-77 | 66.7 | 70.5 | 70.1 | 75.8 |
| 1791 | 100.0 | 100.0 | 100.0 | 100.0 |

## TABLE 2(B)

*Real Wages of Scottish Masons, 1745-1791*

(1791 = 100)

| Year | Money Wages | Real wages expressed in terms of the following indexes : | | |
|------|-------------|--------|--------|-----------------|
| | | Gilboy | Tucker | Botham and Hunt |
| 1745 | 70  | 97.5  | 91.3  | —     |
| 1746 | 70  | 99.7  | 85.4  | —     |
| 1747 | 70  | 96.6  | 85.6  | —     |
| 1748 | 70  | 91.7  | 83.6  | —     |
| 1749 | 70  | 93.6  | 81.7  | —     |
| 1750 | 70  | 98.6  | 80.3  | 111.8 |
| 1751 | 70  | 93.6  | 75.8  | 107.2 |
| 1752 | 70  | 97.5  | 79.2  | 103.4 |
| 1753 | 70  | 96.6  | 77.5  | 101.6 |
| 1754 | 70  | 99.7  | 86.6  | 93.5  |
| 1755 | 70  | 93.6  | 84.7  | 89.2  |
| 1756 | 70  | 73.4  | 66.7  | 82.1  |
| 1757 | 70  | 77.8  | 69.7  | 75.3  |
| 1758 | 70  | 85.0  | 78.3  | 87.6  |
| 1759 | 70  | 92.6  | 82.4  | 102.2 |
| 1760 | 70  | 94.6  | 81.3  | 105.3 |
| 1767 | 70  | 74.5  | 74.5  | 75.8  |
| 1768 | 70  | 84.1  | 75.2  | 80.5  |
| 1769 | 70  | 85.0  | 81.1  | 82.4  |
| 1770 | 70  | 77.8  | 78.9  | 82.3  |
| 1771 | 70  | 70.6  | 73.9  | 77.2  |
| 1772 | 70  | 67.4  | 69.0  | 75.8  |
| 1773 | 70  | 70.0  | 68.9  | 77.5  |
| 1774 | 70  | 71.1  | 70.3  | 73.5  |
| 1775 | 70  | 71.6  | 73.4  | 79.3  |
| 1776 | 70  | 76.4  | 79.4  | 90.2  |
| 1777 | 70  | 70.0  | 72.5  | 82.6  |
| 1791 | 100 | 100.0 | 100.0 | 100.0 |

TABLE 2 (C)

*Real Wages of Carpenters in Selected Scottish Towns, 1790-1830*

Edinburgh

(1792 = 100)

| Year | Money Wages | Real wages expressed in terms of the following indexes: | | |
| | | Gil. | GRS | T |
|---|---|---|---|---|
| 1792 | 100 | 100 | 100 | 100 |
| 1800 | 121.1 | 67.3 | 62.3 | 72.6 |
| 1804 | 231.6 | 159.0 | 156.0 | 154.0 |
| 1810 | 189.5 | 117.9 | 99.5 | 102.0 |
| 1823-42 | 42.1 to 263.2 | — | 193.9 to 210.8 | 181.5 to197.3 |
| 1826-7 | 168.4 to 178.9 | — | 127.5 to 135.4 | 121.2to128.7 |

Arbroath

(1791 = 100)

| Year | Money Wages | Real wages using: | |
| | | GRS | T |
|---|---|---|---|
| 1791 | 100 | 100 | 100 |
| 1818 | 175 | 105.7 | 104.1 |
| 1819-20 | 175 | 119.4 | 109.1 |
| 1821-2 | 175 | 162.2 | 129.1 |
| 1823 | 175 | 152.4 | 134.0 |
| 1824 | 175 | 141.9 | 132.0 |
| 1825 | 212.5 | 154.1 | 147.7 |
| 1826 | 187.5 | 148.5 | 135.5 |

Cupar

(1792 =100)

| Year | Money Wages | Gil | Real wages using: | |
| | | | GRS | T |
|---|---|---|---|---|
| 1792 | 100 | 100 | 100 | 100 |
| 1795 | 111.1 | 86.9 | 78.8 | 89.4 |
| 1808 | 166.67 | 98.9 | 95.0 | 98.5 |
| 1810 | 166.67 | 103.7 | 87.4 | 89.8 |
| 1814 | 166.67 | 117.9 | 90.4 | 89.1 |
| 1819 | 166.67 | — | 103.0 | 99.5 |
| 1826 | 166.67 | — | 125.9 | 118.8 |

TABLE 2(D)

*Real Wages of Masons in Selected Scottish Towns, 1790-1833*

*Arbroath*

(1791 = 100)

| Year | Money Wages | Real Wages expressed in terms of the following indexes : | |
| | | GRS | T |
|---|---|---|---|
| 1791 | 100 | 100 | 100 |
| 1812-3 | 126.7 | 62.0 | 62.8 |
| 1814 | 115.8 | 65.9 | 62.8 |
| 1815 | 100 | 67.8 | 60.0 |
| 1816-7 | 90.0 | 61.6 | 54.7 |
| 1818 | 113.3 | 68.5 | 67.4 |
| 1819-20 | 90.0 | 61.4 | 56:1 |
| 1821-2 | 100 | 92.7 | 73.7 |
| 1823 | 125.8 | 109.6 | 96.3 |
| 1824 | 140.0 | 113.5 | 105.6 |
| 1825 | 140.8 | 102.1 | 97.8 |
| 1826 | 102.5 | 81.2 | 74.1 |

*Cupar*

(1792 = 100)

| Year | Money Wages | Gil. | Real wages using: GRS | T |
|---|---|---|---|---|
| 1760 | 66.67 | 96.3 | - | 76.3 |
| 1792 | 100.0 | 100.0 | 100.0 | 100.0 |
| 1795 | 122.2 | 95.6 | 86.7 | 98.3 |
| 1810 | 200.0 | 124.5 | 105.0 | 107.7 |
| 1814 | 155.6 | 110.0 | 84.4 | 83.2 |
| 1819 | 166.67 | - | 103.0 | 99.5 |
| 1826 | 188.9 | - | 142.7 | 134.6 |

*People and Society in Scotland*

TABLE 2(D) contd.

*Glasgow*

(1792 = 100)

Table (A)*

| Year | Money Wages | Real wages expressed in terms of the following indexes: | | |
|------|-------------|------|-----|---|
| | | Gil. | GRS | T |
| 1792 | 100 | 100 | 100 | 100 |
| 1810 | 170 | 105.8 | 91.5 | 89.2 |
| 1811 | 170 | 89.5 | 92.2 | 91.8 |
| 1812 | 180 | 93.4 | 89.3 | 84.2 |
| 1813 | 180 | 112.6 | 86.9 | 83.8 |
| 1814 | 180 | 127.3 | 96.3 | 97.7 |
| 1815 | 180 | 137.7 | 106.6 | 116.4 |
| 1816 | 180 | — | 109.5 | 126.1 |
| 1817 | 200 | — | 118.6 | 122.2 |
| 1818 | 190 | — | 111.5 | 109.5 |
| 1819 | 150 | — | 89.6 | 92.7 |
| 1822 | 165 to 172.5 | — | 126.8 to 132.6 | 158.5 to 165.7 |
| 1831 | 140 | — | 107.0 | 109.5 |

* This table is based upon the lowest figure (10/-) cited for the weekly wages of ordinary — as against best paid — masons in the O.S.A.

Table (B)*

| Year | Money Wages | Real wages expressed in terms of the following indexes : | | |
|------|-------------|------|---|-----|
| | | Gil | T | GRS |
| 1792 | 100 | 100 | 100 | 100 |
| 1810 | 141.67 | 88.2 | 76.3 | 74.4 |
| 1811 | 141.67 | 74.6 | 76.9 | 76.5 |
| 1812 | 150.0 | 77.8 | 74.4 | 70.2 |
| 1813 | 150.0 | 93.8 | 72.4 | 69.8 |
| 1814 | 150.0 | 106.1 | 80.2 | 81.4 |
| 1815 | 150.0 | 114.8 | 88.8 | 97.0 |
| 1816 | 150.0 | — | 91.2 | 105.1 |
| 1817 | 166.67 | — | 98.8 | 101.9 |
| 1818 | 158.33 | — | 92.9 | 91.3 |
| 1819 | 125.0 | — | 74.6 | 77.3 |
| 1822 | 137.5 to 143.75 | — | 105.7 to 110.5 | 132.1 to 138.1 |
| 1831 | 116.67 | — | 89.1 | 91.3 |

* This table is based upon the highest figure cited for the weekly wages of ordinary — as against best paid — masons in 1792 in the O.S.A.

TABLE 2 (E)

*Real Wages of a Building Labourer in Glasgow, 1792-1831*

(1792 =100)

Table (i)*

| Year | Money Wages | Real wages expressed in terms of the following indexes : | | |
|---|---|---|---|---|
| | | Gil. | T | GRS |
| 1792 | 100 | 100 | 100 | 100 |
| 1810 | 146.67 | 91.3 | 79.0 | 77.0 |
| 1811 | 146.67 | 77.2 | 79.6 | 79.2 |
| 1812 | 146.67 | 76.1 | 72.8 | 68.6 |
| 1813 | 146.67 | 91.7 | 70.8 | 68.3 |
| 1814 | 146.67 | 103.7 | 78.4 | 79.6 |
| 1815 | 146.67 | 112.2 | 86.8 | 94.8 |
| 1816 | 146.67 | — | 89.2 | 102.8 |
| 1817 | 146.67 | — | 86.9 | 89.7 |
| 1818 | 120.0 | — | 70.4 | 69.2 |
| 1819 | 100.0 | — | 59.7 | 61.8 |
| 1822 | 110 to 115 | — | 84.6 to 88.4 | 105.7 to 110.5 |
| 1831 | 120.0 | — | 91.7 | 93.9 |

Table (ii)*

| Year | Money wages | Real wages expressed in terms of the following indexes : | | |
|---|---|---|---|---|
| | | Gil. | T | GRS |
| 1792 | 100 | 100 | 100 | 100 |
| 1810 | 122.2 | 76.0 | 65.8 | 64.1 |
| 1811 | 122.2 | 64.3 | 66.3 | 66.0 |
| 1812 | 122.2 | 63.4 | 60.6 | 57.2 |
| 1813 | 122.2 | 76.4 | 59.0 | 56.9 |
| 1814 | 122.2 | 86.4 | 65.3 | 66.3 |
| 1815 | 122.2 | 93.5 | 72.4 | 79.0 |
| 1816 | 122.2 | — | 74.3 | 85.6 |
| 1817 | 122.2 | — | 72.4 | 74.7 |
| 1818 | 100.0 | — | 58.7 | 57.6 |
| 1819 | 83.3 | — | 49.7 | 51.5 |
| 1822 | 91.67 to 95.8 | — | 70.5 to 73.6 | 88.1 to 92.0 |
| 1831 | 100.0 | — | 76.4 | 78.2 |

* Table (i) is based upon the lowest figure (1/3 per day or 7/6 per week) cited for the wages of building labourers in 1792 in the relevant volume of the O.S.A. Table (ii) is based upon the highest figure cited for the wages of building labourers (1/6 per day or 9/-per week) in the same volume.

TABLE 3(A)

*Real Weekly Wages, recorded in March of Each Year*
*of Weavers of Book Muslins in Glasgow*

(1810 = 100)

| Year | Money Wages | Real wages expressed in terms of following indexes : | | | |
|------|-------------|--------|--------|--------------------------|-------------------|
| | | Gilboy | Tucker | Rostow Gayer, Schwartz | Gourvish Index 2 |
| 1797 | 82.5 | 122.0 | 124.6 | 125.6 | |
| 1798 | 89.8 | 122.5 | 134.6 | 137.5 | |
| 1799 | 91.0 | 89.4 | 126.4 | 116.5 | |
| 1800 | 88.7 | 79.2 | 98.7 | 87.0 | |
| 1801 | 86.4 | 102.2 | 94.4 | 82.1 | |
| 1802 | 91.5 | 124.0 | 117.8 | 114.8 | |
| 1803 | 95.5 | 125.7 | 119.1 | 121.8 | |
| 1804 | 89.3 | 98.5 | 110.2 | 114.5 | |
| 1805 | 104.0 | 119.4 | 116.6 | 119.5 | |
| 1806 | 119.8 | 134.2 | 138.0 | 139.5 | |
| 1807 | 105.1 | 104.7 | 121.4 | 125.7 | |
| 1808 | 89.3 | 85.2 | 98.0 | 97.0 | |
| 1809 | 79.7 | 78.3 | 79.8 | 79.5 | |
| 1810 | 100.0 | 100.0 | 100.0 | 100.0 | 100.0 |
| 1811 | 84.2 | 71.2 | 84.9 | 86.6 | 83.4 |
| 1812 | 89.3 | 74.4 | 82.3 | 79.6 | 79.6 |
| 1813 | 102.8 | 103.3 | 92.2 | 91.1 | 88.2 |
| 1814 | 117.5 | 133.5 | 116.7 | 121.4 | 111.7 |
| 1815 | 95.5 | 117.5 | 104.9 | 117.6 | 98.2 |

TABLE 3 (B)

*Real Wages of Weavers of Hessian Sheeting at Dundee, 1810-30*

(1810 = 100)

| | | Real wages expressed in terms of following indexes : | | | |
|---|---|---|---|---|---|
| Year | Money Wages | Gilboy | Tucker | Rostow Gayer, Schwartz | Gourvish Index 2 |
| 1810 | 100.0 | 100.0 | 100.0 | 100.0 | 100.0 |
| 1811 | 78.6 | 66.5 | 79.2 | 80.9 | 77.9 |
| 1812 | 71.4 | 59.5 | 65.8 | 63.6 | 63.6 |
| 1813 | 57.1 | 57.4 | 51.2 | 50.6 | 49.0 |
| 1814 | 85.7 | 97.4 | 85.1 | 88.5 | 81.5 |
| 1815 | 92.9 | 114.3 | 102.1 | 114.4 | 95.5 |
| 1816 | 50.0 | - | 56.5 | 66.8 | 49.6 |
| 1817 | 42.9 | - | 47.2 | 49.9 | 39.2 |
| 1818 | 57.1 | - | 62.3 | 62.7 | 56.1 |
| 1819 | 50.0 | - | 55.4 | 58.8 | 58.1 |
| 1820 | 50.0 | - | 58.9 | 65.4 | - |
| 1821 | 64.3 | - | 82.4 | 100.3 | - |
| 1822 | 64.3 | - | 91.7 | 117.6 | 79.5 |
| 1823 | 64.3 | - | 90.2 | 101.7 | - |
| 1824 | 75.0 | - | 103.6 | 110.5 | - |
| 1825 | 82.1 | - | 104.5 | 108.2 | - |
| 1826 | 35.7 | - | 47.3 | 51.4 | - |
| 1827 | 39.3 | - | 53.0 | 56.8 | - |
| 1828 | 53.6 | - | 74.7 | 80.0 | - |
| 1829 | 53.6 | - | 76.1 | 80.0 | - |
| 1830 | 42.9 | - | 64.4 | 64.7 | - |

TABLE 4(A)

*Real Wages of Glasgow Mechanics, Machine Makers, 1777-1831*

(1793 = 100)

| Year | Money Wages | Gil | GRS | T |
|---|---|---|---|---|
| | | Real wages expressed in terms of the following indexes : | | |
| 1777 | 58.33 | 65.9 | — | 63.3 |
| 1793 | 100.0 | 100.0 | 100.0 | 100.0 |
| 1810 | 158.33 | 104.2 | 94.5 | 90.6 |
| 1811 | 158.33 | 88.1 | 97.3 | 91.3 |
| 1812 | 158.33 | 86.8 | 84.3 | 83.5 |
| 1813 | 158.33 | 104.6 | 83.8 | 81.2 |
| 1814 | 158.33 | 118.3 | 97.7 | 90.0 |
| 1815 | 158.33 | 128.1 | 116.4 | 99.6 |
| 1816 | 158.33 | — | 126.2 | 102.3 |
| 1817 | 158.33 | — | 110.1 | 99.7 |
| 1818 | 158.33 | — | 103.8 | 98.7 |
| 1819 | 158.33 | — | 111.3 | 100.5 |
| 1822 | 158.33 | — | 173.0 | 129.2 |
| 1824 | 200 to 208.33 | — | 175.9 to183.2 | 158.1 to 164.7 |
| 1831 | 158.33 | — | 140.9 | 128.6 |

TABLE 4(B)

*Real Wages of Glasgow Mechanics, Machine Makers, 1810-31*

1810 = 100

| Year | Money Wages | Gourvish Index 1 | GRS | T |
|------|-------------|------------------|-----|---|
| | | Real Wages expressed in terms of the following indexes : | | |
| 1810 | 100 | 100 | 100 | 100 |
| 1811 | 100 | 103.1 | 102.9 | 100.8 |
| 1812 | 100 | 95.1 | 89.1 | 92.2 |
| 1813 | 100 | 89.3 | 88.7 | 89.7 |
| 1814 | 100 | 95.5 | 103.3 | 99.3 |
| 1815 | 100 | 104.1 | 123.2 | 109.9 |
| 1816 | 100 | 101.7 | 133.5 | 113.0 |
| 1817 | 100 | 94.0 | 116.4 | 110.1 |
| 1818 | 100 | 100.9 | 109.8 | 109.1 |
| 1819 | 100 | 116.0 | 117.6 | 110.9 |
| 1822 | 100 | 121.4 | 182.8 | 142.7 |
| 1824 | 126.3 to 131.6 | — | 186 to 193.8 | 174.4 to 181.8 |
| 1831 | 100 | 136.2 | 149.0 | 141.8 |

TABLE 5

*Real Wages of Edinburgh Printers, 1773-1833/5*

(1791 = 100)

| Year | Money Wages | Gilboy | Tucker | BH | GRS |
|------|-------------|--------|--------|----|----|
| | | Real wages expressed in terms of the following indexes : | | | |
| 1773 | 72.2 | 72.2 | 71.1 | 80.0 | - |
| 1791 | 100.0 | 100.0 | 100.0 | 100.0 | 100.0 |
| 1802 | 92.4 | 72.9 | 64.9 | — | 63.9 |
| 1805 | 102.5 | 68.5 | 62.7 | — | 64.9 |
| 1809 | 126.6 | 72.4 | 69.2 | — | 69.5 |
| 1833-5 | 106.3 | — | 92.6 | — | 101.7 |

TABLE 6(A)

*Real Wages of Miners employed Govan Colliery, 1811-21*
*(including valuation of 'in kind' payments)*

(1811 = 100)

| Year | Total Earnings | Real Wages expressed in terms of the following indexes : | | |
|------|------|------|------|------|
| | | GRS | Gourvish Index 1 | Tucker |
| 1811 | 100 | 100 | 100 | 100 |
| 1812 | 99.3 | 86.0 | 91.6 | 90.8 |
| 1813 | 82.6 | 71.2 | 71.6 | 73.5 |
| 1814 | 86.8 | 87.2 | 80.4 | 85.5 |
| 1815 | 90.7 | 108.6 | 91.5 | 98.9 |
| 1817 | 80.6 | 91.3 | 73.5 | 88.0 |
| 1818 | 70.5 | 75.1 | 69.0 | 75.2 |
| 1821 | 66.9 | 101.4 | — | 85.1 |

TABLE 6 (B)

*Real Wages of Colliers in the South of Scotland 1790-1831*

(1790 = 100)

| Year | Money Wages | Real wages expressed in terms of the following indexes: | | |
|------|------|------|------|------|
| | | T | GRS | Gilboy |
| 1790 | 100 | 100 | 100 | 100 |
| 1810 | 164 | 92.1 | 93.1 | 96.9 |
| 1816 | 133 | 84.3 | 100.8 | — |
| 1820 | 124.7 | 82.5 | 92.5 | — |
| 1824 | 138.1 | 107.1 | 115.5 | — |
| 1831 | 132 | 105.2 | 111.6 | — |

*Source*: G.H. Wood, 'The Course of Average Wages between 1790 and 1860',
*Economic Journal*, ix (1899)

TABLE 7(A)

Money Wage Component of Unmarried Farm Servants,
expressed in terms of real wages, 1790-1814

(1790 = 100)

| | Real Wages measured by the relevant price indexes: | | | | | | | | |
| | 1790 | | | 1794 | | | 1814 | | |
| County | Gil | T | GRS | Gil | T | GRS | Gil | T | GRS |
|---|---|---|---|---|---|---|---|---|---|
| Wigtown | 100 | 100 | 100 | 90.5 | 110.2 | 103.3 | 143.9 | 119.5 | 125.7 |
| Kirkcudbright | 100 | 100 | 100 | 87.3 | 106.4 | 99.7 | 139.0 | 115.4 | 121.3 |
| Dumfries | 100 | 100 | 100 | 84.5 | 102.9 | 96.5 | 134.3 | 111.5 | 117.3 |
| Selkirk | 100 | 100 | 100 | 85.3 | 103.9 | 97.4 | 155.0 | 128.7 | 135.3 |
| Peebles | 100 | 100 | 100 | 92.4 | 112.5 | 105.5 | 167.9 | 139.4 | 146.6 |
| Roxburgh | 100 | 100 | 100 | 84.5 | 102.9 | 96.5 | 125.4 | 104.1 | 109.5 |
| Berwick | 100 | 100 | 100 | 97.5 | 118.7 | 111.3 | 144.7 | 120.1 | 126.3 |
| Haddington | 100 | 100 | 100 | 85.3 | 103.9 | 97.4 | 144.7 | 120.1 | 126.3 |
| Edinburgh | 100 | 100 | 100 | 91.4 | 111.3 | 104.3 | 124.0 | 103.0 | 108.3 |
| Linlithgow | 100 | 100 | 100 | 105.6 | 128.5 | 120.5 | 107.5 | 89.2 | 93.8 |
| Clackmannan | 100 | 100 | 100 | 91.4 | 111.3 | 104.3 | 124.0 | 103.0 | 108.3 |
| Kinross | 100 | 100 | 100 | 99.0 | 120.5 | 113.0 | 134.3 | 111.5 | 117.3 |
| Fife | 100 | 100 | 100 | 99.0 | 120.5 | 113.0 | 134.3 | 111.5 | 117.3 |
| Ayr | 100 | 100 | 100 | 99.0 | 120.5 | 113.0 | 125.9 | 104.6 | 110.0 |
| Lanark | 100 | 100 | 100 | 99.0 | 120.5 | 113.0 | 125.9 | 104.6 | 110.0 |
| Renfrew | 100 | 100 | 100 | 88.0 | 107.1 | 100.5 | 112.0 | 93.0 | 97.8 |
| Dunbarton | 100 | 100 | 100 | 89.1 | 108.5 | 101.7 | 125.9 | 104.6 | 110.0 |
| Stirling | 100 | 100 | 100 | 99.0 | 120.5 | 113.0 | 142.7 | 118.5 | 124.6 |
| Perth | 100 | 100 | 100 | 89.1 | 108.5 | 101.7 | 134.3 | 111.5 | 117.3 |
| Forfar | 100 | 100 | 100 | 95.0 | 115.7 | 108.5 | 143.3 | 119.0 | 125.1 |
| Kincardine | 100 | 100 | 100 | 105.6 | 128.5 | 120.5 | 179.1 | 148.7 | 156.4 |
| Aberdeen | 100 | 100 | 100 | 110.8 | 135.0 | 126.6 | 188.0 | 156.2 | 164.2 |
| Banff | 100 | 100 | 100 | 108.0 | 131.5 | 123.3 | 171.0 | 141.9 | 149.3 |
| Elgin | 100 | 100 | 100 | 95.0 | 115.7 | 108.5 | 188.0 | 156.2 | 164.2 |
| Nairn | 100 | 100 | 100 | 95.0 | 115.7 | 108.5 | 188.0 | 156.2 | 164.2 |
| Argyll | 100 | 100 | 100 | 90.5 | 110.2 | 103.3 | 105.5 | 87.6 | 92.1 |
| Inverness | 100 | 100 | 100 | 90.5 | 110.2 | 103.3 | 105.5 | 87.6 | 92.1 |
| Ross&Cromarty | 100 | 100 | 100 | 79.2 | 96.4 | 90.4 | 167.9 | 139.4 | 146.6 |
| Sutherland | 100 | 100 | 100 | 190.0 | 231.4 | 217.0 | 241.8 | 200.8 | 211.1 |
| Caithness | 100 | 100 | 100 | 171.6 | 209.0 | 195.9 | 179.1 | 148.7 | 156.4 |

*People and Society in Scotland*

## TABLE 7(B)

*Real Wages for All Agricultural Workers in Scotland 1760-1810*

(Real Wages are expressed in terms of money wages, including an evaluation of 'in kind' payments, deflated or inflated by the relevant cost of living indexes)

(1770 = 100)

| Region | 1760-1770 | | | 1770-1780 | | | 1780-179 | | | 1790 All Indexes | 1794 | | | 1810 | | |
|---|---|---|---|---|---|---|---|---|---|---|---|---|---|---|---|---|
| | Gil | T | BH | Gil | T | BH | Gil | T | BH | Gil | Gil | T | GRS | Gil | T | GRS |
| South West | 67.0 | 65.9 | 70.8 | 88.9 | 92.6 | 100.6 | 94.9 | 99.4 | 106.3 | 100 | 91.5 | 111.5 | 104.5 | 147.8 | 140.4 | 141.9 |
| South Central | — | — | — | — | — | — | — | — | — | 100 | 92.3 | 112.5 | 105.5 | 126.1 | 119.8 | 121.1 |
| South East | 55.8 | 55.0 | 59.1 | 59.3 | 61.7 | 67.0 | 63.3 | 66.2 | 70.9 | 100 | 86.6 | 105.5 | 98.9 | 118.2 | 112.3 | 113.5 |
| Lothians | 74.4 | 73.3 | 78.7 | 82.3 | 85.7 | 93.1 | — | — | — | 100 | 84.1 | 102.5 | 96.1 | 116.4 | 110.5 | 111.7 |
| Mid East | 68.0 | 66.9 | 71.9 | 67.9 | 70.6 | 76.6 | 100.0 | 100.0 | 100.0 | 100 | 87.7 | 106.8 | 100.1 | — | — | — |
| Mid West | 69.2 | 68.1 | 73.2 | — | — | — | 98.0 | 102.5 | 109.8 | 100 | 91.9 | 112.0 | 105.0 | 114.4 | 108.6 | 109.8 |
| East Central | 70.6 | 69.5 | 74.7 | 66.4 | 69.2 | 75.1 | 82.5 | 89.5 | 92.4 | 100 | 96.8 | 117.8 | 110.5 | 118.2 | 112.3 | 113.5 |
| North East | 91.5 | 90.2 | 96.9 | — | — | — | — | — | — | 100 | 91.4 | 111.3 | 104.3 | 131.9 | 125.3 | 126.6 |
| West Central | — | — | — | — | — | — | — | — | — | 100 | 90.1 | 109.7 | 102.9 | 108.0 | 102.6 | 103.7 |
| North | — | — | — | — | — | — | — | — | — | 100 | 83.1 | 101.3 | 94.9 | 138.9 | 131.9 | 133.4 |

TABLE 8

*Real Wages of Miscellaneous Groups of Industrial Workers 1790-1831*

(1790 = 100)

*Edinburgh*

| Year | Money Wages | Real wages expressed in terms of the following indexes : | | |
| | | Gil | T | GRS |
|------|-------------|-----|-----|-----|
| 1790 | 100 | 100 | 100 | 100 |
| 1795 | 89.9 | 66.8 | 75.4 | 68.9 |
| 1800 | 133.3 | 70.3 | 83.3 | 74.1 |
| 1805 | 146.4 | 99.3 | 92.2 | 95.5 |
| 1810 | 142.0 | 83.9 | 79.7 | 80.6 |
| 1816 | 139.1 | — | 88.2 | 105.4 |
| 1820 | 142.0 | — | 93.9 | 105.3 |
| 1824 | 181.2 | — | 140.6 | 151.5 |
| 1831 | 147.8 | — | 117.8 | 124.9 |

*Glasgow*

| Year | Money Wages | Real wages expressed in terms of the following indexes : | | |
| | | Gil | T | GRS |
|------|-------------|-----|-----|-----|
| 1790 | 100 | 100 | 100 | 100 |
| 1810 | 147.2 | 87.0 | 82.7 | 83.5 |
| 1816 | 147.2 | — | 93.3 | 111.5 |
| 1820 | 138.9 | — | 91.9 | 103.0 |
| 1824 | 138.9 | — | 107.8 | 116.1 |
| 1831 | 126.4 | — | 100.7 | 106.8 |

*Arbroath*

| Year | Money Wages | Real wages expressed in terms of the following indexes : | | |
|------|-------------|------|------|------|
|      |             | Gil  | T    | GRS  |
| 1790 | 100   | 100  | 100   | 100   |
| 1810 | 159.4 | 94.2 | 89.5  | 90.5  |
| 1816 | 153.6 | —    | 97.4  | 116.4 |
| 1820 | 146.4 | —    | 96.8  | 108.6 |
| 1824 | 147.8 | —    | 114.7 | 123.6 |
| 1831 | 136.2 | —    | 108.5 | 115.1 |

*Source*:  G.H. Wood, 'The Course of Average Wages between 1790 and 1860',
          *Economic Journal*, ix (1899)

Unweighted averages were used by Wood for these calculations.  They clearly relate from the subsequent discussion to members of the artisan class.

The main trades represented in each locality are as follows:-

*Edinburgh* - building, metal wires and brasswork, printing, cabinet making, miscellaneous artisans

*Glasgow* - cotton, shoemaking, building, engineering, pottery, coopers, miscellaneous artisans

*Arbroath* - linen, flax, leather, building, general artisans

CHAPTER 11

# The Experience of Work

## Christopher A. Whatley

Until recently, the systematic study of work, defined here as economically productive labour, had largely been the province of industrial sociologists and social anthropologists, although some historians have made major contributions. Since the early 1970s, however, closer attention has been paid to the workplace, not only for itself but also because of the growing recognition in some circles of the centrality of workplace dynamics and organisation in the development of industrial capitalism. The idea that the effective organisation and control of work lay at the heart of the process of industrial capitalist wealth creation was by no means new, although it had long been overlooked, largely as the result of the tendency of liberal economists to disregard social relations in their analyses of economic and chage.[1]

Hitherto, little serious investigation has been conducted into the labour process and the experience of industrial work in Scotland in the period under review, although agriculture, excluded from the present essay, has been better served.[2] Accordingly, what follows is a preliminary attempt to describe the main features of the 'experience of work' in Scottish industry in the period c. 1760-1830. A simple outline of the dominant aspects of work in the first half of the eighteenth century is followed by an examination of the main forms of workplace organisation in the period of the 'classic' industrial revolution. Thereafter attention is directed towards the processes by which older attitudes to and habits of work were remodelled in accordance with the requirements of 'modern' industry. The experience of women and children, who between them formed well over half of the manufacturing workforce, is examined separately. Where possible the essay tentatively places Scottish experience within the context of the wider debates about the nature of work.

While there are good grounds for supposing that the rate of growth and structural change which occurred in Britain as a whole during the 'classic' period of the industrial revolution was much slower than was once believed, such arguments have less relevance for Scotland where the march towards industrialisation appears to have been amongst the fastest of all the European nations. An economically backward, predominantly agrarian society, with a very small industrial sector and only a poorly developed putting-out system at the end of the seventeenth century, by 1830 Scotland was well on the way to becoming 'irreversibly, a different kind of society', with an economic and social structure little different from the rest of the 'workshop of the world'.[3]

The fact of previous English superiority is critical to an understanding of the labour process in eighteenth and early nineteenth-century Scotland. It will be suggested here that as far as structures and changes in the nature of work were concerned Scotland had much in common with other parts of the industrialising world. Nevertheless, giving additional force to the pace of change and sharpening the character of workplace organisation and relations was the perception amongst the Scottish elite of Scottish backwardness.[4]

A telling indication that the labour process was central to successful Scottish modernisation comes from a report on Carron Company at the end of its first troubled decade: the site of the ironworks was good from the point of view of motive power, raw materials and ease of access to markets, yet, it was noted, these 'favourable appearances' had been 'frustrated' by the difficulties which arose from the establishment of such a works in a 'Country of Idleness'.

## The World of Work before Carron

'Idleness', and other similarly pejorative terms such as 'rogues', 'vagabonds' and even 'cattle', were frequently used by the 'improving' classes, not only in Scotland, to convey their intense disapproval of what appeared to be the unwillingness of the common people of pre-industrialised societies to engage in regular, closely monitored and often centralised work. Wherever men were in control of their own working lives, according to E.P. Thompson, the work pattern 'was one of alternative bouts of intense labour and idleness', while it was unusual for people to remain constantly at a single task.[5] Payment tended to be task- rather than output-related.

All of the currently available indications are that for most Scots a plurality of mainly agricultural occupations was the norm in the late seventeenth and early eighteenth centuries. Most sub-tenant and cottar households for instance seem to have subsisted by combining the income from the sale of some of the produce of their own modest plots of land, and from the wages obtained from agricultural labouring tasks. Occasional employment could also be had as tradesmen's assistants, in building work for example, by labouring for a mason, thatcher or wright.[6]

It is important however to recognise how rigorous was this way of life. Rural underemployment, especially outwith the main agricultural seasons, appears to have been rife and periods of idleness enforced rather than chosen.

Certainly before the mid-eighteenth century Lowland rural dwellers had ceased to be entirely self-sufficient, and depended for at least part of their livelihoods on wage earnings. The search for subsistence meant that rural inhabitants were increasingly to be found encroaching on what urban workers had seen as their prerogative. Most commonly this was in the part-time manufacture of cloth, but involved other urban occupations too, such as two 'vilers' in Dundee, who complained that their privilege of 'playing att all weddings w⁺in ye burgh' was being threatened by others who came in 'from the Cuntry'.

Although full-time work at a single industrial or manufacturing occupation (as distinct from agricultural farm service, already referred to in Chapter 3) was not unknown in Scotland in the early eighteenth century, outside the towns it was unusual, with coalmining and salt manufacturing being the best-known exceptions. Some tasks in the coal industry, though, such as sinking new pits or driving mines, required only the occasional services of men such as George Bower of Baldridge in Fife, who 'when unemployed as a weaver...[worked], not at coalworks, but at sinks or mines'. Full- or part-time, however, in most trades the weather and seasons, as well as changing patterns of demand, exerted powerful influences upon the availability and nature of work.

It was the skilled journeymen from the myriad of urban trades who could most confidently expect to work at their occupations full-time, for life, although not necessarily in the same town throughout. Fortunes fluctuated of course, both between trades and over time. So confident were Dundee wrights of employment in 1695 that they refused to 'fie' or contract with any master for the usual quarter, half or full year: on the other hand the first decades of the eighteenth century saw the decline of the waulking and combmaking trades in the same town, thus making it necessary for men such as Charles Gray, a combmaker, to seek in 1717 an alternative livelihood; in his case as the town's jailor.

Evidence that in pre-industrial Scotland the divisions between work, leisure and obligations outside the workplace were indistinct can be seen at Urquhart colliery in Fife, where almost 22 per cent of the colliers' 'absent days' in the twelve months from May 1743 were voluntarily lost as colliers simply refused to go to work, nursed 'sore heads', the result of self-inflicted damage incurred at drinking bouts such as those that filled the 'daft days' around New Year, while not infrequently colliers chose to remain at home with sick members of their family or to be with their womenfolk during childbirth; others opted to attend marriages or the baptisms of relatives' children, or simply to visit.[7]

However, just how universal these and other indications of an active leisure preference are is not clear. Colliers and salters were reputed to be relatively well paid and could afford to absent themselves from work. Not all workers were in such a favoured position. Working in their masters' workshops or homes, apprentices probably found it hard to slip free for long without being forced to make amends by paying the fines and double days' work for each lost day which were written into most indentures. Others, perhaps out of economic necessity, paid little attention to the holiday calendar.

Weavers often had long periods of respite from their looms, but they were driven by lack of webs to look for alternative sources of employment. Perhaps only for a few decades around the end of the eighteenth century, during the brief so called 'golden age', was weaving work available on anything like a continuous full-time, relatively well-paid, basis, thus making it possible, notably for the best-paid workers in the fine and fancy trades, to engage in learning, poetry and sport. After 1812, when what low-priced webs were available had to be worked hard for long hours before another spell of unemployment in an overstocked labour market began, the earlier pattern of irregular work returned, but now with fewer opportunities to obtain other means of subsistence.[8]

What also has to be considered is that in an age when wage payments were frequently delayed or low, irregular work habits may simply indicate that workers were unwilling to work without reward or for what they judged to be inadequate remuneration: it was preferable to play for nothing than to work for nothing. Although the evidence concerning attitudes to work and financial rewards at the large New Mills textile manufactory in the later seventeenth century is ambiguous, there are indications that some workers 'were moti-vated by the possibility of increased earnings'.[9] However, it seems likely that most ordinary Scots, never having had the means to enjoy the material advantages which in the main were the preserve of their social superiors, could see no point in working beyond the point at which their immediate needs were met.[10]

The idea that clock time was wholly absent from the world of pre-industrialised work should probably be treated cautiously. In the larger Scottish burghs there was certainly an awareness of clock time in the first half of the eighteenth century. In Dundee for instance, in 1717, James Dunbar petitioned the Town Council for the post of town clock keeper, a post which had apparently been held by members of the Smith family for over sixty years. It was an important function; the clocks played a part in determining both the shape of the working day and of leisure activities. Although the time at which urban journeymen commenced work differed between winter and summer so that the benefits of daylight working could be obtained, the normal working day appears to have been similar to that in England, around twelve hours, that is from 6 a.m. until 8 p.m. in summer, with breaks totalling some two hours for meals. There were however discernible variations between trades.[11]

Even in rural areas there are hints that the idea of a normal or customary day's work, measured in hours, was recognised. For instance, although some night work was expected from the new miller's assistant at Bonnyton grain mill in 1714, he would not be required to labour for more than 'ye usual time yt work-men work in the Twenty four hours'. For 'day labourers' too, there were customary limitations on the length of the working day. It was not unusual for additional payments, commonly in the form of a quantity of ale or spirits, to be made to those who had worked after 6 p.m. or into the hours of darkness.

Thus there may have been rather less autonomy, both for employer and employee, in the world of work before the onset of industrialisation than is sometimes suggested. Of course not all masters of urban trades conformed to the decisions of the guildry about working hours. Also, of course, journeymen such as shoemakers who often worked in their own homes could fairly readily leave their lasts and work more or less when they pleased. Mainly for technical reasons some tasks simply could not be carried out within such a rigid timespan. The working hours of outworking country dwellers, such as the growing numbers of spinners and weavers who were struggling with poor materials and low levels of skill to combine work in manufacturing along with what little they could obtain from agriculture, were determined not by guild regulations or efforts through worker solidarity to maintain long-standing practices, but variously by necessity, the availability of work and their own attitudes to income enhancement.

## Changing Structures of Work

The traditional view that industrialisation simply involved the demise of 'older' forms of small-scale work organisation and hand-working methods and their replacement by machines and the factory is no more applicable in Scotland's case than it is anywhere else in the industrialising world. The 'age of manufactures' can best be represented as a 'complex web of improvement and decline, large- and small-scale production, machine and hand processes.'[12]

The form of work organisation most commonly associated with the period under review is the factory. Centralised production however took many forms and was introduced or extended in a wide range of industries. Large manufactories had existed in Scotland in the sixteenth and seventeenth centuries. Although remarkably little is known about these, it is clear that comparatively few were long-lived concerns. Their numbers expanded greatly in the eighteenth century, however: there were 12 pre-1700 paper mills for example, whereas 42 were opened between 1700 and 1800, 38 of which all were built post-1740. A further 37 were established between 1800 and 1825. Between 1728 and 1830 over 700 lint mills were built; over roughly the same period 200 bleachfields were laid out; although some 300 waulk mills had been built in Scotland by 1730, more were added from the 1770s; in wool, some 250 carding mills were built, along with around 100 wool spinning mills by 1838. This list is far from exhaustive.[13]

Many of these, however, were small-scale operations. The numbers employed in a typical paper mill for example were not many more than 10. The more spectacular developments usually, but by no means exclusively, came in cotton spinning, bleaching and iron manufacturing. The first Scottish cotton mill, at Penicuik (1778), was swiftly followed by others; by 1795 there were 91; 120 in 1812. Although they varied greatly in size, several employed many hundreds of people: by 1793 over 1600 had been recruited at Catrine, Ayrshire, where in the 1780s there had only been a handful of cottages. The birth of the modern coke-fired iron industry, marked by the commencement of blasting at Carron in 1760, was followed, although not immediately, by the es-tablishment of several large ironworks, mostly on virgin sites. The nine works which were established between 1779 and 1801 could each number their employees in hundreds, with over 615 working at the largest, Carron, in 1761.

In sharp contrast, however, little organisational or technical change occurred in the struggling salt industry which in the early nineteenth century was carried on using the crude hand techniques of two and three centuries earlier, by a master salter and one or two assistants, in small stone-built panhouses. Handframe knitting, which commenced in the Borders in the 1770s, has been described as 'a semi-domestic form of industrial organisation... in a process of evolution... which had more in common with pre- or proto-industrial stages of...development than the so-called industrial revolution'. In paper making, hand methods were used until the early 1800s, when water- and steam-driven machines were introduced. By 1825 the hand-made era was all but over. In cotton, dual development took place, with the rapid mechanisation of spinning after c.1780, at the same time as the numbers of handloom weavers increased, although from the 1820s there was a rapid growth of factory-based powerloom production.[14]

In recent years much attention has been focused on 'proto-industrialisation', or part-time rural manufacturing, both as a model of industrial organisation and as the first and necessary phase of industrialisation. The most widespread form of manufacturing in Scotland in the second half of the eighteenth century, it was a Europe-wide system in which the interests of underemployed rural dwellers and exporting merchants were fortuitously

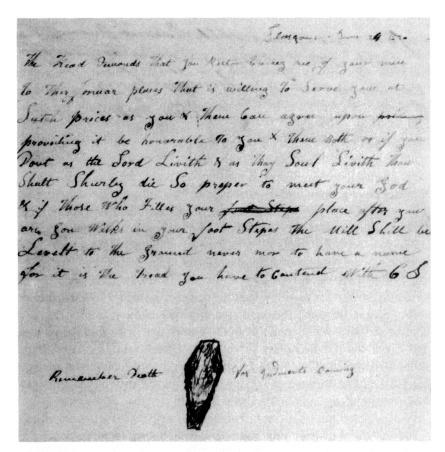

29. Violence, involving vitriol throwing and firearms, was not an uncommon feature of industrial relations in the early nineteenth century. This letter from aggrieved cotton spinners in Milngavie in 1820, warns the mill manager that unless their demands are met, he would 'Shurly die'.

drawn together. The former needed part-time employment to enhance their meagre land-based earnings while the latter, operating in competitive and price-sensitive markets, sought a labour force which was flexible and cheap. During the seventeenth century both linen and woollen goods, most of which were manufactured from raw materials delivered to the country workforce and then collected on behalf of overseas merchants figured modestly amongst Scottish exports. The greatest strides forward in linen production came later, with output doubling every twenty or twenty-five years between c.1730 and 1800. Crucial to the industry's expansion after 1740 was 'its ability to secure increasing supplies of labour at reasonably cheap levels'.[15]

During the 1730s and 1740s, there was a 'considerable extension' of spinning northwards and into the Highlands from the established flax-spinning areas of the central Lowlands and the north-east, bringing large numbers of women as well as children from the informal into the formal, paid world of work. Rural proletarianisation occurred as female spinners came to depend for work on the supplies of flax which were given out and then, as yarn, purchased by urban merchants and their agents, with whom disputes often took place over payment rates, wastage (and embezzlement) and the quality of the work.

As yarn output rose, attempts too were made to established handloom weaving in many rural districts. Traditionally concentrated in the towns, the weaver incorporations still played an important part in the 1740s. High wages for linen weaving, though, and restrictions on the supply of weavers persuaded the Board of Trustees to seek and obtain, in 1751, a measure which removed from the incorporations the right to restrict entry to the trade. That plain linen weaving was not a difficult craft to master also facilitated expansion, and after the middle of the eighteenth century employers apparently found it relatively easy to hire weavers on their own terms and obtain the three- or four-fold increase in their numbers which occurred between the early 1730s and the later 1790s. The rise of the new factory cotton-spinning industry, technically based upon Arkwright's water frame from the end of the 1770s and increasingly upon Crompton's mule, although spinning jennies were also used, led to further increases in the numbers of predominantly male handloom weavers. By 1830 there were around 78,000 handloom weavers in Scotland, more than three times as many as there had been in 1780.

By 1838 two-thirds of all Scottish handloom weavers lived in rural villages or on the edges of towns. Some were employed in loom factories or weaving sheds, more commonly in the finer end of the trade in Glasgow and the west as well as the Borders woollen industry; most linen cloth, however, was woven by individual full-time handloom weavers. They were paid either by the yard or the piece, working on rented or purchased looms in their own home or sheds nearby, more often for putting-out merchants than as independent artisans in the formerly important customer trade. Rural links were not entirely broken, however, notably in the east, where many rural and semi-rural weavers and their families continued to assist in the harvest in the 1830s and afterwards.

## The Struggle for Workplace Control

In spite of the diversity of workplace organisation and the variability of the pace of change, certain features of work experience in manufacturing were to a greater or lesser degree common to most Scottish labouring people after c.1760. Increasingly for employers, 'order and oeconomy' were the watchwords: far greater store was set by the clock and closer attention paid by employers to how the labour time they hired was used. Whatever the length of time worked, employers demanded much more regular habits and a previously unknown intensity of consistent effort. Wherever industrialisation has occurred, critical initial problems for employers has arisen in recruiting, training and retaining a sufficiently large army of willing workers. The rational and methodical management of labour, it has been argued, required 'the fiercest wrench from the past'.[16]

In terms of its human resources Scotland in the middle and later decades of the eighteenth century was by no means an obvious candidate for the factory- and workshop-based stage of industrialisation. Historians in Scotland have tended to consider labour largely in macro-economic terms, stressing the positive contribution which the distinctive features of Scottish demography made to the growth process. While there can be no doubt that a traditionally mobile labour force, and from after 1800 a rapidly growing one, made crucial contributions in the longer run, it may be premature to draw wholly optimistic conclusions about the role of labour in Scottish industrialistion without paying some attention to the very real imperfections which have been identified elsewhere as having existed within the labour market.[17]

Numbers alone were insufficient. There are strong indications that key sectors in Scottish manufacturing in the mid-eighteenth century suffered from severe shortages of skilled labour. Skills, in bleaching, coal and ironstone mining, pottery and glass working, furnace construction and operation and even nailmaking had to be imported from England, with the hope that once taught, Scottish workers would do the same jobs for much less pay.[18]

New attitudes to and habits of work also had to be taught and learned, by a mixture of both 'stick' and 'carrot' techniques. The distinction between work and leisure had to be made clear and nominal working hours filled by consistent productive effort. At Carron, for example, for which Coal- brookdale provided the organisational model, in the mid-1760s, it was anticipated that the completion of the enclosing walls and gates and the appointment of porters would make it easier to check how their employees were utilising their time. Additionally, it would 'add much Order and Respect of the works... and Sobriety of the Workmen'. Drunkenness (and the disorder which often accompanied it), as opposed to moderate drinking, both within the workplace and which kept people from work, posed major problems of control for rationalising employers. Despite efforts to curtail excessive drinking habits, alcohol continued to be an integral part of the working lives of Scots well into the nineteenth century.[19]

The success of efforts to isolate work form the wider social environment (while at the same time increasing attention was being paid to the need for more rigorous social control in the latter arena) were uneven over place and time: the relatively late entry of mill flax spinning in Dundee meant that in 1822 William Brown, a mill manager, still felt it necessary to advise neighbouring firms to keep the gates and doors of their works closed in order to keep out 'strollers' and others who would otherwise distract the spinners. Implicitly rejecting earlier workplace compromises where customary stoppages for local holidays and fairs were tolerated (if disliked) and even made more pleasurable by the calculated paternalism of employers who provided free ale, Brown believed it was 'mistaken humanity' to indulge mill workers in 'ease, idleness or play'.[20]

In this he was not alone: although conditions were not uniform, most Scottish mills by the early 1830s whether steam- or water-powered, or both, had overcome the major technical problems which had led to lengthy stoppages beforehand and were going steadily for twelve hours or so a day, sometimes more, six days a week, Saturdays excepted, for around 306 days per annum, although one Aberdeenshire cotton mill went for 311 days in 1832. Night working in cotton mills was not uncommon after 1800 when trade was good. Workers normally had two short breaks a day for meals, and had Sundays off, but only six or seven other days annually, sometimes less and rarely more. Trade depressions apart, stoppages were usually caused by problems with the supply of water, the time for which often had to be made up.[21]

Workplace regimentation was by no means confined to the mills. In common with many other skilled urban tradesmen in the later eighteenth century, the journeymen bookbinders in Edinburgh's basement workshops had been able to secure a reduction in their hours of work, from twelve to eleven (in 1794), but, they argued in 1811, 'the labour of a Journeyman Bookbinder is now very different from what it was in former times'. Employment then was 'inconstant, and the time... not fully occupied', whereas now, by a 'new division of labour', the work was 'severer'. Scrupulous attention to production costs meant that, wherever possible, customary payments and practices had to be eliminated, as for example the 'play wages' paid at first to the air furnacemen at Carron when the furnaces were being repaired.

Another reason for enclosing works was to prevent theft. Perquisites had long been considered as a customary right by workers who took home and used or sold privately a quantity of material from their employment. During the eighteenth century, however, coal workers, weavers, salters, iron workers, nailmakers and others, like their counterparts south of the border, found that their employers' growing cost- and property-consciousness, often with the help of new laws, was changing the rules of the game and turning such established customary rights into criminal acts. It was no minor problem: at Carron in 1767 it was argued that such was the cost to the firm of theft, unless

30. Gender divisions in the workplace were commonplace. In mining, for example, males invariably cut coal while females carried it to the pit bottom, or even to the surface. *British Coal.*

embezzlement of rod iron by the outworking nailers could be stopped the trade should be given up. Orders were given that 'a striking example be made of the first person [found] Guilty'. Hard labour and whipping were potential punishments. The attack upon and removal of perquisites dealt a double blow to those affected: first, as part of the process of proletarianisation, it took from working people any sense they may have had of being independent dealers in the marketplace with the product their own labour, and secondly, it further shifted the balance in favour of capital by necessitating greater dependence by workers on the wages of their labour.[22]

Workplace discipline was achieved in Scotland in other ways which historians have observed elsewhere. During the early stages of the establishment of a new works, for instance, the performance of workers was often carefully monitored, and where possible those whose conduct was unsatisfactory would be turned off. As rural links weakened and as demographic forces swelled the pool of urban labour from the early 1800s, the threat of dismissal, for offences such as drunkenness, late arrival and shoddy workmanship, became an increasingly potent means of achieving order, especially if this could be accompanied by removing the offender from his or her house.

Long, legally enforceable contracts, which tied workers to a particular employer for a period of months or years, were not new in the second half of the eighteenth century. The system of life binding for coal and salt workers had been made possible by an act of the Scottish Parliament passed in 1606, and other employers had attempted to use similar means to restrict labour mobility. From the seventeenth century at least, and beyond 1830, the indenturing of apprentices was another means used to tie labour to a single employer for a period, as well as to ensure workplace discipline, by laying down strict rules of conduct. A more positive inducement was to transfer the rural practice of paying 'arles' to farm workers who entered with a new master to the industrial sphere. Long used as a means of tempting coal worker parents to bind their children for life, it was also used in the Dundee vicinity by early flax mill proprietors to encourage rural dwellers attending country hiring fairs to engage instead at mill work for periods of six months or a year.

The wider use of written contacts of employment, however, detailing hours of work, wage rates and other related items, was another feature of a more ordered approach to work. It was clearly in the interests of Carron Company, the country's first and leading ironworks, to restrict the outflow of those workers who had been trained at the Company's expense. Accordingly, from an early date, skilled employees, such as moulders, were encouraged to sign contracts for ten, twelve or even fourteen years. For iron workers and even life-bound colliers, there were attractions in a system which provided them with some security of employment (and usually at least subsistence payments) when work was unavailable. At Carron, however, the possession of a particular skill was not to be allowed to tie the Company's hands: all employees were obliged when necessary to revert to the rank of labourer, to be paid at the labourer's rate fixed at the time the contract was signed. At the same time a flow of skilled labour was ensured by insisting that each tradesman instruct a certain number of apprentices; continuity of approved working habits was ensured as soon as it was possible, by taking on as apprentices the sons of reliable current employees.

Fines too were commonly used as a means of regulating conduct, although to be effective these had to form a substantial proportion of a worker's wage. Cash incentives played their part, at least where workers were motivated by the desire to maximise earnings. It was suggested at Salton bleachfield in 1762 that the master bleachers' wages should be related to the field's profits, on the ground that 'this would be an Incentive to Oeconomy & a spur to Industry'. Payment by piece rates shifted a considerable part of the burden of control from master to worker, especially where the latter's livelihood depended upon the labour of an assistant. Employer opinion however was divided on the level at which piece rates should be set. The earlier eighteenth-century view that very low rates would encourage most effort as workers struggled to subsist was still held by some coalmasters in the early 1800s. Others took the view that better workers and enhanced performance would result if there was a prospect of high earnings. Wages and earnings, however, have been more fully discussed in Chapter 10.

Even though substantial but unfinished and uneven progress had been made in the direction of workplace rationalisation by 1830, new methods of working and the elimination of traditional notions of how labour should be controlled and rewarded were rarely introduced easily or without dispute. Combinations and strikes over hours and wages were commonplace and are discussed fully in Chapter 13. However, the collective ability of labour to slow the rate of change, as well as to play some part by negotiation in shaping the way in which work was carried on, was probably greater than has been recognised hitherto. In order for resistance to be effective it was not necessary for formal organisations to exist. It was the attachment of salters to tradition, relatively easy material gain and the sense of individual and collective communal achievement got from outwitting the authorities which kept them quietly embezzling salt into the nineteenth century.

The impact which workers acting collectively to maintain workplace control could have is best seen in coal mining. In spite of their legal status as serfs, from at least as early as the late seventeenth century coal workers had used their collective strength to influence earnings levels, output, and the length of the working day and week. Of little consequence to most coalmasters in the first half of the eighteenth century, when demand was stagnant and economic ambitions were generally modest, from the 1760s, as marketing horizons widened, it became increasingly apparent to the more enterprising coalmasters just how much the industry's competitive weaknesses, particularly in relation to England, were due to the labour force being united in many parts of the Scottish coalfield by the 'fettering bonds of brotherhood'. Hence part and parcel of the 'Emancipation Acts' of 1775 and 1799, which abolished collier serfdom, were the efforts by employers to outlaw collier combinations and thereby regain the managerial initiative. Even so, combinations which embodied traditional collier attitudes to work, including their sense of being skilled and independent artisans, continued to impede the industry's progress, at least until the 1830s.[23]

In certain parts of the textile industry too, it was only after intense struggle that capitalist domination over production was achieved. 'De-skilling', the process which for Marx was inherent in the transfer to modern capitalist industry, where by the division of labour and its replacement by machines, craft skills and other forms of potential worker power were diluted, was in evidence in the Dundee flax heckling trade as well as cotton spinning, where a lengthy struggle for workplace dominance began early in the nineteenth century. Although wages figured prominently in sometimes violent labour disputes, in many cases up until 1825, they were secondary to 'the question of how the mills were to be managed — and who was to be responsible for that management'.[24]

## Women and Children

Yet at the heart of disputes such as these were the interests of skilled adult males, who in the expanding world of Scottish manufacturing industry were a minority. Figures published in 1826 suggest that in manufacturing as a whole in Scotland, women, youths and children formed 63 per cent of the workforce. In less than a handful of industries were no women employed, while youths and children were only absent from leather working. Although not comprehensive, statistics produced in 1834 demonstrate the dependence of key Scottish industries on female labour of all ages. In Lancashire's cotton mills, for example, there were almost as many males as females; in the Glasgow district the ratio was 100:160. The sex ratio was even more skewed in the Scottish flax mills where the ratio of males to females was 100 to 280, a proportion which was 'very different' from that in England.[25]

The contribution which women made to European industrialisation is widely recognised. In Scotland as in many other pre-industrial societies females had long played their part in the domestic household economy. Apart from domestic chores, child-bearing and raising and carrying out certain agricultural tasks, most ordinary Scottish women helped supplement household income by preparing and spinning flax, both to provide their own clothing and for sale to town and country weavers and merchants. Indeed spinning, the 'archetype' of female domestic work, was carried out by Scottish women from virtually all social classes. There were of course marked regional variations; by the mid-eighteenth century the part-time manufacture by females of woollen stockings had become firmly established in Aberdeenshire.[26]

Heavier work was done by women in Lowland coal mines, where there was a clear sexual division of labour. Women (and children) acted as bearers for male coal hewers, to whom they were often related by marriage, and less often as mothers, carrying coal to the pit bottom or in some east-coast pits, to the surface. It was rare, but not unknown, for a woman to work the coalface. Elsewhere, entry to the formal world of work could come with widowhood, when for example, weaver's wives took over the looms of deceased husbands. Their stay was usually temporary though, a holding operation until a son or other suitably trained male was able to relieve them. Older women without support were frequently employed at hard, dirty and poorly-paid casual work which was to be found at many early urban and rural manufacturing enterprises. Many females in Scotland, as elsewhere, made (and continued to make) 'hidden' contributions to production within the context of the family economy, acting as carriers, sellers, organisers and wheelers and dealers in occupations which were apparently male preserves, but which in fact were wholly dependent upon the female contribution. Fishing, for instance, was supported by the activities of women, such as those at Slains, where they were 'generally employed to gather the bait' and at Inveresk on the Forth by the fish-wives who made a major contribution to the household economy from their fish sales in Edinburgh.[27]

[Katherine Logan.]

31. Katherine Logan, who began coal bearing at the comparatively late age of eleven, described her work as 'o'ersair'. The use of child labour in Scottish mines intensified as industrial expansion in the later 1700s revealed shortages of suitable and willing adult female bearers. *Scottish Ethnological Archive, National Museums of Scotland.*

Women, however, with children, were beginning to play a key strategic role in the rise of modern Scottish manufacturing. From the outset, the marked expansion of the Scottish textile industry depended upon the utilisation of the labour of females and young people. Although there is frustratingly little detailed data about working conditions, three tentative conclusions may be drawn. First, manufacturing work in the domestic environment was not resisted, and, as a means of obtaining a cash income may indeed have been welcomed. Secondly, while spinning and indeed other domestic manufacturing occupations were part-time and irregular at first, over time, for many females, the daily, weekly and annual demands of such work on their lives became substantial. Before the end of the century, it is clear that most female domestic industrial work, whether in flax and tow spinning in the east, woollen stocking manufacture in Aberdeenshire, or the burgeoning trade in muslin flowering in the counties surrounding Glasgow, required, often in addition to domestic and agricultural duties, long hours, each day and for most weeks of the year, in return for wages which appear rarely to have exceeded 2s.6d. per week. There seems little doubt that by the end of the eighteenth century the working hours of most females in these sectors were much longer than the ten or twelve worked by male journeymen. The words of the eighteenth-century poet Alexander Ross provide eloquent testimony to the growing female burden:

'The spinning, the spinning, it gars my heart sob
When I think upon the beginning o't.'

Yet, it seems, the alternatives to long hours of poorly-paid work in the home were not favoured by most women, although in parts of the Lowlands full-time spinning had declined by the end of the century as women turned their hand to better-paid agricultural work. They did not however flock immediately to enter the new spinning mills which were built from the late 1770s. Indeed in the early 1800s there were instances of open hostility to the new mills in the east with reports that the women spinners were 'all up in arms' against them while in Forfarshire they threatened to burn them down.[28]

Opposition, not only from females, may have been inspired by fears that livelihoods based upon the household work unit would be threatened. In parishes such as Rayne in Aberdeenshire it was reported that without the income from such work 'the rents of small crofts would not be paid'. Here, as elsewhere in Europe, it was not female manufacturing work which provided a useful supplement to family income, but that of males. Resistance to factories however was universal: new, stark, often large and imposing, they were associated with houses of correction, to which vagrants and petty criminals were sent to work without respite; great emphasis was placed upon the value of independence at work: fear of its loss was evidently still strong amongst Paisley weavers in the early 1830s, when to have turned to mill work could have doubled their incomes.[29]

Yet it is conceivable that there was perceived to be positive merit in the domestic work arrangement. In spite of its arduousness, individuals had some control over their time and effort. Older females who supervised spinning and knitting operations were at least equal partners with their menfolk: in the larger flax-spinning households the mother 'was looked up to as the first and head spinner in the establishment'. The flax-spinning household apparently produced its own culture, of songs, jokes and competition between the spinners, and provided the 'grand Theatre' for courtship. The 'slubber spinners' who 'drew long from the Flax on the rock', and thus produced uneven yarn, were apparently less likely to find marriage partners than the fine spinners, who not only in Scotland were the object of the pragmatically-tinged affections of males who sought the best spinners as partners, and hence a higher standard of living.[30]

Yet while women in the domestic environment may have been able to wrest some advantage from the putting-out system, it was an economic arrangement which was essentially exploitative. In other areas of work, women and children were clearly used as substitutes for more expensive and less malleable adult male labour. With no or little knowledge of, or vested interests in, the formal world of work, they were thought by employers to be ideally suited for those areas of the 'mechanical arts', which according to Adam Ferguson, did best 'where the workshop may... be considered as an engine, the parts of which are men'. In the early 1760s for example, it was made clear to the British Linen Company that the expenses of bleaching, dyeing and finishing were

32. Colliery scene, Lasswade, Midlothian, 1800. In spite of their lowly legal status, coal workers in the eighteenth century valued their leisure time and played an active part in the robust social life of their local communities. *Scotish Ethnological Archive, National Museums of Scotland.*

higher in Scotland than they were in Manchester. As long as this continued, it was argued, 'this country cannot reap the benefit it enjoys, of... Cheap weaving or cheap yarns'. In 1762, it was suggested that the master bleacher at the Company's Saltoun bleachfield should ensure that 'no Men should be employed upon what a woman can perform'. By the end of the century, bleaching and cloth printing were employing many more females than males. By the early 1840s, three times as many females of all ages as males were employed throughout the year at bleachfields in the West of Scotland, virtually all at significantly lower rates of pay, for hours of work which were 'longer than those found to prevail in any other department of labour' in that part of the country. Working and living conditions were often reprehensible.

Although women and children had long assisted male handloom weavers, as weaver incorporation influence diminished, the proportion of women and children actually working looms grew to perhaps a third of the labour force in the 1830s. Sewing and other lighter jobs in the Edinburgh bookbinding trade were being done by children by the early nineteenth century, much to the chagrin of the male journeymen binders who in 1812 protested that such was the nature of the work left to them that they were being brought 'very nearly within the circle of laborious occupations'. In nail making, low mid-eight-eenth-century wages had persuaded many adult nailers in Kirkcaldy to leave the trade and go to sea. The partners of the new Carron Company, however, were anxious to find a market for their rod iron and attempted in the face of competition from the more abundant and efficient nailers of Staffordshire to increase their nail output in the 1760s. Part of their solution was to bind child apprentices, two-thirds of whom around 1767 had been sent from the Charity House in Edinburgh.

The use of pauper and other 'apprentice' labour in the industrial revolution has generated much heated debate ever since the early nineteenth century. Some historians have attempted to justify the practice on the grounds, for example, that children had long been expected to work. While this is true, the evidence from Scotland provides little comfort for those who argue that the pessimistic case is overstated and too dependent upon distortion. Children were often the conscripted shock troops of a generally reluctant Scottish industrial army.[31]

As has been pointed, employers had chronic difficulty in attracting labour to the first, early, mainly rural, cotton and flax mills. It was even true at Carron ironworks, where free housing and even furniture had to be offered to the first recruits. For the mills,however, there were limits to the supply and suitability of 'persons destitute of friends, employment and character'. Prior to the marked shift in favour of capital which occurred in the labour market near the end of the French Wars, employers, on pain of elimination or certainly much-reduced production, were driven to use a corrupted from of the apprentice system as a means of procuring and retaining either orphans or the children of the very poor to act mainly as piecers and machine cleaners. The more 'tractable' they were, and the smaller their size, the better.

The owners of one Inverness thread- and dye-works admitted as much in 1793: it was 'absolutely essential' for carrying on their business that they should employ a number of indentured apprentices 'on a different footing from apprentices in general.' No entry money was paid on their behalf, although in the case of charity house children indentures were usually for seven years instead of the usual three, four or five. Wages, if they were paid at all, were barely above subsistence level, while relatively few boys received any training (other than in regular habits) which would benefit them after the age of around 14, when most began to be turned off as they would have to be paid adult wages. In urban cotton mills, though, a higher proportion stayed on after their mid-teens than in east-coast flax mills, often to work as mule spinners, trained by their fathers. As a means of loosening up the labour market and relieving upward pressure on wage levels from adult male workers children were also used at Carron ironworks, where early on it was determined to 'keep in view the introducing of apprentices… in place of such men as at present have more wages than they will be content with'.

Although conditions varied, generally speaking, the ways in which Scottish 'barracks children' and young people lived and worked were little different from those of the prison factory system used to restrict labour mobility in Meiji Japan: it is not only from the allegedly biased Factory Report of 1832 that evidence comes of recruitment at six or seven years old, exceptionally long hours (longer than those for adults), high humidity and temperatures (especially in cotton mills), ill health and injury, low pay, sexual abuse, fines and physical punishment; Robert Blincoe's Scottish counterpart, James Myles, in his autobiographical *Chapters in the Life of a Dundee Factory Boy*, provides a vivid account of a system which was bad enough in the towns but even worse in the countryside.[32]

If proof is needed that the way the labour of children and young people was used during early Scottish industrialisation was qualitatively different — and worse — than had gone on before, surely it is to be found in the locked doors and windows of many of the early mills and adjoining dormitories. If the testimonies of those involved are considered to have been coloured, their actions may speak to better effect. Frequent attempts were made to run away: even in Glasgow, where the use of pauper apprentice labour was less common, it was 'not easy for the parents to keep their children to the work at first' and child workers could be hard to find during the summer. Children did not only abscond from the mills: fifteen of the twenty five apprentice nailers belonging to the Carron Company around 1767 had 'left the workmen for different causes'. One of the three lads who had formed a 'combination' for the purposes of escaping from an Inverness factory in 1798 and enlisting in the army, declared uncompromisingly that he had left on the grounds that 'he did not like the work'. Dislike had to be intense, for the risks when caught, of being incarcerated and fined or physically ill-treated were high; for some girls who laboured unhappily in Dundee's mills in the early 1800s, prostitution and petty crime were often the only available alternatives. For most mill girls, however, mill work ceased in their early 20s, when they left to get married, their places rarely being taken by married women, but by new child recruits.

By the early 1800s, with population rising rapidly and Irish immigration becoming increasingly important, these were less likely to come from parochial institutions, although some nail and tobacco works continued to draw from this source until the 1840s. Although the child labour force was by 1830 largely recruited from children sent to work by relations, it should be stressed that almost invariably they belonged to 'very poor parents' who had 'not the means of getting food for them' and whose wages made a vital contribution to the family income. On the other hand, the apparent willingness of adult colliers to apprentice their children appears to have been largely motivated by the twin objectives of enhancing family earnings and keeping comparatively

33. Leadhills, c. 1780. Largely because of their malleability, children played a crucial role in the growth of Scottish industry in the eighteenth and early nineteenth centuries. Here boys are shown breaking down lead before it was taken to be smelted. *Private Scottish Collection.*

well-paid work within the collier communities by attempting to exclude 'strangers'.Of the seventy-six boys and girls who became indentured apprentices at Grange colliery between 1783 and 1796, over 90 per cent were related in some way to current colliery employees. Legislation designed to ameliorate some of the worst excesses of the system was ineffective in Scotland until after the Factory Act of 1833.[33]

## Conclusion

By 1830, however, it is clear that the idea of regular supervised work had been accepted, albeit reluctantly, by many labouring Scots, although it should be recognised that large numbers of workers in the mills and mines were increasingly likely to have been Irish or of Irish descent. There were also notable exceptions, such as the framework knitters of Hawick who ignored the town clock calling them to work at 5.20am and continued to exercise a strong leisure preference well into the nineteenth century. These, however, were independent artisans, untroubled till the 1860s by the challenge of mechanisation. The acceptance of greater regularity was partly due to sheer economic necessity, as growing numbers swelled the urban labour market. The tendency of employers to replace earlier long contracts with monthly or weekly engagements increased worker insecurity and encouraged good behaviour. In spite of the evident drawbacks of factory and more closely supervised workshop employment, consistent attendance and effort was rewarded with regular pay, unlike the situation in an increasingly uncertain domestic trade such as handloom weaving. Some millowners softened the blow of mill work by trying to attract families and by offering inducements such as small plots of land on which former rural dwellers could cultivate vegetables; free medical attention and schooling were also available in some places. Within and without the workplace, the assault on plebeian morals and value systems was having some impact too. Robert Owen, building upon the foundations of David Dale's firm, benevolent, but by no means unique system of labour management at New Lanark, reported that his workers had in their new environment become 'industrious, temperate, healthy and faithful to their employers.'[34]

Over the period 1760 to 1830, then, major and diverse changes took place in the way work was organised and experienced. Yet neither 1760 nor 1830 should be seen as sharp turning points, clearly visible dividing lines between old and new. Some older practices carried on, although they often survived only in much amended forms. A great deal more research requires to be carried out in this field, however, before firm conclusions can be drawn and Scottish experience placed firmly within the context of work being done by scholars furth of Scotland. The evidence examined here, however, does provide uncompromising support for the following conclusion. It has recently been said of Scotland after 1830 that the 'upper classes held the whip hand over a divided and largely unorganised working class', in an industrial system based firmly on the singular advantage of cheap labour.[35] While post-1800 demographic forces clearly played their part, so too did the outcome of the battle which was fought between human beings over the form and control of work. The war with labour had not been won by Scottish industrial capital in 1830, but victory was clearly in sight.

NOTES

1. Examples of notable contributions which historians have made to the subject are J.L. and B. Hammond, *The Town Labourer* (London, 1917); S.Pollard, *The Genesis of Modern Management* (London,1965); S.D. Chapman, *The Early Factory Masters* (Newton Abbot, 1967) and, more recently, M. Berg, *The Age of Manufactures: Industry, Innovation and Work in Britain 1700-1820* (London, 1985); the classic modern study of the labour process is H. Braverman, *Labour and Monopoly Capital: The Degradation of Work in the Twentieth Century* (London, 1974); see too E. Garnsey, 'The Rediscovery of the Division of Labor', in K. Thompson (ed.), *Work, Employment and Unemployment* (Open University, 1984), pp. 38-54.

2. See T.M. Devine (ed.), *Farm Servants and Labour in Lowland Scotland 1770-1914* (Edinburgh, 1984). Because relatively little published material on the subject of industrial work in Scotland is available, this essay is largely based on primary research. For the sake of uniformity, in order to save space and to avoid unnecessary interruption of the text, the principal collections of primary sources used are listed here and will not normally be referred to specifically in the notes: SRO (Scottish Record Office), GD 345, Grant of Monymusk MSS;58, Carron Company MSS; GD 406, Hamilton MSS; NLS (National Library of Scotland), Saltoun MSS, MS 17248, 17595; Minto MSS, MS 13304; Cadell of Grange MSS, Acc. 5381; much use too has been made of the records of Inverness Burgh, principally CTI/IB/9, concerning apprenticeships and disputes thereabout; Perth Burgh Records; Dundee Archive and Record Centre, especially TC/CC8, general petitions to the Town Council; legal cases too have provided invaluable information, including SRO, CSP I. Inglis B 6/7, Journeymen Bookbinders (of Edinburgh) v Masters, 1812; Strathclyde Regional Archives, T-MJ 372, papers of Mitchell, Johnston and Co, Solicitors; T-MJ 402, process concerning Pollockshaws printfield, c.1780.

3. N.F.R. Crafts, *British Economic Growth during the Industrial Revolution* (Oxford, 1985); B. Lenman, *An Economic History of Modern Scotland 1660-1976* (London, 1977), p. 102.

4. See J.D. Young, *The Rousing of the Scottish Working Class* (London, 1979), pp. 11-40.

5. E.P. Thompson, 'Time, Work-Discipline and Industrial Capitalism', in M.W. Flinn and T.C. Smout (eds.), *Essays in Social History* (London, 1974), p. 50; see too K. Thomas, 'Work and Leisure in Pre-Industrial Society', *Past and Present*, 29 (1964), pp. 50-66.

6. For a useful succinct survey see C. Larner, *Enemies of God: the Witch Hunt in Scotland* (London, 1981), pp. 40-59; I.D. and K.A. Whyte, 'Some Aspects of the Structure of Rural Society in Seventeenth Century Scotland', in T.M. Devine and D. Dickson (eds.), *Ireland and Scotland, 1600-1850* (Edinburgh, 1983), pp. 32-45; R.A. Dodgshon, *Land and Society in Early Scotland* (Oxford, 1981), Ch. 7; for work in early industry see C. A. Whatley, 'A Saltwork and the Community: The Case of Winton, 1716-19', *Transactions of the East Lothian Antiquarian and Field Naturalists' Society,* 18 (1984), pp. 45-59.

7. Calculated from NLS, Minto Papers, MS 13304, ff. 78-127, List of absentees at Urquhart Colliery, 1743-4; for another example see Whatley, 'Saltwork and the Community', pp. 52-3.

8. A.J. Durie, *The Scottish Linen Industry in the Eighteenth Century* (Edinburgh, 1979), pp. 99-102; N. Murray, *The Scottish Hand Loom Weavers, 1790-1850: A Social History* (Edinburgh, 1978), pp. 14-5.

9. G. Marshall, *Presbyteries and Profits: Calvinism and the Development of Capitalism in Scotland* (Oxford, 1980), p. 186.

10. This characteristic is brilliantly conveyed in the words spoken by Luath in Robert Burn's poem 'The Twa Dogs'; see too P. Mathias, 'Leisure and wages in Theory and Practice', in *The Transformation of England* (London, 1979), pp. 148-67.

11. For a recent discussion of the place of clock-time, see M. Harrison, 'The Ordering of the Urban Environment: Time, Work and the Occurrence of Crowds, 1790-1835', *Past and Present*, 110 (1986), pp. 134-68; for a useful local study see A.M. Smith, *The Three United Trades of Dundee: Masons, Wrights and Slaters* (Dundee, 1987).

12. Berg, *Age of Manufacturers*, p. 91; the seminal article on this subject is R. Samuel, 'Workshop of the World: Steam Power and Hand Technology in mid-Victorian Britain', *History Workshop*, 3 (1977), pp. 6-72.

13. A.G. Thomson, *The Paper Industry in Scotland, 1590-1861* (Edinburgh, 1974), p. 33; for a fuller list see J.P. Shaw, 'The New Rural Industries: Water Power and Textiles', in M.L. Parry and T.R. Slater (eds.), *The Making of the Scottish Countryside* (London, 1980), pp. 291-317.

14. See C. A. Whatley, *The Scottish Salt Industry, 1570-1850; an economic and social history* (Aberdeen, 1987); C. Gulvin, *The Scottish Hosiery and Knitwear Industry, 1680-1980* (Edinburgh, 1984), p.32; Thomson, *Paper Industry*, p.134.

15. For an introductory survey see L.A. Clarkson, *Proto-Industrialisation: The First Phase of Industrialisation* (London, 1985); A.J. Durie, *Scottish Linen Industry* pp.22, 158.

16. Pollard, *Modern Management*, p.189.

17. See for example R.H. Campbell, *The Rise and Fall of Scottish Industry, 1707-1939* (Edinburgh, 1980), pp.2, 17; M. Gray, 'Migration in the Rural Lowlands of Scotland, 1750-1850', in Devine and Dickson, *Ireland and Scotland*, p.116; for an outstanding analysis of the labour market in the period see S. Pollard, 'Labour in Great Britain', in P. Mathias and M.M. Postan (eds.), *The Cambridge Economic History of Europe* Vol. VII (Cambridge, 1978), 2 parts, I, pp.97-161.

18. This theme recurs constantly in the books and papers relating both to Carron and the enterprising Cadell family; see too J.L. Carvel, *The Alloa Glass Work* (Edinburgh, 1935), p.7; B.F. Duckham, 'English Influences in the Scottish Coal Industry, 1700-1815', in J. Butt and J.T. Ward (eds.), *Scottish Themes* (Edinburgh, 1976), pp. 28-45.

19. T.C. Smout, *A Century of the Scottish People, 1830-1950* (London, 1986), pp. 133-9.

20. J.R. Hume (ed.), *Early Days in a Dundee Mill, 1819-23* (Dundee, 1980), p. 20.

21. *Factories Inquiry: Supplementary Report from Commissioners* (P.P. 1834, XX), pp. 1-233.

22. J. Rule, *The Experience of Labour in Eighteenth Century Industry* (London, 1981), pp. 124-46; see too R.W. Malcolmson, *Life and Labour in England, 1700-1780* (London, 1981), p. 148.

23. R. Houston, 'Coal, class and culture: labour relations in a Scottish mining community, 1650-1750', *Social History*, 8 (1983), pp. 1-18; C.A. Whatley, ' "The Fettering Bonds of Brotherhood": combination and labour relations in the Scottish coal-mining industry, c.1690-1775', *Social History*, 12 (1987), pp. 139-54; A.B. Campbell, *The Lanarkshire Miners: A Social History of their Trade Unions, 1775-1874* (Edinburgh, 1979), pp. 15-16 and with F. Reid, 'The Independent Collier in Scotland', in R. Harrison (ed), *Independent Collier: The Coal Miner as Archetypal Proletarian Considered* (Sussex, 1978), pp. 54-74.

24. For a useful discussion of the concept of de-skilling see S. Wood, (ed.), *The Degradation of Work ?Skill, Deskilling and the Labour Process* (London, 1982); for Dundee see J.T. Ward 'Trade Unions in Dundee', in G. Jackson (ed.), *The Third Statistical Account: The City of Dundee* (Arbroath, 1979), pp. 252-3; for cotton see Z.G. Brassey, 'The Cotton Spinners in Glasgow and the West of Scotland c.1790-1840' (unpublished M.Litt. thesis, University of Strathclyde, 1974), p. 117.

25. Sir J. Sinclair, *Analysis of the Statistical Account of Scotland* (Edinburgh, 1825), 2 vols., I, pp. 319-21; *Factory Inspectors Returns: Supplementary Reports* (P.P. 1834, XIX), pp. 278-97.

26. See for example S. Lewenhak, *Women and Work* (London, 1980), pp. 148-61; Berg, *Age of Manufactures*, p. 137; Durie, *Linen Industry*, p. 38.

27. J. Rule, *The Labouring Classes in Early Industrial England, 1750-1850* (London, 1986), p. 13; for a recent contribution in this area see L. Charles and L. Duffin (eds.), *Women and Work in Pre-Industrial England* (1985).

28. Durie, *Linen Industry*, p. 97; Dundee University Archives, MS 11/5/14, C. Mackie, 'History of Flax Spinning from 1806 to 1866'.

29. See *The Statistical Account, XV, North and East Aberdeenshire* (Wakefield, 1982 ed.), pp. xxviii, 442; for a wider view of the significance of female domestic employment to the household see H. Medick. 'The proto-industrial family economy: the structural function of household and family during the transition from peasant society to industrial capitalism'. *Social History*, 3 (1976), pp. 291-315.

30. *Ibid*; Mackie, 'Flax Spinning', pp.16-18.

31. For a recent discussion see Rule, *Labouring Classes*, pp.143-152.

32. K. Taira, 'Factory Labour and the Industrial Revolution in Japan', in *Cambridge Economic History of Europe*, II, pp. 180-5; for a recent survey of conditions in cotton, see J. Butt, 'Labour and Industrial Relations in the Scottish Cotton Industry during the Industrial Revolution', in J. Butt and K. Ponting (eds.), *Scottish Textile History* (Aberdeen, 1987), p. 142.

33. *Reports from the Committee on the Labour of Children in Factories* (P.P. 1831-2, XV), p. 255; Grange colliery figures calculated from NLS, Cadell MSS, Acc. 5381, Box/1, Indenture Book, 1783-1792; for the factory acts see M.W. Thomas, *The Early Factory Legislation* (Connecticut, 1970) and Butt, 'Industrial Relations', p.148.

34. C. Gulvin, *Scottish Hosiery and Knitwear Industry*, pp. 37-38; R. Owen, *A New*

*View of Society and other Writings* (London, 1966 ed.), pp.26-7; see too A.J. Cooke (ed.) *A History of Redgorton Parish* (Dundee, 1984).

35. Smout, *Century of the Scottish People*, p.4

# CHAPTER 12

# The Poor Law

## Rosalind Mitchison

By the mid-eighteenth century the Scottish Poor Law had in Lowland Scotland become capable of marshalling enough in resources to prevent a bad harvest leading to famine and could keep alive for many years individuals of low or non-existent earning power — the old and infirm, the insane, destitute children. A parish could deal with the threat of famine by imposing assessment, which would mean demanding a rate from landowners, and landowners (the 'heritors') could then pass half the burden to their tenantry. This would make up the difference between voluntary funds and the level of need. In such a situation it was the official Poor Law which was dealing with the emergency. But parish records show that it was often easier to keep the source of extra revenue voluntary. The parish would appeal to the landowners for contributions, and draw on reserves. Relief would then continue to be based on 'voluntary' sources, that is on church collections, fines, mortcloth fees and the interest on legacies, as well as special gifts. Landowners might unite at the county level to bring in grain and offer it to parishes below cost: parishes might add further subsidy and sell it either only to the poor or to all who asked.

In this way harvest failure was contained by parish action and by the aid of landowners whether in the relatively informal 'country meeting' or under pressure from those in office, sheriffs and Justices of the Peace. County 'schemes' for the control of vagrancy and the support of the local poor were instituted by those in office and can be traced in the 1770s in eleven counties. Sheriff court material would probably reveal them elsewhere. Country authorities had no direct powers over the parishes, and so in some cases these schemes were ineffective. But the control of vagrancy was a matter attractive to landowners. Vagrants were a potential nuisance, creating fear of theft, and an embarrassment. Justices and sheriffs were the most prestigious members of the gentry, so it was difficult for other landowners to resist their proposals, even if these meant accepting rating. Landowners in the southern counties were particularly susceptible to comparisons with England, which might lead to the adoption of higher pensions and allowances. These may explain the growing differential in the standards of support between the north-east Lowlands and the south. Though in no area could provision be called lavish, it was somewhat more generous in the south. In the north-east the difference what a parish would afford and what would support a destitute household might partly come by response to a presbytery appeal. By the 1820s all the parishes in the Border counties were using assessment, and so were the great majority in the Lothians, whereas in the north-east none were.

Assessment, though it had been ordered in the founding statute of the Scottish Poor Law, had come to be seen by lawyers as only the final device for raising money. If a parish could raise what it thought sufficient by other means, this was held to be in accordance with the law, and it was left to the parish to decide what was needed. There was no generally laid down method by which assessment was made. It could be done by valued rent, by real rent, by goods: it could be selective. In Edinburgh the judges claimed exemption, in some parishes rates lay only on resident landowners. Some long-standing disputes within parishes show that a landowner could delay paying his share for many years. Sessions disliked taking their own landowners to court, well aware that the sympathy of the legal establishement lay with landowning. In 1752 the heritors of Cambuslang had obtained a decision which limited the use of parish funds to poor relief, the salary of the session clerk and the hire of equipment for outside preaching. It had soon become accepted that this decision was impractical: for instance it ignored contributors to the fees of clerks in the higher church courts. But it was a sharp reminder of the prejudices of the judges, and in particular meant that no session could be sure if it sued a landowner, that its members might not be forced to pay for the process personally. For many reasons it was desirable for a parish to maintain good relations with its landowners, so the imposition of assessment required the assent of the upper class.

But the climate of opinion until the second decade of the nineteenth century was in favour of making the Poor Law effective. It is rare to find a Lowland parish in the later eighteenth century neglecting totally the care of the poor, though there were some, even in the south, such as Kilmany in Fife, where the obligation was interpreted on a very narrow base. The number of parishes where the obligation was taken seriously appears to have increased. Parishes regularly put the old and infirm on pension rolls, supported orphans and foundlings by boarding them out with pensioners, paid for the schooling of these children and of others whose parents could not afford school fees, arranged for the care of the insane, made contributions towards the cost of surgery or wet-nursing, joined with other parishes in supporting poor students at the University and buried paupers with a reasonable allocation of ale and tobacco for the mourners, while claiming whatever personal property these paupers left. Where possible they expected paupers to raise some part of their own support by begging. Only when paupers became bedridden would the parish supply a pension on which it was possible to live. Those partially disabled were still expected to work after recovery from surgery or acute illness.

The striking limitation of the Poor Law of Scotland is that it never set up a clear right in a claimant to relief, or even a clearly defined standard of living which it would protect. Law books of the nineteenth century refer to claimants as having rights, but since there was no mechanism by which these could be enforced, they did not exist in practice. The obligation of a session to act charitably was primarily religious. There was no regular system of appeal against a decision of a kirk session. Some cases went to sheriffs, who might order a parish to act, or even set out a specific amount of support due, but even though this had occurred and the session had conformed, the idea that a lay court could order a church court to act had not become accepted. In 1772 in the case of *Paton vs Adamson* the Court Session had destroyed the idea that a sheriff could order a parish to pay a particular sum, but there could still be more limited intervention, by the sheriff and by Justices of the Peace. Appeals could go to the Court of Session, but those that came to be quoted in law books as of authority were on points of definition, usually of settlement.[1] In other words they decided which parish had the obligation of support. The founding Poor Law statute had defined the recipients of relief as the 'poor, aged and impotent' and had contained no orders for the provision of work for the unemployed. Subsequent statutes which had not been put into practice had assigned vagrants as indentured labour to imaginary manufactories or equally imaginary correction houses. Even a statute partly effective, that of 1649, had left uncertainty about the status of the unemployed. In disqualifying the slothful and those able to earn a living, it had not made it clear whether the word 'able' meant physically able or possessed of opportunity. Other uncertainties had not prevented parish obligation to support foundlings, orphans and the insane. The Poor Law, as accepted by lawyers, was what had been developed in practice. Begging, though forbidden by many statutes, was allowed within the parish, though sometimes to make the position of such beggars clear the parish would give them a badge. Vagrants and those in search of work were usually sustained by the parish for one or two nights and then allowed to go their way. Rates were considered necessary only when it was obvious that need exceeded income. In Acts and Proclamations of the 1690s the Privy Council, urgent for aid to the starving, had taken the line that the poor included anyone in serious need, whatever their employment status or physique, and this seems to have been the attitude of most parishes. The word 'able-bodied' had not yet come to be a euphemism for the unemployed. Even the use of the word 'able' to mean capable of some sort of work was not seen as a disqualification for relief: in a list of the poor of the parish of Tranent in the 1750s there was a category labelled 'able', and placed in it was the name Donald Cameron with the comment 'wants a hand'. This category seems to have been of people not totally disabled, and needing some support. Uncertainty over the claims of those partially disabled was not important in a period when the resource of the land was necessary to almost all and when harvest called for all available labour.[2] In the late eighteenth century with the change to a labour force specifically hired over long periods, the expansion of industrial work and a larger share of income coming in the form of wages, the issue arose of whether the Poor Law covered the unemployed, those temporarily unfit for work and those needing help to keep themselves in business. In practice most parishes accepted such cases.

In the Highlands the spectrum of 'the poor' was similar, except that the arrangements for the education of poor scholars was, to a large extent, provided not by the parish but by the SSPCK. The Highlands was a society only partly monetised. There was not the cash in the hands of tenants and cottars to make reasonable contributions to church collections, and as a result there was very little out of which to make a poor fund. Money coming to peasant hands from the sale of cattle or kelp went rapidly to the landowners as rent. In some Catholic areas there was no effective kirk session and no revenue for the poor. It is possible that some chiefs accepted the need to support their followers in bad times, and may even have extended support to some of the families of their men, but chieftainship was in decline in the second half of the century, its ethic superseded by economic advantage, the authority taken over by the central government, and in many cases the person of the chief absent either through the pursuit of a career or through exile. The arrival of starving Highlanders ostensibly looking for harvest work in the Lowlands can be found in newspapers in the later eighteenth century at dates in the year when it was impossible that harvest could yet be under way. Pennant, visiting the Small Isles in 1772, reported the population as starving. We should not be misled by late nineteenth-century opponents of the Clearances when they asserted that in the past times Highlanders had been 'comfortable' in their crofts and take this as evidence that there had been a satisfactory relationship between the productivity of the land and the needs of the inhabitants. Famine was a real risk against which the local social organisation had no adequate defence. We have no information about the level of private mutual support, but well on into the nineteenth century in most Highland parishes the most anyone could expect from the Poor Law would be ten shillings a year and licence to beg, at a time when it would take a shilling to buy enough oatmeal for a week's food.[3]

At the other end of the spectrum of expense came the practice, in some towns, of placing those on relief in poorhouses, where they might be expected to work if they were capable of it. The motives behind this move were mixed. There was often, until it had repeatedly been shown to be a mirage, the idea that the poor could, if their labour was organised, contribute materially to their own support. There were also, in different proportions, the ideas behind the infirmary movement, the desire to provide good care, the desire to discipline and the wish to create professional employment. In practice all these aims proved difficult of achievement. Work would be extracted only if discipline was strong, and discipline meant paid manpower. Poorhouses usually had dietaries and conditions laid down by persons of status and rank, invariably above those likely to have featured in the lives of the poor. For instance on fish days in Ayr poorhouses the main meal centred on either herring or salmon: if the latter, the allocation was at least half a pound a head.[4] At Inveresk the dietary included ale, wheat bread and potatoes; the house had a warm room and comfortable beds, yet even so it was considered too spartan for some delicate paupers. A house such as that in Haddington, holding only a few paupers, mostly small girl orphans and run by an effective housewife who trained them in dressmaking, avoided some but not all of the difficulties. All poorhouses produced a major difficulty for their supporters, in that the removal of beggars from the streets led to a drop in casual almsgiving, so that support had to come entirely from the parish funds, and with the citizenry less conscious of the existence of the destitute. The establishment of a of a poorhouse was usually followed by assessment.

In the bigger cities it is unlikely that the poor could have been supported without such an institution for the seriously infirm. A poorhouse could be a means of rationalising and unifying local support, and relating the administration to the city as a whole. The Town's Hospital in Glasgow seems to have provided centralised and successful management. By contrast the Edinburgh Charity Workhouse was conspicuously badly managed and always in debt.[5]

The expansive tendency of the Scottish Poor Law reached its peak at the end of the century, in the economic stresses of the 1790s and the disastrous harvests of 1800-1. In 1815 many parishes still referred to this difficult time in strong language. The pattern of subsiding food was widely used. There was a much publicised scheme set working in Prestonkirk (East Linton today), an assessed parish, in which oatmeal and barley meal were bought by the parish and purchases at different levels of subsidy were allowed to groups of people according to their level of earnings. The poorest group was defined as 'single women, widows, those unable to work or who cannot procure it, labourers and tradesmen with wages of up to a shilling and fourpence a day'. In this group a family of five would have been allowed to buy about three-quarters of what they needed in cheap grain, but the cost of the remainder would be such that altogether 80 per cent of the wage would go on food. This was a form of 'Speenhamlanding' — the use of money raised as poor's rates to supplement wages, but running at much lower level of support than the system agreed by the Justices at Speenhamland. This pattern of payments to those at work can be found in other parishes. It was common in East Lothian and the Borders, and examples have been found near Stirling.[6] Local studies may well show it to have been very common. The most famous instance of it was what took place in Duns and led eventually to a Court of Session judgement in 1804, *Pollock vs Darling,* which stated unequivocally that the Poor Law was there for the relief of the destitute, however that destitution was caused. But the expansion of relief in these years took place against growing criticism of the system, and in particular much comment on the desirability of halting the spread of assessment. Hostility to the idea of assessment can be found in the *Scots Magazine* of 1773 over the proposal in Edinburgh to raise 10 per cent on valued rents, with some privileged exemptions, to support the poorhouse. Hostility becomes much more apparent in letters to the newspapers in the 1780s. It may have been accentuated by the pamphlet of Joseph Townshend, *A Dissertation on the Poor Laws by a Well-Wisher to Mankind*, published in 1786 and based on the English Poor Law. Townshend proposed the total abolition of poor relief in favour of a system of compulsory insurance. The rising cost of poor relief in England, or the prevailing opinion that it was rising, led to comparisons in Scotland. Self-congratulatory statements were made accompanied by nervous forecastings that Scotland might go the same way as England. In the 1790s the more usual comments of ministers in the *Statistical Account* show the state of clerical opinion. The reports express both a desire to support the poor and, particularly in the later volumes, nervousness for the future. A common theme combining both opinions was the statement that if heritors did not provide more generously for the poor, assessment would be inevitable. 'If the landowners of Scotland understand their own interest,' wrote the minister of Cupar, Fife,'... if they are interested in the comfort of those with whose welfare their own prosperity is intimately connected... while they reprobate parochial assessments and all their baleful conse-quence... they will regularly contribute... to the relief of the poor in those parishes where their property lies.'

The new strand of opinion gained force from the second edition of Malthus's *Essay on Population*, published in 1803. Hitherto the objections were that, since relief damaged the individual's sense of responsibility and independence, it was morally bad. Malthus supplied an economic argument, that by encouraging imprudent marriage, relief kept down the level of wages by increasing the labour force, and so enhanced the poverty it was designed to relieve. It also increased the risk of famine. The new opinion rapidly became

34. An impression of the proposed Charity Workhouse of Edinburgh from William
Maitland's *History of Edinburgh* (1753).

dominant in the pamphlet literature in England, and this literature had a
Scottish component.[7] The anti-Poor Law feeling in England produced various
parliamentary enquiries into the Poor Law, and various abortive bills. In
Scotland the most significant attack on the Poor Law was mounted by T.F.
Kennedy of Dunure, MP for Ayr burghs from 1818. At least in the later stages
of this attack he had help from many in the rising Whig group of young men
within the lawyers' establishment.

In 1815, before he entered Parliament, Kennedy had launched a parish
inquiry on relief costs and assessment, by sending a loaded questionnaire
through the sheriffs to parish ministers. Among other things he asked for
details of Poor Law expenditure for each year since 1790, whether the parish
was assessed, and since when, how many were on the roll of regular poor and
had been since 1790, and whether there were Friendly Societies or Savings
Banks established in the parish. The surviving archive carries replies from 177
ministers, but from only 27 are there full answers to all the questions. The
absence of replies from approximately 700 parishes may not have been just
inertia or the misplacement of documents. Clergy with a high sense of their
calling may well have objected to an inquiry launched through the system of
secular government. The tone of the answers is remarkably uniform on the
subject of assessment . It can be evinced from two samples: St Madoc's, where
the minister admitted that non-resident heritors gave nothing to the poor, and
held that assessment would make the poor 'strangers to modesty, frugality and
industry'; Muiravonside where the statement was that rates would 'take away
all feelings of Charity … and dissolve the whole cement of Society'.[8]

The numerical information submitted does not sustain the idea that poor
relief had drastically increased as a burden. The figures given in the 27 full

replies show a considerable increase in money terms from 1790. In 1800 the amount spent had been nearly three times that of 1790, but after that year it had swung between 20 and 40 per cent higher, ending in 1814 at 86 per cent up. But if this sum is examined in real terms, deflating it by the most esteemed and widely-used series of grain prices, the fiars of East Lothian oats, the increase in 1814 was only 15 per cent up on the 1790 figure. The number of 'regular' poor supported by these parishes had decreased slightly, from 397 to 373. Considering that this period covers great economic change, and in particular, as one perceptive minister observed, the disappearance of part-time earnings in textiles which had been important in many households, the figures hardly justify the heat engendered about the increasing burden of poor relief.

The fears of landowners can be otherwise explained. The end of the war saw a rapid fall in rents from the level they had stood at in the prolonged period of war inflation. Many owners had built an expected level of rental into settlement on marriages and children, and as a result the owner of an estate might have only a small residual income when rents fell. The prospect of a regular charge on land, even if small, was particularly unattractive at such a time. The clergy, ever since the emergence of the threat of radicalism in 1794, took the part of landed society. The change to this opinion is discernible in the tone of the last eleven volumes of the *Statistical Account*. By 1815 political economy and Malthusian arguments had become part of the university education which ministers underwent. Certainly assessment had become more frequent in the period since 1780. One reason for this was that it had become common for parishes to have most of their landowners non-resident and able to evade subscribing to collections. There was also the problem of the growth of dissenting congregations. Dissenters had to support their own ministers, and so not only had little to spare for collections for the parish funds of the established church, but no reason to subscribe. But the poor of such congregations would make requests for relief to the established church. The enhanced personal mobility of the labouring population, as the structure of land occupancy and the system of agricultural labour moved against cottars, made for less informal personal communication between households and less private help.

In some areas landowners had evaded assessment by adoption of an alternative which was called 'voluntary assessment'. In this system the landowners agreed to pay towards poor relief as if they were assessed, either by real or valued rent. In the *Statistical Account* eight parishes in the Lothians claimed to be working 'voluntary assessment'. Any landowner could bring this system to an end with no notice given, simply by refusing his share. No legal action could be brought against him, so a landowner could claim that no permanent charge lay against his estate. The proprietors of Peeblesshire in

1818 stated that the system did not have the tendency, that legal assessment had, of weakening the exertions of the lower orders. The argument seems to have been that uncertainty over the source of relief funds was morally good. A disadvantage, though, which was made clear in legal advice, was that the half of the burden which under legal assessment could be passed on to the tenants could not be so transferred without consent. Obtaining such consent from the tenantry may have been difficult.

The changed climate of opinion on the Poor Law may well explain the discovery by a recent piece of research in the records of over 100 parishes, that the high prices produced by the poor harvest of 1816 did not produce a reversion to Speenhamland practices.[9] Apart from the court decision of *Pollock vs Darling*, which, as always with British justice, took some time to emerge, the Speenhamlanding of 1800 disappeared from sight, and left no trace in the minds of those commenting on the Scottish Poor Law. The Reverend Robert Burns in his extensive *Historical Dissertations on the Law and Practice of Great Britain and Particularly of Scotland with Regard to the Poor* of 1819 stated firmly: 'in Scotland we know nothing of the very impolitic and pernicious practice of making up the deficiency of wages for work done … by grants out of parochial funds'. This should be taken to mean not that ministers knew nothing of the practice but that they had forgotten it.

In the *Statistical Account* of Cupar, Fife, the minister had stressed the need for a clear, statutory answer to two questions, who are the poor with a legal claim to maintenance,and who are the legal administrators of the funds? The latter question was usually settled by a compromise. Since the Humbie case of 1751 the heritors legally had full control over all parish money, but the kirk session was the body that collected the contributions, knew the circumstances of claimants and did the work of distribution. The situation on the former question was more obscure. In 1780 James Anderson of Monkshill had stated that those capable of earning could expect no help from their parish. But numerous kirk session registers of the eighteenth century give instances of aid going to people able to earn. There are instances of help with purchase of a horse for a carter, the payment of a wet nurse to a man whose family had twins, support for a woman nursing a child, aid to families after houses had been destroyed by fire. John McFarlan in his book on the Poor Laws makes it clear that he accepted relief for people prevented from work by a hard frost, or travelling to find work. The whole Speenhamlanding practice of 1800-1 was relief to the able-bodied whether employed or unemployed. As the use of assessment spread, the money from rates was assigned to paying the pensions of those on the roll, though half the collections had also been assigned to this by the Act of 1696. The other half might be used to give emergency payments for special need, and to sustain some in temporary sickness. This part of the expenditure was only nominally under the control of the heritors. As the demand of employers for full-time male muscle in the labour force increased, the issue of those temporarily lacking work tended to become the issue of the 'able-bodied'. There are statements in the legal textbooks of the early nineteenth century which accept the idea of relief for the able-bodied;[10] but after 1820 the literature took the opposite view. The effect of this was to produce the statement in the *Report* of the Royal Commission of 1844, 'the important distinction made by the poor laws of Scotland between the respective titles of able-bodied and impotent paupers, was held for centuries to be the distinguishing excellence of these laws'. Since the phrase 'able-bodied' was of recent coinage, this sentence shows anachronistic thinking. A more direct subversion of the early legalisation is to be found in the book of the Reverend Robert Burns: 'it is the leading principle of the Scottish Poor Laws to avoid any fixed or permanent tax'. The writer has blandly forgotten that the dominant principles of the Poor Laws, expressed in the titles of the early Acts, were the support of the poor and the repression of vagrancy.

The legal views after 1820 were built up by careful glossing of selected statute phrases. In 1819-21 a legal dispute over relief in Paisley, a town suffering from severe and sustained unemployment, had produced the decision that appeals on Poor Law matters could go only to the Court of Session. Such an appeal was difficult for the poor, even though their direct costs were remitted, because this Court sat for only part of the year in a limited number of cities, and all pleadings had to be printed. It was most unlikely that any claimant would put in an appeal. The lawyers could then produce textbooks changing the Law without fear of judicial review. This the Whig group of Edinburgh lawyers proceeded to do. 'Now the expression persons "not able to work for their living" applies to those who are disabled... rather than those whose employment is merely temporarily suspended.' This writer tackled the contradictions of the previous Acts of Parliament and the Proclamations of the Privy Council in the 1690s by preferring the Acts, on the grounds that Proclamations 'must be intended to confirm existing laws', ignoring the subsequent Acts of Parliament which confirmed the Proclamations. Another gloss intruded words into the statutes. Assessment could be used only as the Acts of Parliament authorised, and they authorised it only for those 'whose wants are of a permanent description'. 'No countenance is given to the idea that the wages of labour may be made up, out of the poor rates.' As for *Pollock vs Darling*, which gave such countenance, ' great doubt' existed whether this judgement would now be repeated. Another nineteenth-century authority's gloss was that 'in construing... statutes, it had been held that the words, "poor, aged and impotent" are to be read as "aged poor and impotent poor" '.

These adjustments and rewordings removed authority from *Pollock vs*

*Darling*. The lawyers were aided in this by Malthusian thought: 'since the period when it was pronounced… the dread which was then entertained of persons…incurring the danger of starvation, if not supported by compulsory provision, has been completely removed, by the greater knowledge which has been acquired, as to true causes and remedies of pauperism.'[11]

This systematic reinterpretation of the confused statutory base took place in a world very different from that to which the statutes had pertained. Rapid economic development in the late eighteenth century had led to urban growth. As T.M. Devine's chapter earlier in this volume shows, the accelerating rate of rural-urban migration quickly produced a labour surplus in the larger towns, especially in the crisis years after the end of the Napoleonic Wars.[12] These developments showed up the administrative inadequacy of the Poor Law. The main problem was the relative inelasticity of the parish system of the established Church. It took time for the Church to respond to the movement of population. New parishes involved the raising of new funds, complicated bargaining with landowners, or agreements with the incumbents of existing churches. Though some parishes were created before 1830, many of these did not have full functions. It was only in the 1830s that the Church set out on a major drive to collect money for new churches.[13] By then many areas in the cities were overcrowded with working people who might be forced by change of job, or inability to pay their rent, to migrate frequently, and so did not establish settlement anywhere. They had not the intimate knowledge of each other's affairs which characterised rural life. As early as 1782 the Reverend John McFarlan had recognised that population was shifting to the towns, and that the features which enabled the Poor Law to function in rural parishes did not obtain there. 'It is not uncommon for two private families to live for years in adjoining houses, without so much as knowing each others' names,' he wrote. Fragmentation of society meant that the intimacy of life which had enabled relatives and neighbours as well as elders to pass on information about those in need to a kirk session was not to be found. Residence of at least three years in a parish was required to establish settlement. Even without the new glossing of the law there were many who fell completely through the net of support. By the 1820s this failure had become conspicuous in the towns. In the Lowland countryside and small towns the system was working well enough. Within the councils of the Church and the state these latter places provided the bulk of opinion, and the growing urban crisis was largely ignored.

The rise of dissent made the financial problems of unassessed parishes worse. Evangelicalism also powered the development of charity outwith the Poor Law. There had always been such charity: alms from the rich had been given at rites of passage, craft incorporations had helped some of their members and their dependents when they fell on bad times. But the voluntary origin of most of the money going to relief through the parish had encouraged most charitable impulses to go through the kirk session. In the later eighteenth century voluntary societies, mostly evangelically inspired, were providing specific types of aid for specific causes. Glasgow had had the North Parish Washing Green Society collecting and distributing money since 1792: even older, but only partly charitable in aim were those societies set up to reaffirm specific area links, such as the Buchanan Society of 1725. The Infirmary movement of the eighteenth century set out to aid the poor, and administered large funds and considerable patronage. In the early nineteenth century cities had societies for the repression of mendicancy, which could be seen as an economical form of good works. Though the trickle of voluntary charitable activity had a long way to go before the great era of founding societies of the 1830s and 1840s was reached, it was growing.[14]

The new charitable organisations could have done much to fill areas of need not covered by the Poor Law. Certainly they did something in this direction, and sometimes also acted in collaboration with it. Outside the Border area the Poor Law did not supply much in the way of medical advice and treatment for the poor, but the dispensary movement provided treatment of a kind for people who could not afford it otherwise. In the north-east, parishes often paid a subscription to the Infirmary at Aberdeen to send some seriously ill there.

The Scottish Poor Law kept those it aided alive. That is, they received enough money to live on oatmeal, and also had occasional supplies of clothing or fuel. But a peck of oatmeal a week and four yards of linen every two years was not a standard of living comparable with that of households in work. The Poor Law did nothing to prevent families which had been able to earn adequate support from sinking to a level of extreme poverty. It is possible that some of the charitable societies of the nineteenth century gave help which might prevent poverty to families which conformed to the specifications of the societies' aims. But such aid was not common. The societies did very little and the Poor Law in the towns nothing for the large number of people in extreme poverty who had no right of settlement.[15]

The charitable societies had a significant influence on opinion about the Poor Law. It was already a middle-class view that acceptance of aid from the parish was likely to cause deterioration of character and weaken the attachment to independence. This argument was not applied to private charity, perhaps because the arbitrariness with which it was awarded prevented any sense of claim. Charitable societies were highly selective in the type of person they wished to help; simple destitution had little appeal to them. Malthusian thought had added the argument that relief was likely to accentuate the general level of poverty. Now came the argument that parochial relief was likely to deflect funds which might otherwise have been freely given to particular people, and prevent the exercise of Christian charity, beneficial both to giver and receiver. Arguments such as this added to the distaste of those with property for the imposition of rates and led to the movement for the abolition of the statutory element in the Poor Law in England and Scotland.

In Scotland this attack was led by the most influential churchman of the day, Thomas Chalmers. Chalmers moved, in 1815, from being minister of Kilmany, to a large parish in central Glasgow. In 1817 in an anonymous article in the *Edinburgh Review* he had proposed the ending of a governmental base for relief. Poor relief should involve a personal relationship between giver and receiver, and it could have this only if it was completely voluntary. Assessment-based relief should continue only for established paupers, being legally abolished for new claims. These would be sustained by voluntary collections.

Chalmers went on to attempt to work this system, in the celebrated St. John's experiment. A new Glasgow parish was created and separated from the central system of the Town's Hospital. A body of outside voluntary deacons was brought in and the collections were set aside for the new claims which the deacons could not persuade to withdraw. Each deacon had in charge 400 families. Chalmers stated later that their work did not take more than four hours a week: one of them put it at only six hours a year. It is unlikely that any serious inquiry into alternative resources could have been made, and the deacon's function seems to have been mainly to say no.

The so-called experiment was inherently fraudulent because the population of the parish was not in any real way separated off from that of neighbouring parishes where the burden of relief went up during the experiment's life. But it achieved great publicity, since it was proclaimed as a success by the most celebrated preacher of his day.[16] In spite of this, no assessed parish attempted to follow the scheme.

The gap between the desire of the articulate for the abolition of rates and the reality of the need for them was shown more explicitly over an attempt to carry out the policy made by T.F. Kennedy. Kennedy had, in 1819, tried to get a Bill through Parliament abolishing all appeals against parish decisions on relief. The Bill had failed but the legal decision in the Paisley case two years later had achieved most of its aims. Attempts in 1821-2 to remove the compulsory element in the English Poor Law had also failed. In 1824 Kennedy surreptitiously slid into Parliament a Bill which would have allowed landowners to withdraw altogether from paying assessment provided they took on the support, until these died off, of existing paupers. No new assessments would be allowed. Such rights of appeal as still remained would be abolished. As far as possible the Bill was to make poor relief a voluntary activity.

The Bill raised a storm, in presbyteries, in town councils, in county meetings, in the press, so that it clearly could not go through. It had brought

35. 'The Lame Beggar', by Walter Geikie. *National Galleries of Scotland.*

out the recognition that poor relief by assessment was necessary in the main urban centres. The group of Whig lawyers associated with Kennedy met defeat, and Chalmers had to lead the vote against the Bill in the General Assembly. But the combined skills of misrepresentation of the Church and the Law had a long-term effect in limiting the efficacy of Poor Law reform in 1845.

In spite of upper- and middle-class hostility to assessment, it had been spreading. In the 1790s the *Statistical Account* labelled 92 parishes as assessed. A Church of Scotland report in 1820, which did not receive answers from all parishes, noted 198 assessed. In 1818 on a similarly patchy enquiry the Church had claimed 145. Numeracy was never a strong feature of the ministry and this figure is probably too low. The upward trend, in a hostile climate, is evidence of the inadequacy of voluntary funds. In the 1830s, the *New Statistical Account's* figures suggest that on average 2.5 per cent of the population needed support, irrespective of the surges of the unemployed produced by the swings of the business cycle. The decision to adopt assessment in a parish would occur only after a clear shortfall in voluntary funds. It had to be made jointly by the kirk session and the heritors. For the session to convince heritors of the need, there had to be a full list of the poor. This would often include people asking for but not getting a place on the roll. Even those on the roll might be getting so little that their need to beg was embarrassingly conspicuous. If assessment was adopted it would set total cost at an enhanced level because these shortcomings would be met. So it was difficult for a parish to go back to voluntary funds. This is probably what Chalmers meant when he stated that assessment 'artificially stimulated' claims for relief above their 'natural level'.[17] But even the upward trend in assessment did not meet the needs of the urban situation.

The crisis created by the failure of the old Scottish Poor Law to sustain the unemployed did not arrive until the 1840s, by which time the general urban situation had deteriorated dangerously. It was entirely proper that it was unemployment in Paisley in 1841-2 which forced on reform of the Poor Law, since it had been the crisis there in 1819 that had enabled the lawyers to destroy the appeal system and to rewrite the scope of the law to exclude the unemployed.[18] By so doing they had made certain that the Scottish Poor law became an inadequate instrument for social welfare in an industrialising country.

## NOTES

1. There is a section of W.M. Morison's compilation, *The Decision of the Court Session from its institution until the separation of the court into two divisions in the year 1808, digested under proper heads in the Form of a Dictionary* (usually known as Morison's *Dictionary of Decisions*), 42 vols, (Edinburgh 1871), in vols. XXV-VI. Other cases mentioned can be found in the series of volumes, *Decisions of the Court of Session* (usually known as *Faculty Decisions*), by date.

2. The early development of the Poor Law is described in R.M. Mitchison, 'The Making of the Old Scottish Poor Law', *Past and Present*, 63 (1974), pp. 58-93. The working of the system in the late eighteenth century is shown in J.M. McPherson, *The Kirk's care of the Poor* (Aberdeen, n.d. but probably 1941), and John McFarlan, *Inquiries concerning the Poor* (Edinburgh, 1782).

3. The Report of the Royal Commission, *Poor Law Inquiry (Scotland)* (P.P.1844, XX), is very clear on the deficiencies of relief in the Highlands, and gives detailed evidence in P.P. 1844, XXI.

4. T. Hamilton, *Poor Relief in South Ayrshire, 1700-1845* (Edinburgh, 1942), Ch. 5.

5. R.A. Cage, *The Scottish Poor Law, 1745-1845* (Edinburgh, 1981) Ch. 5.

6. For Prestonkirk see *Caledonian Mercury*, 5 Dec. 1800. For elsewhere, Graham Birnie, 'Tradition and Transition. The Scottish Poor Law, Harvest Failure and the Industrious Poor', unpublished MA thesis, Department of Economic and Social History, University of Edinburgh 1976, Ch. 5.

7. J.R. Poynter, *Society and Pauperism* (London, 1969).

8. The archive is in the possession of Lord Tulliebole at Tulliebole Castle, Kinross-

shire, who has kindly allowed me to study it.

9. June W. Irving, 'The Scottish Poor Law Response to the 1816 harvest failure', unpublished MA thesis, Department of Economic and Social History, University of Edinburgh, 1982, p. 11.

10. G Hutcheson, *A Treatise on the Office of Justice of the Peace, Constable, etc... in Scotland* (Edinburgh, 1806); G Tait, *Summary of the Powers and Duties of a Justice of the Peace in Scotland* (Edinburgh, 1815).

11. Alexander Dunlop, *A Treatise on the Law of Scotland relating to the Poor* (Edinburgh, 1825); David Monypenny of Pitmilly, *Remarks on the Poor Laws and on the Method of Relief for the poor in Scotland* (Edinburgh, 1825); John Guthrie Smith, *Digest of the Law of Scotland relating to the poor* (Edinburgh, 1859). The legal changes are discussed in Rosalind Mitchison, 'The Creation of the Disablement Rule in the Scottish Poor Law', in T.C. Smout (ed.), *The Search for Wealth and Stability* (London,1979), pp. 199-217.

12. See above Chapter 2 and T.M. Devine (ed.), *Farm Servants and Labour in Lowland Scotland, 1770-1914* (Edinburgh, 1984), particularly in the first chapter by the editor.

13. Stewart Brown, *Thomas Chalmers and the godly Commonwealth in Scotland* (Oxford, 1982).

14. E.O.A. Checkland, *Philanthropy in Victorian Scotland* (Edinburgh, 1980); David Hamilton, *The Healers: A History of Medicine in Scotland* (Edinburgh, 1981) Chs .5 and 6; Guenter B. Risse, *Hospital Life in Enlightment Scotland* (Cambridge, 1986).

15. The various pamphlets by W.P. Alison in the early 1840s show this well, particularly *Observations on the Management of the Poor in Scotland and its effects on the Health of the Great Town* (Edinburgh, 1840).

16. R.A. Cage and E.O.A. Checkland, 'Thomas Chalmers and Urban Poverty', *Philosophical Journal,* XIII (1976), pp. 37-56.

17. Chalmers' views on the Scottish Poor Law were clearly expressed in his evidence to the Select Committee on the State of the Need for a Poor Law in Ireland, P.P. 1830 VIII, Second Report of Evidence.

18. T.C. Smout, 'The Strange Intervention of Edward Twistleton: Paisley in Depression, 1841-3', in Smout (ed.), *Search for Wealth and Stability.*

CHAPTER 13

# Patterns of Protest

## W. Hamish Fraser

Social protest can take many forms. At its most spectacular it suggests the armed insurrection or the riot or some public, often bloody, encounter with authority. Such protest are the ones that are well-documented in history. But there can be a whole range of other forms of social protest that leave a much less obvious mark: the boycott, the passive resistance, the silent ignoring, the social crime. Equally hidden, but also manifestations of protest, are apathy, refusal to make an effort, bloodymindedness and drunkenness. Protest can take the form of spontaneous outbursts of anger, breaking forth in response to some apparently minor incident, though perhaps drawing its fuel from long-term grievances. But it can also reflect a more sustained anger and a determination to alter an existing state of affairs, which can be channelled through formalised procedures in trade unions or political organisations.[1] The purpose of this chapter is to look at the circumstances which produced particular patterns of protest in different communities and among a variety of groups in Scotland in a period of extraordinarily rapid economic, social and political change. Inevitably, the focus has to be largely on the documented public protests, but it is well to remember the more latent kind.

## Rural Protest

In a society where, for much of the period, more than two-thirds of the population lived off the land or worked in rural surroundings it was changes in the pattern of land organisation that had the most profound effects on traditional ways of life. The process of enclosure and consolidation, the move away from communal farming to individual holdings and to capitalist enterprise was proceeding at an accelerating pace in eighteenth-century Scotland. Yet, as T.M. Devine has shown, the resistance to these changes in the Lowlands and the Borders was remarkably muted. Apart from the Levellers' Revolt in Galloway in the summer of 1724, when small tenants rose in protest against their eviction and forcibly demolished the dykes that enclosed their former holdings within larger farms, there is only the very occasional minor incident. Social stability appears to have been remarkably little disturbed by the changes.[2]

Part of the explanation seems to lie in the pace of the changes, proceeding piecemeal over generations. A process of social stratification had begun in the rural Lowlands before 1700. Adjustments to new commercial pressures and a growing responsiveness to the market had prepared communities for the acceleration of these processes in the eighteenth century. The timing of the most significant changes was fortuitous. There was no dramatic displacement of population as a result of the changes and the actual level of suffering was not high. An expanding demand for rural craftsmen, and particularly for weavers, helped compensate for loss of small landholdings as sub-tenancies were absorbed. In addition, farmers in several areas of the central and eastern Lowlands were having to compete against the appeal of industrialising towns. As a result, agricultural earnings rose before 1800 and older patterns of long hires, payments in kind and persistence of living-in sheltered farm servants from the worst effects of economic fluctuation in the later eighteenth century. The movement to cash-paid day labourers and the emergence of a huge labour surplus, so extensive in Southern England and which led to the Captain Swing uprising of 1830, did not occur in Scotland.

The easy transition of Lowland Scotland is in sharp contrast to events in the Highlands. There the process of change was altogether more traumatic, as whole glens were cleared of much of their population; and in the Western Highlands there were few of the mechanisms that cushioned change in the Lowlands. While commercial relationships were not absent before 1745, it was not until the aftermath of the Jacobite Rebellion that land in the Highlands lost its significance for military and political purposes and began to be viewed primarily as an economic asset. But even then, only the clan chiefs and their tacksmen kin were involved in farming and in commerce much above subsistence level. For the vast number of Highlanders traditional ties of loyalty and obligation persisted and there was none of the legalism of commercial arrangements such as a lease. Elements of the old survived throughout most of the century, strengthened by the raising of Highland regiments in return for promised land rights and by the need to keep labour available to gather and process kelp.

The change when it came was sharp and harsh, with few of the opportunities for regular alternative employment that existed in the south. The collapse of the kelp industry after 1810 and the failure of new industries to take hold removed the safety valve of non-agricultural employment. Forcible eviction brought a social disruption that sometimes led to protest.

The issue of how much resistance there was still produces something of a

Now is the Time,
Burn the Villain
Fear not– you will
be Supported–

*Burn the Villan*
Dundas

36. Before the King's Birthday riot of June 1792 notices like this were circulating in Edinburgh. The rioting focused on the house of Henry Dundas in George Square.

debate. Many writers in the past have tended to contrast the docility of the Highlanders with the more violent response of the Irish peasantry to change. The supposed 'crime' of the Highland landowners has somehow seemed so much worse precisely because their tenantry, whether through tradition, deference or loyalty, accepted it. In fact, as Eric Richards and others have shown, there were repeated outbursts of protest and resistance to what was being done. Some fifty incidents have been identified between the 1740s and the 1880s. They took a variety of forms. When sheep first came into Lochaber in 1782, the Selkirk sheep farmer was physically assaulted. No doubt other sheep farmers faced the intense, all-pervasive, silent hostility of the local population. There were plenty of examples of petty violence and sheep-stealing, and of the perennial Highland display of defiance: poaching. Only rarely, however, before the 1880s, did members of more than one community co-ordinate their actions.[3]

A particular sense of injustice was a key ingredient in bringing open resistance. It created that moral outrage which Barrington Moore has identified as an essential part of the impetus to rebel. Many of the tacksmen and their followers who, in defiance of their chiefs, emigrated in the later eighteenth century, were making one kind of protest, with a sense of bitterness that past obligations of the chiefs were being violated. Breaches of agreements on the raising of regiments led to mutinies among the soldiers and to protests among their dependants. So the Kildonan tenants who resisted Patrick Sellar's activities in the winter of 1812-3 were indignant that land should be taken from them although they had been promised security when they had 'furnished men for the 93rd Regiment'. They were *'loyal* men whose brothers and sons were now fighting Bonaparte' and they 'were entitled to keep possession of *their* Grounds'. This claim to a moral right to the land both on grounds of custom and on grounds of service (a claim heard in peasant societies throughout world history) was a recurring theme which gave cohesion to much Highland protest.

Many of these protesters were women, just as it had been women who attacked the Lochaber shepherd in 1782. One of the most effective tactics of resistance in the Highlands and in some other rural protests was the use of women (or men dressed as women) to confront authority. Obviously, in many cases women responded spontaneously to being evicted from their homes and needed no lessons in protest. But, as a tactic, the presence of women could be very effective in 'wrong-footing' the authorities. It was difficult for troops to attack them and, if they did act, then the resultant publicity was bad for the authorities. Defeat of the authorities by women was, of course, a deeper humiliation. It could often be accompanied by overt sexual humiliation, as at Gruids in 1821 when the sheriff's officers were stripped before they were sent on their way.

Yet, given the extent of Clearance in the Highlands, one might have expected even more protest. But distance and terrain made co-ordinated action difficult, though it clearly could happen as it did in Ross-shire in 1792, when there was the only really extensive effort to physically drive out the sheep. Over the largest part of the Highlands, the changes taking place were sporadic and gradual and happening over widely separated-geographical areas.

The psychological hurdle of defying a chief to whom one felt an ingrained obligation proved a difficult one for Highlanders to overcome. It was easier to find scapegoats in outsiders, like the southern shepherds or the insensitive agent, and one has many examples of pathetic petitions to the landowner to right the injustices being perpetrated by his agents on the spot. The ministers of religion, generally preaching a doctrine of submission to the will of the landowner, no doubt helped achieve acquiescence, although just occasionally a minister who too enthusiastically assisted in Clearance could find himself physically threatened. And, as James Hunter has argued, the embracing of evangelical sects and of the Free Church in 1843 was a very clear answer to the established church's collusion with the landowners. Perhaps it is to a religion that preached the ephemeral nature of this life, 'a swift thing…a flying vanity, the vicissitudes of which have to be tolerated in expectation of reward in heaven where the rich and mighty would be brought to the level of the poorest' that one must look for an explanation of acquiescence. On the other hand, it was the religion of the Free Church that was in time to give an emotional and ideological cohesion to the crofting community that allowed it to resist the further encroachments of the 1880s. Economic factors too were important, however: acquiescence was strengthened by the increasing desti- tution of many in the Highlands, on occasion accompanied by actual famine. It is not the hungry who rebel.[4]


## Urban Protest

Sudden shortages in food and the accompanying rise in prices were the main causes of urban protest in both small town and city. They could lead to riots and strikes and they were frequently an ingredient in political agitation.

It is with riots that we start. As John Bohstedt says, they were part and parcel of how different elements in the eighteenth-century community interacted. Rioting has to be seen in the context of local politics, part of the theatre of political behaviour, with all the participants knowing their parts and generally adhering to them. Riot crowds 'mobilized networks of people that already existed — networks of kinship and camaraderie, in work, play, markets, work- shop or neighbourhood, as well as institutional networks, such as political and labour combinations'.[5]

All the classic patterns of the riot emerge in the meal mobs, exploding, often with remarkable suddenness, in small towns and in ports. The actions of the mob were open actions, in broad daylight, publicly drawing attention to a grievance and demanding action by the authorities. While some of the actions took place in the countryside, the meal rioters were generally rural craftsmen or town dwellers venturing into the countryside to exert pressure on the producers or to get to the corn mill.

The forced sale of grain was one of the most common features associated with meal mobs. It usually involved negotiations with the authorities, essentially a debate of local politics about the actions necessary to ensure order and social peace. Tayside rioters in December 1772 after negotiations with a magistrate, who agreed to get meal sold at a price acceptable to the rioters, took the keys of a grain store to the sheriff-substitute in Perth to ensure that the sale took place at the agreed price.

Another typical meal riot could involve the *taxation populaire,* the price-fixing riot at which farmers were forced to sell at what the crowd regarded as a fair price. Here the crowd were carrying out the task that they believed the authorities ought to be doing. Logue cites a number of examples of these from the 1799-1801 period when grain prices rose sharply, In Beith, in October 1800, the crowd seized a cartload of meal, and after the church officer had announced it through the streets, it was put on sale at 2s per peck, a little below the market price. It was not *substantially* below: in other words, the rioters on these occasions were prepared to accept compromises. What was being sought was a fair distribution between the farmer and the consumer, and it was accompanied by a popular conception of a 'just' price as determined by custom and experience.

The most common trigger for riots were the attempts to transport grain at a time of high prices to parts of the country where grain was scarce. Well over half of the meal riots identified by Logue were to prevent export of grain or potatoes.

Violence against individuals or property was rare in meal riots but occasionally the most flagrant violators of an accepted moral code would be punished. The middlemen, coming between producing farmer and consumer, were the objects of most hostility: so some of the Tayside meal mobs of 1772 searched for John Donaldson of Elcho, near Perth, a major dealer and exporter, 'threatening in a loud voice that if they could get Donaldson they would put his heart's blood under their feet', and his house was looted. Forestalling and exporting at times of scarcity were very obvious infringements of the rights of the community.[6]

The use of violence was likely to lead to dire retribution and was contrary to the purposes of the rioters. Their main aim was to remind the authorities of their obligations. E.P. Thompson has written of the perceptions of the crowds who made up the eighteenth-century food rioters, with their belief in a 'moral economy' that gave them the right to have food at a price they could afford. When that moral economy was threatened, when practice and custom were undermined, then the crowd would act to eradicate the threat, correct the wrong and punish the violators of the moral code. The riot was the ultimate reminder.

Thomas Muir Esq.r Younger
of
Hundershill

37. Thomas Muir, a Glasgow advocate, was a leading member of the Society of the Friends of the People. In 1793 he was sentenced to fourteen years' transportation to Australia from which he was subsequently rescued by an American ship.

Such compromises had to be made because of the problem of maintaining order in the eighteenth century. The forces of law and order were tiny and there was no easy recourse to forcible suppression of disorder. Although Scotland was well garrisoned with English troops in the aftermath of 1745, it had, before the 1790s, none of the militia and volunteers that could be utilised for the maintenance of the public order in England. Public peace depended on mutual tolerance. The ruling groups had to pay a price for the deference or, at least, acquiescence of the lower orders, a price that involved accepting some measure of paternal responsibility. When that paternalism faded under the pressure of growing acceptance of market forces, then the tensions heightened and the resort to force became more frequent. After 1797, if the usual relationship based on mutual reciprocity broke down, then the local authorities could turn to the Volunteers, but, even then, there were limitations since those part-time soldiers were artisans and labourers themselves, from the same community as the rioters and subject to the same pressure from hunger, neighbours and wives. In an incident in Errol in November 1801 after a meal mob, when the Volunteers were ordered to turn out during a meeting of JPs in the local inn, some women, wives and mothers of the Volunteers took their guns off them so that the crowd could stone the inn with impunity. Elsewhere, there were examples of Volunteers participating in riots.[7]

Whenever possible, then, order in the eighteenth century had to be maintained without resort to force, and to have the authority of provost and constable publicly challenged was something that was bound to cause anxiety to the principal inhabitants. They tended to explain the breakdown of order by blaming outside agitators or influence. As the Inverness magistrates explained to the Lord Advocate after an extensive meal riot in 1793, 'A Pains (sic) Book it is now known had been very industriously circulated among the lower classes of our people'. It was reassuring to know that the fault lay outside the community.

Up until the 1790s the Scottish authorities seem to have been remarkably successful in avoiding the dangers of food riots. There had been two serious ones in Glasgow and in Edinburgh in November 1763 and a spate of them on Tayside in December and January 1772-3. There were incidents in Fife and Galloway in 1783 an another Edinburgh one in the summer of 1784. But, apart from the occasional small incident, there were few compared with many parts of England before the 1790s. Even in the period of sharpest price rises, 1795-1801, Logue identifies only twenty meal riots in the whole of Scotland, compared with forty-three in Devon and forty in Lancashire and Cheshire in the same period.[8] Various factors made for this difference. With harvest failures rare and prices relatively uniform, it was not until the 1780s that there was a substantial increase in the amount of grain being shipped from one region to another. With the different pace of population change by the end of the century, trade grew and the provocation of exports during scarcity became more apparent. However, regulation of markets at times of scarcity continued to be applied for longer in Scotland than in most parts of England. Also other factors operated. Bulk buying of grain by incorporations of trades to sell to their members perhaps eliminated scarcity among a key group in the urban community, while commissioners of supply bought for rural villages. As Rosalind Mitchison shows elsewhere in this volume, many landowners made donations to parish funds at times of distress, and payments in both cash and kind were made to the needy. Co-operative buying by handloom weavers through bodies like the Fenwick weavers' cooperative or the various victualling societies perhaps eased the problem for others. When these mechanisms failed there could be direct intervention by private subscription. In the aftermath of the collapse of the Ayr Bank in 1772, when unemployment was widespread, the 'respectable inhabitants' of Glasgow anticipated trouble by raising a voluntary subscription for the relief of unemployed tradesmen. In the spring of 1783 in Edinburgh some 2,000 families were receiving subsidised oatmeal, thanks to public subscription. Again in March, 1795 (the year which saw the peak of food rioting in England) an eighth of the population of Edinburgh was receiving subsidised bread and there were no meal riots there or anywhere else in the urban centres and industrial areas of central Scotland in the 1794-6 period.

Riot in a large town was potentially much more dangerous than in rural areas. The numbers involved were greater, the amount of property that could be threatened was larger, and the rioters could get closer to the social and political leaders. Certainly troops were more readily available and could be quickly deployed, although, as the events of the Porteous Riot of 1736 showed, even the presence of troops just outside the city walls could not prevent the crowd wreaking its vengeance on the captain of the town guard. Something on that scale was, however, quite exceptional, and that remarkable mixture of social classes in the tenements of the Old Town of Edinburgh left the civic leaders very vulnerable to popular pressure and very sensitive to popular discontents. The magistrates had to walk a difficult line between repression and concession when troubled flared, and on most occasions they opted for concession and negotiation and for ways of avoiding trouble. Only at the very worst food crises were there meal riots in the cities, and the local authorities were generally quick to respond to rising prices to prevent tensions over food getting out of hand.

However, as towns grew in size the complexity of hierarchial social relationships in which the crowd traditionally operated broke down. There was a widening social gap between the propertied and the propertyless. The movement of the well-to-do out of the closes of the High Street to the wide streets and elegant squares of the New Town of Edinburgh between the 1790s and the 1820s epitomised the changes that were taking place in social relationships. The crowd seemed more threatening. There was more property to lose if disorder erupted. There was less of a common understanding of the traditional theatricality of the crowd's actions and a greater readiness to resort to force on both sides. To the political leaders the crowd was a dangerous mob of unknown strangers, whereas in the 1750s and 1760s there had been recognisable, acknowledged leaders with whom the civic fathers could deal. The public assembly in the streets was becoming something to be feared, not to be negotiated with. Also, the crowd itself was more violent. As towns grew rapidly and workers flocked in from surrounding areas, the social networks

The Rev.ᵈ

T : F : PALMER.

Edinburgh published as the Act directs by W. Skirving

38. Thomas Fishe Palmer, an English Unitarian minister who was active in reform circles in Dundee. He was sentenced to seven years' transportation for encouraging the reading of Paine's works and for stirring agitation among low weavers and mechanics.

that were so important an element in allowing crowds to emerge and to know how to act were disappearing. The well-to-do were just as anxious when times were difficult to avoid disorder: charitable collections were made, soup kitchens were provided, but they were seen more as a means of preventing trouble and less as part of a pattern of mutual obligation.[9]

## Industrial Protest

Similar changes in social relationships were also apparent in the workplace, and there too there was a heightening of tension as the period advanced which had implications for the maintenance of public order. The expansion of the

Scottish economy was accomplished only with far-reaching changes in traditional trades and with the development of new ones. These necessitated an expansion of the workforce, increased division of labour and frequently-changing work patterns. Output began to be organised on a more capitalist basis, catering for a wider market, and traditional relationships between master and man began to alter. Older patterns of work relationships based on the assumption that the norm was a progress from apprentice to journeymen to independent master craftsman gave way to a situation where most journeymen remained full-time wage-earners throughout their lives. Where once all could identify with the craft, there now appeared a separation of interests between employer and worker. Journeymen's societies, largely for friendly society purposes, but easily converted to provide the necessary co-ordination in a trade dispute, had begun to emerge early in the eighteenth century. By the second half of the century permanent journeymen's organisations were common among groups such as tailors, shoemakers, masons, wrights and others in all of the main Scottish cities. Such organisations posed new challenges to those in power.[10]

The most frequent cause of dispute was rising prices, and since craftsmen in the cities could less easily exert direct pressure on the producer or the dealer, they pressed for higher wages to meet rising costs. Industrial disputes peaked at times of rising prices, such as in 1763 and 1764, following a number of years of bad harvests.

The dangers of street disturbance in the industrial city were very forcibly demonstrated in Glasgow in 1787. So too was the message that in the context of rapid industrialisation the old patterns and traditional forms no longer applied. Grain prices were high and wages were falling, as cheap Indian muslins swamped the relatively new Glasgow muslin trade. A mass meeting of 7,000 weavers and their families agreed not to take work at the new, reduced prices being offered by the manufacturers. Webs were forcibly removed from looms and paraded through the streets to be handed back to the manufacturers: a typical public ritual, but on an unprecedently large scale. Persistent strike-breakers were manhandled. The weavers' leaders planned a levy to raise funds for weavers to continue to work. To manufactures, new self-made men, with none of the traditions of artisan culture, the issue was a simple one of whether prices were to be regulated 'on the option of the workmen' or 'as in reason it ought, on the demand of the market'. The refusal to work went on for weeks, with weavers assuming that it was only a matter of time before the magistrate would intervene to fix rates. Appeals were directed to the public, arguing that it was wrong to reduce wages at a time of rising prices. Matters got out of hand on 3 September 1787 when a group of Calton weavers forcibly removed webs from looms of weavers who had accepted work at the reduced rates. The webs were paraded through the streets and ritually burned. When the crowd reached the east end of Drygate Street in Calton, it was met by regular troops and magistrates. Stones and bricks were thrown, the troops opened fire and six of the crowd were killed.[11]

The events of 1787 had a traumatic effect on the dominating elite in Glasgow and on the workers. Whereas in the past such an incident would have been regarded as a failure by the authorities, this one was presented as a victory over unacceptable tumult. They sought to prevent a recurrence of such happenings, but not by negotiation and concession, rather by propaganda and social control. Sunday schools were set up by the end of the year and attempts were made to re-organise the administration of the city so that respectable citizens could be made responsible for the different areas of the city and report to the magistrates 'against any disorderly persons therein'. There were demands for police, one of whose functions would be to suppress mobs. Riot in the city was no longer to be seen as a signal of a breakdown in community relations, but as 'seditious insurrections and tumults' that had to be suppressed by force. If propaganda failed, then increased policing had to be used to keep what was increasingly seen as a hostile class in check.[12] It was a pattern that was to become more and more the norm as industrial changes brought major social and ideological changes over the next twenty-five years.

In practice the development of an effective police force proved difficult to achieve. The existing merchant ruling elite in Glasgow was wary about surrendering power or offices to new authorities; the rising business class was concerned about giving power to the burgh authorities over whom they had no democratic check and about paying the cost of improvement. Numerous schemes for a police force foundered on these obstacles, until heightened fears of popular disorder created enough support for a city police force to be established in 1800.[13]

In Edinburgh the symbolic turning-point signalling the end of traditional relationships was the Hogmany Tron riot of 1811-2, when gangs of young men took advantage of crowds to rob them. The authorities took massive retribution. Four were hanged, two transported for life and two for fourteen years. Immediately, the police force was reorganised and strengthened, and Sunday schools and new day schools were opened.[14]

Direct confrontation actually remained relatively rare. Street action was generally a last resort since it was likely to bring down the wrath of the authorities. In Hobsbawm's apt phrase, 'collective bargaining by riot' was largely the act of the ineffectively organised, and journeymen learned rather to use legal processes. Within the Scottish system there existed mechanisms for adjusting wages that removed some of the necessity for direct confrontation. It was legally permitted for journeymen to come together to petition for

CITIZEN SKIRVING
Secretary to the Britifh Convention
A Tried Patriot and an Honefi Man.

39. William Skirving, secretary of the Scottish Friends of the People, and organiser of a convention of reformers in 1793, was transported to Australia for fourteen years. He died in New South Wales soon after his arrival there.

increased wages, first by approaching the incorporation of their trade and, if that failed, by going to the burgh magistrates or to the Justices of the Peace, who since the seventeenth century had had the power to regulate wages and hours of work. If they were dissatisfied with the magistrates' ruling they could then have recourse to civil action at the Court of Session to get the ruling altered.

Such legal intervention was not always to the advantage of the journeymen, since until the 1760s at least the courts tended to see their function as one of keeping journeymen in a position of 'due subordination' to their masters. However, as the century progressed there were signs of the JPs and judges being readier to intervene and to play the role of intermediary. There is evidence that amid the political tensions, industrial unrest and rising food prices of the 1790s and early nineteenth century, local magistrates and national judges were prepared to use their powers to adjust wages to take account of rising prices. The peak of price rises came in 1799-1800, when the price of meal in the rich farming county of East Lothian rose by some 140 per cent. So in 1799 Lanarkshire JPs conceded rises to wrights, when they claimed that 'owing to the present general scarcity and extreme price of necessaries of life they find it impossible with the utmost industry and economy to provide for themselves and their families'. Later in the year, the Midlothian JPs granted a rise to the shipwrights of Leith because of the high price of provisions, and the JPs ruled that the men should get a rise of fourpence a day until the price of meal fell to 1s 6d a peck and 2d day after that until it was 1s 2d a peck, after which they would revert to the old level of wages. When in 1802 the masters sought to reduce the rates, the men again appealed to the JPs who accepted that meal prices had fallen, but went on to say that 'as articles of clothing and house rents are higher', then a small wage increase was allowable. Edinburgh printers, after a prolonged struggle through the courts, got an elaborate table of piece rates, very much in line with their demands, laid down by the Court of Session in 1805.[15] What emerges is that reassertion of traditional paternalist patterns by the landed class that E.P. Thompson has detected at the same time in England. Faced with obvious signs of mounting social tension, the gentry were prepared to use their powers to adjust wages. It was an important safety valve that held open the prospect of legal redress.

It was within this traditional pattern that the Lanarkshire handloom weavers were operating when, in February 1812, they submitted a table of prices to the burgh magistrates of Glasgow and to the Sheriff. Representatives of the weavers and of the manufacturers were summoned, but no agreement could be reached. The weavers now took their table of prices to the JPs, asking for a wage that would enable a weaver 'with fair hours and proper application, to feed, clothe and accommodate himself and his family'. The manufacturers questioned the legality of such an appeal before the Court of Session and, although a number of judges expressed doubts about the ruling, they had no doubt that JPs had the *right* to regulate wages. The Lanarkshire justices reaffirmed their earlier decision and the weavers' association resolved not to accept webs at anything other than the new rates.[16]

The weavers went out of their way to emphasise the legality and the moderation their procedures. The demonstrations and protests through the streets of Glasgow were studiously orderly and ritualised. One model for protest that might have been adopted at this time was machine breaking, which was spreading among the framework knitters of Leicestershire and the shearers of Yorkshire. Although information about events in these areas was available, there was a very deliberate avoidance of any association with Luddism. A system of internal policing existed within the weavers' association to ensure that order was maintained. All along, the concern of the weavers' union was to defend the principle of the regulation of wages by the Justices and, therefore, to operate within legal procedures.

However, at least since the beginning of the century there had been frequent calls from the business community for an end to this kind of interventionism and for the criminalisation of all combination, on the pattern of the English Combination Laws. The new economic orthodoxy shaped by Adam Smith was spreading rapidly. While predominantly gentry JPs and older judges were prepared to uphold traditional patterns, employers and younger lawyers were becoming increasingly critical of them. The issue was debated again and again in the courts in the first decade of the nineteenth century, with the decision always in favour of intervention.

The strongest pressures for change came in the West of Scotland where the most far-reaching and rapid transformation was taking place. Employers had been campaigning for the implementation of combination laws in Scotland, which could only be effectively achieved if wage regulation was eradicated. Their actions had the effect of pushing different trade societies together to form a joint committee to resist the joint employers' campaign. Such collaborative actions were evidence of the appearance of a 'labour consciousness', in John Foster's phrase, that went beyond craft. With probably 30,000 to 40,000 looms standing idle throughout the country and evidence of a new industry-wide awareness, quite different form the more locally-based activities of traditional tradesmen, there was a new level of anxiety. The manufacturers declined to pay the new rates and in collaboration with the legal authorities determined to act against the weavers' association. The leaders of the association were apprehended and a number given prison sentences for combination ranging from two to eighteen months. As even senior judges admitted, this was to fly in the face of previous rulings, but new circumstances, it was argued, required new offences.[17]

Four months later, the statutes allowing JPs to regulate wages in both England and Scotland were swept away by Parliament. Any infringements of the rights of employers to employ whom the wished, when they wished and at the rates they wished, were now denounced as against the laws of nature. Only the market could decide the levels of wages and anything else was 'impracticable'. It made it extremely difficult for Scottish trade unions to retain a legal right to exist.

Denied the possibility of legal redress, and with any belief in the neutrality of courts and justices in the issue of master-and-workman relationships abandoned, it is hardly surprising that many workers, particularly the hand-loom weavers, turned to radical politics. A relatively peaceful period of social relationships gave way to one of bitter conflict.

**Political Protest**

Popular political protest was a rare feature of Scottish society in the eighteenth century. After 1715 criticism of Government could so readily be branded as Jacobite treason that it was generally avoided and the Scottish political system, with its relatively few electors, increasingly became managed by an oligarchy of politicians, first around the Campbell family and later around the Dundas family. Only very occasionally did popular protest burst forth over some political issue. There were sporadic anti-Union riots in 1707. In 1725 the Glasgow crowd wreaked havoc on the property of those who supported the new malt duty. Religious bigotry, despite the fact that only a tiny fraction of the population was Roman Catholic, played its part in riots, not just in Glasgow and Edinburgh, but in relatively small towns, against proposals for some slight Catholic emancipation in 1779. Opposition to the implications of the Patronage Act of 1712, by which the power to present a nominee as parish minister reverted to lay patrons, led to sometimes quite violent anti-patronage riots. These sometimes were a 'radical' assertion of congregational rights, with echoes of covenanting language. Later in the century and at the beginning of the nineteenth they were more generally associated with an Evangelical element within a congregation resenting the intrusion of a Moderate nominee.

Political stirrings of a new kind appeared in the 1780s. As in England, there was a beginning of questioning by those excluded from the spoils of a corrupt political system. Many from the growing middling ranks of Scottish society, conscious of power being pulled ever more firmly into the hands of the Scottish landed classes, demanded burgh reform, with an opening of access to the closed town councils who controlled the selection of burgh MPs. The political debate was widened further by the Revolution of 1789 and by the controversy surrounding Burke's *Reflections on the Revolution in France* and Thomas Paine's replies in *The Rights of Man*. What had been a concern of a relatively small number of the propertied began to widen into an issue of wide public concern.

The year 1792 was particularly volatile. In June, Edinburgh was shaken by the King's birthday riots. This was no spontaneous gathering that got out of hand, but had been anticipated by placards and handbills for days before. It was very specifically aimed at Government, in the shape of the Lord Advocate, Robert Dundas, whose house in George Square came under siege by the crowd. The actual cause of the riot remains obscure, but it perhaps indicates the first signs of a new political awareness, inspired by events in France, among some of those formerly excluded from political debate.[18]

The protests in Edinburgh were followed by similar ones in Aberdeen, Dundee, Lanark, Peebles and Perth, in all of which effigies of Dundas were

40. George Mealmaker, a Dundee handloom weaver, who had been associated with T.F. Palmer in the early 1790s, but had escaped arrest. In 1797 he seems to have been the moving force behind the shadowy United Scotsmen and, in 1798, convicted of sedition, he was dispatched to Australia for fourteen years.

burned. In November and December a new spate of political demonstrations broke out. The Societies of the Friends of the People, where elements from gentry, middle ranks and workers combined to demand political change, spread throughout the country, and Trees of Liberty were planted in Perth, Aberdeen, Dundee and in smaller towns and villages as far apart as Fochabers and Auchtermuchty. Why one small town should be active rather than another is not always apparent. One can only assume that much depended on the role of an influential, local reformer. Given the lack of any tradition of political debate and discussion in Scotland, it is probable that for many of the participants the actual political dimension was slight compared with the excitement of the meeting or the opportunity to express a generalised discontent with their economic state. However, there were signs that at least some of the urban craftsmen were taking the language and slogans of the reformers and learning to adapt and use them for demands that went much beyond what was envisaged by liberal gentry associated with the Societies of Friends of the People. And the Scottish cities were free from the excesses of loyalist mobs.

The authorities' response was devastatingly harsh. There was a series of arrests of reformers in the Spring of 1793, and when that failed to deter continuing demands for reform, leading activists, Muir, Palmer and Skirving together with London reformers who had ventured north of the border, Margarot and Gerald, were despatched to Australia. The tiny group of insurrectionists around Robert Watt was easily broken up and imitators were further deterred by his public hanging. The popular political reform movement was effectively nipped in the bud. Not until the shadowy appearance of the United Scotsmen in 1797, advocating annual parliaments and universal suffrage, were there signs of a renewal of political organisation. There seems little doubt that this underground radical organisation was able to pull into its orbit many workers, especially in the weaving villages of Tayside and Fife, though it was never able to channel other discontents into a political movement. Even the death of twelve protesters, including two women, in the colliery village of Tranent in August 1797 at the hands of dragoons failed to revive political protest. There is no sign that the food riots of 1800, unlike the pattern in the North-West of England, acquired a political dimension.[19]

A shrewd use of a combination of coercion and concession by the public authorities in Scotland had effectively eradicated the popular pressures for political change by the first decade of the nineteenth century. But a hardening of attitudes on economic issues and the adoption of more confrontational industrial policies after 1813 brought a revival of political agitation. Denied the possibility of improvement of their economic position through trade society action or through the intervention of a sympathetic court, not surprisingly many working men turned to political solutions.

The years 1816 to 1820 were ones of growing bitterness and class conflict. Influenced by the writings of Cobbett's *Political Register* and Wooler's *Black Dwarf*, which circulated widely in the West of Scotland, working men identified the economic troubles of these years with the political system. Successful middle-class pressure for the abolition of income tax meant that additional income had to be found from taxes on consumption — salt, beer, sugar, tea, tobacco, shoes, soap and candles. There were signs of a hardening of attitude on the distribution of poor relief.

The groups most affected and most involved in the protest movements and in the radical political organisations were the handloom weavers. Facing sharply declining earnings because of reduced demand and the great influx of poorly skilled workers into their trade, and with their craft organisation effectively destroyed in 1813, it is not surprising that they should have been prepared to consider drastic remedies. By 1819, groups were arming, and supporters of union societies that had previously advocated boycott of taxed goods as the most effective weapon were now won over to support of physical force.[20]

An overheated political situation exploded in April, 1820 with armed insurrection by small groups in the West of Scotland and widespread strikes in Paisley and in Glasgow. We shall never know how far the actions were provoked by police agents to bring the conspirators into the open, but they signalled the coming together of a whole series of discontents. Some were economic: declining and fluctuating earnings, erratic employment. Some were social: bad housing and generally deteriorating living conditions in the rapidly industrialising cities, inadequate provision for relief in times of need. Yet others were about status and class, as handloom weavers saw their social position, their security, their independence and their pride destroyed in half a generation, and a middle-class dominated society being created from which they felt increasingly alienated. Igniting this highly combustible mix was thirty years of radical political agitation against a deeply conservative political structure. There is no doubt about the seriousness of the situation in 1820 in the West of Scotland and of the sense that only a new political system would bring change. It came at the end of a period of fluctuating radical unrest in England, and to a large extent many of the ideas and language came from south of the border. Yet the events in Scotland were more extensive and more serious than anything in England, not excluding Peterloo. The occasional references to an alternative of Scottish separation from England gave them a distinct dimension. Certainly, Lord Sidmouth believed that the Scottish authorities were not to be relied upon to deal vigorously enough with the rebels and set up a special commission to handle the cases, with an English prosecutor and adviser.[21]

The treason trials, the hangings and banishments in the aftermath of the Strathaven and Bonnymuir episodes ended hopes of political redress. It was a decade before the issue of political reform revived among the working class in Scotland.

## The 1820s

At any time, it was only a tiny minority of workers who were involved in overt, potentially insurrectionary protests. For most skilled craftsmen the central and continuing struggle lay in the work-place, where division of labour was bringing the use of cheap, unskilled labour to perform work formerly done by craftsmen. The proletarianisation of the artisan was speeding up and the experience of the handloom weavers, overwhelmed by numbers, was only the most extreme example of a widespread process. That and the economic boom of the early 1820s had the effect of bringing industrial issues once again to the forefront. The sharp rise in the demand for labour speeded up the processes of change. While many made substantial gains in earnings, the erosion of restrictions on who could work at certain crafts intensified. Employers keen to expand output and to reduce costs were devising new management methods and forms of organisation. As Maxine Berg has argued, 'workers adapted their own culture and rhythms of work to new contexts so that the factory never became the capitalist controlled and utterly rational form of work organisation' that employers wanted.[22] In the 1820s many employers were trying to make it just that. Almost all the major disputes of the 1820s were about control of the processes of production in the workplace and about who should decide who should employed. A whole series of disputes in the Glasgow cotton mills, culminating in a strike and general lock-out 1823, were about control in the workplace: about changes in work methods, about employers' rights in fining, on the role of foremen, about who should be employed. It was about how far cotton spinners should have autonomy to develop their own pattern of work and how far these could be imposed by the employers without consultation. It was a battle that was to continue for another fifteen years. Coal miners, less successfully, were trying to do the same in 1824 and 1825.[23] A sense of frustration at what was happening and at their inability to prevent it led them to turn to the use of violence against new workers.

Deprived of the ability to protect themselves through the law or to look to Parliament, and deprived of the hope of achieving redress for their grievances through symbolic gestures, industrial workers diverted their energies into strengthening their own organisations. They also turned their anger against those who most clearly threatened both the present and the future of their trade, the strikebreaker, the half-skilled, the underpaid. Most of the street protest in industrial disputes in the 1820s was against blacklegs. There was still that sense of injustice that stemmed from an awareness that traditional patterns and customs were being overthrown, and there was very little moral disapproval within workers' communities at the often violent attacks on strikebreakers, who were regarded as morally beyond the pale.

The message coming from press, pamphlet, pulpit and school was that the erosion of traditional work patterns was the inevitable and, in the long term, healthy accompaniment of economic growth. To resist it was to take a futile stance against the fundamental laws of political economy. In spite of this increasingly raucous propaganda, there were those who tried to offer alternative interpretations.

The focus of protest changed from the politics of old corruption to the new economic system. Increasingly, craftsmen saw their security, their status, their earnings as having been eroded by the competitive system. A few, encouraged by the ideas floated by Robert Owen and those associated with him, sought refuge in the short-lived co-operative community established at Orbiston near Motherwell in 1825, and that co-operative tradition was to stay alive when the opportunities for industrial action reappeared in the 1830s.[24] Most continued to struggle to retain some control over their working lives by means of trade-union and work-place action.

# ADDRESS
TO THE
## *Inhabitants of Great Britain & Ireland;*
FRIENDS AND COUNTRYMEN,

ROUSED from that torpid state in which WE have been sunk for so many years, We are at length compelled, from the extremity of our sufferings, and the contempt heaped upon our Petitions for redress, to assert our RIGHTS, at the hazard of our lives; and proclaim to the world the real motives, which (if not misrepresented by designing men, would have United all ranks), have reduced us to take up ARMS for the redress of our *Common Grievances.*

The numerous Public Meetings held throughout the Country has demonstrated to you, that the interests of all Classes are the same. That the protection of the Life and Property of the *Rich Man*, is the interest of the *Poor Man*, and in return, it is the interest of the Rich, to protect the poor from the iron grasp of DESPOTISM; for, when its victims are exhausted in the lower circles, there is no assurance but that its ravages will be continued in the upper: For once set in motion, it will continue to move till a succession of Victims fall.

Our principles are few, and founded on the basis of our CONSTITUTION, which were purchased with the DEAREST BLOOD of our ANCESTORS, and which we swear to transmit to posterity unsullied, or PERISH in the Attempt.—Equality of Rights (not of Property,) is the object for which we contend; and which we consider as the only security for our LIBERTIES and LIVES.

Let us show to the world that We are not that Lawless, Sanguinary Rabble, which our Oppressors would persuade the higher circles we are—but a BRAVE and GENEROUS PEOPLE, determined to be FREE, LIBERTY or DEATH is our *Motto*, and We have sworn to return home in *triumph*—or return *no more !*
SOLDIERS,

Shall YOU, Countrymen, bound by the sacred obligation of an Oath, to defend your Country and your King from enemies, whether foreign or domestic, plunge your BAYONETS into the bosoms of Fathers and Brothers, and at once sacrifice at the *Shrine of Military Despotism*, to the unrelenting Orders of a Cruel Faction, those feelings which you hold in common with the rest of mankind ? SOLDIERS, Turn your eyes toward SPAIN, and there behold the happy effects resulting from the UNION of Soldiers and Citizens. Look to that quarter, and there behold the yoke of hated Despotism, broke by the Unanimous wish of the People and the Soldiery, happily accomplished without Bloodshed. And, shall You, who taught those Soldiers to fight the battles of LIBERTY, refuse to fight those of your own Country ? Forbid it Heaven ! Come, forward then at once, and Free your Country and your King, from the power of those that have held them *too, too* long in thraldom.
FRIENDS and COUNTRYMEN, The eventful period has now arrived, where the Services of all will be required, for the forwarding of an object so universally wished, and so absolutely necessary. Come forward then, and assist those who have begun in the completion of so arduous a task, and support the laudable efforts, which we are about to make, to replace to BRITONS, those rights consecrated to them, by MAGNA CHARTA, and the BILL of RIGHTS, and Sweep from our Shores, that Corruption which has degraded us below the dignity of Man.

Owing to the misrepresentations which have gone abroad with regard to our intentions, we think it indispensably necessary to DECLARE inviolable, all Public and Private Property. And, We hereby call upon all JUSTICES of the PEACE, and all others to suppress PILLAGE and PLUNDER, of every description; and to endeavour to secure those Guilty of such offences, that they may receive that Punishment, which such violation of Justice demand.

In the present state of affairs, and during the continuation of so momentous a struggle, we earnestly request of all to desist from their Labour, from and after this day, the FIRST of APRIL; and attend wholly to the recovery of their Rights, and consider it as the duty of every man not to recommence until he is in possession of of those Rights which distinguishes the FREEMAN from the SLAVE; viz: That of giving consent to the laws by which he is to be governed. We, therefore, recommend to the Proprietors of Public Works, and all others, to Stop the one, and Shut up the other, until order is restored, or we will be accountable for no damages which may be sustained; and which after this Public Intimation, they can have no claim to.

AND We hereby give notice to all those who shall be found carrying arms against those who intend to regenerate their Country, and restore its INHABITANTS to their NATIVE DIGNITY; We shall consider them as TRAITORS to their Country, and ENEMIES to their King, and treat them as such.
By order of the Committee of Organization,
for forming a PROVISIONAL GOVERNMENT.
GLASGOW, 1st April, 1820.
Britons.—God.—Justice.—The wishes of all good Men are with us.—Join together and make it one CAUSE, and the Nations of the EARTH shall hail the day, when the Standard of LIBERTY shall be raised on its *Native Soil.*

41. Placards like these appeared all over Glasgow and the West of Scotland on the night of 1-2 April 1820 and triggered a radical uprising.

In less than a century, patterns of protest had changed dramatically. By the 1820s, it was industrial workers who were most identified with popular and working-class protest. Apart from sporadic episodes in the Highlands there were hardly any rural incidents. Food riots were largely a thing of the past. There was no Edinburgh mob of apprentices and craftsmen, and street riots were largely confined to Glasgow and to the other industrial towns of the

West. It reflected the patterns of development in industry and commerce. Workers had had to learn to respond to changed circumstances and to changed attitudes on the part of the authorities, who themselves had adapted as economic circumstances altered. A community-orientated paternalism gave way to the bracing winds of *laissez-faire*.

Clearly, there is much in the Scottish experience that parallels developments elsewhere, though the changes were perhaps sharper in Scotland and taking place over a shorter period. If anything, the extent and levels of popular protest in the eighteenth century are less than one finds in England. There are many fewer meal riots, there is limited political protest and fewer industrial disputes. The mechanisms for preventing protest remained more vigorous in Scotland. Some of these were the intimidation by Lord Braxfield and his ilk of those who questioned the system, but others were the continuing operation of an interventionist local state, in areas of food supply, poor relief and industrial relations. When that was swept away within a relatively short time by governments that were increasingly attentive to the demands of the rising industrial middle class, the result was an explosion of political and industrial violence borne of frustration and a sense of injustice. That way forward ended at Bonnymuir and in the hanging of Baird, Hardie and Wilson in its aftermath. Whig politicians managed to hold out the prospect of political change through constitutional means and to satisfy the aspirations of many of the politically aware. For others there was a swing away from a belief that political reform was a solution to what were essentially the products of an economic system. Rather there was a continuing search for some alternative to the mindless operation of the market, by the building up of effective trade-union organisation and experiments in co-operation. It was a search that was to continue over the succeeding decades.

## NOTES

1. Among the most important studies of popular protests are George Rudé's works, especially *The Crowd in History, 1730-1848* (London, 1964) and *Ideology and Popular Protest* (London, 1980); E.P. Thompson, 'The Moral Economy of the English Crown in the Eighteenth Century', *Past and Present*, 50 (Feb, 1971), pp. 76-136; Louise A. Tilly and Charles Tilly (eds.), *Class Conflict and Collective Action* (London, 1981); J. Stevenson and R. Quinault (eds.), *Popular Protest and Public Order* (London, 1974); Barrington Moore, Jr., *Injustice: The Social Basis of Obedience and Revolt* (London, 1978); A. Charlesworth, *An Atlas of Rural Protest in Britain, 1548-1900* (London, 1983).

2. T.M. Devine, 'Social Stability and Agrarian Change in the Eastern Lowlands of

Scotland 1810-40', *Social History III* (3), (October, 1978), pp. 331-46 and 'Social Stability in the Eastern Lowlands of Scotland during the Agricultural Revolution, 1780-1840' in T.M. Devine (ed.), *Lairds and Improvement in the Scotland of the Enlightenment* (Dundee, 1979), pp. 59-70. For the Levellers see J. Leopold, 'The Levellers' Revolt in Galloway in 1724', *Scottish Labour History Society Journal*, 14 (1980), pp. 4-29.

3. For the fullest discussion of all these issues, see Eric Richards, *A History of the Highland Clearances, Vol.2 Emigration, Protest, Reasons* (London 1985).

4. James Hunter, 'The Emergence of the Crofting Community: The Religious Contribution, 1798-1843', *Scottish Studies*, 18 (1974); T.C. Smout, *A History of the Scottish People, 1560-1830* (London, 1969), p. 330; T.M. Devine, *The Great Highland Famine: Hunger, Emigration and the Scottish Highlands in the Nineteenth Century* (Edinburgh, 1988).

5. John Bohstedt, *Riots and Community Politics in England and Wales, 1790-1810* (Cambridge, Mass., 1983), p. 23

6. For Scottish meal riots see S.G.E. Lythe, 'The Tayside Meal Mobs, 1772-1773', *Scottish Historical Review*, XLVI (1967), pp. 26-36; K.J. Logue, *Popular Disturbances in Scotland, 1780-1815* (Edinburgh, 1979), Ch. 1.

7. Logue, *Popular Disturbances*, pp. 44-5.

8. The English figures are from Bohstedt, *Riots* and from Alan Booth, 'Food Riots in the North-West of England, 1790-1801', *Past and Present*, 77, (Nov., 1977), p. 90.

9. Bohstedt, *Riots, passim.*

10. For a fuller discussion of the emergence of journeymen's organisation, see W. Hamish Fraser, *Conflict and Class: Scottish Workers, 1700-1838* (Edinburgh, 1988).

11. Elspeth King, *The Strike of the Glasgow Weavers, 1787* (Glasgow Museum and Art Galleries, 1987).

12. *Glasgow Mercury*, 19 September, 1787; R. Renwick (ed.), *Extracts from the Records of the Burgh of Glasgow* (Glasgow, 1912), VIII, 10 December 1788; Vol. VIII, 13 November 1794.

13. For a good study of the campaign for a police force in Glasgow see Geraldine Gallacher, 'The First Glasgow Police', unpublished BA dissertation, Department of History, University of Strathclyde, 1987.

14. Andrew G. Ralston, 'The Tron Riot of 1812', *History Today*, 30 (May 1980), pp. 41-5.

15. Fraser, *Conflict and Class*, Ch. 5.

16. N. Murray, *The Scottish Handloom Weaver* (Edinburgh, 1978), pp. 185-9; W. Hamish Fraser, 'A Note on the Scottish Handloom Weavers' Association, 1808-13', *Journal of the Scottish Labour History Society*, 20 (1985), pp. 39-40.

17. For a discussion of this case and others see W.W. Straka, 'The Law of Combination in Scotland Reconsidered', *Scottish Historical Review*, LXIV (2) (1985), pp. 128-42; J.L. Gray, 'The Law of Combination in Scotland', *Economica*, VIII (1928), pp. 332-50; Fraser, *Conflict and Class*, pp. 81-96.

18. Logue, *Popular Disturbances*, pp. 133-146.

19. The political movements of the 1790s can best be followed in C.M. Burns 'Industrial Labour and Radical Movements in Scotland in the 1790s', unpublished

MSc thesis, University of Strathclyde, 1971 and J. Brims, 'The Scottish Democratic Movement in the Age of the French Revolution', unpublished PhD thesis, University of Edinburgh, 1983.

20. W.M. Roach, 'Radical Reform Movements in Scotland from 1815 to 1822', unpublished PhD thesis, University of Glasgow, 1970, p. 54.

21. The careful account of W.M. Roach should be used alongside the more flamboyant one of B. Ellis and S. Mac A 'Ghobbainn, *The Scottish Insurrection of 1820* (London, 1970) for the events of 1820.

22. M. Berg, *The Age of Manufacturers, 1700-1820* (London, 1985), p. 235; R. Price, 'Structures of subordination in nineteenth century British industry', in P. Thane, G. Crossick, R. Floud (eds.), *The Power of the Past: Essays for Eric Hobsbawm* (Cambridge, 1984).

23. For the cotton spinners, see Z.G. Brassay, 'The Cotton Spinners in Glasgow and the West of Scotland, c. 1790-1840: A Study in Early Industrial Relations', unpublished MLitt. thesis, University of Strathclyde, 1974; for the colliers, see A.B. Campbell, *The Lanarkshire Miners: A Social History of Their Trade Unions, 1775-1874* (Edinburgh 1979) and above, Ch. 10.

24. J. Butt (ed.), *Robert Owen, Prince of Cotton Spinners* (Newton Abbot, 1971), Chs. 4 and 6

CHAPTER 14

# The Birth of Class ?

*Tony Clarke and Tony Dickson*

## A Review of the Debate

In the social history of Britain, the period covered by this volume has been presented as having seen the 'birth of class' or the making of a 'class society'. This fundamental change is associated with the industrial revolution and the emergence of industrial capitalism, and has been seen by Harold Perkin as more or less rapidly replacing an eighteenth-century social order in which vertical divisions by trade predominate over 'horizontal' antagonisms between classes. In justly famous articles on eighteenth-century England, E.P. Thompson has acknowledged that the consciousness of trade rather than class may have characterised the urban artisan, whilst denying the existence of consensus or harmony in relations between gentry and plebeians. Rather he employs the terminology of class conflict, whilst acknowledging that popular resistance and riot did not signify a populace which identified itself through the 'modern' language of class. For Thompson, the ruling classes alone showed a perception of their identity of interests.[1] In his view, the 'making of the English working class' occupied the later period from the Paineite and Jacobin societies of the 1790s to the eve of the Reform Bill agitations of 1831-2. Over this period, this class came to feel and articulate an identity of interests across barriers of locality, trade and occupation, to develop class consciousness from the Radical traditions of the eighteenth century, and to express this consciousness in and through working-class organisations — friendly societies, trade unionism and political organisation, culminating in the Chartist agitations of the late 1830s and 1840s. This class consciousness represented for Thompson a recognition of common interests *in opposition to* those of employers and rulers. The effects of the growth of industrial capitalism and the rising tide of political repression during the Napoleonic Wars are credited by Thompson with having driven the working class into a 'state of apartheid', preventing any alliance with radical elements in the industrial bourgeoisie.[2]

Thompson's argument does not command anything approaching universal agreement. There are those who locate the formation of a 'mature' English working class at different times to Thompson. Perkin emphasises the comparatively short period of Reform agitation from the close of the Napoleonic Wars to 1820 as formative for this class. Foster presents the 1830s and early 1840s as marking a qualitative advance in working-class consciousness, at least in Oldham's cotton textile community, and sees the period before 1830 as lacking a crucial component of such a consciousness — mass intellectual conviction of the need to struggle for an alternative social order. For Foster the 1842 'strike for the Charter' in particular reflected such a conviction.[3]

Other critics of Thompson confine themselves rather more to a denial that working-class action and organisation before 1830 showed the unity or continuity implied by his thesis.[4] For example, Glen concludes his study of Stockport by arguing that the 'fragmentation of workers' movements' was becoming the norm by the 1820s. This claim embraces a number of arguments. Support for Radicalism was confined to a minority of workers, even among the handloom weavers, and was declining in the 1820s. Occupational divisions and ethnic antagonisms towards the Irish ensured that where trade unionism made headway it '...in no sense produced a united, militant proletariat of the kind Marx and Engels predicted would emerge'.[5] Industrial struggles are portrayed as deeply sectional and as largely isolated from political radicalism. In this connection, Glen's work exemplifies a much broader debate between supporters of 'holistic' and 'compartmentalist' approaches to labour history.[6] The former type of perspective sees the emergence of class as a historical process to which apparently discrete traditions, movements and organisations may contribute. Thompson's 'holistic' approach seeks to present evidence of an emerging working-class movement in which illegal trade-union activity, including Luddism in the 1810s, overlapped with political agitation. The existence of such a movement is further held to be demonstrated by tracing the role of correspondence, the radical press and travelling delegates and speakers in linking the various regions, and by examining the continuities in personnel and ideas within Radicalism from the 1790s onwards. By contrast, 'compartmentalist' accounts are, according to Donnelly, marked by the claim that there is insufficient evidence to support the argument that industrial and political movements overlapped, or established a significant degree of unity between trades. In this respect, it is important to note that Thompson's argument looks forward to the working-class agitations of the Reform Bill crisis and attempts at General Unionism between 1829- 34, and to the Chartist years, as retrospectively confirming his notion of an emergent working-class consciousness. Glen, in particular, does not address himself to those years, and perhaps in consequence adds to his own presumption of an increasingly weak and fragmented working class.[7]

The debate over class formation and especially the development of the working class in England has been reflected in the literature on Scotland. This is not surprising, since Scotland's economic and social development after 1760 was strongly influenced by the Union with England. The development of trade and industry was tied in many ways to the British state and its colonial empire, notably for example through the role of Glasgow merchants in the tobacco trade. Capital accumulated through such connections helped to fuel industrial development, partly because of the need for manufactured goods to feed the 'store' system, in which such goods were exchanged by merchants for products from the Americas. However, this activity and merchant wealth cannot be held directly responsible for the industrial development after 1780.[8] English technology and, to a lesser extent, capital played a prominent, though not dominant, role in the expansion of cotton spinning by means of water-power in the 1780s and 1790s. In all, Scottish and English industrialisation were part of one common process.[9] How far, then, have historians of Scotland seen the development of a Scottish working class in tandem with the process hypothesised for England by Thompson and his followers?

One school of thought argues that Radicalism in Scotland failed to embody a sense of working-class unity and identity. Smout denies the emergence of working-class consciousness by 1830, arguing for the 'uninflammable character of the Scottish populace as a whole' during the Napoleonic Wars, a character evidenced by the apparent absence of any echo of Luddism in Scotland. Although Smout acknowledges the presence of substantial working-class radicalism in peak years, especially 1792-4 and 1797-1802, when the United Scotsmen formed the focus of such activity, and in the lead-up to the Radical War of 1820, his general conclusions embody a conviction that Radicalism did not transcend the narrow sectionalism to be found in early trade unionism, which was largely aimed at the restriction of entry to particular occupations.[10] Smout's account is thus a compartmentalist one.[11] For example, his argument that 'a decade and a half of silence' followed the repression of the United Scotsmen rests on the assumption that '...Jacobin political activity was sealed off from trade union agitation, and that the different sections of the working-classes were not aware of any common identity of interests'.[12]

Young's writings represent the clearest attempt to apply a Thompsonian 'holistic' analysis to the development of the Scottish working class. By contrast to those who portray this class as less conscious and more passive than its English counterpart, Young argues that there was 'a much bigger and more determined radical working-class movement than Scottish historians have realised'. In portraying this movement, Young argues for the continuity of a Jacobin revolutionary leadership from the United Scotsmen to the Radical War, with substantial working-class support. In 1820, 'a major revolutionary

movement was planning to set up a Scottish republic'.[13] Young shares
Thompson's argument that an 'illegal tradition' of underground trade union
*and* political organisation developed during the Napoleonic Wars, document-
ing some 'Luddite' outbursts of machine-breaking as one indicator to counter
Smout's presumption of a 'decade and a half of silence'. For Young, this
tradition was in Scotland both nationalist and republican, under the joint
influence of Jacobite sentiments and French Jacobinism.[14] It was also class-
conscious to the extent that it opposed private property as such. Here Young's
argument has to contend with frequent disavowals from Radicals themselves,
as in the Address from the 'Committee for forming a Provisional Government'
in April 1820, which called for 'equality of rights (not of property)'. Nevertheless, the writings of the current authors stand a little closer to Young than
to Smout in arguing for 'the making of a class society' in Scotland to 1830, and
for a growing working-class political presence after 1780 exemplified by
considerable support for political change.[15]

## Defining the Issues

To begin to assess the above perspectives in relation to the evidence regarding
class formation and action in Scotland, it is firstly necessary to resolve, at least
tentatively, some of the problems of definition which bedevil the debates.
What is meant by the 'making of a class society' or of a 'modern working
class'? How are such statements to be tested?

A considerable literature has developed around Thompson's conception of
class, which has strongly influenced the terms of debate on this period in
British history:

Classes arise because men and women, in determinative productive relations,
identify their antagonistic interests, and come to struggle, to think and to value in class
ways: thus the process of class formation is a process of self-making, although under
conditions which are 'given'.[16]

This conception is founded in key respects on Marx's notion of class in that,
for Thompson, a consciousness of class rests on the common experiences
shared by a group occupying a common relationship to the means of production. For Marx, the 'common relationship' which defined the working class in
a capitalist society was that of being 'free wage labour' stripped of access to
the means of production (land, machinery or the financial resources to
purchase these) and 'free' to sell their capacity to work to an employer. He
attributed the formation of such a working class in England chiefly to the
enclosure of common lands and the dispossession of the peasantry, beginning
in the late fifteenth century and largely completed before the Industrial

Revolution.[17] It was, however, to large-scale industry that Marx looked for the common conditions which would generate collective organisations and consciousness on a wide scale in this class. Marx was prepared to acknowledge at times that insofar as such organisation and consciousness are not found, then the group concerned do not constitute a class.[18] It is this qualification that Thompson has seized upon. For him, to speak of a class is legitimate only insofar as class consciousness and organisation are present. Thus his critics have accused him of conflating class with class consciousness, and hence of absurdity when he writes of 'class struggle without class' in the eighteenth century.[19]

However, in general Thompson does not deny the influence of objective conditions on class experience and hence on class consciousness and conflict, as some of his critics would argue.[20] It is now generally acknowledged that the force of such objective conditions is heavily present in his writings, as in his discussion of the growing insecurity of artisans and outworkers in the section of *The Making of The English Working Class* devoted to 'Exploitation'. However, such objective conditions are studied through the way they are experienced by working people themselves, rather than examined in their own rights. 'The advent of industrial capitalism in England is a dreadful backcloth to the book rather than a direct object of analysis in its own right.'[21]

To avoid the problem of terminology in Thompson's work we shall refer to class as an objective phenomenon implying a group with a common relationship to the means of production, irrespective of whether class consciousness is present. The question as to whether the period 1760-1830 saw the 'birth of class' in Scotland now needs to be reformulated. It is really two related questions, neither of which implies that classes as objective groupings were absent prior to 1760. Firstly, how far did the processes of economic change produce a class structure increasingly divided between wage labour and industrial capital? This question draws attention to changes within the propertied classes themselves, since this period has typically been portrayed as one in which the economic and political dominance of the landed aristocracy and gentry was challenged by industrialists and an urban middle class. But it also refers to changes which may have been influencing the working class, as in the claim that '...the experience of Scottish labour after 1780 was of proletarianisation, the strengthening of objective boundaries between the classes, intensifying exploitation and heightening economic insecurity.'[22] The second question regarding the 'birth of class' concerns the dimension of class organisation and consciousness. Did the Scottish working class identify itself as having interests antagonistic to those of employers and rulers by 1830? This question raises further ones regarding what criteria for the existence of class consciousness are appropriate at this stage in Scotland's history.

The main emphasis below will be on the issue of class consciousness, but this also entails more limited reference to the objective circumstances to which various classes in Scottish society were responding. We shall begin by examining working-class Radicalism and trade unionism. In particular, how far did Radical politics win mass working-class support and transcend sectional divisions by trade? If Radicalism represented a form of class consciousness, what sort of consciousness was this?

## Radicalism and Working Class Consciousness in Scotland, 1790-1830

There is considerable disagreement over the extent of working-class support for Radicalism in the 1790s and between 1815 and 1820, when Parliamentary reform agitations revived at the close of the French Wars. Whilst Meikle puts the active membership of the United Scotsmen at only a few hundred in the late 1790s, it is difficult, if not impossible, to gauge accurately the degree of wider support for such secret organisations in an era of repression. The Radical activity of the 1790s was geographically dispersed across much of Lowland Scotland, to judge from reported disturbances, and established branches of the Friends of the People (1792-4) and United Scotsmen.[23] Such activity was not the exclusive province of working people, however, and the Friends of the People, in particular, were substantially middle class in leadership and, to a lesser extent, membership. The underground and insurrectionary United Scotsmen on the other hand were more exclusively proletarian.[24] The demands of the more plebeian Radicals for adult male suffrage, vote by secret ballot and annual parliaments struck a chord particularly with artisans and outworkers, notably the handloom weavers. In weaving settlements such as those in Paisley, Radicalism could draw upon literate, close-knit communities which could and did sustain a high level of political culture.[25] In the period 1815-20, however, it is much easier to establish extensive working-class commitment to Radicalism. This commitment does not seem to have been confined solely to the weavers, nor to a limited range of artisanal trades. In the Radical War of 1820, it is generally agreed that the call to strike work was obeyed by 60,000 in the West of Scotland. In addition, Donnelly has argued that the participation of relatively small groups in open insurrectionary activity should not be taken to imply limited support for a Rising. The latter was called off in the belief that the awaited insurrection in England had not occurred.[26] In any case, there is ample evidence of mass participation in Radical demonstrations in both 1816-7 and 1819-20. 40,000 people, mainly operatives, attended a Glasgow Reform meeting in 1816, and an estimated 30,000 met outside Paisley in July 1819 to petition the Prince Regent for

Reform. Much of the town's working population was mobilised in 1819 when crowds controlled the streets in five days of rioting in the wake of a protest meeting over the Peterloo massacre. Even greater numbers, of up to 50,000 in Renfrewshire for example, were achieved in the Reform Bill crisis years of 1831-2, when some Parliamentary Reform was a tangible prospect.[27] Participation in such demonstrations indicates the scale of working-class Radical commitment to reform to have been substantial, although it provides no clear guide to the numbers involved in arming and drilling in insurrectionary preparations in 1819-20.

The evidence from Paisley bears out other indications that weavers dominated numerically in the leadership of Radical organisations, although in Paisley this in large part reflects the preponderance of weavers over other trades, given the role of fancy weaving in the economy.[28] However, the sources suggest a wide appeal for Radicalism across a number of key trades besides the weavers and shoemakers who formed the core of Radical activists in many towns and villages. Of thirty-seven men arrested in Glasgow in 1817 for oath-taking or other treasonable practices, twenty-one were weavers, but there were also four cotton spinners, as well as some from other trades and the middle classes.[29] Donnelly also provides evidence of the involvement of cotton spinners, with many other trades, in the 1820 Rising, as judged by the occupations of those arrested or sought by the authorities. In the strike itself, weavers, cotton spinners, masons, wrights and other trades participated in Paisley, and a similar spread of trades were involved in Glasgow. Thus, 'it would be a mistake to argue, as William Roach does, that the failure of the rising can be largely attributed to the fact that it really only had the full support of one group'.[30] Nevertheless, not all trades were well represented. Agricultural labourers stood aside from the Rising. Colliers' involvement in Radicalism up to 1820 also appears to have been minimal, although Campbell notes that the *Scotsman* reported their participation in the 1820 strike and Young cites an attempt to seize arms from a Volunteer force by 800 colliers in Airdrie on 12 April 1820. Colliers were involved in the Reform demonstrations of 1831-2, which were heavily reliant on the trades unions to provide a mass turnout.[31]

This discussion of the occupational base of Radicalism after 1790 brings us closer to a treatment of the content of Radical ideology and of whether it can be portrayed as a form of class consciousness capable of transcending sectional divisions in the labour force. Calhoun has recently produced a variant of a much older line of argument, that Radicalism appealed to a group of artisans and outworkers influenced by, but not part of, industrial capitalist development, and quite separate from the factory proletariat of the new industrial cities.[32] This account seriously understates the broad base of the

Radical appeal, to include factory trades such as the cotton spinners of Glasgow and Renfrewshire. It also neglects the manner in which handloom weaving was an expanding branch of production precisely because of the impact of industrial capitalism, which dramatically increased the output of yarn prior to a thorough mechanisation of weaving. Thus the number of handloom weavers in Scotland is estimated to have risen from 25,000 in 1780 to 78,000 in 1830 and 84,560 by 1840.[33] Handloom weavers certainly outnumbered the predominantly male elite of cotton spinners who were themselves a minority of the labour force in the cotton mills. One estimate suggests that by the 1830s there were 98 mills in the Glasgow area employing 10,000 people, of whom 1000 were spinners.[34]

In some respects. however, Radicalism and its appeal to working people did rest on cultural traditions carried out by artisans and outworkers. In particular such groups sought to defend a real or imagined 'independence' which had a number of strands. One of these was a belief in the right to control the manner and pace of work, which led many to refuse, for example, the newer forms of work discipline to be found in the factories.[35] A second strain in this culture was an aspiration to control the state of trade to ensure the maintenance of customary levels of remuneration. This strand has been widely acknowledged as an aspect of popular culture from the eighteenth century, implying a belief in the 'moral economy, of just prices and wages which oriented popular protest, notably in the form of 'meal mobs'.[36] More importantly, such a 'moral economy' can also be seen to underpin the weaver's attempts to gain legal and legislative redress for grievances produced from the 1790s by the well-documented decline in their living and working conditions. The 1812 weavers' strike arose when weaver's combinations in the West of Scotland sought to establish minimum prices for their work, first by Parliamentary petition and secondly by appeal to the courts to use their legislative powers to fix a table of prices. Although the courts obliged, the manufactures refused to implement the prices and the courts refrained from enforcing them. The strike was met with repression, and the legislation of 1661 to which the weavers had appealed was repealed.[37]

Radicalism must be seen in the context of such failures to achieve redress from the authorities, together with the suppression of combinations and political repression symbolised by the sedition trials after each wave of Radical activity. Adult male suffrage was a demand for a legislative response to the protection of labour called for, amongst other considerations, by the values of the 'moral economy'. As Stedman Jones has recently argued, the language of Radicalism was a vocabulary of political exclusion, whose success depended on the ability to attribute the economic ills of various groups to a political source. Unless this is borne in mind, it is not possible to understand why real or threatened economic distress should find expression in a movement for universal suffrage.[38] The 'compartmentalist' tradition, represented by Smout for Scotland, is weakened not just by its failure to acknowledge the continuities in the groups and personnel involved in trade unionism and Radicalism respectively, but also in a further respect. The weaver' resort to a variety of attempted remedies, including trade-union pressure and Reform agitations, reflects no sharp division between these remedies, but a learning process reinforcing the perception that failure resulted from the unresponsiveness of the legislature towards the people.

Despite the cultural and sectional divisions within the working class, the evidence regarding the base of support for Radicalism across a number of trades suggests that the Radical movement was capable of generating a degree of working-class identity. Whilst Smout and others stress the sectional exclusivity of the early trade unions or combinations, it is also necessary to emphasise that different trades faced similar problems. For many of the artisanal trades, and especially in the conditions of labour surplus after 1815, their major problem was the difficulty of enforcing apprenticeship regulations and controlling entry to the trade. Demobilisation after the war, Irish immigration and rural-urban migration within Scotland added to this problem. In handloom weaving, even a centre of skilled harness loom work like Paisley saw the virtual ending of formal apprenticeship by 1830.[39] By the 1820s in Glasgow, most master masons were substantial employers, with between 70 and 170 journeymen each. It is argued here, then, that since different trades faced similar problems and shared a common heritage from artisanal culture, this provided a focus for the emergence of collective responses that could transcend 'sectionalism'. Radicalism was probably the most significant of such responses.

It is also clear that those in more industrial occupations, such as cotton spinners and colliers, shared or came to share similar problems to those of the artisans, and responded to some degree in similar terms. Glasgow's Association of Operative Cotton Spinners in 1816 was primarily concerned to restrict the numbers trained for the spinners' role and to limit recruitment to the 'big piecer' position to spinners' male relatives.[40] Culturally, the spinners had a deserved reputation for industrial violence and drunkenness which, we have argued elsewhere, distanced many of them from artisanal culture.[41] But Fraser shows that the spinners' leadership contained elements of church and Mechanics' Institute membership,[42] and we have already seen the involvement of the spinners in radical politics from an early stage. The adult male spinner occupied a well-paid and elite position in the hierarchy of cotton operatives, and exercised authority over the workers, notably piecers and scavengers. Much the same has been established for the collier. Although his position stood somewhat uneasily between artisan and labourer, A.B. Campbell argues that colliers generated a culture analogous to that of the artisan: 'The nature of colliery work during the first half of the nineteenth century — the system of piecework contracts, the freedom from managerial control, and the complex nature of the hewer's tasks — gave rise to a spectrum of values which can be characterised as "independence" '.[43] These values included an emphasis on the hewer's right to control the work process but also to control the market for coal through the collective regulation for output. This operated through the 'darg' or quota which no miner was to exceed in a day's output. This policy of output restriction, together with controls of entry to the trade, formed the basis of the colliers' trade unionism which was most active in Lanarkshire from 1817 to 1818 and from 1824 to 1826. For Campbell, however, it was not until the 1830s that the colliers' strategy met its main threat, from the influx of Irish labour used particularly as 'nob' or 'blackleg' labour during strikes and from the more aggressive strategy of a section of the owners, particularly those linked with the iron masters, seeking greater efficiency and work discipline. The timing of this threat may explain the later conversion of the colliers to mass Radical politics, which was a significant factor in the Chartist era, but not in 1820.[44] The colliers were already present in 1831-2, but for Campbell such participation in Radical politics was exceptional prior to the 1840s.

Thus far, we have argued that Radicalism was capable of forging a degree of working-class identity and consciousness by 1830, in which the vote came to be seen, by many but not all groups, as a key to the redress of the problems of the various trades. Nevertheless the degree of unity was limited by divisions within the workforce, although less by divisions between crafts and perhaps more by those between the artisan and the labourer, the organised and the unorganised. The trades themselves united not just behind the Radical platform as in 1831-2, but also through attempts to found a trade union press and committees of trade delegates. In 1824, the Glasgow Committee of Trades Delegates represented over twenty different trades, whilst the *Herald to the Trades' Advocate* contributed to harnessing of the trades to the Reform Bill agitation in 1831-2. But it should also be noted that the Radical demand for manhood suffrage was inherently inclusive, rather than exclusive, if we leave aside the glaring exclusion of women.[45]

## The Nature of Working-Class Consciousness — Some Qualifications

The debate in the literature addressed by this essay contains further crucial points of contention regarding the character of working-class consciousness before 1830. The following section addresses three issues in an attempt to establish this character more precisely. The first regards the extent to which the Scottish working class adopted a nationalist and revolutionary political outlook. Secondly, the literature raises the problem of the relationship between older forms of popular protest prevalent in the eighteenth-century and newer types of class conflict and consciousness. In particular, how sharp was the division between the outlook of the eighteenth-century crowd and that of trade unionists and Radicals in the early nineteenth century? Finally, how far did working people define their interests in *opposition* to those of employers and the middle classes?

It would probably not be correct to share Young's view that the Scottish working class generated a consciousness that was both nationalist and revolutionary. Young's account of the 1820 Rising shares much common ground with the nationalism of Berresford Ellis and MacA'Ghobhainn, which is well discussed by Donnelly. The latter stresses the internationalist and federalist nature of the 1820 Rising, oriented to joint rebellion with England rather than against Anglo-Saxon domination.[46] In any case, to focus on the insurrectionary phases of Radicalism is to neglect the demands and starting point of working-class Radical movements from the 1790s onwards — reform of the British state through constitutional changes linked to manhood suffrage. Young himself acknowledges that working-class nationalism was 'inchoate and subterranean'.[47] Finally, it is essential to note that Radicalism in any case contained divergent strands. At political demonstrations in Renfrewshire in 1819, the symbolism of Wallace and Bruce could mingle with 'Magna Charta' and the 'rights of Britons'.[48] It can be argued that the main emphasis of working-class Radicalism was on the redress of grievances by peaceful reform if possible, but otherwise by force. Hence the theatre of 'peaceably if we may, forcibly if we must' was played out in 1815-20, 1830-2 and again in the Chartist agitations.

A second set of qualifications as to the character of working-class consciousness in this period needs to be entered. One emphasis in the literature is on the development from 'pre-industrial' forms of popular consciousness and unrest to 'industrial' ones, marked in particular by a transition from crowd actions, as in the meal mob, based on a 'moral economy' of just prices and of obligations of employers and rulers to the people which should override the dictates of the market economy, to the industrial strike as a modern expression of class conflict. Young sees the early 1770s as transitional in this respect, with the wage struggles of Paisley and Glasgow weavers in 1773 as an example of 'more open forms of social struggle'.[49] But it seems more accurate to see the opposition of 'moral economy' to market economy as a *continuing* aspect of popular consciousness which helped to legitimise worker's economic and political struggles, even where these took place in new ways. Thus, notions of traditional and just price are still in evidence in weavers' submissions to Parliamentary enquiries in the 1830s. Real or imagined traditions, like the weavers' Golden Age, continued to play a major part in working-class culture in the early nineteenth century, as focal points for opposition to the effects of industrial capitalism. Furthermore, there does not appear to be a sharp break, as Calhoun imagines for England, between an older populist tradition of the artisans and outworkers and a new reformist and trade-unionist proletariat emerging in the 1820s.[50] The trade unionism of colliers and cotton spinners also drew on this older tradition, as we have seen.

A final aspect of the debate over class consciousness concerns the extent of co-operation between classes which continued to be possible in the Parliamentary Reform Movement, for example, up to and beyond 1832.[51] Such co-operation was possible up to 1832 because '...there were many areas of agreement in the objections of both the middle and working classes to the unreformed system' of Parliamentary representation.[52] Middle-class protest and criticism of the political system was heightened in Scotland by the particularly narrow franchise for the county seats, and for the burghs, whose Parliamentary representatives were elected by self-perpetuating town councils. This franchise partly explains the dominance of the landowners in Parliamentary politics until the late 1820s, typified by the 'politics of management' under Henry Dundas, Lord Advocate from 1775 to 1805. Opposition to this dominance came from a number of quarters, notably the Whig circles centred around Jeffrey and Cockburn, and journals such as the *Edinburgh Review* (1802) and *Scotsman* (1817), although middle-class protest was undoubtedly wider than that encapsulated in the Whig interest. Even in the Chartist period, there was a strong middle-class presence in radical politics, which in part reflected 'how slow the extension of the franchise was in Scotland following the 1832 Reform Act, especially in the recently enfranchised burghs'.[53] Middle-class opposition also expressed itself within the Church of Scotland in the growing Evangelical opposition to the Moderate faction which was allied after 1780 with Dundas and the Tory interest. However, Evangelicals did not win a majority in the General Assembly until 1833.[54]

It is probable that over the period 1760-1830 the urban middle classes were becoming increasingly differentiated socially and economically from the operatives. Residential segregation was becoming more marked, at least in the larger towns, as manufacturers, merchants and professionals moved to residential areas in Glasgow's West End and Edinburgh's New Town after 1780. In Paisley, however, this trend was less marked before 1850.[55] But such social and economic differentiation did not preclude co-operation on the part of 'the people' against 'the Aristocracy', to borrow the Radical vocabulary. Even

Jeffrey and other younger Whigs began to advocate Whig/Radical co-operation after the electoral defeat of 1807.[56] Such co-operation bore most fruit in
the Reform Bill agitations of 1830-2.

In Renfrewshire, the trade unions and middle classes, as well as the Whig
gentry, made common cause in the great reform demonstrations. Montgomery
has shown for Glasgow that there was considerable co-operation between the
Whig and middle-class Reform Association, the more popular Political Union
and the operatives represented by the Committee of Trades. But such co-
operation was clearly coupled with a working-class sense of identity as
operatives distinct from the middle class. 'The Glasgow working classes were
conscious of their own needs, aims and worth. They did not however
formulate these against, or in opposition to others' interests.'[57] This interpretation must be contrasted with that of Young, who follows Thompson for
England in arguing that there was at this time a 'great divide between the
radical working classes on the one hand and the possessing classes, whether
Whig or Tory, on the other'.[58] How is this disagreement to be resolved?

The emphasis of Thompson and Young, for England and Scotland respectively, on the 'illegal tradition' of underground trade-union and insurrectionary activity in isolating the working classes from their employers and the
middle class has to be modified. The working class were never driven into a
'state of apartheid' (Thompson) which prevented inter-class co-operation.
Working-class consciousness acknowledged the opposition of interests between workers and employer, especially in the context of industrial disputes,
but did not attack industrial capital itself as a form of property, nor rule out the
possibility of common ground between classes. In particular, distinctions
continued to be made between 'good' and 'bad' employers in terms of a
popular culture still influenced by traditional notions of the obligations of one
class to another.[59] An instance from the 1830s was the co-operation between
some of the larger, established manufacturers and the weavers in Paisley and
Glasgow in support of Fielden's Bill to establish wages regulation by local
Boards of Trade. The failure of the bill to become law led to a voluntary
agreement on a table of prices, albeit a short-lived one. The established houses
and operatives may have shared an economic interest in wage regulation,
although this was not so for the small 'corks', or merchants with little capital,
who were frequently blamed for contributing to unregulated overproduction.[60]

## Conclusion

This chapter has endorsed the view that a substantial measure of working-
class unity and consciousness emerged in the period under discussion, and

more particularly between the 1790s and the Reform Bill crisis. The evidence from trade unionism and political Radicalism suggests a perception of an identity of interests on the part of working people across a number of key trades and occupations, an identity in part based on older cultural traditions — artisanal aspirations and the 'moral economy' — and in part producing new organisational forms. This consciousness was uneven in its appeal and contained a number of conflicting strands — constitutionalism versus insurrectionism, for example — between which action could move quite rapidly. Some groups of workers, like the colliers before the 1830s, were relatively little involved in wider political agitations. Working-class consciousness and action may not have embraced the agricultural labourer. It was nevertheless not confined to outworkers and the traditional trades and did transcend sectional divisions in the labour force to a substantial extent. At the same time this consciousness entailed a notion of the identity of interests of working people without ruling out co-operation across class boundaries. In particular, however, the participation of a range of trades and trade societies in the Radical activities of 1819-20 and 1831-2 refutes the 'compartmentalist' thesis outlined earlier in this chapter.

Equally significant, perhaps, is that a number of developments may have strengthened the *perception* of increasing differences between classes. As was shown earlier in Chapters 5 and 6 of this volume, there were moves by both landowners and the middle classes, in relation to where they lived and in what kind of houses, to create social distance between themselves and other groups. Such moves by the middle classes in urban areas were heightened by their fears of threats to their property and health through a too close contact with the working class. In addition, as Fraser indicates in the previous chapter, these moves were accompanied by increased calls for a more permanent police and military presence in and around the towns. In parallel, the urban working class found their sense of class heightened by the failure of the state, and its legislative apparatus in particular, to respond to what they saw as legitimate appeals for redress of their grievances, for example in the events surrounding the Weavers' Strike of 1812, and in the Sedition trials of the early part of the century. It was clear from the action of the judiciary in these cases that they saw a real threat to social order from working-class unrest, particularly where it had some middle-class support.

Was the Scottish working class, then, 'made by 1830' as Young has put it? Thompson's language of the 'making' of the working class has been criticised for its finality, that is for the implication that the development of the working class was completed by a certain date and cast in a given mould thereafter.[61] In particular, account needs to be taken of the extension of the franchise in 1832 and the growing working-class disillusionment with the middle-class

Whigs in the later 1830s. The disenfranchised radical public became more nearly synonymous with the working class after 1832, and the actions of an unrepresentative state in refusing assistance to the handloom weavers and in the repression of the Glasgow cotton spinners' strike in 1837 may have strengthened working-class consciousness and contributed to the Chartist agitations. Nevertheless, there is much to be said for treating the years to 1832 as having seen the formation of a Scottish working-class movement. The contrast in scale and coherence between the working-class and trade-union presence in Radical activity in the 1790s, as compared to 1819-20 and 1831-2, ultimately justifies this conclusion.

## NOTES

1. E.P. Thompson, 'Eighteenth century English society: class struggle without class?', *Social History,* 4 (1979), pp.133-165; E.P. Thompson. 'Patrician society, plebeian culture', *Journal of Social History,* 7 (1974), pp. 382-405; H.J. Perkin, *The Origins of Modern English Society, 1780-1880* (London,1969). For the wider debate on the 'birth of class' in England, see R.J. Morris, *Class and Class Consciousness in the Industrial Revolution, 1780-1850* (London, 1979).

2. E.P. Thompson, *The Making of the English Working Class* (Harmondsworth, 1968), and specifically p.195.

3. Perkin, *Origins;* J. Foster, *Class Struggle in the Industrial Revolution* (London, 1974).

4. For references to and a review of Thompson's critics, see F.K. Donnelly, 'Ideology and early English working class history: Edward Thompson and his critics', *Social History,*1 (1976), pp. 219-38.

5. R. Glen, *Urban Workers in the Early Industrial Revolution* (London, 1984), p. 76.

6. Donnelly, 'Ideology', p. 223; T. Dickson and T. Clarke, 'The making of a class society', in T. Dickson (ed.), *Scottish Capitalism* (Edinburgh, 1980), p.174.

7. N.Kirk, 'The myth of class? Workers and the industrial revolution in Stockport', *Soc. for Study of Lab. Hist. Bull.,* 51 (1986), p. 41.

8. T.M. Devine, 'Colonial commerce and the Scottish economy, c.1730-1815', in L.M. Cullen and T.C. Smout (eds.), *Comparative Aspects of Scottish and Irish Economic and Social History, 1600-1900,* (Edinburgh, 1977), pp.177-190. Also B. Lenman, *Integration, Enlightenment and Industrialisation* (London, 1981), Ch. 3.

9. T.C. Smout, *A History of the Scottish People 1560-1830* (London,1972 ed.), pp. 224, 236.

10. Smout, *History,* pp. 413, 417.

11. Dickson and Clarke, 'The making', pp.173-4, 180; J.D. Young, 'The making of the Scottish working class', *Soc. for Study of Lab. Hist. Bull.,* 28 (1974), pp. 66-7.

12. Young, 'The making', p.66.

13. J.D. Young, *The Rousing of the Scottish Working Class* (London, 1979), pp. 60-1, 83.

14. Young, *The Rousing,* pp. 57-8.

15. Dickson and Clarke, 'The making'; *idem,* 'Class and class consciousness in early industrial capitalism: Paisley, 1770-1850', in T Dickson (ed.), *Capital and Class in Scotland* (Edinburgh, 1982), pp. 60-5.

16. E.P. Thompson, *The Poverty of Theory and Other Essays* (London, 1978), pp. 297-8.

17. K. Marx, *Capital,* Volume 1 (Harmondsworth, 1976), Ch. 27.

18. Morris, *Class,* p.25.

19. P. Anderson, *Arguments within English Marxism* (London 1980), esp. p.42.

20. R. Johnson, 'Edward Thompson, Eugene Genovese, and socialist-humanist history', *History Workshop,* 6 (1978), pp. 79-100; C. Calhoun, *The Question of Class Struggle* (Oxford, 1982).

21. Anderson, *Arguments,* p.33; K. McClelland, 'Some comments on Richard Johnson...', *History Workshop,* 7 (1979), pp.101-15.

22. Dickson and Clarke, 'The making', p.167.

23. H. Meikle, *Scotland and The French Revolution* (Glasgow,1912), p.192.

24. For middle class Radicalism, see Ch. 6 above.

25. Clarke and Dickson, 'Class and class consciousness', pp.16-18.

26. F.K. Donnelly, 'The Scottish rising of 1820: A reinterpretation', *Scottish Tradition,* 6 (1976), pp. 27-37.

27. Clarke and Dickson, 'Class', pp. 38-40, 42-3; Young, *Rousing,* p.79.

28. Clarke and Dickson, 'Class', pp.14, 42.

29. Young, *Rousing,* p.59.

30. Donnelly, 'Scottish rising', pp. 32-3; I. Hutchison, 'Glasgow working class politics', in R.A. Cage (ed.), *The Working Class in Glasgow, 1750-1914* (London, 1987).

31. A.B. Campbell, *The Lanarkshire Miners* (Edinburgh, 1979), pp. 74-6; Young, *Rousing,* p. 62; A.Wilson, *The Chartist Movement in Scotland* (Manchester 1970), p. 28.

32. Calhoun, *Question,* pp. 7-11.

33. Estimates compiled by N.Murray, *The Scottish Handloom Weavers, 1790-1850* (Edinburgh, 1978).

34. H. Fraser, 'The Glasgow Cotton Spinners, 1837', in J. Butt and J.T. Ward (eds.), *Scottish Themes* (Aberdeen,1976), p. 81. For Paisley, see Clarke and Dickson, 'Class', p.23.

35. Clarke and Dickson, 'Class', p.17 *et seq* and see also above Ch.10.

36. E.P. Thompson, 'The moral economy of the English crowd in the 18th century', *Past and Present,* 50 (1971); K.J. Logue, *Popular Disturbances in Scotland, 1780-1815* (Edinburgh,1979), esp. pp. 210-3.

37. W.Ferguson, *Scotland: 1689 to the Present* (Edinburgh, 1968), pp. 273-4. See also Ch. 13 which shows that in some locations in the early nineteenth century the

judiciary did regulate wages in favour of workmen, but also charts the decline of such practices in the face of newer and harsher political economy.

38. G. Stedman Jones, 'The language of Chartism', in J. Epstein and D. Thompson (eds.), *The Chartist Experience* (London 1982), p. 8. Stedman Jones' perspective on the significance of the language of Radicalism and Chartism is reviewed and criticised in J. Foster, 'The declassing of language', *New Left Review,* 150 (March/April, 1985), pp. 29-45. There is some truth in Foster's argument that Stedman Jones interprets this language without reference to the particular contexts in which it was used. More specifically, we would argue that the institutional links between trade unions and Radicalism are critical in interpreting the meaning and extent of working-class support for the latter.

39. Murray, *Scottish Handloom Weavers*, p. 28 ff.

40. Fraser, 'Glasgow Cotton Spinners', p. 82.

41. Clarke and Dickson. 'Class', pp. 21-3.

42. Fraser, 'Glasgow Cotton Spinners', pp. 86-7.

43. Campbell, *Lanarkshire Miners*, p. 2.

44. Campbell, *Lanarkshire Miners*, Ch.3 and pp. 251-2; Wilson, *Chartist Movement*, pp.190-5.

45. F. Montgomery, 'Glasgow and the struggle for Parliamentary reform, 1830-32', *Scottish Historical Review*, 61 (1982), pp. 130-145; F. Montgomery, 'The unstamped press: the contribution of Glasgow, 1831-1836', *Scottish Historical Review*, 59 (1980), pp.154-70; D.Thompson, 'Women and nineteenth century Radical politics', in J. Mitchell and A. Oakley (eds.), *The Rights and Wrongs of Women* (Harmondsworth, 1976).

46. Donnelly, 'Scottish rising', p. 35.

47. Young, *Rousing*, p. 81.

48. Clarke and Dickson, 'Class', p. 41.

49. Logue, *Popular Disturbances,* pp.159-60; Young, 'The making', p. 63.

50. Calhoun, *Question*, p.xiii. For analyses of the wider conflict between arguments based on free market thinking and popular cultural conceptions of economic justice in the early nineteenth century, see P. Richards, 'The state and early industrial capitalism: the case of the handloom weavers', *Past and Present*, 83 (1978), pp. 91-115; J. Smail, 'New Languages for labour and capital', *Social History* , 12 (1987), pp. 49-71.

51. Montgomery, 'Glasgow'; Clarke and Dickson, 'Class', pp. 42-3, 45-52.

52. Montgomery, 'Glasgow', p.137.

53. K. Burgess, 'Workshop of the World', in Dickson (ed.), *Scottish Capitalism*, p. 211; Ferguson, *Scotland*, p. 288 ff.

54. Smout, *History*, p. 219. On the political power of the landowners, challenged but not eliminated by 1832, see Ch. 5 of this volume.

55. M.McCarthy, *A Social Geography of Paisley* (Paisley, 1969), Ch. 5.

56. Ferguson, *Scotland,* p. 271; Meikle, *Scotland,* p. 236.

57. Montgomery, 'Glasgow', p.144.

58. Young, *Rousing*, p.79.

59. Stedman Jones, 'The language', considers this distinction and Radical and

Chartist attitudes towards industrial capital in a wider British context. See pp. 19-25.

60. Richards, 'The State', pp. 103-6.
61. Anderson, *Arguments,* pp. 43-9.

# Index

Aberdeen 22, 36, 60, 76, 91, 112, 129, 131, 136, 157, 179, 263, 283, 284
Aberdeen Philosophical Society 131
Aberdeenshire 179, 236, 240, 241
Absenteeism 71
Accounts 115
Adam, Robert 102
Africa 70
Airdrie 36, 159
Alford 166
Allan, James 135
America 73
American Revolution 143
American War of Independence 82, 85
Angus 41, 60, 66, 67, 91, 179, 197
*Annals of the Parish* 93, 115, 138
Anti-Burghers 150-1, 160
Anti-Catholicism 154, 283
Applecross 167, 168
Apprentices 20-1
Arbroath 36, 214, 215, 226
Ardchattan (Argyll) 180
Argyll estates 71
Argyll, Dukes of 21, 83, 96, 104, 130
Argyllshire 21, 73, 77, 172, 179, 181
Ashton, T.S. 188-9
Associate Presbytery 150-1, 152
Association of Operative Cotton Spinners 300
Assynt (Sutherland) 148
Atlantic 133
Auchtermuchty 284
Australia 285
Austria 17, 28
Ayr 32, 256
Ayr Bank 276
Ayrshire 22, 53, 60, 63, 64, 92, 154

Badenoch 76
Baird, John 289
Baking 5
Balfron (Stirlingshire) 152
Banff 17, 60, 179
Bankers 111, 115
Banking 39
Baptism 10, 11
Baptists 150
Battle of Bonnymuir 124, 286, 289
Beattie, James 129
Beith 273
Belfast 115

Belfast Lough 87
Belgium 29
Bendochy (Perthshire) 173
Bereans 151
Berg, Maxine 286
Berwickshire 53, 59, 60, 91
Birth control 18
Black, Adam 137
Black, Joseph 130
Black Watch 83
Blacksmiths 66
*Blackwood's Magazine* 138
Blair, Hugh 130
Blincoe, Robert 245
Bohstedt, John 272
Bookbinders 236, 243
Borders 5, 17, 36, 92, 178, 232, 234, 253, 257, 263
Boswell, James 114
Braxfield, Lord 289
Brechin 36, 166
Brewing 5
Bridge of Allan 37
Bridgewater estates 85
Bristol 77
British Fisheries Society 81-2
British Linen Company 243
Brougham, Henry 133, 174
Brunton, Mary 133
Buccleuch, Duke of 97, 102
Buchan 67
Buchanan, Dugald 127
Buchanites 160
Building labourers 217, 228
Burghers 150
Burial registers 20
Burke, Edmund 283
Burns, Robert 127, 128, 138
Bute 91
Bute, Earl of 130

Cabinet makers 196
Cadiz 33
Caithness 18, 77, 179, 198
*Caledonian Mercury* 21, 133
Calhoun, C 298, 303
Calton (Glasgow) 278
Cambuslang 158, 253
Camerons of Lochiel 77-8
Campbell, A.B. 298, 301
Campbell, George 130, 131

310